Essential ICT

for WJEC

WJEC
CBAC

AS Level | Stephen Doyle

OXFORD

OXFORD
UNIVERSITY PRESS

Great Clarendon Street, Oxford OX2 6DP

Oxford University Press is a department of the University of Oxford.
It furthers the University's objective of excellence in research,
scholarship, and education by publishing worldwide in

Oxford   New York

Auckland   Cape Town   Dar es Salaam   Hong Kong   Karachi
Kuala Lumpur   Madrid   Melbourne   Mexico City   Nairobi
New Delhi   Shanghai   Taipei   Toronto

With offices in
Argentina   Austria   Brazil   Chile   Czech Republic   France   Greece
Guatemala   Hungary   Italy   Japan   Poland   Portugal   Singapore
South Korea   Switzerland   Thailand   Turkey   Ukraine   Vietnam

Oxford is a registered trade mark of Oxford University Press
in the UK and in certain other countries

British Library Cataloguing in Publication Data

Data available

ISBN 978-1-85008-413-6

FD4136

10 9 8 7 6 5 4 3 2

Printed in Spain by Cayfosa-Impresia Ibérica

Paper used in the production of this book is a natural, recyclable product
made from wood grown in sustainable forests. The manufacturing process
conforms to the environmental regulations of the country of origin.

Editor:	Geoff Tuttle
Project development:	Rick Jackman (Jackman Publishing Solutions Ltd) and Samantha Jackman
Concept design:	Patricia Briggs
Layout artist:	GreenGate Publishing Services
Illustrations:	GreenGate Publishing Services
Cover design:	Jumpto! www.jumpto.co.uk
Cover image:	Courtesy of Chris Harvey/Fotolia.com

Contents

Unit 1 Information Systems

Introduction to the AS Units

There are two units for the AS Information and Communications Technology:

- Unit IT1 Information Systems
- Unit IT2 Presenting Information

For the AS level the balance of the marks for the two units is:

Unit IT1 Information Systems: 60%
Unit IT2 Presenting Information: 40%

Unit IT1 Information Systems

Assessment for Unit IT1 Information Systems

This consists of a question paper with answers written in an answer booklet which is marked externally by WJEC. There are no optional questions in the paper for Unit 1.

There are two sections to the paper:

Section A

- This will account for 75% of the marks for IT1.
- Consists of structured questions designed to assess your breadth and depth of knowledge of Section A of the IT1 specification.
- Is a written paper of 2hr 15 min duration.
- Quality of written communication (clarity of answer, grammar, spelling and punctuation) are assessed in two questions.

Section B

- This will account for 25% of the marks for IT1.
- You will be required to prepare a spreadsheet on a specific topic given to you by the WJEC examination board in advance of the examination.
- You will use spreadsheet software to complete this work and then produce a hard copy (i.e., a printout on paper).

- You will take your printout into the examination and use it to answer the questions in Section B.
- Your spreadsheet will be handed in at the same time as your completed examination paper.

The organisation of Unit IT1 Information Systems

Unit IT1 is divided up into the following topics:

1 Data, information and knowledge
2 The value and importance of information
3 Quality of information
4 Validation and verification
5 Capabilities and limitations of ICT
6 (a) Uses of ICT in business
   (b) Uses of ICT in education
   (c) Uses of ICT in healthcare
   (d) Uses of ICT in the home
7 Presenting information
8 Networks
9 Human–computer interface (HCI)
10 Social issues
11 Database systems
12 Modelling

1 Data, information and knowledge

There is a subtle difference between the terms data and information and you need to be able to define and use these two terms correctly. You will also learn about how knowledge is needed to interpret information. You will learn the definitions of the terms and be able to use them to describe ICT systems. You will learn about the reasons for encoding data and the problems it sometimes causes.

2 The value and importance of information

Information is the lifeblood of all organisations and without it they could not function. ICT systems provide information on which staff and managers can base their

decisions. In this topic you will learn that information has a value and what the costs of gaining information are in terms of money, time and human resources.

3 Quality of information

The result of processing data is information and here you will learn about the factors that affect the quality of information. You will learn about how the quality of information must be maintained if users are to have any confidence in it.

4 Validation and verification

Here you will learn about the nature of errors and how they occur and what can be done to reduce errors to a minimum. You will learn about verification and validation methods and how these checks can ensure that data entered into a computer system is reasonable and sensible. You will learn that it is impossible to eliminate all errors from data entry.

5 Capabilities and limitations of ICT

ICT systems have huge capabilities in areas such as repetitive processing, speed of processing, data storage capacity, speed of searching and accessibility to information and services. You will learn about what ICT can do and the sorts of things that can limit its effectiveness.

6(a) Uses of ICT in business

Here you will learn about CAD (computer-aided design) and CAM (computer-aided manufacturing) and how they are used by a variety of different businesses. You will also learn about the computer systems used in shops, such as e-commerce, bar coding, automatic stock control, etc.

6(b) Uses of ICT in education

As you will already know, schools and colleges make extensive use of ICT for both teaching and learning and also administration. You will learn about computer-based learning, computer-based training, distance learning, video-conferencing, chat rooms for learning, etc. You will also learn about the variety of systems that schools and colleges use for student registration and also about the systems used for storing student records.

6(c) Uses of ICT in healthcare

Here you will learn about the many ICT systems used in healthcare. You will learn about the computer-controlled scanning devices such as MRI and CAT scans and how sensors are able to record important patient measurements.

In addition, you will learn about the computer-based administrative systems that support patient well-being which include electronic patient records, blood bar coding and tracking, the use of the Internet, distributed medical databases and other developments.

You will learn about the use of expert systems that can be used to aid diagnosis and enable inexperienced doctors to make expert diagnoses.

6(d) Uses of ICT in the home

Most people now use ICT in the home for entertainment and on-line home banking. Here you will look at a variety of forms of entertainment making use of ICT, from digital photography to cinema and theatre booking using the Internet.

Many people now use the Internet for on-line home banking and we will look at the systems for making on-line payments and the security implications of such systems.

7 Presenting information

In this topic you will be looking at the necessity for information to be presented in a range of different formats and via different media. You will learn to be mindful of the intended audience and to choose the most appropriate format and media for them.

In addition you will learn about the important aspects of word-processing/DTP, presentation, database and web authoring software.

8 Networks

This topic looks at networks that enable data to be transferred from one place to another. You will be looking at the characteristics of networked computers and stand-alone computers and the relative advantages and disadvantages of networks. There is a difference between the terms the World Wide Web and the Internet and here you will learn what this difference is. You will also look at the uses of communication technologies and various aspects and features of the Internet.

9 Human–computer interface (HCI)

Human–computer interaction is an important aspect of ICT because it is concerned with the way humans and computers interact with each other. In this topic you will look at the need for effective human–computer interfaces and you will learn about the types of HCI to choose from.

10 Social issues

The widespread use of ICT has led to huge changes for society and it is now hard for us to see how we could get by in our lives without such systems.

This topic looks at a whole range of social issues from health and safety issues to all the laws that needed to be introduced to cope with the misuses of ICT systems. In this topic you will learn about the laws relating to ICT use such as the Data Protection Act 1998, the Computer Misuse Act 1990 and the Copyrights, Designs and Patents Act 1988.

11 Database systems

This topic provides an introduction to databases and looks at the difference between a flat-file and a relational database. You will learn about the main features of relational databases and how the security of such databases is ensured by the use of a hierarchy of passwords.

12 Modelling

In this topic you will be introduced to the topic of modelling. You will learn what a computer model is, what its components are and how a model can be created using spreadsheet software.

You will also learn about some of the more advanced spreadsheet modelling concepts.

As part of the assessment for IT1, you will be required to produce a spreadsheet model, so in this topic you will learn about what you have to produce for this.

In addition you will learn about how a model can be used to produce a simulation and about a range of applications for simulations. You will learn about the advantages and disadvantages of using simulation models and the special hardware requirements for complex simulations.

Unit IT2 Presenting Information

Assessment for Unit IT2 Presenting Information

For this unit you will undertake DTP and multimedia tasks and present your work for internal assessment (i.e., assessment by your teacher/lecturer) and moderation by the examination board WJEC.

This unit requires you to use ICT hardware and software to solve a problem involving three separate tasks. These tasks require you to produce:

- a document such as a leaflet or magazine
- a document containing automated routines (e.g. mail merge)
- a presentation to an audience such as a webpage or a slide-type show.

You must look clearly at the table in the specification from WJEC which lists all the features (basic and advanced) that should be included in each task you submit.

A copy of the page from the specification is shown on page ix for your reference:

Background

Analysis of existing data processing activities

Tasks	Examples	Basic features	Advanced features
	Candidates must attempt all tasks	Candidates should use **all** of these features	**At least five** of the following are required to access the higher mark ranges
Task 1 DTP Design and produce a document of at least two A4 sides and containing at least 150 words	• Leaflet or magazine	• Use of different styles • Use of different font sizes • Use of bold, centre and underline • Right or fully justify • Autoshapes • Bullet points • WordArt • Shading effects • Headers and footers • Use of at least two forms of electronic combination of graphical images, e.g. scanned images, graphics from the Internet, clipart from disc, digital camera images, graphs from a spreadsheet, graphics from a paint or CAD package • Tables	• Customised tables • Different paragraph formats • Different line spacing • Superscript and subscript • Page or frame borders • Set and use own tabs • Set and use own indents • Watermarks • Pagination • Use of layering (forward and behind) • Create own style sheets
Task 2 Automated documents Design and produce documents containing automated routines	• Mail merge letters including macros	• Import data from an external source • Design and use of professional format and layout for data • Ensure automated routines work	• Individual macros or modules created using internal programming capabilities of the software package • Individually designed templates (other than the normal template or standard templates provided by wizards in the software package)
Task 3 Presentation Design and produce a presentation of at least six slides/pages for an audience	Either a • Slide-based presentation Or • Web pages	• Background styles • Animation effects • Transition effects • Hypertext • Hotspots • Bookmarks	• Use of sound • Use of original video • Use of original animation/Flash graphics

The organisation of Unit IT2 Presenting Information

Unit IT2 will give you skills, knowledge and understanding in presenting information. Unit IT2 is divided up into the following tasks:

• Task 1 DTP
• Task 2 Automated documents
• Task 3 Presentation

Introduction to the features in the student book

The philosophy behind the student book

This student book has been based on extensive research from schools and colleges on the different ways ICT is taught and this book has been developed with all the findings in mind. As this is a new specification, many students and teachers/lecturers will be finding their way and the aim of the book is to provide a depth of coverage for the material for Units IT1 and IT2. This book covers all the material for the WJEC AS level in ICT.

This book should be used by the teacher/lecturer in conjunction with the teacher support materials. Of course this book can be used stand-alone, but if you are a teacher then there are many resources in the teacher support materials to help your students succeed and maximise their marks. The Teacher Support CD-ROM contains the following non-digital resources: Answers to the Questions, Activities and Case studies and also provides additional Questions and Case studies.

The Teacher Support CD-ROM also includes a wealth of digital materials such as PowerPoint presentations, missing word tasks, and free text tasks. These will all help your students consolidate their understanding of the topics.

The structure of the student book

The WJEC AS-level consists of two units with each unit being divided into topics. In this book each topic has been further divided up into double-page spreads. This allows division of each topic into bite-size easily digested chunks of material. For consistency and to make the student book easy to use, all topics are structured in the same way.

Topic introduction pages

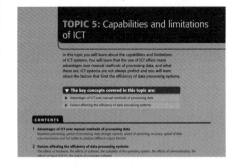

The first page of each topic consists of an introduction to the material in the topic and includes the following features:

Topic introduction: just a couple of paragraphs introducing students to the subject matter in the topic.

Key concepts: this lists the key concepts covered in the topic. These key concepts are identical to those in the AS WJEC specification.

Contents: the contents lists the spreads used to cover the topic and each spread covers key concepts.

Introduction: introduces the content on the spreads.

The content: what you need to learn is presented in the content and this material has been written to give you the essential information in order to answer examination questions.

Key words: these are specialist terms used in the content spreads and it is important that you not only remember these words, but you can use them with confidence when describing aspects of ICT systems. There is also a glossary at the back of the book which can be used for reference.

You will find out: this tells you what you will learn from the content of the spreads.

Topic spreads

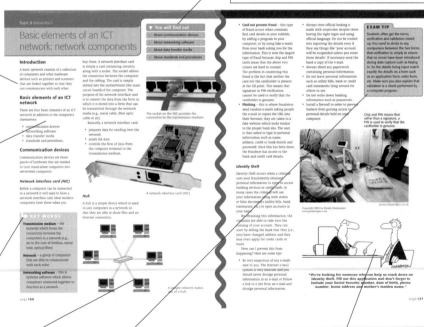

Diagrams and photographs: brings the topic to life with relevant and carefully researched images.

Exam tips: useful tips based on the problems that students have when they answer questions on the topics.

Cartoons: relevant cartoons drawn by the cartoonist Randy Glasbergen add a bit of humour and fun to the topics.

Questions, Activities and Case study spreads

These are usually included at the end of the content spreads and are used to consolidate learning. There are some occasions where Activities or Questions are included within the content spreads. Each block of questions covers a certain number of pages and most of the time this will be a double-page spread. This allows you to look at the spreads and then practise the questions. The answers to all the questions are available in the teacher support materials, which are available separately on CD-ROM and complement the student text.

► Questions 1   pp. 00-00

1 Managers in organisations have to base their decisions on the information they receive. It is therefore important that the information supplied to them is of good quality.
   (a) Give three features that information must have in order for it to be good quality information. (3 marks)
   (b) Give one reason why a firm making use of quality information will probably do better than a firm without quality information. (1 mark)
2 One quality of information is that it should be able to target resources of an organisation so giving the organisation a competitive advantage.

Explain clearly, by giving an example, what this means. (2 marks)
3 A sales manager for a large car dealership says that he is always provided with 'quality' information from the firm's management information system. With the aid of examples, where appropriate, describe five characteristics of quality information. (5 marks)
4 Explain, by giving examples in each case, two problems caused by the use of out-of-date information. (2 marks)

Questions: are included at the end of each topic and refer to the content in the spreads and are clearly labelled so that you can either do them after each double-page spread or all in one go at the end of the topic. The questions are designed to be similar to AS examination questions and have marks to give students the opportunity to understand how answers are marked.

The answers to the questions are included in the Teacher Support CD-ROM.

► Activity 1: Useful websites

The following website contains an interactive demonstration of some of the features of the software used with electronic whiteboards. Take some time to look at this and write down a list of the features.
http://www.prometheanworld.com/uk/server/show/nav.1693

Activities: offer interesting things for you to do which will help add to and reinforce the material in the spreads.

► Case study   pp. 00-00

Using fingerprinting in schools

Many schools are now using fingerprinting methods to help with pupil registration. One such school in South Wales has been using fingerprinting methods for a couple of years now. The system works by the pupils placing their finger on a scanner which is installed outside the classrooms. The scanner reads certain aspects of the print to identify the pupil and then records the attendance details on the computer.

The head teacher of the school has sung the praises of the system, saying how it has helped reduce truancy because pupils now know that it can be immediately identified by the system. Teachers at the school have welcomed the system because it frees them from having to do this important but time-consuming task.

If a pupil fails to register at the start of the day, a text message can be sent to the parent's mobile phone

alerting them of the non attendance of their child. This makes it virtually impossible for a pupil not to attend school without their parents knowing.

Many pupils like the system because it gives them more time to chat with friends and find out what is going on in the school with their form teacher.

Some parents and pupils were initially worried that fingerprints were being routinely taken and stored by the school and that this was personal data which could be misused. However, the company who supplied the system explained to parents that no full fingerprints are stored by the system. Instead the fingerprint is stored as a code and it is this code that is matched. They were reassured that a fingerprint cannot be re-created from this code and that it is only used by the school for identification purposes and not for some other sinister use.

1 Many schools use fingerprinting as a method for recording the presence of pupils at school.
   (a) Fingerprinting is an example of a biometric input device. Explain briefly what this sentence means. (2 marks)

   (b) Give three advantages of using fingerprinting to register attendance. (3 marks)
   (c) Many parents may be worried that the system stores their child's fingerprints. Write a sentence to explain how you might address this worry. (2 marks)

2 Describe one way in which the fingerprinting system helps prevent truancy in schools. (2 marks)
3 Give one example of how this fingerprinting attendance system could possibly be misused. (2 marks)

Case studies: real-life case studies are included that relate directly to the material in the topic. Case studies give a context in which you can answer the examination questions. Often examination questions on ICT ask not only for a definition or explanation but also an example. Case studies build up your knowledge of how the theory you learn about is used in practice.

Case study questions: will give you practice at answering questions which relate to real-life situations. The questions have been carefully constructed to be similar to the examination questions you could be asked and relate directly to the case study and other material contained in the content spreads.

If your teacher has the Teacher Support CD-ROM, they will have the answers to these case study questions.

Exam support

Worked example: is an important feature because it gives you an insight into how the examination questions are marked. At AS level you can have the knowledge but still fail to get a good mark because you have failed to communicate what you know effectively. It is essential that you understand just what is expected of you when answering questions at AS level.

Student answers: you can see an examination question with examples of two different student answers. For each student answer there is a corresponding sample Examiner's comment.

Examiner's comment: offers you an insight into how examiners mark student answers. The main thing here is to be able to see the mistakes that can be made and ensure that you do not make similar mistakes. By analysing the way answers are marked you will soon be able to get more marks for the questions that you answer by not making common mistakes.

Examiner's answer: offers some of the many possible answers and an indication of how the marks are distributed between the answers. It should be borne in mind that there are many possible correct answers to some questions and that any mark scheme relies on the experience of the markers to interpret the mark scheme and to give credit for answers that do not appear in the mark scheme.

Summary mind maps

Mind maps are great fun to produce and a very good way of revising. They are included at the end of each topic to summarise the material contained in the topic. Sometimes there will be only one mind map and other times there will be several – it all depends on how the material in the topic is broken down.

As well as using these mind maps to help you revise, you should produce your own.

Why not produce them using the computer? There are many good pieces of mind mapping software.

Worked example 1

1 ICT systems offer many advantages over corresponding manual systems.
 Describe three such advantages. **(6 marks)**

Student answer 1

1 Faster processing because you can do things quicker.
 You can produce the output in lots of different formats depending on the audience, such as graphs, presentation, as a file to be used as the input into another computer system. With the manual system you were limited to output on paper.
 You search better for stuff on the computer than you could search through a load of paper files. Paper files can only be stored in one order but records in computer files can be ordered in many ways.

Examiner's comment

1 The first advantage gains a mark – the student needed to explain what 'things' can be done quicker.
 The second advantage gains two marks as they have adequately explained the advantage and also given a comparison.
 The third advantage is marred a little by the word 'stuff' – what stuff? However, they have given a valid advantage and explained it further by giving an example.
 (5 marks out of 6)

Student answer 2

1 Speed of processing, as faster processing means it is quicker to extract data from a large database.
 Data storage capacity, as a huge amount of data can be stored in a very small space, either on a server or CD/DVD. The same volume of data would take up a huge amount of space.
 Speed of data communication, as files can be sent over networks such as the Internet very quickly using broadband. If you wanted to send paper documents quickly, it would still take hours and be very expensive.
 Accuracy. The data stored on the computer is likely to be more accurate because validation checks will have been used to make sure that only sensible and allowable data is entered.

Examiner's comment

1 In the first answer the student mentions that it is 'quicker to extract data....', but you do not extract data from a database, you extract information. The student has not been penalised on this answer. The student has not made it clear with the final sentence 'The same volume of data would take up a huge amount of space' that they are referring to the manual system. Only one mark is given here.
 The other two descriptions are of correct advantages and there is some comparison to the manual method of performing the task, so full marks for both these answers.
 (5 marks out of 6)

Examiner's answers

1 There are no marks for just giving the name of the advantage without a sentence explaining it. One mark for the advantage, and the second mark for further explanation, or an example to a maximum of 6 marks.
 Repetitive processing can be performed such as using templates or style sheets so that a page of a document does not have to be completed from scratch.
 Large data storage capacity means that data can be stored in a small space and also that the data is portable. Large quantities of paper files take up a huge amount of space.
 Speed of processing is much faster with ICT systems. Processes such as searching for information, sorting information, performing calculations, etc., are performed much quicker by computer.
 Accuracy is improved when computers are used. Validation checks make sure that only allowable and sensible data is entered.
 Speed of communication is improved as e-mail, file attachments, file transfer, etc., can be used to transfer information very quickly. Sending letters manually takes a long time.
 Speed of searching is improved as it is much faster to type in search conditions and extract specific information from a database rather than have to wade through files manually.
 The same information can be output in lots of different formats. For example, information can be output as a file for use with another system, a presentation, a report, a website, etc.

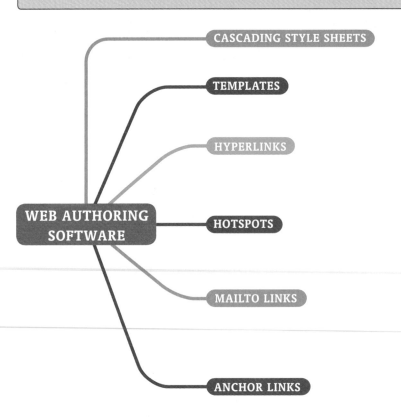

CASCADING STYLE SHEETS

TEMPLATES

HYPERLINKS

WEB AUTHORING SOFTWARE

HOTSPOTS

MAILTO LINKS

ANCHOR LINKS

TOPIC 1: Data, information and knowledge

In this topic you will learn about what constitutes data, information and knowledge.

You will learn that there are different forms of data and that it is sometimes necessary to encode data during collection or during input to enable effective processing.

You will learn about the problems associated with the encoding of data.

▼ The key concepts covered in this topic are:

▶ The relationship between data, information and knowledge

▶ The reasons for encoding data and the problems associated with encoding

CONTENTS

Unit IT1 Information Systems

The relationship between data, information and knowledge

Introduction

In this section you will learn about three important terms: **data**, **information** and **knowledge**. You will see by the use of examples how these terms are different and see how they may be used when describing ICT systems.

What exactly is data?

There are a number of forms that data can take. Data can be:

- numbers
- words
- images
- sound.

Data are details that are meaningless because they lack relevance. If you look at data, it is either no use to you or not in a form that you can use.

Ways in which data can arise

There are lots of ways data can arise and these are summarised in the following diagram:

The differences between data and information

Data are the raw values put into, stored and processed by a data processing system and that information is produced together with a context that adds meaning.

Raw data is relative because data processing often occurs in stages so the 'processed data' from one stage can be the raw data for the next stage of processing.

| £23,712 | £28,932 | £35,067 |

The above set of numbers is data. It tells us nothing because there is no context. We do not know if they are a premiership player's weekly wage, the price of a car or the value of sales of own brand baked beans in a week. No new knowledge is gained by looking at these figures and on their own, they are impossible to understand.

If we are told that the data refers to the first three months' sales of baked beans in a store, then 'the first three months' sales have steadily increased' is information. 'Sales for the second month have increased by 22% and for the third month by 17.5%' is information.

KEY WORDS

Data – raw facts or figures or a set of values, measurements or records of transactions

Information – consists of processed data or data with a context

Knowledge – is derived from information by applying rules to it

Information informs you of something you did not already know or it is presented in a way that has meaning and is useful. Converting data (sometimes called raw data) is what ICT systems do.

Information

Information comes from the processing of data. People or computers can find patterns in data which gives them information and the information enhances their knowledge about the subject.

Information is data which has been:

- processed
- converted to give it meaning
- organised in some way.

Knowledge

Knowledge is how to interpret and apply information by applying rules and once this is done, decisions can be made on the information received.

The relationship between data, information and knowledge

Here are a few examples to help you understand the relationship between data, information and knowledge.

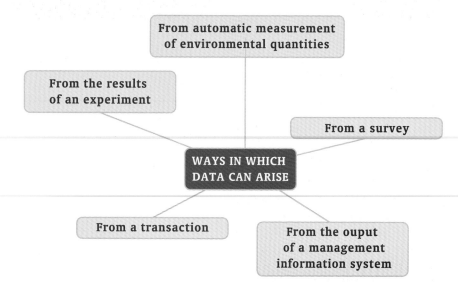

From automatic measurement of environmental quantities

From the results of an experiment

From a survey

WAYS IN WHICH DATA CAN ARISE

From a transaction

From the ouput of a management information system

Here is a list of numbers: 4.31, 4.18, 4.29, 4.32, 4.19 and 4.21. It is impossible to know what they mean as there is no context, so these numbers are data.

If, however, we know that they are race times; 4.31, 4.18, 4.29, 4.32, 4.19 and 4.21 minutes, we are adding a context, so this set of numbers becomes information. Processing of the data in some way, for example finding the fastest time, also produces information.

Knowledge is applying rules to the information. For example, in this example the rule is that the runner with the fastest time wins the race.

Here is another list of numbers without a context.

07:30 | 160/94 | 08:30 | 155/92 | 09:30 | 150/90 | 10:30 | 148/91 | 11:30 |146/90

These are raw numbers without a context and have not been processed in any way, so this is data.

If you are told that they are a list of blood pressure readings taken at hourly intervals, then a context has been added, so this is information.

Processing of the data by putting it into a table also means we now have information.

Time reading was taken	Patient blood pressure
07:30	160/94
08:30	155/92
09:30	150/90
10:30	148/91
11:30	146/90

Taking blood pressure readings

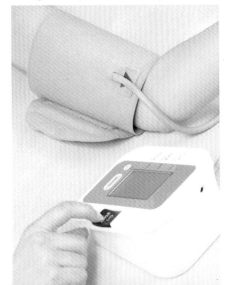

The doctor can then apply the knowledge they have about blood pressures which is summarised here:

Systolic pressure/Diastolic pressure
120–140/70–90 represents normal blood pressure

140–159/90–94 represents mild high blood pressure

160–179/94–119 represents high blood pressure

The doctor can apply the knowledge to the information in the table to draw conclusions about the patient's health and take appropriate action.

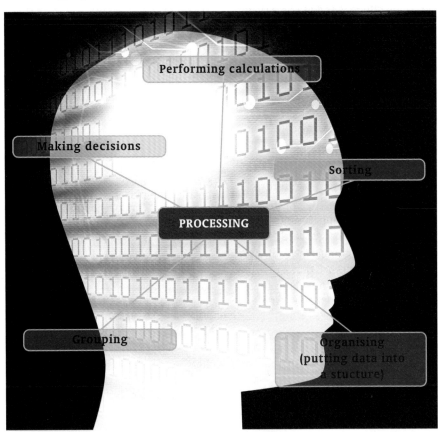

EXAM TIP

When asked to describe the difference between data and information you need to be very precise in your answer. In many ways it is better to remember a definition word for word, rather than try to put your own definition together.

You may be asked to give an example to show that you understand the difference between the two terms. Remember, when giving your answer, that data is not a single value.

A word of warning about the terms information and data

In general usage, the words information and data are often used interchangeably. However, in ICT there is a very clear and distinct difference between the terms and you must be very precise in using and explaining them.

It is extremely important that you can distinguish between data and information.

Examples of processing are shown in the diagram below:

Producing useful information

To be useful, information has to be meaningful to the person using it. Many information communications systems fail to give users the information they need and this is frustrating to users.

The reasons for encoding data and the problems associated with encoding

▼ **You will find out**

▶ About what encoding is

▶ About the reasons for encoding data

▶ About the problems associated with encoding

▶ About the reliance on value judgements

Introduction

In this section you will learn about how data is sometimes encoded on collection or input into an ICT system. There are a number of problems that encoding data causes and you will learn about them in this topic.

The reasons for encoding data

Encoding data

Data is often coded during collection or when input into an ICT system. The reasons for this are:

- coded data takes less effort to type in
- more data can appear on the screen
- takes up less storage space (less important as storage media is cheap)
- it is easier to check that a code is accurate using validation checks.

Examples of encoding

There are many examples of encoding data and here are a few:

Country of origin for cars:

    GB = Great Britain
    D   = Germany
    IRL = Ireland
    CH = Switzerland

Sizes of clothes:

    S   = Small
    M   = Medium
    L   = Large
    XL = Extra large

Airport codes:

    LHR = London Heathrow
    MAN = Manchester
    RHO = Rhodes

Problems associated with encoding

The main problem with the encoding of data is that it coarsens precision. This means that the encoded data is less accurate than the data from which it came. This is best seen by taking an example. Descriptions of criminals on a police computer system might include the eye colour of the criminal. It might be decided to use:

Eye colour	Code
Blue	BL
Brown	BR
Green	GR
Grey	GY

Suppose we are entering the details of a criminal into a database and on the form we are using we see the description of the person and their eye colour is described as being blue/green. We now have a problem about which code to use. The database will only allow us to put the eye colour as blue, brown, green or grey, so which one do we choose? Because we would now realise that the data for the eye colour for all other entries could be inaccurate, we may just settle for one colour and not worry any more about it. It does, however, compromise the integrity of the database system and we will now have less faith in the results it produces than before. When we search the database for eye colours, we now realise that blue eyes and green eyes are not all those colours but they could also have in them blue/greens as well. The coding system employed has now made us unsure about the data and the stored data is not as precise as the original data.

Encoding sorts data into specified formats to allow storage.

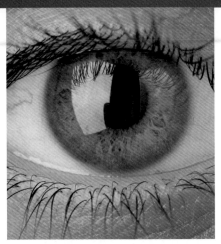

Hazel eyes: encoding data doesn't always ensure accurate results.

The reliance on value judgements

Encoding data often involves the person collecting or entering the data in making judgements about which code to use.

Here are the heights of 10 people:

Mohammed	5 ft	5 inches
Chloe	4 ft	11 inches
James	6 ft	6 inches
Asia	5 ft	9 inches
Courtney	5 ft	0 inches
Jack	6 ft	5 inches
Leroy	5 ft	10 inches
Charles	4 ft	10 inches
Mary	6 ft	10 inches
Jane	6 ft	2 inches

Imagine the problems you could get if you left it to different people to decide which of the following height codes to put each of these people in:

T = Tall
M = Medium
S = Short

Value judgements can be different for different people.

When you apply for university or a higher education institution, you have to fill in a form called a UCAS form and on part of the form your teacher/lecturer will write a character reference for you. Such a volume of text is difficult to store and interrogate, since to do this would involve breaking value judgements down into set answers. So instead of free text, your teacher may be asked to answer certain specific questions by choosing from a range of possible answers.

Here is a question along with the code used for the answer:

On a scale of 1 to 5 how would you describe the pupil's/student's punctuality?

1 Never late
2 Occasionally late but with a good excuse
3 Lateness is occasional without any excuse given
4 Regularly late
5 Invariably late

In the database you could include a field in which you enter one of the above numbers. To some extent this still depends on the person entering the data, but since there are many choices, it is more accurate than some of the other coding methods which could be used. A balance always needs to be struck between keeping the coding possibilities to a minimum, whilst keeping them large enough to make them an accurate reflection. When devising coding systems for fields in databases, you need to bear this in mind.

Tall, medium or short? Value judgements can result in errors in data collection.

Questions and Activities

▶ Questions 1 | pp. 2–3

1 Look at the following:
12, 23, 3, 42, 76, 16, 29
   (a) Can you understand what these numbers mean? (1 mark)
   (b) Explain, giving a reason, whether the numbers are data or information. (2 marks)

2 Data can take different forms.
Give the names of **three** different forms that data can take. (3 marks)

3 By giving a suitable example, explain the difference between data and information. (3 marks)

4 An IT manager explains that 'data is processed to produce information'.
Give **three** distinctly different examples of processing. (3 marks)

▶ Questions 2 | pp. 4–5

1 Data is often coded so that less data needs to be entered into the computer, which saves time typing and also reduces the likelihood of the user contracting RSI.
Give **one** different reason why data is sometimes coded. (2 marks)

▶ Activity 1 Is it data or information?

For this exercise you need to decide whether each of these examples is data or information.
1   A bar code on a tin of baked beans.
2   A graph showing the way sales have varied over a twelve-month period.
3   Your bank balance has jumped 102%.
4   12.78.
5   A graph showing how the annual mean temperature varies with latitude.

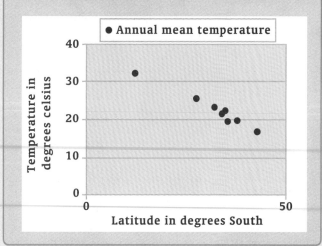

▶ Activity 2 What codes are these?

Codes are all around us. Here are some popular codes. Can you work out what the codes are used for and where you have seen examples of each code being used?
1   10/12/76
2   M or F
3   L23 5TA
4   01519307766
5   90-12-45
6   LPL, MAN, LGW, LHR
7   GB, F, CH, D

Exam support

Worked example 1

1 (a) Define the terms data, information and knowledge. (3 marks)

(b) Give two reasons for encoding data. (2 marks)

(c) Encoding data causes a number of problems. By referring to an appropriate example, describe one problem with the encoding of data. (2 marks)

Student answer 1

1 (a) Data is information before it is processed.
Information is data that has been processed.
Knowledge is what you know about the information.

(b) To make it harder for people to understand as you need to decipher it.
Putting data into a code summarises it so there is less to type in.

(c) It coarsens the precision of the data.

Examiner's comment

1 (a) The definition of data is true but it is not really appropriate to explain it this way.
The definition of information is fine.
The definition of knowledge is vague and gains no marks.

(b) For the first answer the student is confusing coding with encrypting.
The second answer is fine.

(c) The reason given is correct but the student has not given an example.

(3 marks out of 7)

Student answer 2

1 (a) Data consists of raw facts and figures at the collecting stage, before they are processed.
Information is either data that has a context or data that has been processed in some way (e.g., sorted, presented clearly, had calculations performed, etc.).
Knowledge is the rules that are used to interpret and apply information.

(b) The amount of data that needs to be entered can be reduced using encoding. For example Female and Male can be encoded as F and M and this means faster data input.
Because coded data is shorter, it takes up less disk space, which means the processing of the data is faster.

(c) Encoding data can mean that it is less accurate than the original data. For example, if the height of a person was encoded as T for tall, M for medium and S for short, it could mean that it is left to the person entering the data which category someone with a height of 5ft 7ins would be put into.

Examiner's comment

1 (a) All these definitions are correct and expressed clearly, so full marks here.

(b) Both are valid reasons for encoding, so full marks.

(c) This is a very good description on how encoding can involve making value judgements and how this coarsens precision. This gains full marks.

(7 marks out of 7)

Examiner's answers

1 (a) One mark each for suitable definitions similar to the following:
Data – raw facts or figures or a set of values, measurements or records of transactions
Information – consists of processed data or data with a context
Knowledge – is derived from information by applying rules to it

(b) One mark each for two reasons such as:
Less time is spent typing the data in, so data entry costs are lower
The fewer the keystrokes made, the less chance of making transcription/keyboarding errors
Less memory is needed to store the shortened data

(c) One example for one mark and a relevant description for the second mark.
The data is coarsened. An example would be in a police computer where eye colour is entered in one of the following categories: blue, brown, grey or green. Suppose a person has blue/green eyes, where would they be put?
– it is then down to the person typing in to decide.

Summary mind maps

Ways in which data can arise

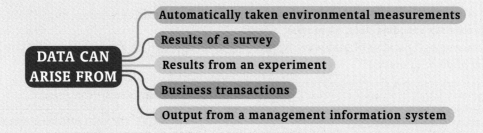

DATA CAN ARISE FROM
- Automatically taken environmental measurements
- Results of a survey
- Results from an experiment
- Business transactions
- Output from a management information system

Encoding data

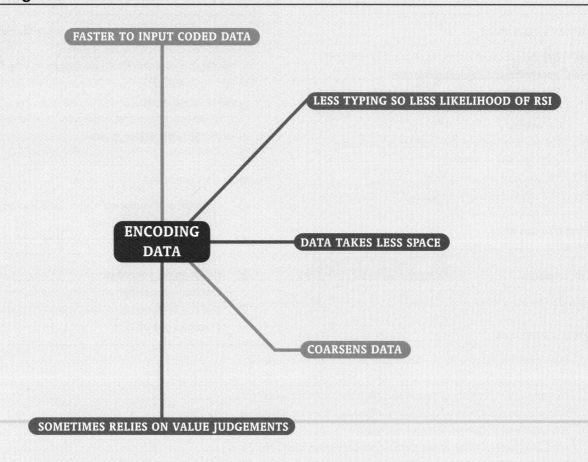

ENCODING DATA
- FASTER TO INPUT CODED DATA
- LESS TYPING SO LESS LIKELIHOOD OF RSI
- DATA TAKES LESS SPACE
- COARSENS DATA
- SOMETIMES RELIES ON VALUE JUDGEMENTS

TOPIC 2: The value and importance of information

Information is the lifeblood of any organisation and without accurate up-to-date information organisations could not function properly and businesses would fail.

In this topic you will be looking at the value and importance of information and what the essential qualities of information are. You will look at why managers need information and how they use this information to make decisions. You will also look at the costs of obtaining good quality information in terms of money, time and human resources.

▼ The key concepts covered in this topic are:

▶ The importance of up-to-date, accurate and complete information

▶ The costs of obtaining good quality information in terms of money, time and human resources

CONTENTS

Unit IT1 Information Systems

The importance of up-to-date, accurate and complete information

Introduction

In this topic you will learn about the importance of information to an organisation and how it is important to keep this information up-to-date, accurate and complete.

You will learn how information has a value and that this value can be measured in terms of money, time and the human resources needed to produce the information.

Why managers need information

Before looking at why managers need information, it is important to consider the role of a manager and the tasks involved in management. Managers are present in many layers in an organisation, from the junior managers, middle managers through to the senior managers and directors. What they do depends on their level within the organisation. Junior managers tend to deal with management at an operational level and therefore they deal with management of the day-to-day issues in an organisation. Senior managers deal with strategic matters and make major decisions.

All managers have to make decisions using information obtained from the day-to-day operations as well as from external information, and the types of decisions can be classed under the following headings:

- planning
- directing
- controlling
- forecasting.

The lower layers of management are responsible for:

- the day-to-day management of the operations staff
- allocating work to subordinates
- arrangement of staff rotas, dealing with staff sickness/absence
- motivating staff
- handling a departmental budget.

The higher levels of management are responsible for:

- strategic planning – this involves the setting of overall objectives and policies
- market share
- cash flow
- profits
- growth in profits.

Information is needed to fulfil all the above roles and it is important to note that the different levels of managers need different types of information. For example, the directors of an organisation would not need information on which customers had not paid their bills, but they would need information on projected turnover and profit for the business.

All information may be classed as a commodity and like all commodities it has a value and may be bought and sold. The monetary value information may have depends on:

- the accuracy of the information
- the potential and intended use of the information.

It is important to know that information which is collected and stored, but never used, has no actual value since no decisions will be based upon it, so it is superfluous and should never have been collected in the first place.

Financial markets (stock market and money market) are subject to rapid change and information systems are needed which react to these changes, and from the data supplied can tell the broker whether they should buy or sell. Obviously, since large amounts of money are involved, it is important that the information produced by the computer is accurate. The timeliness of this information is also important, since if the value of the pound were to fall rapidly, then the broker would need to quickly sell pounds and buy a different foreign currency whose value was rising. The speed with which the information is obtained and the speed with which any resulting transaction can be made will be reflected in the profit.

How information aids decision making

Information aids decision making in the following ways:

- The more information there is that is relevant to making the decision, the less risk there is in taking the decision.
- Information enables a manager to take remedial action – for example, if a customer owes a large amount of money then no orders should be sent to them until they are up-to-date with their account.

- Simulations can be performed using spreadsheet software to experiment with 'what-if' scenarios using the information in order to arrive at a decision.

Using information to monitor progress

Information can be used to monitor progress. For example, companies can use ICT to see how well they are performing against targets set. Personnel such as sales staff can judge their performance using information about their previous year's sales or by comparing their performance with other sales staff. Monthly sales figures can be compared with previous monthly sales figures from other years.

Using information for the targeting of resources

Organisations only have a finite amount of resources. By resources we mean:

- money
- human resources (e.g., people with suitable expertise)
- time
- hardware
- software
- materials.

All these resources need to be correctly allocated and this can be achieved by using ICT.

For example, ICT can be used for:

- creating production schedules
- planning projects
- stock control systems that ensure that stock is always available when needed.

The competitive advantage information gives

Most businesses have competitors which are organisations selling similar products or services to the same type of customer. It is therefore important for organisations to remain competitive. In order to remain competitive it is necessary to:

- Use market research information collected from customers to understand why they choose the organisation or products or services.

- Ensure that customer orders are always satisfied by having accurate stock information.
- Be able to anticipate customer demand from previous sales information. For example, you could predict the amount of barbecue food sold during a hot spell from information from previous sales during hot spells.

The importance of up-to-date, accurate and complete information

Information is only of use if it is:

- up-to-date
- accurate
- complete.

Up-to-date

Information should always be date stamped so that there is no danger of using out-of-date information. If the information is personal information, then under the terms of the Data Protection Act 1998 there is a legal requirement for the information to be kept up-to-date.

There are a number of consequences of using information that is not up-to-date:

- If the information being kept is personal and the person whom the information is about suffers loss as a result of information being wrong because it was not updated, then the organisation can be sued.
- There is a legal requirement for information to be kept up-to-date under the Data Protection Act 1998 and not keeping it up-to-date could lead to prosecution.
- You could send a letter to a customer threatening legal action for a bill that your records show had not been paid when the customer had paid but this had not been updated on the computer.
- A letter could be sent to someone who had died, which would distress the family of the bereaved.

Accurate

Information from a computer system must be as accurate as it can be because errors can result in the following problems:

- Customers being sent the wrong items – this costs money to sort out and will upset the customer.
- Customers being invoiced the wrong amount – this will waste time sorting out and will also upset the customer and damage any trust they had in the organisation.
- Buyers basing their stock ordering decisions on incorrect sales information resulting in stock having to be sold off cheaply.
- Misreading gas or electricity meters resulting in embarrassing mistakes, with ordinary domestic customers being sent bills for thousands of pounds.
- Typing the details in from a customer over the phone and mishearing them and typing in the wrong address resulting in goods being sent to the wrong address.

Complete

It is important that all the information is complete, as incomplete information can cause a number of problems including:

- An order might be only partly fulfilled because an item was not in stock at the time. Then the rest of the order is not sent later, resulting in an upset customer.
- A manager has asked for a sales report and some of the information she asked for on the report is missing, resulting in her having to base a decision on only part of the information, which is more risky.
- Not including the postcode on a letter, resulting in the letter being received late.

The costs of obtaining good quality information

▼ **You will find out**

▶ About the costs associated with data collection

▶ About the costs associated with data entry

▶ About the costs associated with processing and maintenance

Introduction

Information has a number of associated costs. The collection of high quality information requires people and resources to be directed towards it. The question is whether the rewards the information brings are worth the costs in providing it.

Many systems, such as those in schools and colleges, come with management information modules, which enable high quality management information to be produced from information already held in the system. In other applications, the information is not available because the data used to supply the information is not available, because it has not been collected.

In this topic you will learn about the costs of obtaining good quality information in terms of money, time and human resources.

Do the rewards information brings outweigh the cost of collection?

The costs associated with data collection (direct and indirect)

Information is never free, since there is always an associated cost of collecting it in the first place and it is important that the costs of obtaining the information do not outweigh the financial benefits from having the information to start with. To make sure that this is always the case, management usually perform a costs/benefits analysis, which makes sure that the costs in collecting the information do not outweigh the benefits obtained. For example, if certain information results in an increase in profit to the organisation of £200, yet costs £250 to collect, then it is not worth having the information to start with. Usually the information provided by a system will do some of the following:

- reduce costs
- eliminate losses
- reduce wastage
- use resources more effectively
- provide better management information to aid more accurate decision making.

Costs associated with the collection of data include:

- costs of employing an expert to design data collection forms
- the setting up of questionnaires to collect data
- the production of on-line forms to collect data from customers
- the travelling costs and other expenses involved in people performing interviews
- the costs of staff employed to work through documents to collect the information
- the costs for specialist staff to collect data from other systems
- the costs of buying information from a third party.

Data collection can be direct or indirect. Data which is collected directly by the organisation is called direct collection. An example of direct collection is where a store collects information itself about the increase in sales as a result of an advertising campaign for a certain product.

Indirect data collection is where the data is obtained from a third party rather than the organisation collecting it itself.

The costs associated with data entry

The costs associated with data entry can be divided into:

- Human resource costs – the costs of any staff performing data entry, the costs of training these staff, the costs of any specialist staff needed for programming, etc.
- Time costs – the entry of data, especially using keyboards, takes time. This can slow down the whole process from collecting the data to the production of the final information.
- Hardware costs – sometimes by spending money on automatic methods of data entry using bar coding, optical mark reading, magnetic ink character recognition, speech recognition, etc., the human resource costs can be lowered.

The costs associated with processing and maintenance

Once data has been collected and then input into an ICT system, the next stage is to process it. There are also a number

Some methods of transferring data can be expensive.

- Processing large amounts of data takes time and many ICT systems have many millions of records to process to extract certain information. Reports are printouts obtained by applying search criteria to a database or other information system. Some reports are complex and demand a lot of processing time for their production. Once a report is produced, it must be checked and then distributed to all the interested parties.
- The backing up of large amounts of data is necessary but time consuming.

Processing data to provide high quality information takes time.

of maintenance activities that will need to be performed such as:

- keeping data in the database or other system up-to-date
- taking backup copies of data for security purposes
- small changes to the structure of the program or database so that the relevant processing can occur.

There are costs associated with the processing and maintenance of data and these costs arise in a number of ways:

Financial costs

- Data may need to be transferred from one place to another using expensive communication lines.
- Outside firms may be used to ensure that the data is backed up off-site.
- Consumables costs such as printer paper and toner/ink cartridges.

Human resource costs

- In some cases, such as the processing of questionnaires, staff will be needed to oversee the batch processing performed using OMR or OCR and deal with any rejected forms.
- Specialist staff will be needed to give the instructions to the database to process the data by extracting specific details.
- Software can be pushed to the limit by users' demands for more information. These demands may not be satisfied unless a programmer uses some fancy programming tricks to enable the software to do something it was not really designed to do.
- Staff may need to be employed to analyse the information from the system and to produce more meaningful reports for different groups of people.

Questions

▶ Questions 1 | pp. 10–13

1 A school information management system contains information about pupils. As well as the usual personal details about pupils, such as contact details, e.g. names and addresses, there is some information of a very personal nature, such as ethnicity, religion and some medical information that school staff might need.

(a) Give two reasons why the data contained in this system must be kept up-to-date. (2 marks)

(b) There are a number of costs associated with keeping data up-to-date. Name and describe two such costs in relation to this school information management system. (4 marks)

2 The head teacher and senior managers of a school use the school's information management system for the making of day-to-day decisions.

Describe, by giving one example, a decision that could be made and the consequences of basing this decision on information which is not up-to-date. (3 marks)

3 The costs of collecting, inputting, processing and maintenance of data to produce information are not just quantified in financial (i.e. monetary) terms. State two other costs associated with producing quality information. (2 marks)

4 In a marketing campaign, customers have to fill in questionnaires for which they get a free voucher to spend on products. The questionnaires are then collected, batched together and read using an OMR reader.

(a) Describe two costs associated with the collection of data for this system. (2 marks)

(b) Describe two costs associated with the processing and maintenance of the data. (2 marks)

Exam support

Worked example 1

1 (a) **All organisations require up-to-date, accurate and complete information but there are financial costs in getting such information. As well as financial costs there are other costs. State two of these costs and give an example for each cost explaining how the costs arise. (4 marks)**

   (b) **There are a number of implications for an organisation if the information is not of good quality. Give distinctly different examples of a problem that could arise if the information is not:**

   (i) **up-to-date**

   (ii) **complete**

   (iii) **accurate. (3 marks)**

Student answer 1

1 (a) Financial costs – it costs a lot of money to collect data and then pay people to input it into the computer system.
        People cost – people are needed to do the collecting of the information and then type it into the computer system and these people will need to be trained so there are training costs as well.

   (b) Up-to-date – letters could be sent out to someone who had died, causing stress to the family.
        Accurate – mistakes in invoices can cause embarrassment and mistrust in customers and the organisation might lose business as a result of this.
        Complete – the designer of a system may forget an important piece of information.

Student answer 2

1 (a) Human resource costs – need suitably qualified people to extract the required information from a large database.
        Time costs – the time it takes to create queries or write programming code to extract the information asked for from the ICT system.

   (b) Up-to-date – a summons could be issued to someone who has actually paid their bill because their account had not been updated causing mistrust and distress for the customer.
        Accurate – validation checks need to be in place so that only sensible and reasonable data can be entered.
        Complete – an order might be only partly fulfilled because an item was not in stock at the time. Then the rest of the order is not sent later, resulting in an upset customer.

Examiner's comment

1 (a) This student has not read the question, as they want 'other costs', so no marks for this part. By people cost the student means human resource costs and because of the good explanation given, they are not penalised for this. Two marks for this part.

   (b) The first two answers are fine and gain full marks. The third answer does not adequately explain the problem of the information being incomplete and so gains no marks. **(4 marks out of 7)**

Examiner's comment

1 (a) Two good answers so full marks here.

   (b) A suitable example has not been given for the answer 'accurate' so no marks for this part. **(6 marks out of 7)**

Examiner's answers

1 (a) One mark for the type of cost and one mark for an example related to the cost × 2.
        The time cost in the collection of the data for processing which can be very time consuming.
        The human resources cost because suitably qualified people are needed to collect the data and enter it into the computer system.
        Human resource cost as staff will need to be re-trained to collect the data and also enter it into the system for processing.

   (b) Three appropriate examples with one mark for each.
        Up-to-date – wasting money by sending mail-shots or promotional material to past customers who have since moved.
        Complete – not including a postcode on an address label meaning that delivery is delayed.
        Accurate – mistakes in a meter reading by a utility company resulting in a bill for a ridiculous amount.

Worked example 2

2 All firms collect data in order to produce information and this collection of
   data and subsequent processing of the data has a cost associated with it.
   (a) Describe two costs associated with data collection. (2 marks)
   (b) Describe two costs associated with data entry. (2 marks)
   (c) Describe two costs associated with processing and
        maintenance. (2 marks)

Student answer 1

2 (a) Human resource costs, as people are needed to design
       questionnaires to give to the general public to give
       feedback about the food and service at a restaurant.
       Financial costs, as money is needed to fund the staff
       wages, the paper used, the time for interviews to take
       place, etc.
  (b) Human resource costs – training staff to enter data
       accurately into the computer system.
       Time costs – entry of the data into a computer by
       keyboarding takes time and this time needs to be made
       available.
  (c) Time costs, as processing large amounts of data and
       producing meaningful results in the form of reports
       takes a large amount of time.
       Maintaining a database containing data costs a lot of
       money because people are needed to delete data and so
       on.

Student answer 2

2 (a) Expert staff need to be employed from outside to design
       the questionnaires scientifically so that the results are
       statistically valid. There is no point processing data
       which has not been collected properly.
       Human resource costs. Staff need to be trained on how
       to interview people to collect the information by giving
       personal interviews and filling in questionnaires.
  (b) Time costs. The entry of data by keying in takes a long
       time and resources need to be diverted away from the
       day-to-day operations in order to do this.
       Financial costs. People need to be employed or existing
       staff need to be paid overtime in order to key in all the
       data that has been collected.
  (c) Time costs. A firm needs to spend time on a regular basis
       keeping their data in databases up-to-date. If the data
       held is personal data, it must by law be kept up-to-date
       as a requirement of the Data Protection Act 1998.

Examiner's comment

2 (a) This is a good answer with the costs clearly
        identified and a good description for each
        cost.
   (b) Both answers are correct and well described.
   (c) Both answers are correct and well described.
        (6 marks out of 6)

Examiner's comment

2 (a) Here the student has not said whether their
        answer relates to financial costs or human
        resource costs. The description is fine but they
        can only be given one of the two marks.
   (b) A good answer worth two marks.
   (c) Only one cost has been quoted here.
        Sometimes, it is easy to forget that you have
        only answered part of the question – so watch
        out for this.
        The answer given is good but only worth one
        mark because the other part is missing.
        (4 marks out of 6)

Examiner's answers

2 (a) One mark for the cost which must be a cost for data collection and not data input and one mark for a suitable description.

Financial costs
- paying outside organisations to conduct market research
- costs of printing out and sending questionnaires
- costs of paying experts to conduct a survey

Time costs
- the time it takes to conduct market research
- time away from other business activities
- time needed to process the results and write reports

Human resource costs
- staff needed to design questionnaires
- staff need to be allocated to the project and taken away from other jobs
- staff need to be trained
- travelling expenses and other costs for staff

(b) Financial costs
- people need to be employed or existing staff need to be paid overtime in order to key in data
- hardware devices such as scanners may need to be bought to input data collection forms/questionnaires automatically
- software may need to be purchased to enable characters on forms to be read automatically using OCR
- outside staff may need to be paid to key in data

Time costs
- time to enter the data into the system using a keyboard
- the time taken to deal with problems with rejected forms or incomplete questionnaires

Human resource costs
- training costs on dealing with input
- cost of external staff who enter data

(c) Financial costs
- maintaining a database containing data costs because people are needed to delete data and so on

Time costs
- processing large amounts of data and producing meaningful results in the form of reports takes a large amount of time

Human resource costs
- cost of staff who have to analyse the data, produce graphs, presentations and reports

Summary mind map

Costs of good quality information

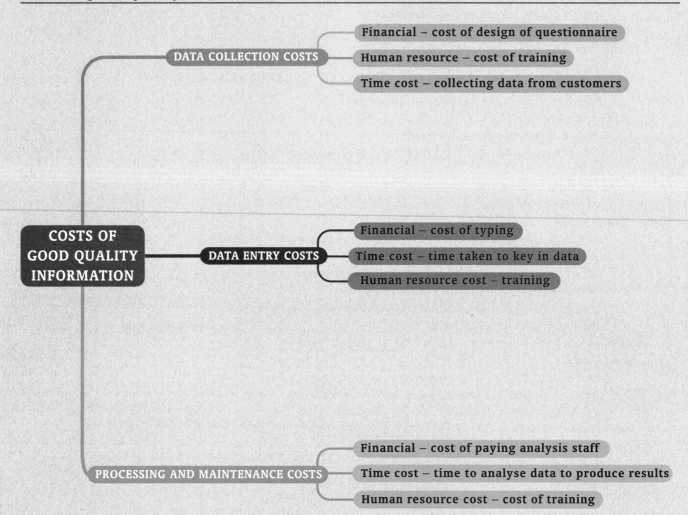

TOPIC 3: Quality of information

In order for information to be useful to the people in an organisation, it needs to be good quality information. In this topic you will learn what qualities of information determine whether it is good quality information. You will learn about the importance of keeping information up-to-date and also that in many cases there is a problem processing the information because there is so much of it.

▼ The key concepts covered in this topic are:

▶ How information can improve the quality of decision making

▶ Quality of information

▶ The importance of keeping data up-to-date

▶ Processing huge amounts of data

▶ How to find information

CONTENTS

Unit IT1 Information Systems

How information can improve the quality of decision making

▼ You will find out

▶ About how information can improve the quality of decision making

▶ About quality of information

▶ About the importance of keeping information up-to-date

▶ About processing huge amounts of data

Introduction

Management decisions are based on information and if the information is high quality then the decisions made are more likely to be good ones. If, however, the information on which the decisions are based is of poor quality, then the decisions could well be bad and be costly for the organisation. In this section you will learn about what constitutes good quality information and why such information is needed.

Quality of information

Some information is better than other information. For example, you need to decide how reliable the information is. This is particularly important, as decisions are usually made on the basis of the information. The quality of the information is a measure of:

- the accuracy of the information
- the relevance for a particular use
- how up-to-date the information is
- the completeness of information
- how easy the information is to understand
- how well information is targeted
- how much user confidence there is in the information.

Here are some examples of the above:

Accuracy

Credit card statements must have the correct rate of interest applied to the balance, otherwise customers will complain and the card company could be prosecuted.

Targeted and well-timed information can aid decision making.

The relevance for a particular use

A group has asked their record company for a breakdown of their royalties for all months over the last three years and the record company only gave them the total royalties for each year. The group wanted to look at the seasonal variations in their royalties but the information given would not show this.

How up-to-date the information is

Food is usually date stamped so that after a certain date it would be best not to eat it.

Information should be date stamped, as using out-of-date information could result in problems such as bills being sent to the wrong address, decisions being based on incorrect information and so on.

All reports and printouts from a computer should be date stamped so that the user knows how recent the information is.

A report showing out of stock items in a store printed out on Monday should not be used to place orders for more stock on a Friday, as many more items would have gone out of stock by then and there is the possibility that more stock may have replaced previously out of stock items.

The completeness of information

It is hard in any organisation to base decisions on incomplete information. For example, a customer may ring up and order some goods and the salesperson may say that they will be delivered the next day. The salesperson may not have a stock list so they have incomplete information regarding the stock position. It is therefore important that the salesperson has all the facts, such as the current stock position, when taking orders.

How easy the information is to understand

The meaning of any information should be clear to the user and any abbreviations or codes used should be explained. Information cannot be used properly unless it is understood. It is also

important that information is unambiguous, since it could mean that members at a meeting could be talking at cross purposes.

There is a requirement under the Data Protection Act 1998 that if the data subject requests information about themselves, the information must be presented clearly with any codes explained.

Complex data, particularly in the form of numbers in tables, are quite difficult to understand and interpret. It is much better if such information is presented pictorially so that comparisons between figures can be made quickly and any trends can easily be spotted. It should not be up to the reader to do this further analysis, so the information you supply should always be in the form that makes it easy to understand.

How well information is targeted

Information needs to be targeted at the person who is going to use it. Management frequently receive reports containing detailed figures and diagrams, when all they really need is an overview of the situation. The lower the level of management, the more detailed the information needs to be. The lowest level of management needs details on daily operations in order to make decisions about scheduling, stock control, payroll, staff rotas, etc. Top managers and directors should not have to wade through mountains of detail just to get the information they need in order to arrive at a decision. All they need is to be able to identify problems and trends at a glance, so just a summary is needed.

How much user confidence there is in the information

Sometimes, when users ask for information from the system, they spot some aspect of the information that they know is definitely wrong. This causes them to suspect other aspects of the information. For example, the system may tell them that there are five items of a certain product in stock when they know that there are actually only two.

When this happens the user has no confidence in the system providing the information and rather than use the system to tell them how many items of a product are in stock, they would prefer to go and check.

The importance of keeping data up-to-date

There is a requirement under the Data Protection Act 1998 for anyone who processes personal data to keep that information accurate and up-to-date.

It is very difficult for a business to do this alone. For example, if you move house, you are likely to tell your bank, credit card companies, utility companies (gas, electricity, telephone, etc.) but unlikely to tell the company you booked a holiday with last year so they can stop sending you brochures.

There are companies that keep details of people who:

- have moved house (including their new address)
- have deceased
- have asked not to be sent unsolicited mail (i.e., mail that they have not asked for)
- have never responded to a mail-shot.

The companies provide a service where you can update your data with all the changes.

You are probably wondering where these organisations get this data. Here is where it comes from:

- The moving details come from the utility companies who are contacted with the new address details when people move.
- The deceased data comes from the Registers of Births, Marriages and Deaths.
- The people who do not want to be sent mail-shots comes from a database set up by the Mailing Preference Service (MPS).
- Data concerning people who have never responded to a mail-shot comes from all the companies who send mail-shots who pool this information together.

Sometimes you can have too much data.

Processing huge amounts of data

Sometimes the main problem with data is that there is too much rather than too little. Within hours of the terrorist attack on the London Underground on 7 July, police were gathering huge amounts of data which included:

- CCTV footage
- mobile phone records
- witness statements.

They managed to process all of the available data and managed to arrest the people involved.

Processing huge amounts of data requires a powerful computer coupled with sophisticated software.

How to find information

▼ You will find out

▶ About on-line information sources (intranet and Internet)

▶ About information on CD-ROMs

▶ About non-ICT sources of information

Introduction

Much of the information needed by an organisation comes from within the organisation, and the organisation's ICT systems can be used to extract this information.

Many companies use information supplied from outside the organisation. For example, organisations subscribe to other organisations that supply credit information about their customers. There are also organisations that collect marketing information about each one of us, such as our likes and dislikes, what we buy, where we take our holidays, etc. Companies often pay for lists of customers who have certain requirements that could be met by the company.

On-line information sources

Much of the information management needs in order to make decisions can be obtained from on-line systems. This information can include information from the organisation's own systems as well as from the systems of others. For example, if a manager wants to know what percentage of goods have been returned by their customers as being faulty, then the internal systems will tell them this. If a large utility company needs to update its records with people who have changed address who have failed to tell them, then this can be bought from an external organisation that specialises in collecting this information.

Intranet

Many organisations use an intranet as an internal network to enable information to be shared. Intranets use Internet technology for internal networks used only by the staff of the organisation.

Users of the intranets are able to use web browser software to access data in any database that the organisation wants to make available. For example, sales staff could gain access to stock information using the intranet.

Intranets are good ways of making information available to lots of people, as they are used to using the Internet and they can quickly figure out how to search for specific information as the techniques are just the same.

Internet

Huge amounts of information can be found on the Internet and many companies subscribe to on-line services which provide them with the information they need. For example, high street travel agents have access to flights and holidays that are not available to book direct. They can access these systems using the Internet.

Here are some examples of information from the Internet that could be used by managers of an organisation:

- Tax information – to see how best to use the tax laws to lower the amount of tax paid by a business.
- Information about the Data Protection Act and other laws – to ensure that the company is complying with the law.
- Details of utility suppliers and their costs – so as to minimise the costs to an organisation.
- Research into competitors' products or services – so as to ensure that the company remains competitive.
- Information from the government's National Statistics Office can be used to find information useful for planning.

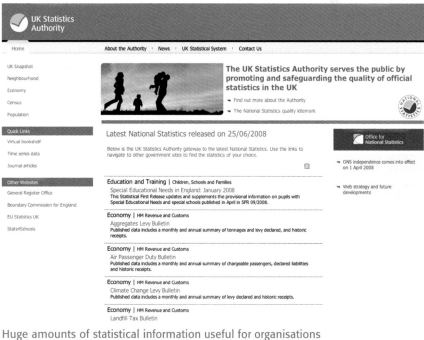

Huge amounts of statistical information useful for organisations are available from the National Statistics website. Take a look at the site at http://www.statistics.gov.uk/.

CD-ROMs are ideal for holding static data (i.e., data that does not vary much from day-to-day).

Postcode finder

To find the postcode for any UK address, please enter as much information as possible.

You can still do **15** more searches today.

Building number:		e.g. 17 (Do not use hyphens, e.g. 164-180)
Building name:		e.g. Montgomery House or Primrose Cottage
Street:		e.g. High Street or High St
Town:		e.g. Cambridge

Find a postcode ▸

This on-line postcode finder by the Royal Mail enables a postcode to be found. If you want to use the search facility more than 15 times, you need to pay a subscription.

Just Built™
Just Built™ puts you in touch with the UK's newest addresses.

Redirect Check
Prevent identify fraud with Redirect Check.

National Change of Address
Keep in touch with customers who move.

Universal Suppression Service
Clean your mailing lists and remove old data.

Here are some other services provided by Royal Mail. Think about how useful each set of information would be to a business or organisation.

CD-ROMs

The advantage in using CD-ROMs to hold information is that the information on the CD-ROMs cannot be altered and the fact that CDs can hold a large amount of information.

CD-ROMs are used less for the distribution of large amounts of information, mainly because most information does change and it is easier to access the information on-line.

Examples of information from CD-ROM include:

- A CD from the Royal Mail containing full listing of all known UK addresses, updated quarterly.
- A CD from a customer database to give travelling salespersons contact details and details about past orders.

Non-ICT sources of information

It is easy to assume that all the information that organisations use is available using ICT, but this is not the case. For example, if you go into a doctor's surgery you will still see lots of paper files. This is because there was a period where patient details were not computerised and transferring them on to a computer takes time.

Although computers are used in most organisations, there are smaller organisations that have yet to make the change. Maybe the owners are older and cannot be bothered to learn new systems or maybe with the small amount of paperwork, the paper-based system works well.

Non-ICT sources of information would include:

- directories (phone directories, Yellow Pages, etc.)
- maps
- paper invoices, bank statements, orders, P60s, credit card statements, utility bills, etc.
- old paper-based records
- reports
- letters
- newspapers
- journals
- manuals.

Yellow Pages: one of many paper-based sources of information.

Questions

▶ Questions 1 pp. 20–21

1 Managers in organisations have to base their decisions on the information they receive. It is therefore important that the information supplied to them is of good quality.
   (a) Give three features that information must have in order for it to be good quality information. (3 marks)
   (b) Give one reason why a firm making use of quality information will probably do better than a firm without quality information. (1 mark)

2 One quality of information is that it should be able to target resources of an organisation so giving the organisation a competitive advantage. Explain clearly, by giving an example, what this means. (2 marks)

3 A sales manager for a large car dealership says that he is always provided with 'quality' information from the firm's management information system. With the aid of examples, where appropriate, describe five characteristics of quality information. (5 marks)

4 Explain, by giving examples in each case, two problems caused by the use of out-of-date information. (2 marks)

▶ Questions 2 pp. 22–23

1 Managers gain much of their information from their on-line systems. Give three information sources that a manager could use, where the information obtained is not from an ICT source. (3 marks)

2 Mangers frequently need information that is not available on-line. Give two examples of such information and explain briefly why each piece of information is needed. (2 marks)

Exam support

Worked example 1

1 In order for management to make good decisions, it needs good quality information. One feature of good quality information is that it is accurate.
   Give four other features of good quality information. (4 marks)

Student answer 1

1 The information must be relevant as users of the information do not want to waste time reading information that is not relevant to their purpose.
   The information must be accurate because in most cases it will be used to base decisions on.
   The information must be collected for a purpose otherwise there is no point in producing it.

Examiner's comment

1 Because the word in the question is 'Give four other features', no explanations are needed so students giving these simply waste their time which could be better spent on more detailed explanations for other questions.
   The first answer is correct.
   The second answer gains no marks because they had to describe 'four other' features. Accuracy was mentioned in the question.
   The third answer is not an answer to this question and gains no marks.
   (1 mark out of 4)

Student answer 2

1 Relevant
   Understandable
   Complete
   Up-to-date

Examiner's comment

1 All of the answers are correct.
   (4 marks out of 4)

Examiner's answers

1 Notice the word 'give' in the question. This means that a complete explanation is not needed.
   One mark each to a maximum of four for four of the following:
   Accurate
   Correctly targeted
   Understandable
   Complete
   Relevant
   Up-to-date
   Has user confidence

Worked example 2

2 The owner of a tool hire company is moving over to using an ICT system for recording loans and returns of equipment. As well as recording information about the loans, the customers and the tools, the owner would like management information that would enable him to run the business more profitably.

(a) Explain, by giving an example applicable to his business, how management information could make his business more profitable. (3 marks)

(b) Management information can aid the owner in decision making. Give one example of a decision the owner could make and describe what management information from the ICT system he would need to make the decision. (2 marks)

(c) State two advantages that up-to-date, accurate and complete information will give the owner. (2 marks)

Student answer 1

2 (a) He could use the management information to make decisions that will make the business more profitable.

(b) He could use the system to find out which tools have been taken out the most and then use this information to ensure that enough of these tools are available to satisfy customer demand.

(c) The manager can target resources so that money is used to buy those pieces of equipment that are the most profitable to hire. The manager can make sure the information is complete and from the information he can identify trends.

Examiner's comment

2 (a) This answer gains no marks. The student should have explained what the information is and how the information makes the business more profitable.

(b) This answer explains what information is needed and also explains why the information is needed. A good answer that is worth both the marks.

(c) The first answer is correct. The second answer is ok as complete information is needed to spot trends. **(4 marks out of 7)**

Student answer 2

2 (a) He could use the customer and rentals information to find out who the best customers were over a year and then give them a special discounted hire rate. This would encourage the customer to remain loyal to the hire firm, which in turn will increase their profit.

(b) What equipment to buy. He could do a search and find out which equipment is hired the most and make sure that he buys more.

(c) He could target customers who used to hire equipment but have not hired equipment lately. Special offers may entice them back. Customer records need to be kept up-to-date so that you are not wasting time and money sending mail shots to customers who have moved. They can buy this information from the Royal Mail.

Examiner's comment

2 (a) This answer adequately explains what the information is and how it can improve the profitability. Full marks here.

(b) The decision is clear (i.e. what equipment to buy) and the answer explains what needs to be done to find this information. Two marks for this answer.

(c) Both of these answers are good so full marks here. **(7 marks out of 7)**

Examiner's answers

2 (a) One mark for the example, one mark for a clear description of the information that would be needed and one mark for an explanation (or implied reason) why the profitability is increased. Typical answers include:

Finding out the cost of the tool, how many times it is hired out and the hire fee, to work out the profit from the tool in one year. This would enable the owner to identify those tools not earning their keep.

Identifying who the best customers are by listing the amount spent per year at the hire store so that some loyalty discount is offered to them to make sure they do not start using a different hire firm.

(b) One mark for a clear statement of the decision and one mark for the information the system would need to supply for the decision to be made.
Example:
Deciding which extra tools to buy. Use the equipment and rentals data to produce a report outlining the number of times each tool has been hired out so that the most popular tools can be identified so more can be bought.

(c) Any two (one mark each) from:
Enables customers to be targeted for promotions, etc.
It enables accurate decisions to be made.
It allows trends to be spotted (e.g., a particular piece of equipment becoming more popular).
It allows the progress of the firm to be monitored by comparing actual sales with projected sales.

Summary mind maps

Quality of information

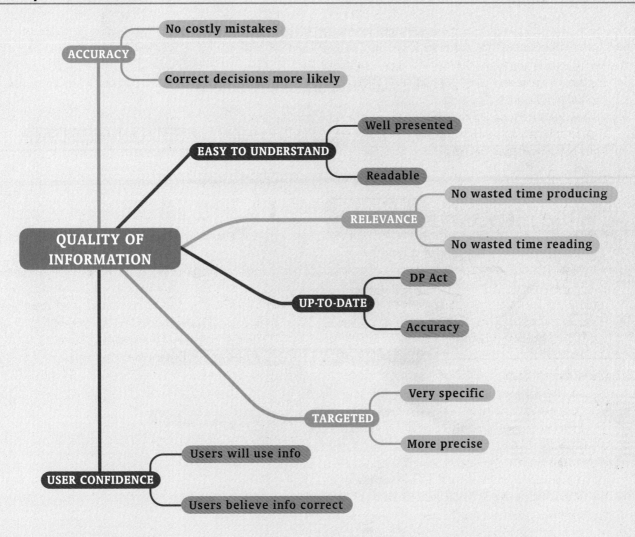

ACCURACY
- No costly mistakes
- Correct decisions more likely

QUALITY OF INFORMATION

EASY TO UNDERSTAND
- Well presented
- Readable

RELEVANCE
- No wasted time producing
- No wasted time reading

UP-TO-DATE
- DP Act
- Accuracy

TARGETED
- Very specific
- More precise

USER CONFIDENCE
- Users will use info
- Users believe info correct

How to find information

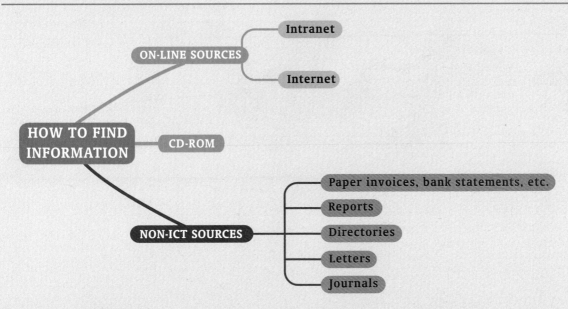

HOW TO FIND INFORMATION

ON-LINE SOURCES
- Intranet
- Internet

CD-ROM

NON-ICT SOURCES
- Paper invoices, bank statements, etc.
- Reports
- Directories
- Letters
- Journals

Summary mind maps continued

Examples of information a manager might need from the Internet

TAX INFORMATION TO REDUCE TAX BILLS

INFORMATION ABOUT COMPETITORS

DETAILS OF LAWS AND REGULATIONS BUSINESS MUST ADHERE TO

EXAMPLES OF INFORMATION A MANAGER MIGHT NEED FROM THE INTERNET

SUPPLIERS INFORMATION

STATISTICAL INFORMATION FOR PLANNING

DETAILS OF VENUES FOR COURSES/MEETINGS

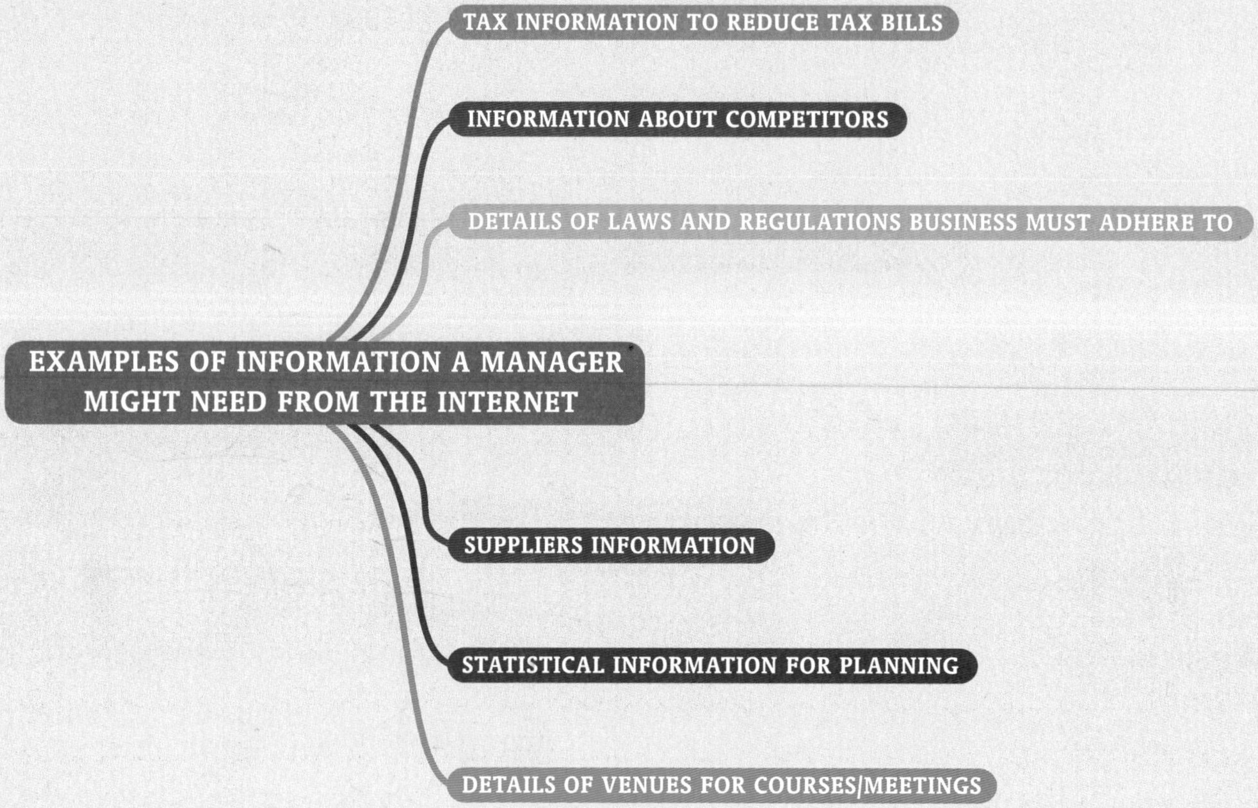

In this topic you will learn about what data errors are and the problems they can cause if data containing them is processed. Data errors can occur during input, transcription, processing and transmission and you will learn about how it is impossible to eliminate these errors from occurring. You will learn that it is possible to reduce the errors as much as possible by making use of a number of checks called validation and verification checks. You will learn about these checks and learn that they can only reduce errors.

▼ The key concepts covered in this topic are:

▶ How data errors occur

▶ The purpose of validation

▶ The purpose of verification

▶ Creating validation checks

CONTENTS

How data errors occur

▼ You will find out

► About the problems inaccurate data can cause

► About the errors that can occur during data input, transcription, processing and transmission

Introduction

The processing of incorrect data can produce ridiculous and embarrassing output. Errors can take time and effort to sort out and can be distressing to any people affected by incorrect personal data. When an ICT system is developed, it is essential that error checking is incorporated into the design. In this section you will be covering the types of error that can occur and how error checking techniques can increase the accuracy of data entry.

Problems with inaccurate data

The processing of accurate data is essential for any ICT system. Errors in data can cause all sorts of problems such as:

- incorrect decisions being made resulting in loss of money
- goods being sent to the wrong address
- having to spend time sorting out mistakes
- loss of goodwill
- loss of trust
- being prosecuted under the Data Protection Act 1998 for not keeping personal data accurate.

It is essential that techniques are built into any data entry method so that errors can be reduced, or in some cases eliminated.

How data errors can occur during input, transcription, processing and transmission

There are a number of ways in which data errors can occur. They can occur during:

- transcription
- input
- processing
- transmission.

How data errors occur during transcription

Transcription errors are mistakes humans make when either keying in data or filling in forms such as optical mark forms. Often they occur through carelessness and are not picked up by verification methods such as proof reading. Transcription is the process of copying data from a source document such as an order form or an application form. Transcription errors are those errors that are introduced during the keying in process

Careful training of staff and stressing the importance of accurate data entry may help to reduce transcription errors. Validation performed by the computer program that accepts the data can help, but the incorrect data being entered is often valid data which means that it is impossible to detect.

How data errors occur during input

Input data even though it has been verified (i.e., checked against the source documents) and validated, can still be incorrect. Incorrect data can occur in a variety of ways and it is usually any human involvement at either the data collection stage or the input stage that provides the weak link in the system. The only way to avoid errors is to keep human involvement to a minimum and therefore use direct methods of data capture such as MICR, OCR, bar coding, etc., whenever possible.

Keyboarding can introduce a large number of errors during input. Even automated methods of data entry,

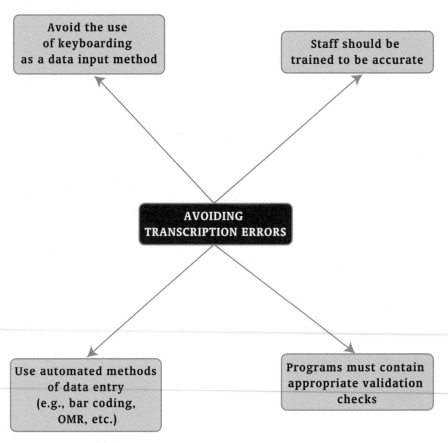

Summary of the ways the number of errors introduced during data entry can be decreased.

such as optical mark recognition or magnetic ink character recognition, can have problems with errors. For example, a form may not be read by the reader, because it may not have been marked correctly. It is important that the system does not try to guess at what the mark should be, as this would introduce incorrect data. Instead, the system should reject the form and leave it for a human to decide what to do.

Bar code readers in supermarkets make a beep that tells the operator that an item has been scanned correctly. This means that the person can scan the products in again if they do not hear the beep, or if that fails, manually enter the number at the bottom of the bar code.

How data errors occur during processing

Mistakes that could occur during processing include:

- A programming error that remained undiscovered during testing and only comes to light when a series of conditions apply. This can cause programs to crash (i.e. stop running).
- The use of the wrong version of a data file for processing data rather than the latest version. For example, you could use an older version of a spreadsheet by mistake or you could use the wrong set of data to perform a mail merge.
- Incorrect formulas in spreadsheet that were not detected and corrected during the testing, means that incorrect processes are being performed, leading to wrong information being output.
- Damage by viruses – viruses are able to delete data or otherwise render it unreadable.
- Equipment malfunction – hard disk drives are like any mechanical device in that they break down occasionally. This can cause the loss of data, so it is important to always back up files containing programs and data.

How data errors occur during transmission

When data is passed through a communication medium (wireless, metal wire, optic fibre), it is important that the data is not corrupted in any way and if it is, it is equally important that this is detected and the data is re-transmitted.

The checking of data after it has passed along a communication line is performed using a parity check. Parity checking works in the following way. The computer adds up the number of bits in one byte and if the parity is different to the parity setting, the computer will report an error. It is possible to use either even or odd parity. Taking odd parity, for instance, suppose we are sending the letter C along a communication line.

In ASCII code, the series of bits used to represent C is 1000011. Since there are three 1s in this code and odd parity is being used, a 0 is added to the left-hand side of the group of bits so that the total for the byte is odd. If even parity were being used, a 1 would need to be added so that total for the byte would then be an even number.

Communication devices have a chip inside them to deal with parity checks: the sending device adds the parity bits and the receiving unit calculates what the parity bit should be. If an error has occurred, transmission parity will no longer be observed, and the corruption is detected. The problem with parity checks is that if more than one error occurs and the errors compensate for each other, parity can still appear to be correct.

Binary codes are sent along communication channels (i.e., wires, fibre optic cable and wireless) and checks must be in place so that the data is not corrupted in any way during transmission.

The purpose and types of validation

Introduction

There are a number of validation checks that can be used to validate data being entered into an ICT system. The more validation in place, the less likely ridiculous data is to be processed.

The validity and correctness of data

For a piece of data to be valid, it has to obey certain rules. For example, if a field has been set for the entry of a number, and a letter is entered instead, then the letter is not a valid piece of data for that field. As you can set fields in databases to accept only certain types of data, this would be spotted by the database and the piece of data would not be accepted.

If the surname 'James' was entered incorrectly as 'Jones' then it would be accepted into the database, as 'Jones' is as much a piece of valid data as 'James'. Both pieces of data are valid yet one is incorrect. You can see that there is a difference between the correctness and validity of data.

Types of error which can occur during data entry

The commonest errors during data entry using a keyboard can be put into two groups:

- transcription errors
- transposition errors.

Transcription errors

Transcription involves the transferring of data (written or printed on a form) to the computer, usually by keying it in. Transcription can also involve typing what a person says into the computer. Unfortunately human operators who have to key in the data are faced with a number of problems, namely:

- Problems with understanding speech – the person not speaking clearly enough into the phone.
- A caller not spelling out unusual words or names – the person doing the keying in, guesses the spelling.
- Poor handwriting – the source document (application form, order form, payment slip, etc.) has writing on it which cannot be read.
- Misinterpretation – the person keying in misinterprets information on the form or what was said over the phone.
- Typing mistakes – the keyboard operator reads or hears the right information but makes a mistake when typing it in.

Transposition errors

Transposition errors are easy to make when typing at high speed and involve the accidental swapping around of characters. Examples of transposition errors include typing in:

- 'fro' instead of 'for'
- the account number 100065 instead of the correct account number 100056
- the flight number AB376 instead of BA376.

It has been estimated that around 70% of keyboarding errors are transposition errors. Transposition errors can be spotted during the proof reading process and it is also possible to spot some of them by using spellcheckers.

Important numbers such as account numbers, employee numbers, VAT numbers, National Insurance numbers, etc., make use of check digits which enable checking on the accuracy of the input of these numbers.

Validation

Validation is a check performed by a computer program during data entry. Validation is the process which ensures that data accepted for processing is sensible and reasonable. Validation is performed by the computer program being used and consists of a series of checks called **validation checks**.

When a developer develops a solution to an ICT problem, they must create checks to lessen the likelihood of the user entering incorrect information. This is done by restricting the user as to what they can enter, or checking that the data obeys certain rules.

Validation checks

Validation checks are used to restrict the user as to the data they can enter. There are many different validation checks each with their own special use including:

- Data type checks – these check if the data being entered is the same type as the data type specified for the field. This would check to make sure that only numbers are entered into fields specified as numeric.
- Presence checks – some database fields have to be filled in, whilst others can be left empty. A presence check would check to make sure that data had been entered into a field. Unless the user fills in data for these fields, the data will not be processed.
- Length checks – checks to make sure that the data being entered has the correct number of characters in it. For example, a six-digit account number will be checked to make sure it contains exactly six digits.
- File/Table lookups – are used to make sure that codes being used are the same as those used in a table or file of codes. For example, a car parts firm has lots of parts, with each part being given its own code. If a person types in a code for a part, it will be checked against the table to ensure it is a valid code.
- Cross field checks – the data in more than one field often need to be checked together to make sure they make sense. For example, when data is entered for a department in an organisation, the extension number is compared to make sure that it is a valid extension for that department.

- Range checks – are performed on numbers. They check that a number being entered is within a certain range. For example, all the students in a college are aged over 14, so a date of birth being entered which would give an age less than this would not be allowed by the range check.
- Format checks – are performed on codes to make sure that they conform to the correct combinations of characters. For example, a code for car parts may consist first of three numbers followed by a single letter. This can be specified for a field to restrict entered data to this format.

Remember

Not only is there a requirement that data is error free, it is essential that data is kept up-to-date. Data that is not kept up-to-date will be accurate at the time it was entered but changes to details such as name, address, phone number, etc., will mean that errors start to creep in. If personal data is stored, then there is a requirement under the Data Protection Act 1998 to keep such details up-to-date.

Check digits

Check digits are added to important numbers such as account numbers, International Book Numbers (ISBNs), Article numbers (the numbers under the barcode), etc. These numbers are placed at the end of the block of numbers and are used to check that the numbers have been entered correctly into the computer.

ISBN 978-1-85008-280-4

9 781850 082804

The 13-digit number shown underneath the bars is encoded in the bars, which means they can be scanned to give the number rather than having to type it in.

When the large number is entered, the computer performs a calculation using all the numbers to work out this extra number. If the calculation reveals that the extra number (called the check digit) is the same as that calculated by the other numbers, it means that all the numbers have been entered correctly.

The limitations of error checking

Despite all the checks put in place errors will still occur. It is very easy for someone to think they know how to spell a person's name when they don't. There are many names that sound the same but are spelt differently. All you can do is put in as many checks as possible to reduce the probability of errors occurring.

In order to reduce errors it is best to:

- reduce the amount of typed input to a minimum – to reduce errors it is much better to capture data automatically using optical mark/character recognition, bar coding, etc., rather than type it in
- allow a user to type in their details – they will be unlikely to make a mistake with their own details
- allow a user to check their details and confirm they are correct
- use as many validation and verification methods as is possible.

The purpose of verification

▼ **You will find out**

▶ About what verification is and the different methods of verification

▶ About how content can be verified and validated

Introduction

Many applications still require that data is keyed into the computer system using a keyboard. In many cases the person doing the keying in will either be looking at a form containing the data or may be listening to someone give them the details over the telephone. In this topic you will be looking at verification of data and how it plays its part ensuring the accuracy of information.

Verification

Verification means checking that the data being entered into the ICT system perfectly matches the source of the data. For example, if details from an order form were being typed in using a keyboard, then when the user has finished, the data on the form on the screen will be identical to that on the paper form (i.e., the data source). There are three methods of verification:

- proof reading
- double entry of data
- sending back printouts.

Proof reading involves one user carefully reading what they have typed in and comparing it with what is on the data source (order forms, application forms, invoices, etc.) for any errors, which can then be corrected.

In **double entry of data**, two people use the same data source to enter the details into the ICT system and only if the two sets of data are identical, will they be accepted for processing. The disadvantage of this is that the cost of data entry is doubled.

Sending back printouts is another way to check that information is correct by printing the information out and sending it back in hard copy form to the person who supplied it, in the hope that they will be able to spot anything that is wrong. This is the procedure when you book a holiday over the phone. The travel agents will send you a printout of the confirmation of the booking which you should check carefully and then let them know if there are any mistakes.

Verifying and validating content

If you are developing a multimedia ICT solution to a client problem, there are many ways of checking content so that the final solution is accurate and fit for purpose. Content means the material you are putting on the website, presentation, etc., such as text, images (photographs, cartoons, line drawings, sketches), video, sound, etc.

During the development of multimedia products it is necessary to check the content or the arrangement of the content by:

- Checking the accuracy of any content supplied. Any factual information included should be checked.
- Checking the readability of the content based on the characteristics of the user/audience such as age, ICT experience, etc.

- Spellchecking – there is nothing worse than clients, users or audiences spotting spelling mistakes. Use the spellchecking feature of the software tools to make sure that these do not occur.
- Grammar checking – correct grammar is essential and so use the grammar checking feature of the software tools to check this automatically. You should also allow others to read through the content to check that it makes sense.
- Checking all the content is present – it is easy to leave out a bit of text or an image. Proof reading by yourself or others will be able to spot this.

▶ **KEY WORDS**

Verification – checks that the data being typed in matches exactly the data on the document used to supply the information

Validation – the process which ensures that data accepted for processing is sensible and reasonable

Proof reading – carefully reading what has been typed in and comparing it with what is on the data source (order forms, application forms, invoices, etc.) for any errors, which can then be corrected

Spellchecker – facility offered by software where there is a dictionary against which all words typed in are checked

Grammar checker – used to check the grammar in a sentence and to highlight problems and suggest alternatives

Data should be verified so that it is fit for purpose.

- Ensuring that there is no duplication of content – one common mistake is to say the same thing twice. Proof reading will be able to spot this.
- Checking consistency of layout – webpages or slides with similar content should have a consistent design. Again this can be spotted and corrected by proof reading.
- Checking images – images should be checked to make sure they are the correct size and of an appropriate resolution.
- Checking that the font and font size are appropriate for the characteristics of the user and/or audience.
- Checking that images are suitable for the text.

Examples of verification

Double entry of data

When creating passwords, they are often keyed in twice by the user and only if both versions match will they be accepted as the user's new password. If a user were to make a mistake with a single password, they would not know what the password they typed in was and this can cause many unnecessary calls to the helpdesk.

Proof reading

Suppose you are entering pupil details into a pupil database for a school. The parents will usually provide the information on a form that has been sent to them. The details on this form are then keyed into the database.

Typing mistakes are easily made and it is easy to misread information on a sheet.

Once the person inputting the information has finished, they will carefully work through the information contained in each field with what is supplied on the application form to check that the information is the same.

Sending back printouts

If you buy a book or CD, for example, using the Internet, you will have to make your selections usually by adding your purchases to the shopping trolley. When you reach the checkout and pay for your purchases you will then receive a confirmation e-mail which acts as your receipt and also a way of you checking your order. Most people print out this e-mail for checking as they find it easier to check that way and it is useful for future reference.

When goods are ordered in a more traditional way (i.e., without the use of the Internet), a printout of the order is sent to the customer that they can check. Any problems with the order can be notified and corrected before the goods arrive.

Avoiding human error

The human factor is often the cause of errors and methods which avoid the use of humans for the input of data are preferable to reduce errors. Most errors are introduced during keyboarding so, if possible, keyboarding needs to be replaced by direct input methods, but they are not always appropriate.

Direct input methods do improve the accuracy of input but these methods can still introduce errors. For example, a scanner used to read the marks on an optical mark form may read imperfections in the paper or card as marks.

Using scanners such as bar code or optical mark readers enables data to be captured more accurately than by typing the details in. They are also a faster and cheaper way of entering data.

Collecting data over the phone makes verification more difficult as there is no paperwork to refer to. So the customer details need to be carefully verified at the time (e.g., name, contact details, order details, etc.).

Creating validation checks

▼ You will find out

▶ About how to produce validation checks using database software

▶ About how to produce validation checks using spreadsheet software

Introduction

When you create an ICT solution you need to bear in mind that other users may well use the solution who may not be as careful as you are when entering data. It is essential that you try to restrict as much as possible the data that a user can enter by using validation checks.

Here you will learn how validation checks can be created using both database and spreadsheet software.

Validation and databases

When databases are created, validation rules are created for some of the fields in the database. Not all database fields can contain validation checks. For example, a person's surname can be almost any combination of characters so it would be hard to distinguish between a correct and incorrect one. You can, of course, specify the type of data that can go into each field and the length (i.e., the number of characters) for each field.

There are many different validation checks for databases depending on the type of field being validated. Many checks are performed by the database software itself. For example, if a field is specified as being numeric, letters cannot be entered.

The actual instructions for the validation check given to the database are called validation expressions. As well as creating the validation expressions, the database designer needs to produce the messages that will appear should the user type in data for the field which breaches the rule. Ideally such text should give them some idea about what is wrong with the data.

Look at the following table. It shows validation expressions for fields using the database software Microsoft Access. The second column contains the validation message which will appear if the user types in data unacceptable for the field.

Validation expression	Message appearing if expression is not valid
>50 And <100	The number entered must be over 50 and under 100. Note this does not include the numbers 50 or 100.
>=10 And <=20	The number entered must be between 10 and 20 including the numbers 10 and 20.
>0	A positive number must be entered.
<>0	A non-zero number must be entered.
>#12/01/07#	A date after the date 12/01/07 must be entered.
>=#01/01/08#	A date on or after the date 01/01/08 must be entered.
Like"????Y"	The data entered must be five characters long ending in the letter Y.
= 3 Or 4	The data being entered must be 3 or 4.
>=#01/01/07# And <#31/12/07#	The data being entered must be in the year 07.
"Male" Or "Female"	Only the words Male or Female can be entered.
<=Date()	The date entered must be today's date or sooner.

Validating entry into spreadsheet software

Many ICT solutions created using spreadsheet software need the user to supply their own data. Validation checks can be created on a cell or a cell range in order to restrict the data a user can enter. In this section you will learn about the various methods used to validate data entry into spreadsheets.

⤷ KEY WORDS

Validation expression/rule – the command that a developer must type in order to set up the validation for a particular field/cell

Validation message – the message the user will see if they type in data that does not meet the validation rules for the field

Creating a successful database includes adding validation checks.

▶ Activity 1: Validating cells and creating validation messages

In this activity you are going to find out how validation checks can be applied to cells in the spreadsheet package Microsoft Excel.

1 Load Excel and create a new worksheet.
2 Suppose data is being entered into cells from A3 to A5. We need to put validation checks in all these cells. To choose a range for the validation check, highlight all the cells from cell A3 to cell A5.
3 Click on  and select Validation... from the pull-down menu like this

4 The following Data Validation screen appears:

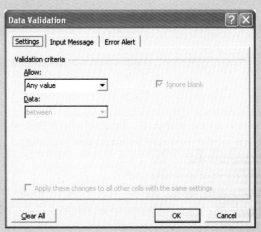

Click on the pull-down menu under Allow

5 Here you can select the type of data that you want to go into the cell. In this worksheet whole numbers need to be entered in the selected cells so click on **Whole number**.
Notice from this list, all the different ways you can specify for data being entered into a cell. Once you have specified a particular type of data it can prevent other different types of data from being entered.

6 Now click on the Data: pull-down menu.

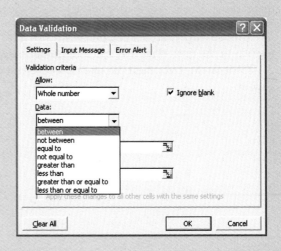

Select **between** from the list.

Creating validation checks continued

7   In the <u>Mi</u>nimum box enter 1 and in the Ma<u>x</u>imum box enter 100 like this:

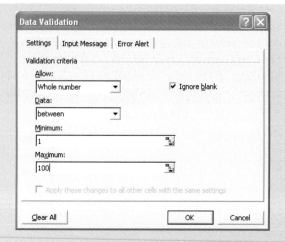

8   You have now added a validation check that will only allow whole numbers between and including 1 to 100 to be entered.

9   **Adding an input message**
An input message appears when the user selects the cell. It lets the user know what values it is acceptable to enter.
   Click on the Input Message tab and the following window appears.
   Enter the text as shown into the <u>T</u>itle: and <u>I</u>nput message: boxes

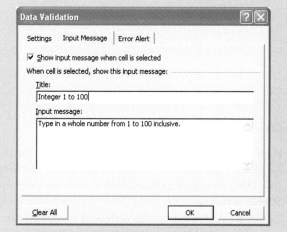

10 **Adding a validation message**
When a user tries to enter invalid data into a cell containing a validation check, the following message appears:

   This message is not very helpful because it does not explain to the user what they can and cannot enter.
   Click on the Error Alert tab and enter the text as shown:

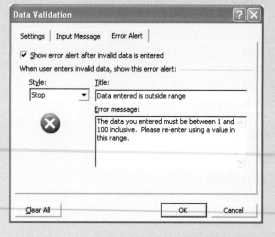

11 Click on OK to make all the changes.

12 You now have to test this validation check.

       You need to check that:
- It only allows whole numbers to be entered.
- It only allows numbers between 1 and 100 to be entered.

It is best to create a table and then enter in the values into cell A4 of the spreadsheet and record what happens. You should never assume that a validation check will work as expected without checking it.

13 Type each of the numbers into cell A3 in turn and then copy and complete the validation table shown below.

Validation check for cell: A3			
Value entered	**What should happen**	**What actually happens**	**Action needed**
0	Not accepted	Not accepted	None
1			
2			
20			
99			
100			
101			
7.5			
-2			
A			

       Remember – always ensure that your validation checks work as expected. Do not simply assume they will work.

14 To complete the validation you need to check that all the cells in the range from A3 to A5 have the validation check. You can do this by entering valid and invalid values into the cells.

Restricting the user to a list

One way of helping a user enter correct data is to supply them with a list of items to choose from. Using a list prevents the user from entering data that is not on a list. The only problem with lists is that they are only appropriate when there are only a small number of choices, for a field such as M or F, ranking of 1 to 5, etc.

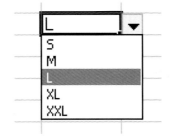

Here the sizes of a shirt are shown as a list from which the user can select.

Questions

Questions 1 pp. 30–31

1 There are a number of ways in which data errors can occur.
By giving an example in each case, describe how errors can occur during:
(a) Input (2 marks)
(b) Transcription (2 marks)
(c) Processing (2 marks)
(d) Transmission (2 marks)

2 If inaccurate data is processed, it can have a number of different consequences.
Describe three distinctly different consequences of processing data that is incorrect.
(6 marks)

Questions 2 p.32

1 Think about the types of mistake you make when typing information into a computer. Write a list of **three** different mistakes you can make. (3 marks)

2 A computer manager says 'data can be valid yet be incorrect'. By giving **one** suitable example, explain what this statement means. (3 marks)

Questions 3 pp. 33–34

1 A college keeps all of its staff details in a file held on their administration ICT system. Shown below is a section of the file showing the data entered into some of the fields.

Surname	Forename	Dept Number	Dept Name	Ext Number
Peter	Hughes	112	Accounts	318
Suzanne	Roberts	121	Accounts	671
Charles	Jones	361	Personnel	432
Jenny		712	Student services	543
James	Wong	361	Accounts	543
Suzanne	Roberts	121	Accounts	671

(a) During the entry of this data, the validation checks were turned off. By referring to the data held in the above table, state **four** problems that have occurred. (4 marks)
(b) For each **one** of the problems identified in (a), state the name of the validation check that could have been used to prevent the problems. (4 marks)
2 (a) Explain clearly the difference between data validation and data verification. (2 marks)
(b) Give three different ways in which data being entered into a database can be verified. (3 marks)

Questions 4 pp. 36–39

1 Using the validation expressions in the table on page 36 to help you, write down a sentence explaining how each validation expression works.
(a) "Junior" Or "Senior"
(b) = 1 Or 2
(c) >=Date()
(d) Like"A????"
(e) Like"???????"
(f) <20
(g) >=1 And <=50
(h) >=#01/02/08#
(i) >=#01/01/08# And <=#31/12/08#
(j) "M" Or "F"

2 Explain the difference between a validation rule and a validation message. (2 marks)

Case study

▶ **Case study 1** pp. 30–39

British Gas sends out £2.3 trillion bill

Utility British Gas has admitted sending one of its customers a bill for £2,320,333,681,613. Brian Law of Fartown, Huddersfield, received the bill last month as a final demand after failing to pay an earlier bill of £59. The sum of £2.3 trillion was apparently due for electricity supplied to Mr Law's new home in Fartown. And the letter from British Gas threatened to take him to court unless he paid the amount in full. Mr Law, who runs an exhibition company called Prodis Play in Leeds, had delayed paying the original bill last year because he was away on business.

A penny a day

According to the local newspaper, the Yorkshire Post, Mr Law attempted to call British Gas to resolve the matter but with little result. 'After two hours, I did get through to somebody, and said I had received this bill,' Mr Law told the newspaper. 'I started reading the figure out and the girl I was speaking to said there must have been a mistake. Eventually, I talked to a chap who promised to sort things out and he asked me to fax the bill through. I did that and rang again on the Wednesday, but this gent wasn't in and neither was his manager. I kept leaving all my phone numbers but nobody rang back.' Eventually, Mr Law decided that he would only be able to resolve the matter by going to court and offering to pay a penny a week.

'Simple mistake'

However, after enquiries by the press, British Gas responded, saying it was a 'simple, clerical mistake'. The figure on the final demand was in fact the meter reference for Mr Law's property. 'The clerical error meant that the reference ended up in the bill's total box', said a spokesman for the company in Leeds. The company said it had 'a very amiable conversation' with Mr Law about the mix-up, adding, 'he seemed to see the funny side'. Mr Law will now be setting up a direct debit arrangement to pay his future bills. 'There is certainly no question of us taking him to court or cutting off his supply', the company added.

(Article which appeared on BBC website March 2003 http://news.bbc.co.uk/1/hi/business/2818611.stm)

1 Processing accurate data is a requirement for any ICT system. In this case study inaccurate data was processed to produce ridiculous results.
Explain **two** different consequences to an organisation of processing inaccurate data. (4 marks)

2 The diagram on page 42 shows a gas bill.
(a) Explain clearly how the customer in the case study above came to get his extremely large bill. (1 mark)
(b) (i) Give the name of a suitable validation check that could have been used for the amount of the bill. (1 mark)
(ii) Describe how the check you have described in part (i) can prevent the error described in the case study from occurring. (1 mark)

3 The customer reference number is a unique number given to each customer and contains 9 digits.
(a) The first customer entered onto the system has customer reference number 000000001
(i) Write down the maximum number of unique customer reference numbers it would be possible to have with this ICT system. (1 mark)
(ii) Name and describe a validation check that could ensure that only numbers are entered into this field. (2 marks)
(iii) Name and describe a validation check that could be used that would ensure that only 9 digits could be entered for the customer reference number. (2 marks)

(b) A payment slip similar to that on page 42 is used when a customer pays a bill. Each payment a customer makes is given a unique number. This payment number is a 23-digit number. A bar code is used so that this large number can be entered automatically into the ICT system.
(i) Give one reason why bar coding is used here for data input. (1 mark)
(ii) Bar coding often makes use of a check digit. Briefly explain the purpose of a check digit. (2 marks)

Topic 4 Validation and verification

Your gas bill

Mr A Nother
123 Park Avenue
Northbridge Wells
Countyshire
NW55 2PL

Customer account
912345678

Telephone
01912 345678

Website
www.home-energypower.com

	Previous	Present	Units/kWh	Total
Reading	11942 E	12150 E	208 = 2311.47 kWh	

Charges	Standard		Meter number 99999	
965 kWh at 4.266p per kWh (1 May 07 to 12 Jun 07)				£41.17
1346.47 kWh at 2.173p per kWh (1 May 07 to 12 Jun 07)				£29.26

	Total
Subtotal (excluding VAT)	£70.43
VAT at 5.0% on £70.43	£3.52
Charges for this period	£73.95
Previous bill 1-May-2007 12345666	£77.42
Payment received – Thank you 8-Jun-2007 01234567	£77.42

Amount to Pay   £73.95

- -

Transfer
Cash Company

bank credit

Reference (Customer number)		Credit account number	Amount due
`123`	`912345678`	`1234 56`	£ 73.95

Cheque acceptable

Cashier's stamp and number	Signature	Date	

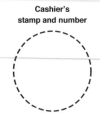

`9123 4567 8912 3456 789`

Any?Bank

Sort code
`11-22-33`

	CASH	
	CHEQUE	

£ _____

Exam support

Worked example 1

1 Read the following sentence:
   Validation checks can ensure that data is reasonable or sensible, but they cannot ensure that data are correct.
   By giving a suitable example, explain carefully what this sentence means. (4 marks)

Student answer 1

1 Data might be wrong but it still passes the validation check. An example is where a person makes a spelling mistake when typing in a name. The name will still be accepted even though it is wrong.

Examiner's comment

1 The first sentence is true but it needs to mention that the validation checks will check for data that is obviously incorrect or ridiculous data.
   The spelling mistake is a bad example to choose as it is hard to validate a person's name. You can only really use a data type check. The answer does not fully answer the question asked. (2 marks out of 4)

Student answer 2

1 The user types in a quantity of laser printer toner cartridges they want to order. They want to order 2 but instead they incorrectly type 20. There is a validation check called a range check which will only query or not accept the quantity if less than 0 or greater than 150. Since 20 is in range it will be accepted even though the number 20 is incorrect. Hence the quantity 20 is incorrect yet still valid and will be accepted for processing.

Examiner's comment

1 Here a clear example has been given for a field that has a stated validation check (i.e., a range check) and there is a clear explanation of how data can be valid yet incorrect. (4 marks out of 4)

Examiner's answers

1 Two marks for explanation and two marks for the example.
   Any example here which picks up the fact that validation can only restrict the data but it cannot ensure the correctness of data.
   The user enters a date such as 09/11/75. The validation check on the date field will check that the date is not impossible or a date into the future and perhaps a check to make sure that the date does not make the person ridiculously old. However, if the user makes a mistake whilst typing in and transposes two digits and enters 09/11/57, then as this is a valid date it will not be picked up by the validation check. Hence the validation check can only check that the data is sensible or reasonable.

Worked example 2

2   A tool hire company uses database software to record the details of all its customers. Before a customer can hire tools, the company must record the following details: title, forename, surname, address, postcode and date of birth. Name and describe a validation check that can be used when data is entered into each of the following fields. The validation check must be different in each case. **(8 marks)**

(a) Surname   (c) Date of birth

(b) Postcode   (d) Title

Student answer 1

2 (a) Format check   (c) Range check

  (b) Format check   (d) Format check

Examiner's comment

2 The student should have looked at the mark scheme and noticed that there are a total of 8 marks which means two marks for each part.

   As stated clearly in the question they needed to name the type of check and also to describe the check. This student has only named the check. Always look at the mark related to the parts of the questions to prevent this kind of mistake which is so common. This student has reduced the marks they can now get by half.

   Answer (a) is incorrect – a format check is used for codes where there is a combination of letters and numbers.

   Answer (b) is correct for the postcode.

   Answer (c) is correct for the date of birth.

   A format check is inappropriate for a name. It is hard to validate a name so a data type check is the only simple check besides checking against a list or a file of names. **(2 marks out of 8)**

Student answer 2

2 (a) A presence check which means that the field cannot be left blank. The name would be needed to contact the customer.

  (b) Postcode could be cross-checked against a database obtained by the Royal Mail of all the postcodes to check that it is a valid postcode.

  (c) A range check so that the age as calculated from the date of birth does not make the person ridiculously too young or too old.

  (d) Title can be validated using a check to make sure that there are no numbers in the person's title.

Examiner's comment

2 Answers (a) to (c) give both a correct name for a suitable check and a suitable description of the check. In part (d) the person has not given a name to the check, so only one mark for this last part. The check they have described is a data type check.
   (7 marks out of 8)

Examiner's answers

2 One mark each for the name of a validation check and one mark for a correct description for each field.

   (a)   Data type check – to make sure there are no numbers in the name.
        Presence check – to check that data has been entered into the field.

   (b)   Format check – so that the postcode contains the correct combinations of letters and numbers for it to be a valid postcode.
        Table lookup – could be cross-checked against the database obtained from Royal Mail to make sure that the postcode actually exists.
        Length check – to make sure that the correct number of characters for a postcode have been entered (e.g., 7, 8 or 9 characters).
        Cross field check – could check that the postcode matches the address field.

   (c)   Format check – check that the data entered is in the correct format for a date, e.g. DD/MM/YY.
        Range check – to make sure that the date is not in the future or does not make the customer too old or young.

   (d)   Length check – to make sure the title does not contain too many characters.
        Presence check – to ensure data has been entered for the field.
        Table lookup – to check that a valid title has been entered by comparing the title with a list of titles in a table.
        Data type check – to make sure that the title does not contain any numbers.

Summary mind maps

When data errors occur

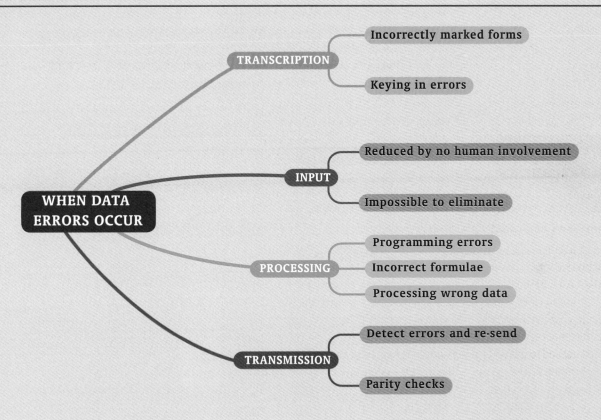

TRANSCRIPTION
- Incorrectly marked forms
- Keying in errors

WHEN DATA ERRORS OCCUR

INPUT
- Reduced by no human involvement
- Impossible to eliminate

PROCESSING
- Programming errors
- Incorrect formulae
- Processing wrong data

TRANSMISSION
- Detect errors and re-send
- Parity checks

The purpose and types of validation

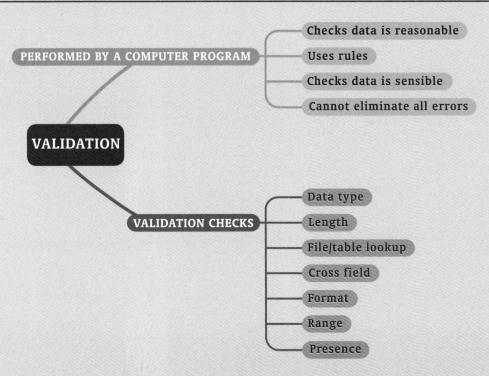

VALIDATION

PERFORMED BY A COMPUTER PROGRAM
- Checks data is reasonable
- Uses rules
- Checks data is sensible
- Cannot eliminate all errors

VALIDATION CHECKS
- Data type
- Length
- File/table lookup
- Cross field
- Format
- Range
- Presence

Verification

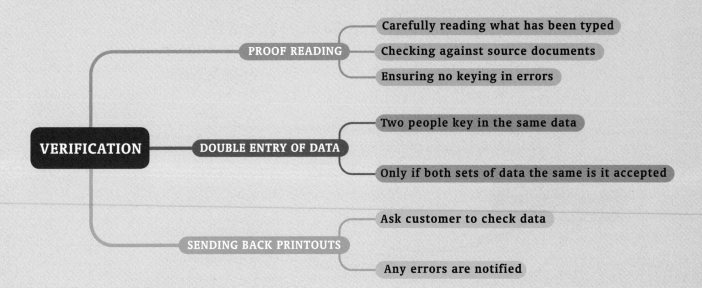

VERIFICATION

- **PROOF READING**
  - Carefully reading what has been typed
  - Checking against source documents
  - Ensuring no keying in errors

- **DOUBLE ENTRY OF DATA**
  - Two people key in the same data
  - Only if both sets of data the same is it accepted

- **SENDING BACK PRINTOUTS**
  - Ask customer to check data
  - Any errors are notified

TOPIC 5: Capabilities and limitations of ICT

In this topic you will learn about the capabilities and limitations of ICT systems. You will learn that the use of ICT offers many advantages over manual methods of processing data, and what these are. ICT systems are not always perfect and you will learn about the factors that limit the efficiency of data processing systems.

▼ The key concepts covered in this topic are:

▶ Advantages of ICT over manual methods of processing data

▶ Factors affecting the efficiency of data processing systems

▶ Limitations of data processing systems

CONTENTS

Advantages of ICT over manual methods of processing data

Introduction

Computer systems now perform many of the routine activities performed when processing transactions such as orders, purchases, payments, etc.

The main advantages of ICT over manual methods of processing data are:

- repetitive processing
- speed of processing
- data storage capacity
- speed of searching
- accuracy
- speed of data communications
- the ability to produce different output formats
- the ability to search and combine data in many different ways that would otherwise be impossible
- improved security of data and processes.

Repetitive processing

Processors are so fast that there are not many tasks that challenge them. What computers are very good at is fast repetitive processing where similar tasks are repeated over and over again with just a few small changes. Fast repetitive processing is required in many applications such as billing systems for producing utility bills or credit card statements.

Some simple examples of how fast, repetitive processing can help most users with their work include:

- performing a mail merge
- sending the same e-mail to everyone in your e-mail address book
- replicating a formula down a column or across a row in a spreadsheet
- setting up a style sheet so that all the documents based on it have a similar design.

Speed of processing

Speed of processing depends on:

- the speed of the processor
- the speed of communication if the processing is being performed on-line
- the speed at which the data arrives for processing – this is usually dependent on the speed that the input devices work.

The faster the data can be processed then the faster the results or output is produced. In some business systems speed is crucial to their operation. For example, all monthly paid staff will need to be paid on a certain day of the month. Utility bills are all sent out at roughly the same time, which means processing needs to take place very quickly.

Data storage capacity

Because the cost of storing data has come down over the years, many organisations are storing a lot more data than they used to. They have come to realise that the more data they hold about products, sales, customers, etc., the more they can process this data to produce useful information. For example, a supermarket, through its loyalty scheme, would be able to identify those goods that a customer is not buying in the store and must be buying somewhere else. They can then target the customer with special offers for these products. Without the huge quantities of information about customers obtained through rewards/loyalty schemes, and the cheap availability of large amounts of storage this would be impossible.

Processing of credit card accounts

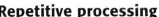

Production of accurate weather forecasts

Processing transactions in e-commerce systems

FAST REPETITIVE PROCESSING

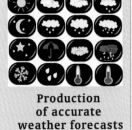

Production of utility bills

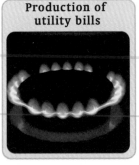

Producing itemised phone bills

Storing data can help companies produce useful information.

Often processing needs to happen quickly to ensure results.

The use of the Internet and networks enables fast access to information and fast action.

Speed of searching

Manual searching for information can take ages. Computer-based searches are extremely fast and it is easy to create search conditions that will enable only very specific information to be extracted.

Accuracy

Humans make mistakes but computers, when they have been correctly programmed, do not. This means that accuracy of computer-based systems is much higher than that possible with manual systems.

Speed of data communications

Most people who have an Internet connection have a broadband

Computer-based systems can be more accurate.

connection which means they have very fast access to information.

Most companies now communicate with each other using networks, because manual methods are too slow. For example, many companies promise delivery of goods within 24 hours from placing an order. Without the use of networks or the Internet for the placing of an order, this would be impossible.

The ability to produce different output formats

Arranging information to make it as easy to understand as possible is one thing computers are very good at. Altering the output format in different ways can be done using software such as word-processing or DTP.

Complex numerical data can be put into different formats such as:

* text
* tables
* graphs
* pictures.

Putting text into tables can easily be done using word-processing software.

Changing the output format from numbers to graphs is made very easy using spreadsheet software. Drawing neat graphs manually is very time consuming.

In many cases a picture can save a thousand words. Can you imagine building flat-pack furniture without a picture to help?

Being able to change output formats is a big advantage of ICT.

The ability to search and combine data in many different ways that would otherwise be impossible

Modern databases enable huge stores of data to be searched using complex search conditions. Sometimes only part of the data is known. For example, the police can search for all white Ford Fiestas with registration numbers that start with the letters MT and end in 08. This would have been virtually impossible using a manual system.

Improved security of data and processes

There are many reasons why the security of data and processes is improved by the use of ICT systems and here are some of them:

* **Data is easily backed up** – with ICT systems data is easily backed up because data can be copied. Copying manual data takes a long time plus you have to have somewhere to store it.
* **Fewer mistakes are made during processes** – lack of human involvement in the processes means fewer mistakes are made.
* **Better security of data** – data is protected by passwords. Also, only certain staff are given permission to make changes to data.

Factors affecting the efficiency of data processing systems

▼ **You will find out**

▶ About those factors that affect the efficiency of data processing systems

Introduction

Data processing systems are frequently called transaction processing systems because they are the systems that record, process and report on the day-to-day business activities of an organisation. Data processing concerns all the routine transactions that need to be performed on a day-to-day basis. These include such things as processing customer orders, dealing with returns, arranging deliveries, processing payments made, dealing with queries, processing the payroll, dealing with stock and placing orders with suppliers.

The effects of hardware

One factor that limits an IT system is hardware. Software uses the capabilities of the hardware. This means that certain software will only run on hardware of a certain minimum specification. This is why, when you purchase software, there is always a list on the back of the package, quoting the minimum specification or system requirements.

Here is an example of hardware requirements for a CAL (computer-aided learning) program for young children:

CPU: Pentium II 400 MHz
RAM: 128MB
Video: 640 × 480 (24 bit colour)
CD-ROM: 6 speed
40MB hard disk space

The speed at which processing occurs depends on the type and speed of the processor, and the amount of random access memory (RAM).

The amount of RAM is important because with large amounts of RAM, more program instructions and data can be held in memory at one time and this speeds up processing.

Computers systems should always be purchased with plenty of excess storage capacity to allow for future uses and further expansion of the organisation/business.

The effects of software

There is always a choice of software, so this should be carefully researched. In some cases different types of software will do the same task. For example, word-processing software could be used to produce a simple magazine, but for a more complex magazine DTP software would be better.

Poor software is frequently a source of frustration for users. Sometimes it is difficult to use or does not work in the way you expected. The worst types of software have bugs or errors which cause the computer to crash unexpectedly and in some cases cause users to lose work.

In cases where there is no suitable software available, it will be necessary to write the software from scratch. This is an expensive and time-consuming option but it may be the only choice for a very specialist application.

The suitability of the operating system

Some of the newer applications software needs the latest version of operating system software in order to run. It is important, before buying new applications software, that you look to make sure what operating system must be used to run it. Normally software will contain details of the operating systems that can be used with the software in the list of the systems requirements.

Here is part of the system requirements for a CAL (computer-aided learning) program for young children:

Windows: 98, 2000, ME, XP, Vista
Mac OS9, OS X

Some new applications software will not run using older operating systems

and some of the older applications software will not run with new operating systems.

The effects of communication

Anyone in an organisation who will be involved in working with a new system should be consulted and involved in its development. There are many examples where staff who will use the system have not been consulted during its development. There must be sufficient communication between the developers and the users of the system at all stages of development.

The effects of input (GIGO)

The output from a system should always be considered first because this determines what needs to be input and also the processing that needs to be done. Many systems have been developed with these deficiencies:

- The system cannot produce some output because further inputs are needed that were not considered at the time of development.
- The inputs are not accurate because the data validation and verification techniques are not comprehensive.

GIGO stands for garbage in garbage out and is a term frequently used with ICT to refer to the fact that the output information is dependent on the accuracy of the input data. No amount of processing or fancy presentation of the information will make up for the fact that incorrect data has been processed, rendering the output useless if it cannot be relied upon.

Limitations of data processing systems

Introduction

Data processing systems are designed to complete tasks in the most efficient way. The success with which they do this depends on a number of factors which are discussed here.

Problems and limitations

The nature of computer software

Software is probably the most noticeable aspect of a system to a user, because they will be using it on a day-to-day basis and any problems with it will soon be noticeable. The trouble arises when software is chosen by someone who knows little about the tasks performed by the user. The user then finds that the software does not live up to expectations.

Software can be bought off the shelf or it might be developed specifically for an organisation. Bespoke (tailor-made) software is software specially written for an application. Many large organisations prefer to write their own software rather than have to fit their own procedures around an existing package. The final result is a solution that meets their needs perfectly.

There are a number of software limitations:

- Ability to transfer data – data is frequently passed from one piece of software to another. If one piece of software could not read the data produced by a different piece of software, it would be a serious limitation.
- Bugs – software frequently contains bugs which cause the system to crash. Software needs to be thoroughly tried and tested before being passed to the user.
- Compatibility – you may not have an operating system capable of running the applications software. Also, you may not be able to pass the data from one piece of software to a different piece of software.
- Poor design of software – poorly designed software causes user frustration and stress and can also cause RSI if excess keyboard input is unnecessarily needed.

Changes in circumstances during development

In order to survive, businesses must adapt quickly to change. This means that they must change their systems on a regular basis in order to cope with the new demands of the business. Some systems take a long time to design and implement and during the time spent creating the new system, the needs of the business change. What this means is that the new system may no longer satisfy the needs of the business.

Organisations constantly changing

Organisations are constantly changing and there is a necessity for the information systems they use to change as well. For example, they may merge with other organisations, or they may be bought out.

Speed of implementation

Businesses need to react quickly to change. This means that systems need to be developed quickly in order to be useful. This can cause problems because when systems are developed in a rush there can be problems such as insufficient testing of the software. This can cause the software to crash unexpectedly.

Compatibility

If a new system is being developed there are a number of things to consider:

- Will the new system work with the existing data? This is extremely important with database systems as you would not want to spend time and money re-keying data that was already in digital form. Luckily, suppliers of software usually make sure that data can easily be imported from other database software.
- Will the old system work with new data? Sometimes data can be bought from elsewhere. For example, a large mail order business which is no longer operating may sell its customer data to a similar business.
- Will the new software work with the existing software? One system often needs to work with other systems. For example, a stock control system would need to work with a purchasing system so that goods running low in stock can be purchased automatically. This means that the software needs to be compatible.
- Will the new system work with the existing hardware?

Insufficient testing

Software often needs to be written in a rush and testing often suffers as a result. Insufficient testing means:

- thorough user testing has not taken place, resulting in software that is frustrating to use
- the software does not do exactly what was required of it
- the software does not produce the correct results owing to a formula being wrong
- the software contains bugs which cause the computer to crash.

Limitations of data processing systems continued

Poor communications with user

When a new system is designed or new software produced, the user's needs should be determined. The user and anyone who has a vested interest in the system should be consulted at all stages in the development. Poor communications between the developer and the user can lead to the system not matching the user's needs. This will not produce a good system and usually causes user frustration.

Sometimes the person developing the new data processing does not contact the potential user of the system enough. Instead they go away and devise the system they think the user wants or needs. Here are some things that should be asked:

- Have all the relevant people in the organisation who have an interest in the system or will be using the system been consulted?
- Have these people been involved in the system development at all stages?
- Does the system produce management information as well as perform the basic data processing tasks?
- Has enough thought been given to future expansion of the system?

Abilities of the user

Users of ICT systems have different educational backgrounds and different knowledge and skills in ICT. Before developing a new system, the developer should find out about the skills of typical users and the new systems should be developed with this in mind. Not taking into account user skills can lead to:

- increased user frustration as they struggle to use the new system
- increased training costs as more training is needed because the system is difficult to use
- frequent calls to the help-desk which will cause delay in completion of tasks
- resistance by users to use the software.

Poor post-implementation procedures

Once a new system has been implemented, you cannot simply leave the users to get on with it. Post-implementation procedures ensure that:

- the system is performing as it should do and if not then it should be altered so it does
- bugs and problems with the software are recorded and reported so that they can be corrected
- suitable support is given to users, if needed, usually by the help-desk.

Maintenance procedures

Systems need to be maintained so that they function correctly. Maintenance problems include:

- Not taking regular backup copies of programs and data causing risk to the organisation in losing important data.
- Not updating software regularly. If virus checking software was not updated regularly, new viruses could be introduced onto the system.
- Not changing passwords on a regular enough basis. This can compromise the security of the data.

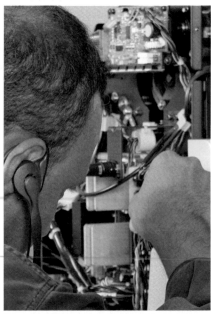

Poor maintenance can result in expensive faults.

Cost

Cost always is a limiting factor when trying to produce the best ICT system or trying to run a system. Cost will limit:

- the amount of time that can be spent producing the system
- the amount of new hardware and software that can be bought
- staff training to use the system
- the ability to keep updating the software to take advantage of new functionality.

Developers who develop new systems are given budgets, as are departments who perform the data processing using the systems on a day-to-day basis. Poor planning or budgeting of either of these can lead to overspending.

Hardware

All systems must be fully justified financially. They must be capable of generating savings or efficiencies, or provide greater opportunities for profit. A system that costs, say, £20,000 to develop that only saves say £4000 per year for five years is not worth going ahead with.

Similarly, there has to be good reason for replacing older hardware with newer hardware.

Support

Some users of data processing systems may feel they are not given appropriate support with the systems. For example, they may feel that:

- hardware problems are not dealt with quickly enough
- problems with programs not producing the correct output are not corrected
- the help-desk set up to help them only serves to confuse them more, so they do not bother using it
- they have not been given appropriate user training on a new system
- they have not had on-going training to take full advantage of the capabilities of the system
- they have no way of recording faults with hardware or problems with software.

Questions

Questions 1 pp. 48–49

1 A large utility company sends electricity bills to all its customers. These bills are sent out over a couple of days every three months.
Describe **three** capabilities of ICT systems which make them ideal for the processing of the data needed to produce electricity bills. (6 marks)

2 In a newspaper article it said that one of the capabilities of ICT systems is that there is improved security of data and processes.
Give **two** reasons why the data in ICT systems is more likely to be secure compared to a manual system. (4 marks)

Questions 2 pp. 48–50

1 The Internet is an ICT system and your use of the Internet is limited by a number of factors. Name and describe **four** factors that limit your use of the Internet. (8 marks)

2 ICT systems are limited in what they can be used for. State **four** limitations of ICT systems. (4 marks)

Questions 3 pp. 51–52

1 The use of data processing systems can be limited by a number of factors.
For example, the type of operating system being used can limit the applications software that can be run.
Describe how each of the following factors can affect the efficiency of data processing and give an appropriate example of the factor in each case.
(a) Change in circumstances during development. (2 marks)
(b) Poor communications with user. (2 marks)
(c) Insufficient testing. (2 marks)

2 There are many factors affecting the efficiency of data processing systems. Describe **two** such factors and explain how each can affect data processing. (4 marks)

3 Systems making use of software tools can often be developed in a hurry. This causes a number of problems such as inadequate testing.
(a) Explain what is meant by inadequate testing. (2 marks)
(b) Give **two** consequences of inadequately testing software. (2 marks)

Exam support

Worked example 1

1 ICT systems offer many advantages over corresponding manual systems.
   Describe three such advantages. (6 marks)

Student answer 1

1 Faster processing because you can do things quicker.
   You can produce the output in lots of different formats depending on the audience, such as graphs, presentation, as a file to be used as the input into another computer system. With the manual system you were limited to output on paper.
   You search better for stuff on the computer than you could search through a load of paper files. Paper files can only be stored in one order but records in computer files can be ordered in many ways.

Student answer 2

1 Speed of processing, as faster processing means it is quicker to extract data from a large database.
   Data storage capacity, as a huge amount of data can be stored in a very small space, either on a server or CD/DVD. The same volume of data would take up a huge amount of space.
   Speed of data communication, as files can be sent over networks such as the Internet very quickly using broadband. If you wanted to send paper documents quickly, it would still take hours and be very expensive.
   Accuracy. The data stored on the computer is likely to be more accurate because validation checks will have been used to make sure that only sensible and allowable data is entered.

Examiner's comment

1 The first advantage gains a mark – the student needed to explain what 'things' can be done quicker.
   The second advantage gains two marks as they have adequately explained the advantage and also given a comparison.
   The third advantage is marred a little by the word 'stuff' – what stuff? However, they have given a valid advantage and explained it further by giving an example.
   (5 marks out of 6)

Examiner's comment

1 In the first answer the student mentions that it is 'quicker to extract data….', but you do not extract data from a database, you extract information. The student has not been penalised on this answer. The student has not made it clear with the final sentence 'The same volume of data would take up a huge amount of space' that they are referring to the manual system. Only one mark is given here.
   The other two descriptions are of correct advantages and there is some comparison to the manual method of performing the task, so full marks for both these answers.
   (5 marks out of 6)

Examiner's answers

1 There are no marks for just giving the name of the advantage without a sentence explaining it. One mark for the advantage, and the second mark for further explanation, or an example to a maximum of 6 marks.
   Repetitive processing can be performed such as using templates or style sheets so that a page of a document does not have to be completed from scratch.
   Large data storage capacity means that data can be stored in a small space and also that the data is portable. Large quantities of paper files take up a huge amount of space.
   Speed of processing is much faster with ICT systems. Processes such as searching for information, sorting information, performing calculations, etc., are performed much quicker by computer.
   Accuracy is improved when computers are used. Validation checks make sure that only allowable and sensible data is entered.
   Speed of communication is improved as e-mail, file attachments, file transfer, etc., can be used to transfer information very quickly. Sending letters manually takes a long time.
   Speed of searching is improved as it is much faster to type in search conditions and extract specific information from a database rather than have to wade through files manually.
   The same information can be output in lots of different formats. For example, information can be output as a file for use with another system, a presentation, a report, a website, etc.

Worked example 2

2 A school uses word-processing software for sending letters to parents, writing reports for governors' meetings and spreadsheet software for the analysis of examination results and working out department budgets.

Explain by referring to the examples given, how the following offer advantages to the school when using word-processing and spreadsheet software.

(a) Repetitive processing. (2 marks)

(b) Compatibility. (2 marks)

(c) Accuracy. (2 marks)

Student answer 1

2 (a) Bills can be produced quickly using meter readings. The meter reading is taken and the previous reading is subtracted to work out the gas or electricity used. The computer can then work out the cost of the gas, add on VAT and the name and address details.

(b) Being able to import data directly from the other systems such as the school's information management system into word-processing software. For example, children who had been late could have letters sent to their parents. Compatibility with existing software. For example, the school will need to check that the word-processing and spreadsheet software they want to use will run with their existing operating system software.

(c) Documents can be checked for accuracy of spelling and grammar using the spellchecker and grammar checking facilities of the word-processor before being sent to parents.

Examiner's comment

2 (a) Here the student has not read the question properly. They have written about repetitive processing without referring to the examples given in the question.
This answer gains no marks.

(b) Two advantages have been identified and clearly explained so full marks for this part.

(c) The student has given two suitable examples referring to the same piece of software. These are not distinctly different enough for the two marks so only one mark is given.
(3 marks out of 6)

Student answer 2

2 (a) Use of templates so that all the word-processed reports created by the school have a common appearance and the person who supplies the information does not have to worry about layout, fonts and font sizes.
Use of mail merge will enable a personalised letter to be sent to groups of parents with details of school trips, arrangements for parent evenings, etc.

(b) The files produced by the other systems such as the pupil database should be compatible with the word-processing software. This is important as a pupil file can be used to supply the data needed to perform the mail merge.

(c) Accuracy of spreadsheet is ensured by including validation checks that prevent ridiculous data being entered.

Examiner's comment

2 (a) A good explanation of two different examples of repetitive processing and the student has clearly referred to the use in schools. Full marks here.

(b) Although only one piece of software has been referred to, the student has given a comprehensive answer. Two marks for this answer.

(c) The explanation given is good but further amplification or reference to another point is need for the two marks. Only one mark is given here. **(5 marks out of 6)**

Examiner's answers

2 (a) Any suitable example of repetitive processing. One mark for an advantage for spreadsheet and one mark for an advantage for word-processing. Accept two examples from the same item of software for two marks.

Two marks can also be given for a very comprehensive answer covering the one point. Examples include:

Use of automated routines such as macros, wizards, etc.

Use of mail merge

Replication of formulas

Use of templates

Use of headers and footers

Use of style sheets

Use of formatting techniques

They must give an example of use for the mark – the name is not sufficient.

(b) Any suitable advantage related to spreadsheet and/or word-processing such as:

Must be possible to import data into other school systems

Must be possible to export data from the word-processing or spreadsheet software into the school's existing systems

Must work with the operating system software used by the school

Must work with existing hardware the school has such as printers, etc.

(c) One mark each for two descriptions of advantages referring to word-processing or spreadsheet software or both.

Can use spell/grammar check to check accuracy of spelling of documents/spreadsheets

Can use validation checks to ensure only reasonable and sensible data is accepted for processing

Ease of importing of data from other packages means no re-keying of data so fewer mistakes

Use of copy and paste means data does not have to be re-keyed so fewer mistakes

Summary mind maps

Advantages of ICT over manual methods of processing data

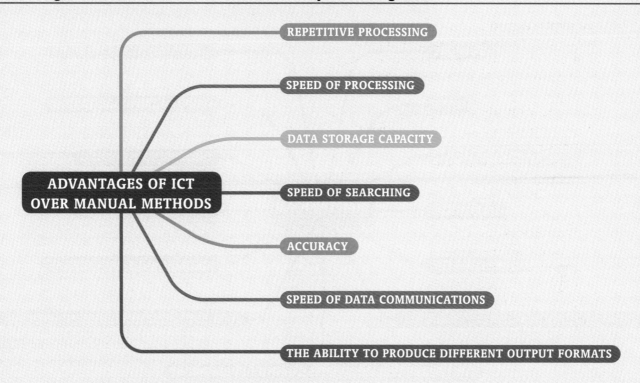

Factors affecting the efficiency of data processing systems

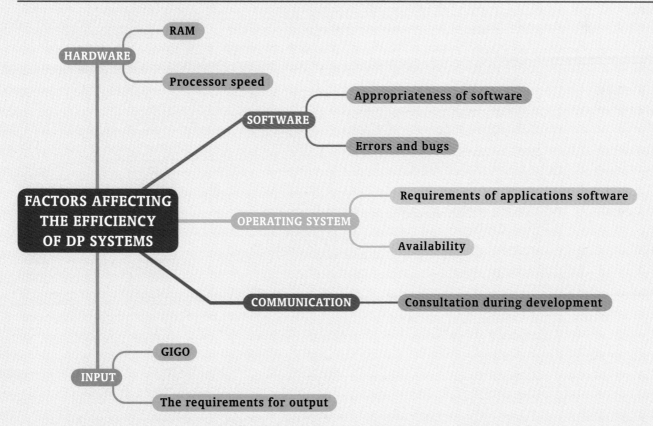

Summary mind maps continued

Limitations of data processing systems

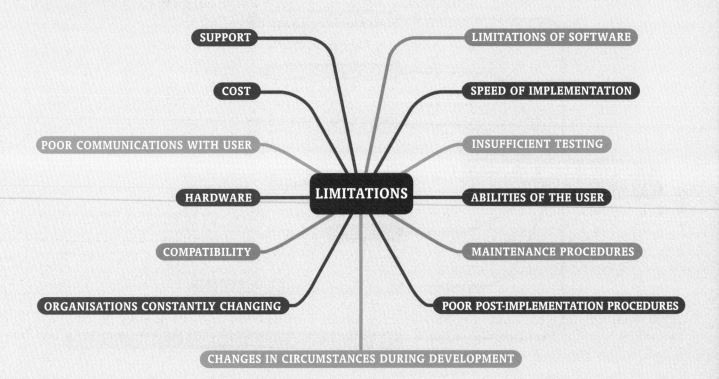

TOPIC 6(a): Uses of ICT in business

In this topic you will learn about how ICT is used for business for the design and manufacture of components or goods using CAD and CAM software and also how computerised shopping systems work.

▼ The key concepts covered in this topic are:

▶ Computer-aided design (CAD) and computer-aided manufacturing (CAM)

▶ Computer-based shopping systems

CONTENTS

Unit IT1 Information Systems

Computer-aided design (CAD) and computer-aided manufacturing (CAM)

Introduction

In this section you will be looking at how computers can be used to help design new products and components. You will also look at how the designs can be used as the input to computer systems that will enable the actual products or components to be manufactured automatically.

CAD and CAM

CAD (computer-aided design) is the use of computer systems in engineering, architecture, kitchen design, etc., to support the design of products, buildings or the placement of objects (kitchen units, bathroom furniture, etc.). CAD can also cover the design of products such as packaging.

CAM (computer-aided manufacturing) is the use of computers to control the manufacturing process in some way by controlling manufacturing equipment such as lathes, drills, millers and robots. Many CAM systems are able to take the design produced using CAD and feed it into a CAM system that actually makes the product or component.

Robots are are used in computer-aided manufacturing.

CAD/CAM systems are used to integrate the design and manufacture of components. Once the design has been created using the CAD package the information can be programmed into the CAM system, where the actual component is manufactured using tools such as lathes, milling machines, drills, robots, etc.

Features of CAD packages

Here are some of the many features of CAD packages:

- Zoom – the ability to zoom in or zoom out from a particular part of a design.
- 2D and 3D – the ability to change from 2D drawings to 3D surface models.
- Rotation – ability to rotate a 3D design so the design can be seen from different angles.
- No need to build a prototype – designers can see designs without the need to build a prototype (actual model).
- Shading – can add shading to a diagram to aid visualisation.
- Layering – layers can be used, with each layer adding more detail to the drawing – for example, one layer shows the walls of the building, another layer shows the electrical circuits, another shows the plumbing, etc.
- Walk-through – the CAD package allows a person to enter the building and investigate the views from the inside before the building is built.
- Costing – in kitchen design CAD software, as each appliance or unit is added, it is recorded, so a list of what is needed and the costs can be added up to give a final amount.

Advantages of using CAD

There are many advantages of using CAD for producing drawings and here are some of them:

- Easily stored and transferred – drawings are digitised and can be sent via e-mail to others working on the project.
- Easily altered – existing drawings can be easily altered rather than starting from scratch.
- Can manipulate image – ease of manipulation of images on the screen.
- 3D available – can produce drawings in 3D, which is especially useful for diagrams of kitchens, gardens, buildings, etc.
- Scaling – drawings are easily scaled up and down.
- Can use libraries of artwork to include in the diagrams – for example, trees, people, plants, etc., can be used in a 3D drawing of a proposed building to add realism.
- Can produce lists of components automatically – can be used to create lists of dimensions and parts needed to create the product/component.
- Stress/strain calculations can be performed – this means the software will only allow you to design buildings that are safe.

- Hatching/rendering – hatching means adding different types of shading to an image to add realism. Rendering means using a computer to draw an image on a computer screen and this often means using ray-tracing to turn an outline sketch into a detailed image of a solid object.

Features of CAM packages

The main features of CAM are as follows:

- Uses a computer, CAM software and a device or devices that produce the product, which are controlled by the software.
- Takes the input from CAD packages and uses the information to produce a set of instructions to give to machinery to manufacture the article or component.
- Used to program and control equipment (robots, milling machines, lathes, drills, cutters, etc.).
- Products are made automatically.
- The CAM equipment can be re-programmed to make new products or components with different dimensions.

Advantages of using CAM

- Cheaper manufacture – the manufacture is automatic so costs of manufacturing a product are reduced.
- Faster time from design to manufacture – can produce new components/products more quickly.
- Better quality – products created using CAM are produced to a better quality (i.e. no human involvement so no mistakes).
- Lower wage costs – very little human involvement means the goods can be produced more cheaply as the wage costs are lower.
- Machines can be re-programmed – the machines which use CAM (lathes, millers, drills, robots, cutters, etc.) can be re-programmed to enable them to make new products.
- Can make small quantities that would normally be uneconomical – small quantities of a product to the customer's design can be made cheaply.

Examples of CAD

- producing kitchen or bathroom designs for customers
- producing the designs for a component that is to be manufactured
- used by architects for designing buildings
- used by gardeners/landscapers to design a garden
- used to produce engineering drawings
- used to produce maps and plans.

Examples of CAM

- used to manufacture components used in car engines and gearboxes
- used to manufacture double glazed windows and conservatories.

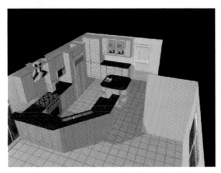

Kitchen design companies use CAD.

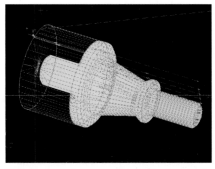

This engineering component is changed from a 2D drawing to this 3D model.

Landscape designers and achitects use CAD software when designing for clients.

This CAM system produces CDs and places them in the plastic cases ready for despatch.

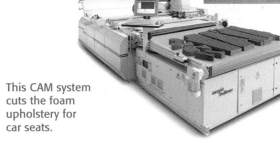

This CAM system cuts the foam upholstery for car seats.

Computer-aided design (CAD) and computer-aided manufacturing (CAM) continued

Hardware requirements for CAD and CAM

CAD and CAM are demanding applications requiring high-specification computer hardware.

Input devices

Besides the keyboard, CAD systems make extensive use of the mouse and most CAD systems use a mouse with two buttons and a scroll wheel, although some use a specially designed mouse such as the space mouse.

The main input device for CAD systems is the mouse.

Space mouse – this makes use of a mouse and a set of buttons which allow the user of CAD to position and manipulate objects in 3D space.

Processing

CAD/CAM packages place huge demands on the processor of a computer.

Speed of processor

CAD software needs to perform many complex calculations when scaling, transforming (moving, rotating, stretching, reflecting) images or producing 3D models from 2D designs. The speed at which this can be done depends on the speed of the processor.

The processor is the brain of the computer and the speed of the processor is the main influence on how fast the CAD system appears to a user. In order to speed up CAD systems, dual processors are used, which means that program instructions can be dealt with faster by allocating them between the processors.

CAD requires lots of processing power, so faster processors should be chosen where possible.

Memory

Memory is used to hold programs and data which may need to be accessed immediately by the processor. Large amounts of RAM (random access memory) should be included and there should be the space to add more RAM as future upgrades of the CAD software may require it.

Graphics card

In most cases, if an ordinary PC is used with CAD, it may be necessary to change the graphics card, as most graphics cards are designed with business uses and games in mind. CAD places lots of demands on the graphics card.

The best graphics cards will offer performance (speed), stability and image quality. A 3D-capable graphics card will be needed in order to turn 2D designs into 3D designs. The CAD software will say which graphics cards are compatible, so you need to look carefully at the system specification for the software.

Output devices

The output devices for CAD are slightly different than for other systems mainly because of the detail that is generally needed on the screen and the size of the printouts that need to be produced.

Screen

CAD designers spend a lot of time looking at the screen so the screen needs to:

- be as large as possible so as to reduce eye strain – a minimum size of 17 inches should be used
- have a minimum resolution of 1024 × 768 pixels (a pixel is the smallest dot of light on the screen)
- be flicker free with a very stable picture
- have a non-reflective coating on the screen to reduce glare.

Printers/plotters

A4-sized printouts and below can be printed out on an ordinary ink-jet or laser printer but in many cases detailed plans need to be printed on larger sheets of paper, so specialist plotters are used.

Drum plotters – these are used when drawings, plans and maps need to be printed on large sheets of paper.

With a drum plotter the paper moves as well as the pens.

Machinery

Output from a CAD design can be input into a CAM package which can then control machinery to make the item. The output from the CAM package is the instructions to control devices, such as millers, lathes, cutters, drills, etc., that are used to automatically manufacture components or products.

This laser cutter is used to cut shapes out of thin metal using a laser beam and uses CAM software to give it the measurements and other details.

CAD and CAM software

There are a number of pieces of CAD and CAM software. Most of this type of software requires a lot of training before it can be successfully used but the pieces of software described here are the ones used in schools because of their simplicity. They can of course be used in businesses.

Pro/Desktop

This is a piece of CAD software and allows the visualisation of 3D objects on the screen which can be viewed from any viewpoint. Using the software you can assemble and explore different arrangements of 3D parts. You can also experiment with the colour and texture of the parts and look at them using different views.

There are a series of shapes contained in a library which you can select and drop onto the working area of the screen where the shapes can be sized and combined with other shapes to form an assembly.

Once a shape has been assembled in 3D, the material can be chosen and the mass and volume of the object can be determined. In addition drawings (other than 3D) can be produced, which can aid manufacture.

The main advantage of this piece of software is that it allows the designer to generate, design and model alternative ideas.

ArtCAM

ArtCAM is a CAD design and a CAM package that allows you to take your 2D designs and turn them into 3D designs. For example, you can either create the 2D design using the software or you can import it from another graphics or design package. It can then be turned into the 3D model which can include relief (i.e., different depths used on faces) and shading can be added to improve realism. Using the software you can add textures and text on curved surfaces. Once the model has been created it can be exported into a CNC machine which includes lathes, laser cutters and routers.

One of these images has been produced using the ArtCAM package and the other is the actual sign made in wood. The rendering is so realistic it is hard to tell which picture is the image and which is the actual object. The real wood object is the one on the right.

ProSketch

This piece of software is aimed at graphic design and design of textiles. Using the software allows users to create initial sketches of garments and other textile products.

Like all design software there is a library of objects, which in this case include zips, buttons, sleeves, button holes, collars, etc. Background images can also be selected so that the garments designed can be showcased in the best way possible.

Using another piece of software from the same company, users are able to select from a whole range of colours and textures of fabrics for their design, which include stripes, spots, all-over colours, checks, over prints, etc. The software makes it easy to make changes to designs and improve on designs.

Design libraries can be set up so that rather than always starting from scratch, existing designs can be modified to form new designs, thus saving time. Dimensions can be added to the designs which aid manufacture.

One very useful feature of the software is the powerful simulation feature that allows you to drape the designed garment onto a drawn design such as a figurine (i.e., just like a mannequin in a shop).

You can even take a photograph of a person and then produce a model of them wearing the garment.

Websites for CAD/CAM

Here are a number of websites which you will find useful. Some of these websites will even allow you to download a trial version of the software to explore.

When looking at these websites, think about the features they offer the user and the applications to which they are most suited.

- http://www.prodesktop.net/
- http://www.artcampro.com/
- http://softwaresolutions. fibre2fashion.com/productDetail. aspx?refno=1760

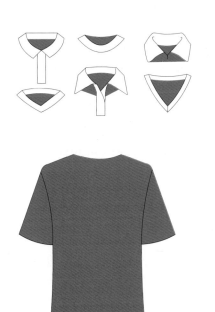 

This football shirt design has been created using CAD software. Notice how the user has made designs for a number of collars to see which one looks best.

Computer-based shopping systems

▼ You will find out

▶ About payment methods

▶ About on-line shopping

▶ About e-commerce

▶ About electronic funds transfer (EFT)

▶ About electronic point of sale (EPOS)

▶ About bar codes

▶ About other methods of data entry

▶ About automatic stock control

▶ About pricing

▶ About just in time control systems and their advantages and disadvantages

▶ About human–computer interfaces

▶ About loyalty cards

Introduction

In this topic you will be looking at the way ICT is used in the retail environment. The retail environment is one of the most competitive businesses, and shops need to react quickly to changes in customer shopping habits in order to remain competitive. The huge rise in shopping on the Internet, particularly at busy periods such as Christmas, has placed many demands on shops. Most shops have websites and some of these websites enable customers to place orders for goods on-line.

Payment methods

There are a number of different ways payments may be made electronically and these are looked at in the next section.

Electronic funds transfer (EFT)

Electronic funds transfer refers to the payment for goods, where the payment is made from one account to another. EFT payments can include:

- credit and debit cards
- payments made using an intermediary such as PayPal or Nochex
- payments made using an electronic purse (i.e. where you credit money to a card before use)
- payments made between one bank account and another using on-line banking.

More details of these methods can be found in Topic 6(d) on Uses of ICT in the home (in the on-line home banking section).

Credit/debit card is the main payment method for on-line shopping.

Payments made using on-line banking

Many people now use on-line banks and when they have an on-line account, transferring money to pay for goods is made easy. It is easy using an on-line account to transfer money from one account to another provided you know the sort code and account number.

Advantages of electronic payments from a customer's perspective

- Faster receipt of goods or services – no wait for post or cheques to clear.
- Quicker to enter card details rather than send a cheque in the post.
- If a credit card is used for items costing over £100, then the credit card company will take up any complaints you have with the store.

KEY WORDS

Electronic funds transfer (EFT) – The process of transferring money electronically without the need for paperwork or the delay that using paperwork brings

Advantages of electronic payments from a store's perspective

- Payment is made immediately so cash flow is improved.
- EFT can be integrated with accountancy systems, so fewer account staff are needed thus reducing business costs.
- No wasted time dealing with cheques that bounce (i.e., get returned because the customer does not have enough money in their account).
- Faster delivery can be offered, which can improve turnover.

Stores such as Tesco make use of the latest ICT developments to make their business profitable and to allow them to expand rapidly.

Disadvantages of electronic payments from a customer's perspective

- Payments are easy, so a customer may make impulse purchases they later regret.
- There may be a tendency to spend too much on credit cards.
- There is a danger in entering card details that they will fall into the wrong hands and be used fraudulently.
- Not everyone has a computer or Internet access.
- Erosion of privacy as more companies hold data about you and what you buy.

More and more cash-rich but time-poor people choose do their shopping on-line, despite there often being an extra charge for delivery.

Disadvantages of electronic payments from a store's perspective

- Stores have to pay a commission for electronic payments to the company being used to make the payment (e.g., credit/debit card company, PayPal, Nochex, etc.). For an on-line credit card payment the commission is typically 3.1%.
- Stolen credit cards may be used to pay for products or services. It is the seller of goods or services who has to bear the cost of fraudulent transactions.
- There need to be procedures in place to ensure the security and privacy of customers' data, particularly their credit or debit card details.
- It is quite expensive to set up a payment system.

Performing stock control by linking to the POS terminal

Bar coding on goods allows them to be identified as they pass through the checkouts so that they can be deducted from stock. This forms the basis of the sales-based ordering system which automatically re-orders goods from the warehouse using the sales-based information from the checkouts. If, for example, 200 tins of baked beans were sold from a certain store in one day, then 200 would be automatically re-ordered and delivered to the store the following day from one of the stores distribution centres.

On-line shopping

On-line shopping is growing rapidly as shoppers pushed for time abandon high street stores for the ease of shopping from their own homes. On-line shopping was first of all popular for CDs, DVDs, books and groceries, but many more people are now using the Internet to buy virtually anything.

Computer-based shopping systems continued

E-commerce

Commerce means all those activities needed for the successful running of a business, which would typically involve the following:

- buying
- distributing
- marketing
- selling
- paying.

If some, or all of the activities listed above are performed using electronic systems, such as the Internet or other computer networks, then the business can be said to be involved in e-commerce.

E-commerce is not just about the selling of products, it also involves the selling of services, and involves such technologies as:

- on-line marketing
- electronic funds transfer (EFT)
- just in time control systems/supply chain management
- on-line transaction processing
- electronic data interchange (EDI)
- automatic stock control systems
- automated data entry systems.

E-commerce uses the latest communication and associated technology such as:

- Internet
- mobile phones
- extranets
- e-mail
- databases.

There is no doubt that there has been a huge change in the way people work and play and many of these changes have been brought about by the use of e-commerce. People are now able to shop and bank from the comfort of their homes and they now have a global marketplace to pick their goods and services from.

Some businesses could not exist without e-commerce technology. The phenomenal rise of low-cost airlines is due in part to the e-commerce technologies that enable operating costs to be kept low.

In this section you will be looking at the social implications, the benefits and drawbacks of e-commerce and some typical e-commerce businesses to see how they work.

The main parts of an e-commerce system

The main parts of an e-commerce system are as follows:

- A catalogue of products that includes a search facility and also provides a link to the stock control system.
- A shopping cart/basket – allows shoppers to browse and add and remove items from their basket.
- Checkout – when shoppers have finished shopping they can checkout where they enter their details (name and contact details) and pay for their goods.
- Payment – here the credit or debit card details are encrypted and validated and the transaction is either accepted or declined. Once payment has been authorised, an e-mail is sent to the customer confirming the order.

Benefits of e-commerce

Both the customer and the business benefit from the use of e-commerce in the following ways:

- Always accessible – there are no opening hours for an e-business. The information on the site is available 24/7. Your customers can access the information from your site anywhere and at any time.
- Low start-up and running costs – it is relatively cheap to start in e-commerce, since all you really need is a computer connected to the Internet and something to sell. Many businesses have started in a small way, selling on the auction site e-Bay and have then created their own website to attract customers. Once the site is up and running, the running costs are quite small compared to traditional businesses because the premises and staff costs are lower.
- Easily updated – the problem with printed material is that by the time it is prepared and printed it can be out of date. Information on the website can be updated daily or even more regularly, so the information is always up-to-date. Many products are bought abroad, so they have a price that needs to be converted into pounds. As the rate of exchange alters daily, then their cost to the supplier will change. This means that it is possible to have a price for goods which changes daily. Computer manufacturers such as Dell have prices which change from day to day.
- Search facilities – goods can be found quickly on e-commerce sites using a search facility.
- Low distribution costs – you do not need the usual costs involved with other forms of promotion such as stamps and envelopes. Once they have been produced, websites are not labour intensive and the routine updating is fairly easy.
- Global marketplace – it is possible to have goods delivered to you from any part of the world, so it is possible to find the cheapest product not just in this country, but in the world. Many on-line businesses are global and anyone who has an Internet connection can make purchases anywhere in the world.

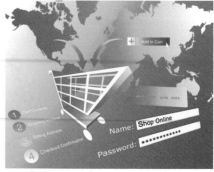

E-commerce allows shoppers to buy goods from anywhere in the world.

Here is a banner advert supplied by CD-wow. This could be put on your e-commerce site so that when a customer clicks on it, they are taken to the CD-wow site.

- Competitive edge – there are nearly always savings to be made when products or services are bought using the Internet. This is because the costs of running an Internet business are lower than a typical bricks and mortar business. These lower costs give the e-commerce business a competitive edge compared to a traditional business but as more and more people develop e-businesses, the competitive edge will be eroded.
- Gathering customer information – if you buy goods from a traditional store, they know little about you, and if you pay cash, they no nothing about you at all. If they have a special sale, or new products that may interest you, it is difficult for them to let you know. With e-commerce, this problem does not exist, because you have to enter personal details such as your name and address, e-mail address, phone number and payment details. It is also easy for them to collect further information and they also know what you have bought. They can send you e-newsletters via e-mail about products you may like and special offers, etc.
- Alternative income sources – if you have a popular e-commerce site which gets lots of hits, then you may consider some alternative income sources such as:
  - Banner advertisements for other companies.
  - Links to other websites.
  - In many cases the banner advertisement also provides the link to the business advertised.
  - You will get a commission if a user visits your website and then follows a link to a website of one of your trading partners and then makes a purchase.
  - If you have a very popular website then this income can be very significant and help towards the costs of your own e-commerce site.

Drawbacks of e-commerce

E-commerce is not without its drawbacks and in most cases these are on the consumers' side. These drawbacks are summarised in the diagram below:

- Unemployment – computers automate many of the administrative tasks performed by people, so this can lead to more people being unemployed.
- Lack of interaction with people – for some people, such as the elderly and the disabled, going to the traditional shops provides a good way of interacting with others. When this is removed, people can become introverted and mistrustful of others.
- Lack of exercise – walking around traditional shops is good exercise, but sitting at a keyboard ordering goods and services on-line provides little exercise.
- Problems when things go wrong – when goods or services are ordered on-line, you can have problems when things go wrong. If you have received goods through the post and they are faulty or the wrong ones, then it is a hassle parcelling them up and sending them back. Dealing with delivery problems can be difficult.
- Lack of consumer trust – bogus websites, problems with copying credit cards, and bad experiences of customer service have put some consumers off shopping using the Internet.
- Problems with international legislation – goods bought abroad because they are seemingly cheaper, end up being more expensive when customs duty is added.
- Goods bought from abroad means profits stay abroad – many goods such as cars, CDs, fashion items, etc., are cheaper abroad. There are many search engines that find the cheapest place to buy these items. The high street stores and the general economy suffer as a result.
- Security problems – many people are scared about inputting their credit card details when paying for goods or services. They are worried about ID theft and their card details being used fraudulently and there is also the problem that the site could have been set up simply to steal money from them.

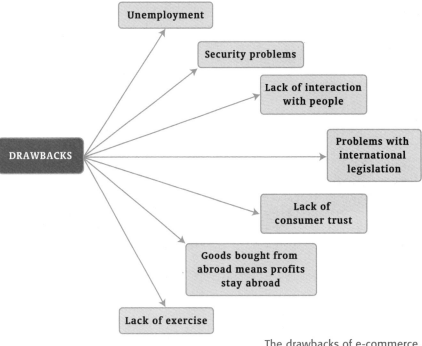

The drawbacks of e-commerce.

Computer-based shopping systems continued

- parcel tracking systems
- linking books to borrowers in libraries
- luggage labelling at airports.

Electronic point of sale (EPOS)

POS terminals

Point of sale terminals are placed in stores where customers pay for goods. There are a variety of input devices used with a POS terminal and these include:

- touch screen displays
- keyboards
- magnetic strip readers (for reading credit/debit card and loyalty card details)
- bar code readers.

Bar code recognition

Bar code recognition involves using a series of light and dark bars of differing widths to enter a code which is usually printed underneath the bar code.

Using the code, the system can determine from a product database the country of origin, the manufacturer, the name of the product, the price and other information about the product. Suitable applications for bar code recognition include:

- recording of goods in supermarkets
- warehouse stock control systems

ISBN 978-1-85008-280-4

A bar code.

Advantages of bar code input

- Faster – scanners are sophisticated and can read bar codes at different angles.
- More accurate – compared to typing in long codes manually.
- Low printing costs – can be printed on labels. You can buy special software which allows an ordinary printer to print bar codes.

Disadvantages of bar code input

- Can only be used for the input of numbers.
- Expensive – the laser scanners in supermarkets are expensive, although hand-held scanners are relatively cheap.

Other methods of data entry

There are a number of other input devices used by stores, such as:

- Hand-held input devices – these are portable devices used for stock-taking in stores. Sometimes they have bar code readers attached to them so they are able to read the bar codes on the shelf labels. The hand-held device then uses wireless communication to send the data to the main computer system.
- Magnetic strip readers – magnetic strips can be seen on credit cards, debit cards

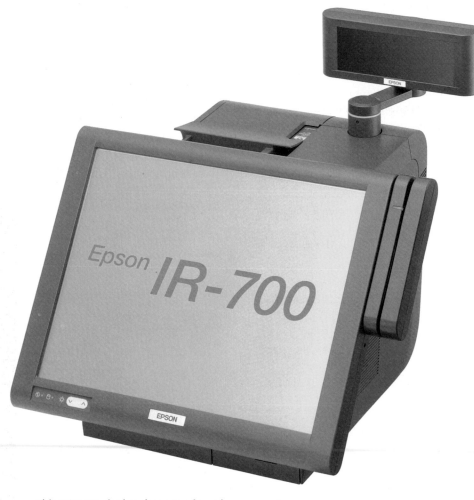

This POS terminal makes use of touch screens.

Chip and PIN readers are used by customers to enter their PIN at the point of sale terminal.

and loyalty (i.e. Reward) cards. Although chip and PIN readers are used to read credit or debit card details, magnetic strip readers are still used to read the magnetic strips on reward cards. Advantages of magnetic strip input include:

- Fewer errors – there are fewer errors made because there is no keying in of data.
- Added security – because there are security details encoded in the card which do not appear on the card, making it harder but not impossible to commit fraud.
- Very quick – the card is read quickly, which is particularly important in a shop.
- Data cannot be read without a properly programmed machine – decreases the likelihood of fraud.
- Chip and PIN reader – these have now replaced magnetic strip readers for the reading of credit or debit card details. Rather than signing to verify you are the owner of the card, you have to enter a four-digit personal identification number (PIN) to verify that you are the true owner of the card.

There is more information on chip and PIN readers and cards in the banking section later on in this book.

Automatic stock control

All supermarkets hold stock that needs to be controlled for the following reasons:

- Keeping large quantities of stock is expensive and if the quantity kept can be decreased, then the resources released (money, staff, space) can be put to better use in the organisation.
- If insufficient stock is kept, customers' requirements may not be met and customers may choose to shop elsewhere.
- Many of the stock items in a supermarket are perishable, which means they only have a limited shelf life.

There are a number of costs associated with keeping stock:

- The cost of buying the stock.
- The cost of the premises to house the stock.
- Higher staffing costs as more people are needed to find and move stock.
- Higher wastage due to damage, or goods going off if they are perishable or go past their sell by date.

Feedback systems are used in some forms of stock control to reduce the variation between the stock kept and the stock required to satisfy the customer orders. This reduces the higher than necessary stock levels which exceed the customer demand. Because there is constant feedback, comparisons are constantly being made between the set stock level and the actual stock used.

The main objectives of an automatic stock control system are:

- to maintain adequate stock just to meet customer demand
- to re-order goods automatically when stock falls below a minimum level
- to monitor and adjust stock levels, i.e. to optimise the stock level
- to produce stock valuations for accountancy and audit purposes
- to provide management with up-to-date and accurate stock information.

Just in time stock control systems

Many supermarkets and stores make use of a just in time stock control system. The system makes use of the 'just in time' concept, where goods are delivered to the stores as fast as they are being sold. This new system will cut the stocks of products in each store by about one fifth and this will free some of the staff who would normally be putting the extra goods on the shelves to concentrate on giving a better service to the customers.

The new system replaces the old system of ordering fresh and packaged products and it will allow individual stores to respond to changing demand throughout the day automatically. The old system placed orders that depended on the average demand for the products over the previous five days and this prevented the opportunity to respond to unexpected rushes on products. The system will ensure that they do not run out of items like salads or ice-cream during hot weather or soup during cold weather.

With the latest system, the deliveries are spread out to four or five per day rather than a single large delivery in the morning. Savings in human resources are also expected and these staff can now concentrate on some more customer-focussed tasks being developed.

Advantages of just in time stock control

- Smaller stores can be used because not as much stock is held.
- Store is able to respond to changing demand through the day.
- Easier to cope with several small deliveries than one large delivery.
- Ensures that they do not run out of fast-selling items.

Disadvantages of just in time stock control

- Expensive to introduce.
- Stores are more responsible for their own ordering so more admin staff are needed.
- True stock may differ due to theft and damages.

Computer-based shopping systems continued

Pricing

Many prices of goods change on a regular basis. This causes problems for shops as they are often charged more by their suppliers and need to pass this price increase onto their customers.

Goods are not priced individually on supermarket shelves. Instead the database of all the goods contains the price, which may be altered by a computer in the store. The bar code on the goods links the item to the correct record in this database. Once the price is changed, the bar code links to the new price. The store then needs to print out a new shelf label which contains details of the goods, a bar code and the price.

This method of fluid pricing enables stores to pass price increases from their suppliers onto their customers. This increases the profitability of the store.

This is an electronic shelf label which means when the price on the database of products is updated, it automatically changes on the shelf label.

Human–computer interfaces

Staff working in supermarkets and other stores, need to be protected against some of the medical problems caused by the use of ICT systems such as:

- eye strain
- back ache
- repetitive strain injury
- stress.

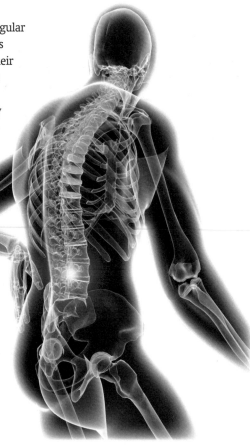

Backache is common among computer users and needs to be prevented by the use of ergonomically designed workstations.

Stores have moved away from using the keyboard for the entry of data and moved towards laser scanners and touch screens. This will hopefully eliminate many of the health problems.

Loyalty cards

Most supermarkets and stores use loyalty cards (sometimes called reward cards) to encourage customers to shop regularly at the store. In this section you will look at what these cards are and the ICT implications for their use.

To be able to communicate with customers you need their addresses. In the past, if they bought goods, you did not know who they were (if they paid cash) or where they lived.

Many stores have loyalty cards. Each time the card is used, points are added. When the number of points earned reaches a certain value, customers are given vouchers that can be used in the store instead of cash.

The scheme works like this:

- The customer fills in an application form to join the scheme.
- The customer is given a card that contains a magnetic strip.
- Each time the customer goes to the store they take the card with them.
- When making the purchases whether by cash, debit card or credit card, the loyalty card links the customers to their purchases.
- The card adds a certain number of points based on their bill and the items bought, to the total.
- As stores can link what the customer buys to the customer details, they can send special offer vouchers for the things the customer buys.

The use of loyalty cards

There is a case study called Loyalty cards – linking you to your purchases in the case study section, which you should read to find out more about the use of loyalty cards.

All the large stores make use of reward/ loyalty cards.

Case studies

▶ Case study pp. 60–63

Using CAD and CAM in the fashion industry

CAD is used in the fashion industry to design items of clothing. The designer used to use a sketchpad to draw the designs. They worked using pencil, so that if they made a mistake or something needed to be altered, then they could just rub it out. With CAD it is much easier. They can easily make adjustments and keep saving the previous designs so that they can go back to them.

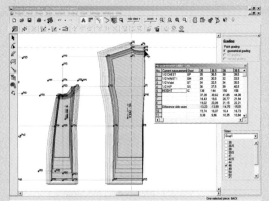
Here a pair of trousers is designed using the CAD software.

Once a design has been finalised, the CAM (computer-aided manufacture) machine can be programmed to cut out the fashion designs that were designed using the computer. The main advantage in using ICT in this way is that fewer people are needed. You no longer need a person to use the design to actually cut the cloth to produce the pieces to be stitched together.

In addition to this, the use of CAM along with CAD can considerably reduce the time between the design of an item of clothing and its production and the cutting machines can be reprogrammed to make different garments.

1 Explain why CAD and CAM are often used together. **(2 marks)**
2 Give one advantage in using CAM in the fashion industry. **(1 mark)**
3 Explain three features of CAM. **(3 marks)**

▶ Case study pp. 60–61

Garden design with Great Gardens Ltd

CAD software is used by Great Gardens Ltd to help with the design of gardens for their clients. The clients are shown a series of gardens the company has designed and the client can see what aspects of the designs they like within the allocated budget.

Using 3D modelling, the software allows the 2D design of the gardens to be turned into a 3D view. The client can then see what the garden looks like at various angles using the walk-through feature. The CAD software will also allow the client to see what the garden looks like at different seasons and it can also show them a garden at night with the various lighting effects.

The garden designer produces a list of the features the client would like to see included, measures the client's garden and then starts work on the design. They will sometimes start with a design they have already produced and make alterations to this according to the client's requirements, or if one is not available, they will start from scratch.

Structures such as paths, patios, decking, walls, pergolas, greenhouses, sheds, fences, etc., are added first

2D plans can be converted to 3D models to show clients.

and there is a large library of these structures to choose from.

Water features such as ponds and waterfalls can be added and to aid the designer in designing these, a wizard takes the designer through the steps.

Case studies continued

Trees and plants can then be added from the huge database. Here the garden designer will need to look for combinations of colours, whether the plants flower at the same time, autumn colour, whether the plants will thrive in the conditions in the garden, etc.

Gardens need to look good immediately they have been made as well as many years into the future. Here the garden designer can use a feature of the software called Plant growth projection. This feature is used to visualise what the garden will look like in Year 1, Year 2, etc.

Complex components such as ponds have their own wizard to guide users through the steps involved in their design.

The owner of Great Gardens Ltd said the main advantage of the software is that it is so easy to experiment to see what works and what doesn't. The collection of structures is easy to use and the ability to make changes to designs quickly, whilst the client is with you is a big plus.

'We have designed hundreds of gardens and we find that many clients choose some of our existing designs with minor alterations which saves us lots of time.'

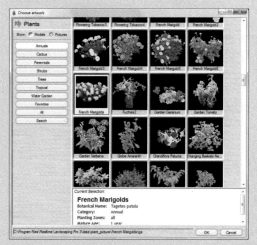

These screenshots show some of the features of garden design software.

1 Garden design software is an example of CAD software.
  (a) What is meant by the abbreviation CAD? (1 mark)
  (b) Give three features that the garden design software has in this case study. (3 marks)

2 In the past, the garden design company would have produced the garden design by hand using pencil and paper. Many visits to the client's house would be needed in order to finalise the design. Describe three ways in which life has been made much easier for the garden designer when designing gardens. (3 marks)

3 Explain what is meant by the term 3D modelling as used in the case study. (2 marks)

4 Here are some of the features of CAD software used for designing gardens:

  Plant database   Zoom
  Lighting effects   Walk-through
  Seasonal   Structure
     views   library

  Select four of the above features and for each one describe the advantage it gives when the designer is designing a new garden from scratch. (4 marks)

John Laing using computer-aided design

John Laing are one of Britain's largest construction companies and they construct large buildings such as office blocks, hospitals and schools. It is not surprising that for these complex buildings they make extensive use of CAD.

The CAD software allows architects to create an electronic representation of a building in 3D. This is important because in the past 2D plans were produced and in many cases the designs needed to be changed when an actual model of the building was created by a model builder. The CAD software allows the buildings to be viewed at the design stage and no physical model is produced.

Since the designs of the building are stored as computer files, everyone involved in the project can access them using the company's network. In addition, if alterations need to be made to the design, then the alterations are made and everyone can then access the new design. The company has found that design mistakes can be quickly identified and rectified and this has saved the company lots of money if these are sorted out before construction.

The CAD software allows the user to add textures, colours and finishes to the designs and allows walkthroughs using photo-quality images. This gives the designers the opportunity to view the final effects in seconds.

1 The ability to change a 2D plan to a 3D visualisation of a building is one advantage in using CAD software.
Describe two other advantages in using CAD software. (2 marks)

2 Discuss the special requirements that the running of CAD software has for the computer hardware that needs to be used. (5 marks)

3 Name and describe three distinctly different features of CAD software. (3 marks)

Tesco: Designing store layout using CAD

It is no longer necessary to use drawing boards for planning new stores and redesigning existing ones. Instead, computer-aided design (CAD) is used. This has reduced the time taken to plan new stores: a data bank holds designs and plans from existing stores which can be adapted, rather than new ones having to be generated each time. CAD is also able to show three-dimensional views of the stores, and colours, lighting and different

finishes on materials can be altered simply by moving the mouse. When a new store is planned, photographs of the proposed site can be used in conjunction with CAD to see what the area will look like with the Tesco store in place.

CAD is also used to design the warehouse layouts, and the roads and areas surrounding the distribution centres. This is important, since the access roads need to be suitable for large articulated vehicles, and there must be ample room around the distribution centres for them to turn round.

1 Name and describe three features you would expect to find in CAD software. (3 marks)

2 Give two advantages for Tesco in using CAD software for the designing of their stores. (2 marks)

3 People who use CAD software frequently work for long hours at the computer, which means they could experience a number of health problems.
Name and explain three health problems they could experience and for each health problem, suggest a way the health risk could be minimised. (3 marks)

Case studies continued

▶ **Case study**   p. 70

Loyalty cards – linking you to your purchases

Loyalty cards are used to link you to your purchases to analyse your purchasing habits.

Loyalty cards are very popular with shoppers because when you shop you collect points, which entitle you to freebies or savings. What do the shops get out of it though? The answer is quite a bit really. Apart from the likelihood of you returning to make more purchases to collect more points, most retailers find that shoppers using loyalty cards will spend more in their stores.

Before loyalty cards, the stores used to use newspaper and TV adverts to get our interest. By using loyalty cards they can actually target particular shoppers with advertising for those products they are most likely to buy.

An example of this would be if they wanted to increase their market share for the sale of pet food. As not everyone has a pet, they would need to target the marketing at those people who owned pets. Using a loyalty card, the purchases you make are linked to you, so if you bought cat food on a regular basis, then it is almost certain that you owned a cat. The pet food marketing material could therefore be sent to you.

You can see that it is possible to send different targeted marketing material to different customers with free vouchers or money off vouchers for the items they buy or are most likely to buy.

In addition to this, through the use of loyalty cards, retailers know what you bought and in some cases more than you do yourself. For example, do you know how many toilet rolls you get through in your house, because they do!

Retailers have a very powerful tool to build up huge databases full of information about our buying habits. For example, they could find out if we are living a healthy lifestyle. They could find out how much alcohol a particular person or household drinks.

One concern of loyalty schemes is that a few privately owned businesses are building up huge databases full of personal information about each one of us. Clearly this is an intrusion of privacy but you do volunteer to join a loyalty scheme and therefore volunteer the information you give them. Some people would say that the information you give them is a fair swap for the benefits you receive.

The problem might be that in the future the government might introduce legislation which allows the government to use the data held in these databases for its own purposes.

In the United States a court found that a man could pay more maintenance to his family because they found from a retailer's records that he had a history of buying very expensive wine.

1 Many retailers have a loyalty scheme which rewards shoppers who make regular purchases. The use of loyalty schemes has led to the development of large databases of customer information. Much of this information is concerned with personal information about customers and their purchases.

(a) Some of the information collected will be sold to other organisations. Describe two possible uses these organisations could make of the data they purchase. **(4 marks)**

(b) Some customers may object to personal information being passed to other organisations. Describe one reason they would object. **(1 mark)**

(c) Describe why other organisations would want to purchase some of the customer information that the retailer has collected. **(2 marks)**

Questions and Activity

▶ Questions 1 pp. 60–63

1 (a) What do the abbreviations CAD and CAM stand for? (2 marks)
   (b) Describe two features that you would expect to find in
       (i) CAD software
       (ii) CAM software. (4 marks)
2 Explain two uses to which CAD/CAM software can be put. (2 marks)
3 An engineering company uses CAD systems to design components for car engines and gearboxes.
   (a) Give two advantages that CAD packages offer compared to producing designs and scale drawings manually. (2 marks)
   (b) CAD software places demands on the computer used to run it.
       Describe the special hardware requirements for the successful running of CAD software. (3 marks)

   (c) The engineering company is thinking of using CAM to help manufacture the components using information from the CAD software.
       Give two advantages in using CAM. (2 marks)
4 (a) Explain what is meant by a CAD system and give two distinctly different applications for it. (4 marks)
   (b) Explain what is meant by CAM. (3 marks)
5 A garden design company is using a CAD package to help design gardens for their customers.
   Discuss the advantages and disadvantages of using CAD software for this purpose. (6 marks)

▶ Questions 2 pp. 64–70

1 Many supermarkets make use of 'just in time' for stock control.
   Explain how a 'just in time' stock control system works and discuss the advantages and disadvantages it offers the store. (8 marks)
2 Many stores have a loyalty scheme to enable stores to find out more information about their customers.
   (a) Explain how a loyalty card scheme works. (4 marks)
   (b) Give the name of the hardware device needed to read the information off the customer's loyalty card. (1 mark)
   (c) The use of loyalty cards raises a number of security and privacy issues.
       Explain:
       (i) one security issue
       (ii) one privacy issue. (2 marks)

3 Bar coding is used extensively in stores for the recording of stock and purchases.
   (a) Explain what a bar code is and how it is used in stores to record stock and sales. (3 marks)
   (b) Explain three advantages to the store in using bar codes to record sales. (3 marks)
   (c) Explain one disadvantage in the store using bar codes. (1 mark)
4 Discuss the range of input devices used in supermarkets and other stores.
   In your discussion you should mention the hardware used, the data recorded and the information output and the relative merits and disadvantages compared to alternative methods of inputting the data. (10 marks)

▶ Activity

You are looking for a chart CD. Write a list of the advantages in buying it from an on-line store such as Amazon or CD-wow. Now write a list of the disadvantages.

Exam support

Worked example 1

1 Loyalty schemes are very popular in stores for encouraging shoppers to make purchases at the store on a regular basis. When customers join the scheme they fill in an application form and when this is done, the details are entered into a database and a swipe card is sent by post to the customer.
   When customer details are entered into a database they are verified and validated.
   (a) Define the term verification. Name and describe one verification method that can be used during the entry of customer data. **(3 marks)**
   (b) Define the term validation. Name and describe one validation method used during the entry of customer data. **(3 marks)**

Student answer 1

1 (a) Verification means that the program checks the data for mistakes when it is being entered into the computer. You could look at the data to see if there are any mistakes and then correct them.
   (b) Validation is a check that the computer program does to make sure that wrong data is not put into the computer. Range check – ensures that only numbers entered within the range specified are accepted for processing and if not, they are rejected.

Examiner's comment

1 (a) This student has mistakenly given a definition for validation rather than verification. The example given does apply to verification but there is no name given. One mark is given for this section.
   (b) The definition includes the error in thinking that validation can check that wrong data is not put into the computer. Validation can only check that the data is sensible and cannot check simple errors like misspelling a person's name. No marks for this definition.
   The explanation for range check is good.
   (3 marks out of 6)

Examiner's answer

1 (a) One mark for a suitable definition such as:
      Verification means checking that the data being entered into the ICT system perfectly matches the source of the data.
      No mark for the name of the method but up to two marks for the description.
      Proof reading/visual check – carefully reading what they have typed in (1) and comparing it with what is on the data source/application form to find errors (1).
      Double entry of data – two people use the same data source to enter the details into the database (1) and only if the two sets of data are identical, will they be accepted for processing (1).
   (b) One mark for a suitable definition such as:
      Validation – the process which ensures that data accepted for processing is sensible and reasonable.
      No mark for the name of the method but up to two marks for the description.
      Presence checks – some database fields have to be filled in whilst others can be left empty (1) so if data for an essential field is left blank the data for the other fields will not be accepted for processing (1).
      Data type checks – check if the data being entered is the same type as the data type specified for the field (1). This would check to make sure that only numbers are entered into fields specified as numeric (1).
      Range checks – are performed on numbers to check that a number being entered is within a certain range (1). For example, if you have to be over a certain age to have a loyalty card, then if a date of birth were entered and this gave an age less than this, the data would not be allowed by the range check (1).
      Format checks – are performed on codes to make sure that they conform to the correct combinations of characters (1). For example a date of birth may have to be in a certain format (e.g. dd/mm/yy) and unless it is in the correct format it will be rejected (1).

Worked example 2

2 An architect uses specialist CAD software to design a new school.

(a) Select any four of the following features of CAD software and describe an advantage of each to the architect when designing a new school from scratch.

      Rotate
      Zoom
      Costing
      Walk-through
      Hatching/rendering
      3D modelling. (4 marks)

(b) The architect and the people in her office use CAD software for long periods working on very detailed designs and drawings. State one health problem that could result from the use of a CAD system and explain how this health problem could be prevented. **(2 marks)**

Student answer 1

2 (a) Zoom – you can see detail in the garden such as plants and trees
      Save – you can save the designs for later
      Rotate – you can rotate the plan so it can be printed in landscape or portrait orientation
      3D modelling – a 3D model of the design can be produced.

(b) Eye strain – looking at the screen for long periods can give you eye strain. This can be solved by taking Paracetamol.

Examiner's comment

2   (a)   This answer was completed by a quite weak student who has not properly grasped what is required here.
        The 'zoom' answer refers to a garden but the question refers to the design of a building. The student has not read the question properly.
        Save is not mentioned in the question so no marks here.
        The student has failed to understand what rotate does in CAD software.
        The answer on 3D modelling could simply be given by anyone guessing.
        No marks for any of these answers.

    (b)   Only one mark here for the nature of the health problem. **(1 mark out of 6)**

Student answer 2

2 (a) Zoom – you can see a particular part of the diagram closer by using zoom.
      Walk-through – you can actually walk through the building to see what it looks like.
      Costing – this lets you work out the costs of all the components in the building
      3D modelling – this allows a two-dimensional plan to be turned into a three-dimensional picture.

(b) Repetitive strain injury (RSI) – this is caused by the repeated use of the mouse or keyboard and it causes pain in the joints of the hands. To reduce the likelihood of RSI, you can use a wrist rest.

Examiner's comment

2   (a)   All of these answers are related to features of CAD software. There are a few problems with some of the descriptions of the features. For example, walk-though does not allow you to walk through the building. This is a computer model that allows you to pretend you are walking through the building and it models what you would see.
        The description of costings is too general and this information could be guessed from the name costings. Students need to be clearer by explaining the advantage the costings would give the architect.
        Two marks are given for this answer.

    (b)   This answer clearly explains the nature of the problem and identifies what can be done to help prevent the problem from occurring.
        (4 marks out of 6)

Examiner's answers

2 (a) The answer must not give general features (for example, relating to garden design software) and must be relevant to the architect designing a new building.

Any four features (one mark each) such as:

Rotate – you can see the design from different angles, which enables the architect to see the overall design – saves having to make a physical model.

Zoom – can hone in on a particular part of a diagram to see it in more detail and be able to read the details on the diagram.

Costing – this allows the architect to add items to the drawing and the costs of these items are added to the total cost to check that the design is not exceeding the budget.

Walk-through – the architect and clients can virtually walk through a building and observe the building from the inside.

Hatching/rendering – can see the effect of different finishes such as slate, tile, brick, etc.

3D modelling – allows the 2D plan to be used to produce a three-dimensional representation allowing the architect to see the design from different aspects.

CAD software enables architects to be more innovative.

(b) Repetitive strain injury (RSI) – caused by the repeated movement of the mouse and use of the keyboard.
Use a wrist rest/mouse pad with a rest.
Eye strain – caused by looking at the detail on the screen for long periods. Alleviated by the use of larger screen/frequent breaks (say for 5 min in every hour)/change in activity/frequent eye-tests, etc.
Back ache/back strain – use an adjustable chair with adjustable arms, seat height, back support, etc.
Stress – caused by the pressure of the work and the complexity of the software. Make sure unreasonable deadlines are not given/changes in activity/training to make software easier to use, etc.

Summary mind maps

CAD systems

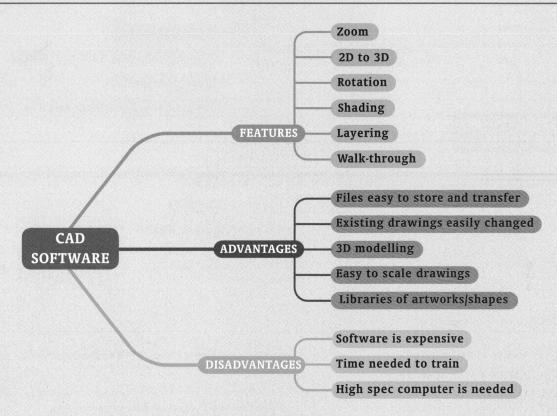

CAD SOFTWARE

FEATURES
- Zoom
- 2D to 3D
- Rotation
- Shading
- Layering
- Walk-through

ADVANTAGES
- Files easy to store and transfer
- Existing drawings easily changed
- 3D modelling
- Easy to scale drawings
- Libraries of artworks/shapes

DISADVANTAGES
- Software is expensive
- Time needed to train
- High spec computer is needed

CAM systems

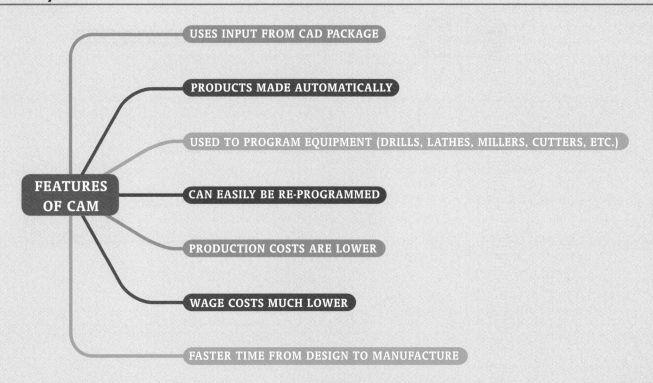

FEATURES OF CAM
- USES INPUT FROM CAD PACKAGE
- PRODUCTS MADE AUTOMATICALLY
- USED TO PROGRAM EQUIPMENT (DRILLS, LATHES, MILLERS, CUTTERS, ETC.)
- CAN EASILY BE RE-PROGRAMMED
- PRODUCTION COSTS ARE LOWER
- WAGE COSTS MUCH LOWER
- FASTER TIME FROM DESIGN TO MANUFACTURE

Summary mind maps continued

Payment methods

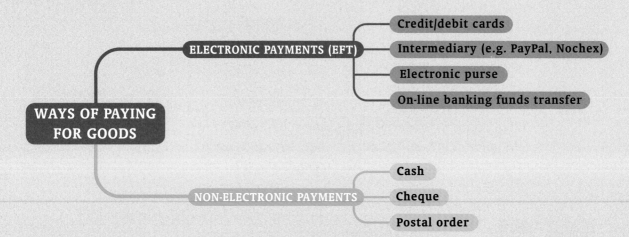

ELECTRONIC PAYMENTS (EFT)
- Credit/debit cards
- Intermediary (e.g. PayPal, Nochex)
- Electronic purse
- On-line banking funds transfer

WAYS OF PAYING FOR GOODS

NON-ELECTRONIC PAYMENTS
- Cash
- Cheque
- Postal order

Bar coding

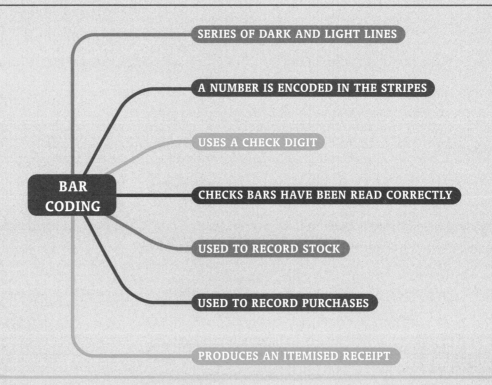

BAR CODING
- SERIES OF DARK AND LIGHT LINES
- A NUMBER IS ENCODED IN THE STRIPES
- USES A CHECK DIGIT
- CHECKS BARS HAVE BEEN READ CORRECTLY
- USED TO RECORD STOCK
- USED TO RECORD PURCHASES
- PRODUCES AN ITEMISED RECEIPT

In this topic you will learn about how ICT can be used for teaching and learning in schools and colleges and also how these organisations use ICT to help with administration. You will see how ICT can be used to help students understand their subjects and how it can be used to help them revise for examinations.

Schools and colleges employ lots of staff and have hundreds or even thousands of students about whom information needs to be kept. Much of this information needs to be kept for many years in case a school or college reference is needed in the future.

Schools and colleges have legal requirements to keep certain information and they all have budgets to control. It is no wonder that ICT has been used to help them save time with this administration, so they can concentrate on the teaching and learning.

▼ The key concepts covered in this topic are:

▶ Use of computers for teaching and learning

▶ Use of computers for school/college administration

CONTENTS

Unit IT1 Information Systems

Use of computers for teaching and learning

▼ **You will find out**

▶ About computer-assisted learning (CAL)

▶ About computer-based training (CBT)

▶ About distance learning

▶ About videoconferencing

▶ About on-line learning/e-learning

▶ About chat rooms for discussion with tutors/experts

▶ About features of software packages

▶ About revision programs

▶ About authoring software

▶ About interactive whiteboards

Introduction

In this section you will find out how ICT improves teaching and learning in schools and colleges.

Computer-assisted learning (CAL)

Computer-assisted learning covers a whole range of computer-based packages which aim to provide interactive instruction in a particular area or on a certain subject.

There are a variety of ways CAL can be run on a computer:

- The software can be run straight from a CD or DVD.
- It can be installed and run from a network on its own or in conjunction with a VLE (virtual learning environment).
- The software can be run over the Internet.

Typically, CAL would contain some or all of the following features:

- Tutorials – to instruct students in the subject.
- Simulations – to help students understand complex situations.
- Animations – help students understand how things work.
- Drill and practice – help students consolidate the learning.
- Tests – let students know how well they have learnt the topic.
- Games – introduce fun into the learning process.

Computer-based training (CBT)

Computer-based training (CBT) uses ICT systems for training in the workplace, usually by making use of PCs or portable devices. It is important to note that CBT is not about just training people to use computers, although it can be used for this. It is about using computers to train people to do different tasks and also to train them how to react in different situations. CBT can be used for:

- Health and safety training – to teach people about how to spot dangers in the workplace.
- How to perform a particular job – for example, how to operate a piece of equipment or machinery.
- Induction courses – used to introduce new employees to the company or business.
- Flight simulation courses for pilots – so that pilots can experience different types of emergencies.
- Instruction on how to use a particular piece of software.

Features of CAL/CBT

- Highly interactive – users supply answers to questions and situations.
- CAL/CBT both make use of multimedia features.
- Used for tutorials – allow the user to learn something new.
- Uses models/simulations – so that the user can experiment to see what happens in different situations.
- Used for revision – tests students with interactive activities that allow students/users to assess their progress in the area of revision.
- Encouragement – it does not matter if a user gets answers wrong – they can try again and the answer is often shown after a certain number of attempts.
- Games to make learning fun – even the most serious topics can be made fun when turned into a game.
- Testing and assessment – here the user can take a test/assessment to see how well they have understood the learning/training. The results from the test/assessment are given immediately including information on what they did well and what they did less well.
- Can be used for learning at a distance – no need for formal learning with lessons in set places at set times, etc.

KEY WORDS

Computer-assisted learning (CAL) – using a computer interactively for the learning process

Computer-based training (CBT) – using a computer interactively for training, usually on a person's occupation

On-line/e-learning – using ICT to help in the learning process

Advantages of CAL/CBT

- Students have flexibility as to where and when they want to learn.
- Materials are provided in lots of different ways such as text, voice, video, animations.
- Can access the material using a variety of different hardware such as laptop, PDA, mobile phone with MP3 player, iPod, etc.
- Can learn in many different environments such as in a car, while out running or walking, etc.
- Keep people using them interested and motivated by the variety of activities.

Disadvantages of CAL/CBT

- The software is often complex and uses lots of animation and graphics which makes it expensive.

- Students often need the interaction of their classmates in order to learn.
- Can present an opportunity for students to have a break rather than work on the CAL/CBT package.
- It is hard for teachers to gauge progress using some of the packages.

The Open University was set up to offer distance learning courses.

Before a teacher is qualified to teach in schools, they need to pass tests in numeracy, literacy and ICT. All these tests are done on-line and marked immediately by the computer. This screenshot shows one of the tasks they have to complete as part of the ICT test.

Distance learning

Distance learning is learning which takes place away from the confines of a traditional teacher/lecturer in a room teaching a group of students. Instead the learning takes place at a different place to the teacher. In many cases distance learning makes use of videoconferencing so that the students can see the teacher and the teacher can see the students. Distance learning is done in some schools where only a few students want to take a particular AS or A2 level course and the school cannot justify the expense of taking on a specialist teacher. Many universities also offer distance learning courses which allow adults to fit in degree study with their job and family commitments.

Distance learning can make use of all the latest ICT developments such as:

- E-mail – students are free to e-mail their tutors with problems they are having with the subject.
- Chat rooms – students can chat in real time amongst themselves or with their tutor in a group tutorial.
- Videoconferencing – allows a teacher/lecturer to give a lesson/lecture to a group of students who may all be located in different places.

Videoconferencing

Videoconferencing enables two or more individuals in different locations to see and talk to each other and exchange audio, video or any other digital file, enabling users to share computer applications and even work concurrently on the same file.

Videoconferencing is used widely in schools for:

- Distance learning – some schools use outside organisations to provide teaching via distance learning and videoconferencing in order to provide a wider range of subjects at AS and A-level.
- Conferences for schools – school students are given lectures using videoconferencing with scientists or mathematicians on real-life topics. Schools from around the world can take part in these conferences.
- Virtual trips to places of interest – students are able to virtually visit museums, art galleries, businesses, etc., and talk with their staff using videoconferencing.
- Collaborative working – students from different schools and colleges, which may be in different countries, can work together on a project.

On-line learning/e-learning

Authoring software can be used to create multimedia products which can be used to teach a particular subject. If the multimedia product is placed on-line, so that it can be accessed using the Internet, it is called e-learning. Another name for e-learning is simply on-line learning.

You can do a whole variety of courses on-line such as:

- GCSE and A-levels
- degree courses from many universities
- language courses
- courses for professional qualifications
- job-based courses.

Most on-line courses have knowledge sections which lay out what you need to know, then revision sections where you consolidate this knowledge, and finally testing sections where you are tested on what you have learnt.

Advantages of distance/on-line learning

- Students can work at their own pace.
- They do not have to worry about getting things wrong – the computer will not judge them like a teacher.
- Students get immediate feedback on tests, which enables them to monitor their progress.
- No set lesson times – students can decide where and when they want to study.
- Can fit learning around work and family commitments.
- Wide range of subjects – may not be able to do a particular subject locally.

Disadvantages of distance/on-line learning

There are a number of disadvantages of distance/on-line learning, namely:

- No social side – people enjoy the social side when learning with others.
- Lack of flexibility – human teachers can explain things in different ways to help you.
- Expensive – on-line courses can be expensive compared to other methods.
- It is harder when working in isolation – no classmates to help.
- Need to be motivated – in a class situation the teacher/lecturer can motivate you.
- Need more self-control – to do the work in your own time.

Topic 6(b) Uses of ICT in education

Use of computers for teaching and learning continued

Multimedia – making use of many media, such as text, image, sound, animation and video

Chat rooms for discussion with tutors/experts

Chat rooms do have many problems, and students are often prevented from going into them using filtering systems. However, carefully controlled and moderated chat rooms are very useful for students who are learning a subject on their own.

Here are some educational uses to which chat rooms have been put:

- can be used to question an expert in a particular field
- are used to hold tutorials with course tutors
- are ideal for students who are learning a foreign language.

Features of software packages

There are many different types of software package used for teaching and learning.
- presentation software
- software to be used with interactive whiteboards
- tutorial software
- revision software.

Most software used for teaching and learning makes full use of multimedia features as summarised here:

Revision programs

Revision programs are software that helps you revise for your exams and they provide a good and often fun way of building up knowledge about a subject and again most of them make use of multimedia features.

Revision programs can come on CD or be used direct from a website.

Authoring software

You may think that authoring is something writers do when they produce a book. Now, in ICT, authoring has taken on an additional meaning. Authoring is the process

of creating a multimedia product such as a website, an interactive presentation, an interactive learning tool for CAL/CBT or instructional software for an electronic whiteboard.

Instead of combining text and graphics like a traditional author would do, other multimedia elements are combined to produce a multimedia product which makes use of the following:

- text
- graphics
- audio
- video
- games
- quizzes
- tests
- links to websites
- animations.

The authoring software is used to add a structure to all the above components so that the multimedia product functions as a whole and enables the material to be used interactively.

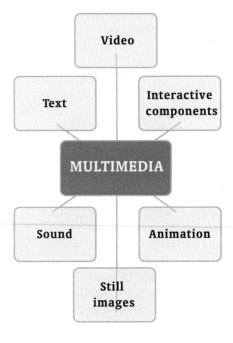

If you want to create a multimedia product you have two choices:

- You can design the product and then use a programming language to produce it.
- You can use authoring software.

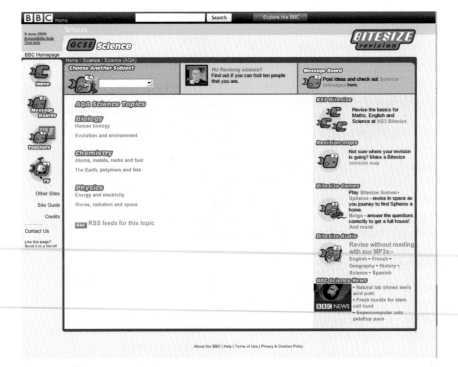

The BBC offers CAL on their BITESIZE revision site.

"How can I trust your information when you're using such outdated technology?"

"There aren't any icons to click. It's a chalk board."

Advantages of using authoring software

The advantages of creating multimedia products using authoring software rather than by producing programming code are:

- A novice can generally use the authoring software – for example, a classroom teacher could produce e-learning materials easily for their students.

- No programming needed – it allows the author to focus on the instructional development of the content rather that the programming.
- Faster to develop an e-learning product – it speeds up the process from initial development to the final published software.
- They automatically add the background programming code to allow the e-learning course to communicate test results, bookmarking and other information back to the author.

Disadvantages of using authoring software

- Not as flexible – you have to adapt the way you want to solve the problem to the way the authoring will allow.
- Not able to perform certain tasks – there are some things you may want to do that you can only do by using programming.

Interactive whiteboards

Interactive whiteboards are widely used in classrooms and lecture theatres and allow lessons or lectures to be more engaging and exciting.

An interactive whiteboard is a large interactive display which makes use of a computer and a projector. The working area and the user interface around the edge are projected by the computer onto the interactive whiteboard. The user then controls what happens by using a special pen, their finger or other input device.

Interactive whiteboards are modern replacements for ordinary whiteboards and flipcharts and they can be used to show anything that can be made to appear on a computer screen.

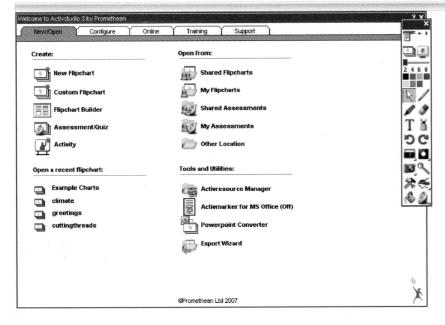

Some of the features of the software that can be used with an interactive whiteboard.

Use of computers for school/ college administration

▼ **You will find out**

▶ About computer-based methods of registration (e.g., OMR, wireless systems, smart cards, fingerprint recognition and retinal scanning)

▶ About student record keeping

Introduction

In this section you will find out how ICT helps save time on administrative matters in schools and colleges and frees teachers and lecturers from many of the routine tasks such as student registration.

ICT systems used for school/college administration

Schools and colleges employ staff, pay for goods and services, keep records of student attendance, keep records of students, etc. It is not surprising that they use ICT systems to help with these administrative tasks wherever possible. In the following sections you will learn about two main systems used in schools/colleges: the system used for student registration and the student record-keeping system.

The old paper-based registration system

The old paper-based registration system worked as follows:

- Marks were made on a sheet of paper, called a register, containing a list of student names.
- The marks were completed by the form teacher in the morning and after lunch.
- The registers were collected and kept at a central point for reference and health and safety reasons.
- The marks were added up by the form teachers each term so that attendance statistics could be produced.

There were lots of problems with this manual system, such as:

- Registers were often left unattended which meant pupils could easily alter the register.

- Mistakes in register entries meant registers were hard to understand.
- Statistics for attendance tended to only be produced each term.
- Teachers were responsible for the accuracy of the registers.
- Students could register themselves and then play truant by not attending the lessons.

The next step was the processing of the registers by computers and this meant someone had to enter all the marks from the register into the computer. The attendance marks were entered by keying in using a keyboard.

Because of the problems in inputting such a large amount of data, other direct methods of input were used that removed the need to type in marks.

Computer-based methods of registration

Any ICT system used for student registration in schools or colleges should:

- capture student attendance accurately
- capture the student attendance automatically
- be very fast at recording attendance details
- as far as possible avoid the misuse of the system
- enable not only morning and afternoon attendance to be recorded but also to record attendance at each lesson
- be relatively inexpensive
- be able to interface with other ICT systems used in the school, such as the system for recording student details.

There are a number of ICT systems currently used in schools and these will be looked at in the following sections.

Optical mark recognition (OMR)

Many schools use a system making use of optical mark recognition for student registration, where the teacher or lecturer marks a student's attendance by shading in boxes using a pencil. The forms are passed to the administration office where they are collected and batched together and processed automatically using an optical mark reader. As the forms are read automatically, it removes the problems of making mistakes when the marks are typed in using a keyboard. Once input, the data about attendance is processed and reports can be generated outlining students for whom attendance is a problem.

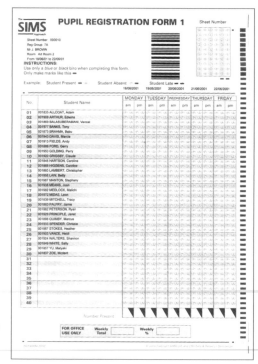

An OMR form which is used to enter student registration information into the schools information management system.

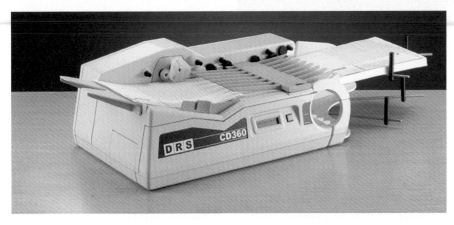

An optical mark reader – the device used to input the data on the marked registration forms into the system.

This is the least technologically advanced of the ICT methods we will look at for registration and it suffers from the following problems:

- registration is not checked in real time, so it is not possible for the admin staff to take immediate action
- teachers may leave the registers on their desks and not return them for processing
- registers can easily be altered by students
- registers have to be physically passed to and from the admin office
- if the OMR forms are folded or not filled in correctly, they are rejected by the reader.

Wireless systems

RFID (Radio Frequency Identification) obtains data stored on a tag (a small chip) using radio signals, which means that the reading device and tag do not have to come into contact with each other. This means that the data on the tag, which is usually attached to a credit card sized plastic card, can be read from a distance. This system is therefore a wireless system.

The main advantage of using this system is that there is no need to remove the card from your pocket or bag as the tag can still be read. This means that pupils only have to remember to have their card with them, so as they enter school their attendance is automatically recorded.

All this comes at a price and the main disadvantage with the system is the cost.

Smart cards

A smart card is a plastic card the same size as a credit card that contains either a microprocessor and memory chip or just a memory chip. Smart cards hold much more information than cards that only contain a magnetic strip and they sometimes perform encryption so that if the card is lost or stolen it cannot be misused.

Smart cards can be used in schools in the following ways:

- for monitoring attendance
- for the payment for meals in the school canteen
- for registration of students

- for access to the school site, buildings and rooms to improve security
- for access to certain facilities such as the computer network, photocopier, etc.
- to record borrowings and returns of school library books, digital cameras, musical instruments, etc.

In some schools, smart cards are used to purchase food in the school canteen. The cards can be topped up with money at the start of the week or daily and this reduces the time it takes for meals to be bought as no time is spent exchanging cash.

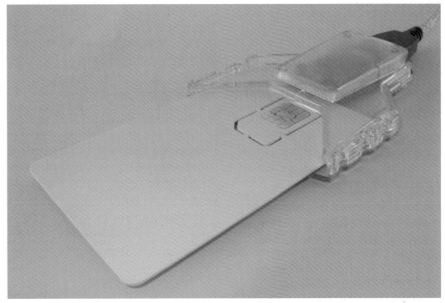

A reader used to read data from the chip in a smart card.

An RFID tag which enables data stored on the chip at the centre to be read at a distance.

Use of computers for school/college administration continued

Computer-based methods of registration (continued)

Swipe cards

Students are given a swipe card which they use for registration purposes by swiping the card using a card reader. Swipe cards consist of a plastic card with a magnetic strip containing a limited amount of data on it. The swipe card is used to identify the student to the registration system and some other systems such as the library system and the school meals system. The same card can be used for access to school buildings.

There are a number of advantages in using swipe cards and these include:

- the cost of the cards and the readers is low compared to other methods
- readers can be made which are almost vandal proof.

The disadvantages include:

- cards are often lost, meaning that students have to be registered using a keyboard
- students can be swiped in by someone else.

Biometric methods

Biometric methods provide a fast and easy way of recording students' attendance at school or college. Biometric methods make use of a feature of the human body that is unique to a particular person in order to identify them. Biometric methods include:

- fingerprint recognition
- retinal scanning.

Biometric methods are ideal for primary schools where the children are too young to look after smart cards or swipe cards and older students do not have to remember to bring a card with them to school.

Measurements are taken at certain points on the fingerprint and then stored as a code.

Fingerprint recognition

Everybody's fingerprint is different, so fingerprinting provides a unique way of identifying people. Many schools now use fingerprinting systems in a scheme which has government approval to improve attendance in schools.

Fingerprint scanners can be installed outside classrooms to allow students to record their attendance.

Fingerprint recognition works in the following way:

- A student places their finger into the fingerprint scanning device.
- The scanner acts as an input device and stores some of the features of the fingerprint as a mathematical code.
- The software then compares the code with all the fingerprint codes it has stored previously.
- The person whose finger has been entered is identified from the student database.
- The details of their attendance are recorded.

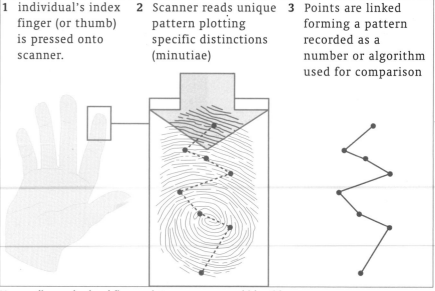

1 individual's index finger (or thumb) is pressed onto scanner.	2 Scanner reads unique pattern plotting specific distinctions (minutiae)	3 Points are linked forming a pattern recorded as a number or algorithm used for comparison

How police and school fingerprint scanners record identities.
The whole fingerprint is not stored, only certain points that are used to distinguish between prints.

Retinal scanning

The retina is a thin tissue situated at the back of the eye, which contains millions of tiny blood vessels that are uniquely arranged. Like fingerprints, the pattern of these blood vessels can be used to uniquely identify a person.

Input devices, called retinal scanners, can send a low-level light beam into a person's eye and then analyse the reflected pattern. This pattern is coded in a similar way to the way fingerprints are coded and this code is then stored on a computer database. This then allows a student to approach the scanner to record their attendance at school or class, so the system can be used to identify students in school registration systems.

The advantages of using ICT systems for registration

- The details are recorded almost in real time – this means it is immediately possible to identify students who are not present.
- Teachers have the administration burden removed – the responsibility for attendance marking is moved away from teachers.
- Not possible for students to abuse the system – students are not able to mark themselves or other people in.
- Promotes health and safety – in the case of a fire, the system can provide information on everyone in the building.
- Encourages students to be responsible – students are given responsibility for recording their attendance.
- As the system is easy, it is possible to check the attendance for each lesson rather than just twice a day.
- If a student arrives very late – the system will record how late they were and their attendance is still recorded.
- Can be accessed using any terminal – the attendance details can be accessed from any computer on the network and this means more than one person can use the same data at the same time.

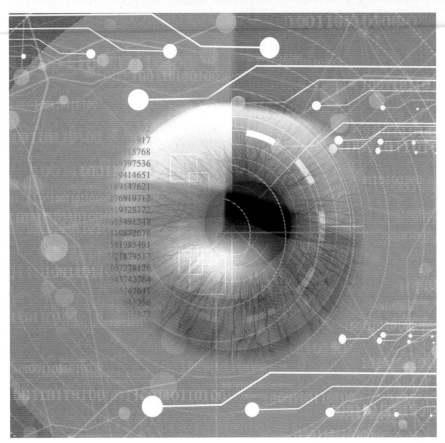

Retinal scanning provides unique identification of a person.

- No need for registers to be physically moved from place to place.
- Reports can be generated quickly for any student – no need to add up totals manually.
- As the data is held on computer, it takes up much less space than lots of paper registers which need to be kept for several years.

The disadvantages of using ICT systems for registration

- Biometric readers are very expensive.
- Human rights issues when fingerprint systems are used, even though the actual fingerprints are not stored and cannot be re-created from the code.
- Readers must be kept clean or false reads can be produced.
- The system can develop faults, so a suitable backup system must be available in these circumstances.

Other uses for biometric systems in schools

Biometric methods are not only used for recording attendance. They can also be used for:

- recording borrowing and returns of library books or other equipment
- recording use of photocopiers
- recording cashless meals for pupils who have free school meals
- entry control to buildings and rooms.

Many libraries in schools use fingerprinting systems rather than cards to record who is borrowing a book.

Use of computers for school/college administration continued

Student record keeping

Schools and colleges keep the information about their students in a large database and this database would typically contain the following fields for the information about each student:

- Unique Pupil Number (UPN) (a unique number for each student)
- Surname
- Forename
- DOB
- Gender
- Position in family
- Ethnic origin (although this is 'sensitive' data under the Data Protection Act 1998, the DfES require statistics about ethnicity)
- Language of home (if other than English)
- Religion (although this is 'sensitive' data under the Data Protection Act 1998, the school has good reasons for collecting the information)
- Names of parents and/or guardians with home address, telephone numbers and e-mail address
- Name of the school, and the date of admission and the date of leaving
- The name of the pupil's doctor
- Emergency contact details.

The above are the minimum fields needed in a student record. Also included in the database management system will be the following:

- Any reports written about the student
- National Curriculum results sheets
- Any important medical information about the student
- Information on exclusions
- Information on any major incidents involving the student (e.g., accident or other incident)
- Examination results
- Correspondence with outside agencies or parents for major matters
- Child protection reports/ disclosures.

As you can see, there is a large amount of information stored about each student and much of this information is sensitive personal information. The school has a responsibility under the Data Protection Act 1998 to ensure the privacy and the security of the information it holds about its students.

Schools information management systems

There are many different pieces of information stored by a school – the student records and the records of attendance are just two. By integrating all the systems, it is possible to extract the data needed from the system in the form of reports.

The main advantages in using schools information management systems are:

- they reduce the workload for teachers in the classroom and in the school office
- they can provide up-to-date information for parents
- they can support decision making for school managers
- they can tackle truancy effectively
- they can be used to plan timetables
- they can be used to strengthen home–school links.

Use of ICT systems to support administration in schools and colleges

Here are some examples of other ways schools use computers:

- Internet – used for research by staff, used to find careers/ university info, etc.
- Intranet – used to exchange information between staff and also for internal e-mail.
- Word-processing – used for the writing of schemes of work, lesson plans, references, reports, etc.
- Spreadsheet – used for managing school/department budgets, used for keeping test marks, etc.
- Presentation software – used for the preparation of lessons by staff, staff development, etc.
- Electronic data interchange – used to exchange information about exam entries and results with examination boards.
- Timetabling software – used to plan timetables and allocate resources (i.e., staff and rooms).

A pupil record from the schools information management system. Notice that included in the details is a photograph of the pupil.

Case studies

▶ Case study pp. 86–89

Using fingerprinting in schools

Many schools are now using fingerprinting methods to help with pupil registration. One such school in South Wales has been using fingerprinting methods for a couple of years now. The system works by the pupils placing their finger on a scanner which is installed outside the classrooms. The scanner reads certain aspects of the print to identify the pupil and then records the attendance details on the computer.

The head teacher of the school has sung the praises of the system, saying how it has helped reduce truancy because pupils now know that it can be immediately identified by the system. Teachers at the school have welcomed the system because it frees them from having to do this important but time-consuming task.

If a pupil fails to register at the start of the day, a text message can be sent to the parent's mobile phone alerting them of the non attendance of their child. This makes it virtually impossible for a pupil not to attend school without their parents knowing.

Many pupils like the system because it gives them more time to chat with friends and find out what is going on in the school with their form teacher.

Some parents and pupils were initially worried that fingerprints were being routinely taken and stored by the school and that this was personal data which could be misused. However, the company who supplied the system explained to parents that no full fingerprints are stored by the system. Instead the fingerprint is stored as a code and it is this code that is matched. They were reassured that a fingerprint cannot be re-created from this code and that it is only used by the school for identification purposes and not for some other sinister use.

1 Many schools use fingerprinting as a method for recording the presence of pupils at school.
   (a) Fingerprinting is an example of a biometric input device. Explain briefly what this sentence means. (2 marks)
   (b) Give three advantages of using fingerprinting to register attendance. (3 marks)
   (c) Many parents may be worried that the system stores their child's fingerprints. Write a sentence to explain how you might address this worry. (2 marks)

2 Describe one way in which the fingerprinting system helps prevent truancy in schools. (2 marks)

3 Give one example of how this fingerprinting attendance system could possibly be misused. (2 marks)

▶ Case study pp. 86–89

Privacy issues of using fingerprint recognition systems in schools

A person's fingerprint is unique to that person and does not change with age. This means that once a fingerprint has been taken and stored it can be used for the person's entire lifetime.

Some computer experts reckon that fingerprint systems will be used to uniquely identify each one of us and this means that if someone could steal our fingerprint they could steal our identity.

The manufacturers and the schools who introduce these fingerprint recognition systems say that 'the system does not store a fingerprint, only a code which uniquely defines a fingerprint'. Some people argue that this is just like storing the fingerprint itself, as the police and security services also use these codes to uniquely identify criminals.

Some people say that the fingerprint can be recreated from the code and even if it cannot be done now, what about in the future?

With all the problems with sensitive personal data going missing from government departments, many people argue that schools, having a limited budget, cannot possibly provide the security needed to keep fingerprint data safe.

1 Biometric input methods are used in schools to monitor student attendance.
   (a) Give the name of the biometric method used for input in this case study. (1 mark)
   (b) Give one reason why biometric methods are better than other methods such as OMR, smart card or swipe card for the monitoring of attendance. (1 mark)

2 Many people are worried about the routine fingerprinting of pupils for use in the system outlined. Explain two concerns a parent might have about their child being fingerprinted. (2 marks)

Questions and Activities

▶ Activity 1: Useful websites

The following website contains an interactive demonstration of some of the features of the software used with electronic whiteboards. Take some time to look at this and write down a list of the features.

http://www.prometheanworld.com/uk/server/show/nav.1693

▶ Activity 2: The schools information management system (SIMS)

SIMS is a very popular ICT system used in schools for the day-to-day running of the school. In order for you to understand what a school record and reporting system can do, you are advised to look at the following site where there are several product demonstrations.

http://www.capitaes.co.uk/SIMS/Downloads/demos.asp

▶ Activity 3: Why is the following data needed by schools?

One school pupil database contains the following fields. For each field write a sentence to explain why the data is needed by the school.

- DOB
- Language of home
- Religion
- Emergency contact details
- Unique Pupil Number
- Gender
- The name of the pupil's doctor.

▶ Questions 1 `pp. 82–90`

1 Most schools now use databases to store details about each pupil. The table shows some of the fieldnames and data types stored in one pupil database.

Fieldname	Data type
UniquePupilNumber	Integer
Firstname	
Surname	Text
FirstLineAddress	Text
SecondLineAddress	Text
Postcode	
LandlineNo	Text
DateOfBirth	Date
FreeSchoolMeals(Y/N)	

(a) Give the most appropriate data types for the fields:
   (i) Firstname
   (ii) Postcode
   (iii) FreeSchoolMeals(Y/N) (1 mark)
(b) Give the names of three other fields that would likely be used in this database. (1 mark)
(c) Explain which field is used as the unique field in the database and why such a field is necessary. (2 marks)
(d) It is important that the data contained in this database is accurate.

Describe how two different errors could occur when data is entered into this database. (2 marks)
(e) Explain how the errors you have mentioned in part (d) could be detected or prevented. (2 marks)

2 Interactive whiteboards are used extensively in schools.
Explain, by referring to an example you have seen, how the use of these boards improves teaching and learning for students. (4 marks)

3 Here is a statement which appeared recently in an article in the computer press on training methods:
'Computer-based training/computer-assisted learning is little more than an electronic page-turning exercise that is hardly any different from reading a manual or book.'
From your experience of CBT/CAL packages, write a short piece in reply to the above argument, saying whether you agree or disagree with the statement and supporting your argument with examples of CBT/CAL which you have used or seen. (8 marks)

▶ Questions 2 `pp. 82–90`

1 A student's date of birth is incorrectly input as 3/4/90 instead of 4/3/90.
The date of birth is accepted into the system for processing.
(a) Explain with reference to the example in the question what is meant by a transposition error. (1 mark)
(b) Explain by reference to the example why data can be both valid and incorrect. (2 marks)
(c) Explain how verification could be used to spot the error. (2 marks)

2 When a pupil joins a school, they are given an eight digit unique pupil number.
(a) Give one reason why each pupil at the school is given a unique number. (1 mark)
(b) Name and describe two validation checks that could be performed on this number. (4 marks)

3 ICT-based student registration systems in schools offer the advantages of speed and accuracy to the form teacher. Discuss two other advantages to the school in using ICT to register students. (4 marks)

Exam support

Worked example 1

1 Schools use ICT to remove some of the administrative burden. For example, registering pupils' attendance can be done using ICT rather than by using a paper-based register where the form teacher would record attendance.
   (a) Describe three different methods by which ICT systems can be used to record pupil attendance. (6 marks)
   (b) Give two advantages in using ICT systems to record and process students' attendance details. (2 marks)

Student answer 1

1 (a) The pupils can mark themselves in using biometric methods. The teacher can enter the pupils' marks into a computer. The teacher can put the marks on a form which is then entered into the computer.

  (b) The teacher does not have to calculate the total attendances for each pupil or the percentage attendance details, so there is no time wasted and it is more accurate.
  The teacher does not have to bother marking the pupils in because the computer does it for him.

Examiner's comment

1 (a) Although the student has mentioned 'biometric methods' there is not enough detail for even one mark here. The student needed to explain what the biometric method is and how the attendance mark is produced.
  The second answer only gains one mark. The student should state the actual method used (i.e. using a keyboard).
  Although the students sounds as if they mean using optical mark forms to input the attendance details into the computer using optical mark recognition, it is not up to the examiner to 'guess' what a student means. This answer therefore gains no marks.

  (b) One mark is given for the first answer as the second answer is far too vague.
  Statements like the 'computer does it for them' gain no marks. **(2 marks out of 8)**

Student answer 2

1 (a) Biometric testing using fingerprints. The pupils register their presence in school by placing their finger in a scanner. The scanner scans their finger and identifies who they are and inputs their details and the time of their attendance.
  Pupils use swipe cards containing a magnetic strip which identifies the pupil to the system. The magnetic strip reader reads the pupil details encoded in the magnetic strip which is used to identify the pupil from the database. Their attendance is recorded.
  Biometric testing using retinal scanning. The pattern of blood vessels on the back of the eye is unique to a particular pupil and this fact is used to identify the pupil to the attendance system.

  (b) Teachers do not have to waste time recording attendance and they can spend more time teaching.
  Pupils are responsible for their recording of attendance. This makes them more responsible and more like adults.

Examiner's comment

1 (a) A biometric method is one method of input used in a school registration system. The student here has given two answers that refer to biometric methods (i.e. fingerprinting and retinal scanning) which means only one of them can be included. Students have to be careful to always give distinctly different answers when asked to give a certain number of methods, functions, features, types etc. This is a very common mistake.
  The other method of input gains the marks.

  (b) Both of these answers are correct.
  (6 marks out of 8)

Examiner's answers

1 (a) One mark for the name of the input method and one mark for a description of how the system is used to mark attendance.
The three methods must be different so students cannot give more than one biometric method.

Biometric method (retinal scanning, fingerprint scanning, face recognition, etc.). Students are recognised by the scanner and their attendance details are recorded.

Swipe cards – each pupil is given a plastic card containing a magnetic strip which contains identification details which is read by the reader.

Wireless terminals – here the teachers are given laptops to record each pupil's attendance and the details are sent wirelessly to update the school's administration computers.

(b) One mark for each explanation of advantage × 2
Explanations include:

Takes the burden of attendance away from the teachers.

Makes the pupils more adult by making them responsible for recording their attendance.

Attendance statistics are available immediately so parents can be notified if their children are not present.

Harder for pupils to get marked in and then go home.

Worked example 2

2 **Many schools use CAL packages to help with teaching and learning. Schools also make use of distance/on-line learning to help with teaching and learning.**
(a) Give two advantages and two disadvantages in using distance/on-line learning. (4 marks)
(b) CAL packages are sometimes used with pupils who have learning difficulties. Give two advantage and two disadvantages in using CAL packages with these students. Your answers must be different from those for part (a). (4 marks)

Student answer 1

2 (a) There is no teacher around to tell you off when you get something wrong.
There are ways in which you can move back to a topic you feel you did not understand.
Learning is a social thing and you do not have the chance to interact with your classmates with on-line learning.
There is no-one around to help you if you get stuck but if you had a proper teacher then they might be able to explain it a different way to help you understand.

(b) The CAL package will not judge you if you make mistakes, unlike a teacher who may think you are stupid.
The CAL package will make use of multimedia effects which means that it will encourage reluctant learners to learn because it will be fun.
CAL packages cannot be used at home.
CAL packages are expensive because they take a long time to produce.

Examiner's comment

2 (a) The two advantages are sensible and well expressed, so full marks for these.
Again both disadvantages are acceptable answers and are well expressed so full marks for these.

(b) The first, third and fourth answers are justifiable reasons and they are all relevant to a pupil with learning difficulties.
The second answer is incorrect as many CAL packages can be run over a network such as the Internet. **(7 marks out of 8)**

Student answer 2

2 (a) You can access the teaching materials from any computer, which makes it very flexible when you do the course.
You can take the course 24/7, which makes it more flexible than traditional lessons which have to be arranged according to a timetable.

(b) You can learn at your own pace and not the pace of the rest of the class.
CAL packages often make learning a game, which is fun and keeps the pupils engaged in their learning.
The teacher could think you were learning on the computer when you weren't reading the information and simply guessing at the answers.
There is no competition with your classmates to see who does best, so this can de-motivate you.

Examiner's comment

2 (a) These two answers are very similar as they both refer to the fact that on-line courses offer flexibility (e.g. time and location). Students have to be careful they do not write an answer that is just slightly different, as marks will not be given for both answers. The answers to this type of question must be distinctly different. Only one mark is given here for one advantage.
No disadvantages are given here. It seems likely that the student has forgotten to read this part of the question. It is always worth reading the question and your answer again at the end of the question to check for this.

(b) All the answers here are correct so full marks for this part to the question. **(5 marks out of 8)**

Examiner's answers

2 (a) One mark each for two advantages such as:
Students can work through the material at home or in the library
Useful when students cannot attend school for personal reasons (e.g. illness, etc.)
Students become more responsible for their learning which is useful practice for entry into HE
Students can repeat the lesson if there is something they do not understand
Classes are able to be run with fewer students than normal
Classes can take place at any time – there need not be a set timetable.
One mark each for two disadvantages such as:
Students need to be motivated otherwise they won't complete the tasks
Can be expensive
Lack of support and encouragement from a teacher
No encouragement or collaborative learning from others in the class.

(b) One mark each for two advantages such as:
Students are able to work at their own pace
They do not have to worry about getting things wrong as there is no human to judge them
They can repeat parts many times until they fully understand them
The multimedia aspects of the software can be used to suit the different types of learner
Adds more fun to the learning process
Can use special input devices such as touch screens to help students who find it hard to use a keyboard and mouse
Learners can gauge their own progress.
One mark each for two disadvantages such as:
Lack of teacher encouragement
Pupils may just think of it as a game and not learn anything
There is no collaborative learning
Does not teach them to interact with humans.

Summary mind maps

CAL/CBT

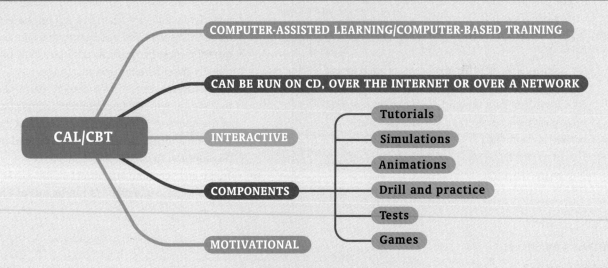

ICT-based student registration system

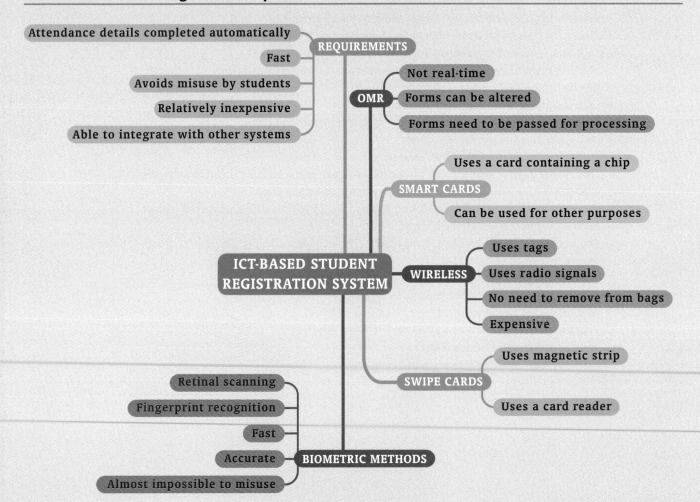

In this topic you will learn about how ICT is used for healthcare in hospitals and by general practitioners. You will see how some of the material you have already covered is used to make the NHS an efficient organisation. You will see that ICT is not just used for patient record keeping, it is also used for jobs involving patients' health.

▼ The key concepts covered in this topic are:

▶ Medical databases

▶ Scanning, life support and computer-controlled equipment

▶ Expert systems

CONTENTS

Unit IT1 Information Systems

Medical databases

▶ You will find out

▶ About electronic patient record keeping

▶ About blood bar coding and tracking systems

▶ About the use of the Internet, intranets and extranets

▶ About distributed medical databases

▶ About backup and recovery procedures

Introduction

In this section you will be looking at some of the ICT systems that are used to record information about patients and their medical conditions. There are also systems that interface with the patient record systems in order to ensure the safety of the patient.

Patients are at the heart of the NHS and having accurate information about each patient is fundamental to this.

Electronic patient record keeping (EPR)

In the past all patient records were kept on paper and this caused many problems which included:

- Many medical staff needed to access the same patient records and sometimes they needed them simultaneously. The only way two doctors could access them at the same time would be to photocopy them which is expensive and wasteful.
- Huge numbers of paper-based records caused storage and retrieval problems.
- Handwritten notes written quickly meant that others could not always understand them.
- Patient records frequently went missing, as doctors kept them on their desk rather than returning them to the medical records department.
- Patient records filed in the wrong place meant many tests had to be repeated, wasting time and money.
- Problems with notes not arriving ready for patient appointments.
- Handwritten prescriptions could not be understood by the pharmacist and this wasted time.

If you have visited a hospital or your GP lately, you will notice that many of the paper-based systems in use have been replaced partially or completely by electronic systems.

Storing the patient details on a large database which is available for all healthcare workers to access if they have the required permissions is a huge improvement. Anyone in any part of the system can access the information and many people can access the same patient's record at the same time.

There are many advantages in storing data electronically rather than on paper and these include:

- Patient details are available to be viewed wherever there is a terminal. In some cases the details can be accessed on mobile devices such as laptops and PDAs.
- There is only one set of data kept so it is easier to ensure the consistency of the data.
- Security is improved because the data can be protected using different permissions for different staff.
- It is much easier to back up the data.
- You do not need to transport patient files from place to place as with the paper system.
- Patient information is available in many different places instantly. For example, it is available at the bedside, in the consultant's office and in the emergency department.

New and future developments of medical databases

The NHS National Database

A database is currently being developed which will be the world's largest database containing secure information about patients' healthcare. The new database provides patient care records which will allow patient healthcare professionals quick access to reliable information about the patient. This huge database will store information on allergies, current prescriptions and bad reactions to medicines as well as all the patient information held by GPs and hospitals. The new database will contain information on more than 70 million patients and there will be 400,000 registered users of the system.

The Electronic Prescription Service

Electronic Prescription Service is a new service and will enable prescribers – such as GPs and practice nurses – to send prescriptions electronically to a dispenser (such as a pharmacy) of the patient's choice. This will make the prescribing and dispensing process safer and more convenient for patients and staff. About 70 percent of prescriptions issued are for

"I'm prescribing a squiggly line, two slanted loops, and something that looks like a P or J."

Electronic patient record systems print out the prescription. This eliminates problems with hurried handwritten prescriptions not being understood.

repeat medication, which can be time consuming using the current paper-based system, so this new system will save doctors time and allow them more time with patients.

Patient identification

When a patient arrives at the hospital they are allocated a unique number, which in some cases is their NHS number. This number is important as it provides the key field for the patient database and it is used to distinguish between patients with the same name living at the same address.

Patient identification is extremely important in hospitals, so each patient is issued with a wristband with a bar code on it. This system provides the critical first step in making sure that patients are correctly identified.

The bar coded wristband contains the following information about the patient:

- patient names
- date of birth
- blood type
- NHS number or some other number that uniquely identifies the patient.

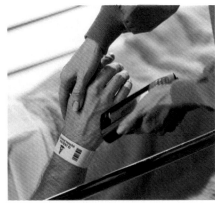

A bar coded patient wristband.

Blood bar coding and tracking systems

Blood transfusions can cause a big risk to patients, if either the blood or the patient is incorrectly identified. Putting the wrong blood into a patient can prove fatal, so it is important that identification mistakes do not occur. Also there needs to be a way of determining who gave the blood and who received it, as many infections can be passed through blood products. If in the future it was identified that either

the donor or the recipient had a medical problem, then both could be identified.

Blood bags used for blood transfusions are routinely bar coded with certain information at the blood bank before being delivered to the hospital.

How blood tracking works

Tracking blood is extremely important, so hospitals use a computerised ICT system for this purpose, which works in the following way:

1. Blood is taken from donors and is then tested to determine certain characteristics of the blood such as blood group (A, B, AB, O, etc.).
2. Blood is stored at the National Blood Transfusion Service. Cross matching takes place and bar coded labels are produced during testing and attached to the blood bags.
3. Matched blood is sent to the hospital where it is kept in a blood bank/fridge. The details of the blood contained in the bar code are scanned in before a blood bag is placed inside the fridge.
4. Hospital staff remove the required blood by first scanning their ID card. The magnetic locks on the blood bank/fridge then unlock, allowing the blood to be removed. The identification bar code on the blood is scanned and the blood taken to the ward. In this way blood is tracked into and out of the fridge.
5. The patient who requires the transfusion has their bar code on their wristband scanned using a handheld PDA. If it matches then the blood transfusion is given.

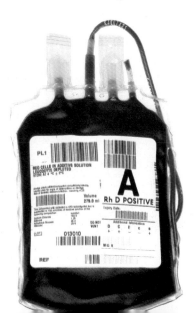

Information contained in the bar code is scanned into the system before the blood is transferred to the fridge.

Advantages of the blood tracking system

- The system provides a full audit trail by identifying the member of staff who removed the blood, the time/date, location, and time spent out of the fridge.
- Eliminates the need for staff to keep paper records so saves time.
- Eliminates the need for space to store the paper records, which means costs are lower.
- Cross matching information electronically eliminates the risk of patients being given the wrong blood, so saves money by patients not making claims.
- Provides security by only allowing certain staff to access blood in the fridge.
- Used for stock control so that the blood to match the patient's needs is always available.
- Can find the donor or receiver of the blood if there has been a danger of cross-infection.

Other uses for bar coding in healthcare

Bar coding is a fast and efficient input method and is used in medical applications apart from patient identification and blood tracking such as:

- identifying laboratory specimens (blood, urine, etc.)
- some patient paper-based records contain a bar code on them for identification.

PDA with bar code reader used to scan in patient details.

Medical databases continued

Use of the Internet, intranets and extranets

Internet technology allows healthcare trusts to reduce their networking costs and allow access to their ICT systems from anywhere at any time subject to the correct authorisation.

Use of the Internet

Hospitals allow staff to access the Internet from the organisation's extranet or intranet. Firewalls are used to ensure that people cannot access the hospital systems from the Internet without permission.

The Internet can be used by hospitals to:

- send e-mails to patients they find difficult to contact by phone
- communicate with patients using a hospital website
- allow staff to perform research
- enable patients to communicate with their friends and family
- send information on lab tests or X-rays requested by doctors in primary (e.g., GP) or secondary care from hospital or lab servers.

Intranets

Intranets are private networks that use the same technology as the Internet for the sending of messages and data around the network. Only hospital staff are allowed access to the intranet. Many hospitals use intranets as a way of transferring patient data to different devices (e.g., PCs, laptops, PDAs) around the hospital.

Extranets

Extranets are networks that use the same technology as the Internet but allow people who are not employees of the hospital or trust to access and exchange certain information. They must, however, be authorised to use the extranet which is protected by usernames and passwords. Extranets can be used by:

- suppliers – so that they are able to check that vital drugs and equipment never run out
- other agencies (e.g., social workers, care homes, etc.) who work with patients but outside the hospitals
- general practitioners – who can check on the condition of their patients in hospital.

Distributed medical databases

A distributed medical database is a collection of patient information spread over two or more servers in a network. There are many different systems used in health trusts and as a patient you can end up having your details stored on more than one of them. Using Internet technology it is possible to build a system that can access all the information about a particular patient, even if the information is stored on different servers at different locations.

When a healthcare professional needs to see a patient's medical record, the distributed parts are found and merged to form a single record. Ideally, the user will be unaware that the record is in different bits scattered throughout the network.

Distributed databases have the advantage that:

- security can be improved as the data is not all kept in one place – databases can be easily replicated
- speed of access is improved because one server does not have to deal with all the requests for information from users.

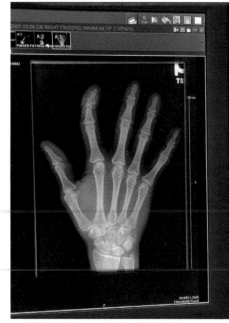
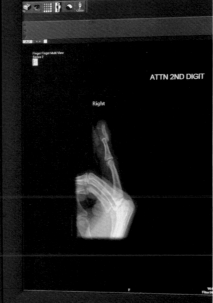

X-rays are now digitised so they can be stored with the patient records.

ICT systems enable doctors to spend more time wiht patients.

Considerations for backup:

- Whether any downtime is acceptable – if downtime is not acceptable then a RAID system should be used.
- How much data needs to be backed up – tape stores the most.
- Where the data is to be stored – copies of data should be kept off-site.
- How often copies of the data should be taken – this depends on how often the data changes.
- When the data should be backed up – data is usually backed up when the system is being used the least – usually this would be at night.

Backup and recovery procedures

Medical databases lie at the heart of patient care and it is crucial that this data is kept secure and backed up regularly.

Recovery procedures must be in place so that staff can recover any lost data, and it is essential that the procedures are tested to make sure that the systems can be recovered in the event of a problem.

Ensuring the privacy of patient records

The privacy of patient records is taken very seriously by hospitals and medical staff and they have to make sure that personal medical details are only disclosed to authorised staff. The privacy of the EPR system is assured by:

- Access levels – these control what a user can do. For example, read only access would only allow a member of staff to view certain data but not copy, delete or alter the data in any way.
- 128-bit encryption – this ensures that data being sent along networks is coded, so that even if it were intercepted, the data would not make sense. The data is only able to be decoded and hence understood by the correct recipient.
- Password – a system of passwords ensures that users are only allowed access to those parts of the patient records needed for their particular job. For example, admin staff would not have access to medical records, whereas doctors and nurses would.
- Audit trails – these are provided so it is possible to see who viewed or altered information contained in the database.

These file servers are used to hold all the patient details in a large hospital.

Scanning, life support and computer-controlled equipment

Introduction

In this section you will look at how ICT systems are used to diagnose a patient's illness and also how a patient's condition can be monitored and if necessary controlled by ICT systems.

Sensors (analogue and digital)

There are many physiological measurements that need to be recorded for a patient in hospital. In order to free up time from medical staff, this routine recording of data can be performed automatically using sensors.

Sensors are devices that can be used to detect physical, chemical and biological signals and provide a method of measuring and recording

them using processors or computers. There are two different types of sensor:

- Analogue sensors – used to measure an analogue quantity, which is a quantity that can have an almost infinite set of values such as temperature, pressure, etc.
- Digital sensors – these are sensors that can detect digital quantities. For example, a switch can only have two positions (on and off or 0 and 1) and so can be represented as a digital quantity.

If an analogue sensor is connected to a computer, then the signal it produces will need to be converted into a digital signal before it can be processed or stored by the computer. The reason for this is that computers are nearly always only capable of processing and storing digital signals.

Data measured by sensors and its uses

Sensors are used in medicine to measure the following:

- temperature
- blood pressure
- central venous pressure (to determine the amount of blood returning to the heart and the capacity of the heart to pump blood into the arteries)
- pulse
- blood gases (e.g., concentration of dissolved oxygen)
- blood sugar
- brain activity
- electrical activity of the heart (ECG (electrocardiogram))
- intra cranial pressure (pressure inside the skull)
- breakdown of gases from a patient's breath
- respiratory rate.

Intensive care units are used for seriously ill patients who need continual care. In order to reduce the burden on staff, many of the routine physiological measurements are made using sensors. ICT systems are used to continually monitor the patient's well-being and if any of the measurements made goes

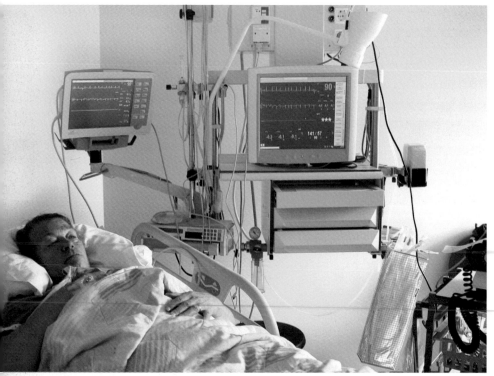

Patients have many sensors attached to them.

outside a certain range, then the medical staff are alerted, so that they are able to take remedial action. Patients have a much higher likelihood of survival if the medical staff are alerted as soon as the vital signs, as detected by the sensors, move outside their normal ranges.

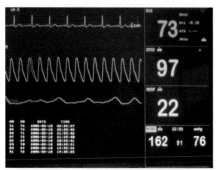

Displays from vital signs sensors are shown together on a screen near the patient in the intensive care unit. If any readings go outside normal range an alarm sounds to alert medical staff.

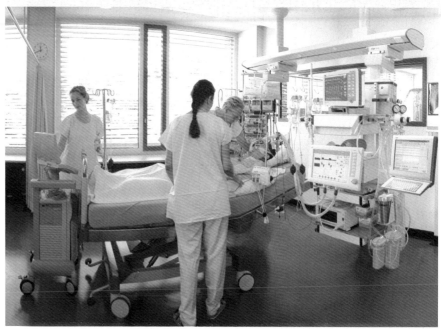

As well as taking measurements automatically, the combination of sensors and ICT can be used to control a patient's condition.

Advantages of using sensors for patient monitoring

There are many advantages in using sensors and ICT systems for patient monitoring and these include:

- Measurements are never missed as they are taken automatically.
- Real-time monitoring – patient's vital readings are taken in real time, which is much better than taking readings every so often. If any measurements fall outside the acceptable range, an alarm sounds to alert medical staff.
- Frees up medical staff from taking routine measurements to allow them to focus on administration of drugs, etc.
- Reduces costs – one member of staff can be responsible for more patients in intensive care units.
- Trends in the patient's condition can be spotted – the side-by-side graphs on the screen make it easy for doctors to spot trends in the patient's condition.
- More accurate readings – sensors produce more accurate readings than people, who can make mistakes when taking readings.

Monitoring and control of a patient's condition

Sensors can be used to monitor patients but as well as the data being used by a computer to assess whether the condition of the patient is worsening and to alert the medical staff, the data can also be used to control medical equipment that takes over the function of some of the organs of the patient.

Life support systems use the data from sensors to control medical equipment that assists or replaces important bodily functions and so enables a patient to live who otherwise might not survive. Data from sensors can be used to control:

- respiration – a ventilator is used, which is a machine that pumps air in and out of the patient's lungs
- excretion
- heart function – machines can take over some of the functions of the heart
- kidney function – dialysis machines are used when kidneys fail to function correctly
- intravenous drips containing fluids.

Copyright 2001 by Randy Glasbergen.

—GLASBERGEN

"Whenever your cholesterol goes too high, a sensor will send a signal that automatically locks the kitchen door and turns on your treadmill."

Scanning, life support and computer-controlled equipment continued

Scanning devices

Scanning devices are used to build up a model of the internal structures of a patient which aids diagnosis and ensures patients get the correct treatment.

MRI (magnetic resonance image)

An MRI scanner makes use of magnetic and radio waves to build up a picture of the inside of a patient. MRI scans do not use X-rays, which means they do not cause any damage to the patient.

The patient lies inside a large, very powerful cylindrical magnet and powerful radio waves are sent into the patient's body. The hydrogen atoms in the patient's body emit radio waves of their own and the scanner picks these up and turns them into a picture.

A computer is needed to analyse the data from these radio waves and produce an image on the screen. The image is modelled from the location and the strength of the radio signals it receives.

The MRI scan is used to produce clear pictures and it is the best technique for doctors to use when they are checking for tumours.

MRI scans can also be used for:

- examining the heart and its blood vessels for damage
- examining joints and the spine for damage
- checking the function of certain organs such as the liver, kidneys and spleen.

CAT (computerised axial tomography)

A CT scanner is a special and more complicated type of X-ray machine. Unlike ordinary X-ray machines, which only send out a single X-ray, CT scans send out several X-ray beams at different angles to the body. The X-rays are then detected after they have passed though the patient's body

where their strength is measured. Those beams which have passed through denser parts of the body will be weaker than those which have passed through soft tissue. The scanner can therefore assemble a picture based on signal strength and after processing these signals on a computer, the system produces a two-dimensional picture on a screen.

CT scans are more detailed than ordinary X-rays and some of the latest CT scanners can even produce three-dimensional images. They allow virtual images to be produced, which enables doctors to see what a surgeon would normally see during an operation without actually operating.

CT scans are mainly used for pinpointing tumours in the body and for planning the use of radiotherapy for the treatment of tumours. As CT scans use more X-rays than a traditional X-ray, they can cause side effects and they are not performed unless absolutely necessary.

Advantages of scanning devices

- Higher cure rate – early detection of tumours means the patient is more likely to be cured.
- Reduces unnecessary operations – can reduce unnecessary investigative operations, thus reducing costs for the NHS and unnecessary stress for the patient.
- Helps surgeons plan operations – enables the surgeon to look at the position and shape of internal organs so they can understand what they have to do before they operate.
- Faster diagnosis – reduces patient stress as they do not have to wait as long for results.
- Scanning can be done routinely – can detect illnesses so that the treatment can be started before symptoms appear.
- Safe in the case of MRI scans – MRI scanning is a very safe scanning method, but CT scans are not, as they involve the use of X-rays.
- Can look at internal organs, and tumours in 3D using computer modelling to see the best way of performing an operation or giving a patient radiotherapy.

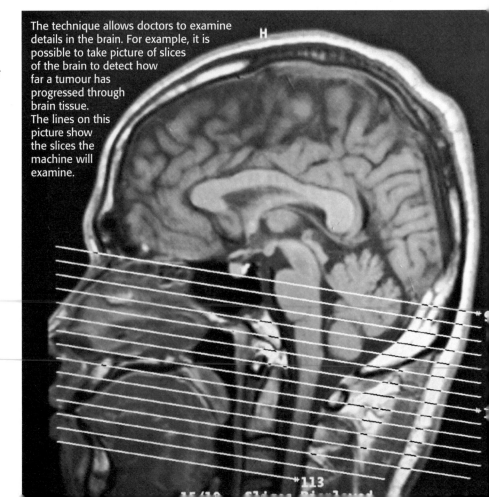

The technique allows doctors to examine details in the brain. For example, it is possible to take picture of slices of the brain to detect how far a tumour has progressed through brain tissue. The lines on this picture show the slices the machine will examine.

Disadvantages of scanning devices

- Sophisticated computer-controlled scanning equipment is very expensive.
- Can break down – more sophisticated equipment means more things to go wrong.
- Can be dangerous for staff to use – CT scans can expose the patient and staff to ionising radiation, so they need to take care.
- With MRI scans, the patient needs to keep still for times up to about an hour in very enclosed space and this is uncomfortable and distressing for some patients.

Backup and recovery procedures

Scanners make use of sensors and these sensors need to give the correct readings in order to monitor the patient's condition correctly. Sensors have a self-test facility where they are able to check their own readings. This is extremely important in intensive care units where incorrect readings from sensors could cause a critical change in the patient not to be recorded correctly and sounding the alarm.

Many of the scans recorded are kept with the patient records so that they can be consulted using any terminal in the hospital. All this data, contained in a large database, is backed up in real time, which means there is no downtime for this crucial system.

The hospital has its own backup recovery plan that will be put into operation should any of the data or programs be lost or any of the networks or hardware fail to work correctly. The plan makes use of the following:

- mirrored hard drives
- backup tapes which use a tape rotation system
- off-site archiving of data.

Power problems can occur from time to time but all the scanners and ICT systems in hospitals have an uninterruptible power supply (UPS) which keeps the power running when the supply to the hospital has been cut.

New and future developments

Modern medicine has started to focus more on patient care outside of hospitals and in particular prevention. For example, more routine testing is planned, because if many diseases are detected early enough, they can be cured.

The development of sensor and communications technology will enable tasks that are normally performed at a GP surgery or hospital outpatients to be performed in people's homes. Advances in sensor technology will create a series of smart sensors which have a small computer chip incorporated into them which will enable data to be not only collected but processed as well. The next step from this is to use the data from a processor to work an actuator which will allow a measured amount of drug to be administered into the patient's body only when the system recognises that it is needed.

Many new sensors are being developed that will detect certain bacteria without a sample needing to be sent to the laboratory for analysis. This can be done whilst the doctor is with the patient and the patient can be prescribed suitable medication immediately.

Smart blood pressure sensors will manage the drugs for patients with high blood pressure and an immediate alert is sent to the central monitoring unit if sensor measurements for heart function and other vital signs indicate a problem.

Home healthcare – videoconferencing and sensor technology will enable patients to talk to doctors and consultants from their own homes using their home computers. This would enable huge cost savings as hospitals could be much smaller with fewer administration and other staff.

One major health problem is diabetes and intelligent sensors have been developed that are put on the patient. One glucose (a sugar) sensor sits on the patient's arm a bit like a wristwatch, and a small electric current is sent out and this opens up pores in the skin which can be used by the sensor to measure the glucose concentration. A glucose reservoir can be implanted in the patient so that the system automatically gives them glucose if the sensor detects it is needed. This removes the need for the patient to inject themselves.

Engineers for the Japanese company Toto have designed a toilet that analyses urine for glucose concentrations, registers weight and other basic readings, and automatically sends a daily report by modem to the user's doctor.

You will have read a lot about the problems with MRSA, the flesh eating bug which seems to have got a hold in many hospitals. In the future, sensors will be developed that can sniff out bugs given off by patients or staff. The people can be kept away from seriously ill people and so stop bugs spreading.

Special hospital beds may be developed which include sensors that can monitor vital signs and blood chemistries and are also equipped to control mechanical ventilation, suction, intravascular infusion and cardiac defibrillation. All of these things can be done immediately in response to data received from the sensors. By using these special beds, an intensive care unit will no longer be needed and this will reduce the chance of cross-infection.

Limitations

There are some limitations in the use of scanning, life support and other computer-controlled equipment which include:

- Bandwidth is sometimes limited, which means scans cannot be stored with other patient record details – it takes too long to transfer the files, they take up too much storage space, etc.
- Life support malfunctions can cause the death of seriously ill patients.
- Ethical problems – when should life support systems be turned off?
- All this equipment is very expensive and could be better used for prevention rather than cure.

Expert systems

Introduction

In this section you will learn about ICT systems that mimic the expertise of human experts and how these systems are used by less experienced staff to help make accurate diagnoses and ensure that the patient receives the most appropriate drug for their condition.

What is artificial intelligence?

Artificial intelligence is a reasoning process performed by computers, which allows the computer to:

- draw deductions
- produce new information
- modify rules or write new rules.

The computer, just like a human, is able to learn as it stores more and more data.

Neural networks

Neural networks are biological systems that are used by the brain for learning new things. By understanding how the brain works, scientists can develop ICT systems making use of artificial neural networks that mimic the way the brain works. The main advantage of artificial neural networks is that they can learn by example just like the human brain, which means they are useful for pattern analysis or data classification.

Ordinary ICT systems are good at:

- fast processing of data
- obeying a set of instructions given as the program code.

Ordinary ICT systems are not good at:

- adapting to circumstances
- dealing with data in parallel (i.e., computers like to process data in a linear fashion)
- dealing with data that is imprecise or contains errors.

ICT systems making use of neural networks have the following advantages in that they:

- are good where algorithms cannot be developed (i.e., where it is difficult to develop a computer program because the nature of the problem being solved is not understood enough)
- are good where there are plenty of examples the system can learn from
- are good where a structure can be identified from existing data.

ICT systems making use of neural networks have the following disadvantages in that:

- they are only suited to certain tasks
- the examples used to teach the system must be chosen carefully, otherwise time is wasted and the system can produce unpredictable results
- because the neural network learns on its own, its operation can be unpredictable.

How parallel processors work

The main aim of artificial intelligence is to get computers thinking like humans and to do this it is necessary to build a computer that works in a similar manner to the human brain. Most computers are used to dealing with one thing at a time, albeit very quickly, which means we are tricked into thinking it is doing more. The human brain is much more powerful owing to the fact that it consists of more than 1000 billion nerve cells called neurons through which the brain's commands are sent in the form of electronic pulses. This enables the brain to process many pieces of data at the same time, which allows us to think, talk, listen, and walk all at the same time. The human brain is able to process data in parallel and this is called parallel processing.

Specialist computers such as supercomputers are available that

can carry out parallel processing and these computers are used for very complex computer tasks where millions of individual items of data need processing very quickly, such as in the production of weather forecasts.

Using a single processor the problem is programmed as a series of instructions which are processed by the processor (central processing unit) in turn.

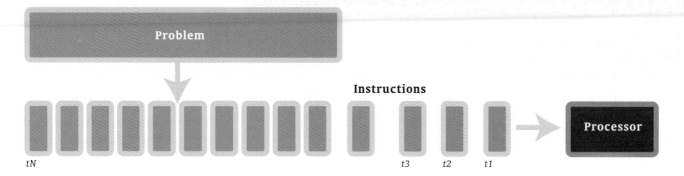

tN   t3   t2   t1

With parallel processors the problem can be divided into parts that can be solved at the same time and then the programming instructions for each part can be written.

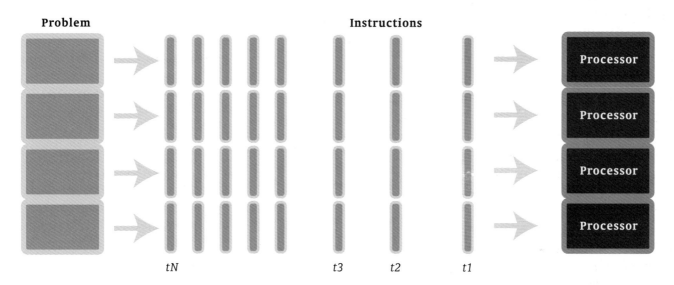

tN   t3   t2   t1

In parallel processing the problem is broken down into tasks which can be processed simultaneously. Each processor works on part of the problem so the results are obtained more quickly.

What is an expert system?

An expert system is an ICT system that uses artificial intelligence to make decisions based on data supplied in the form of answers to questions. This means that the system is able to respond in the way that a human expert in the field would to come to a conclusion. A good expert system is one that can match the performance of a human expert in the field.

The three components of an expert system

Expert systems consist of the following components:

- Knowledge base – a huge organised set of knowledge about a particular subject. It contains facts and also judgemental knowledge, which gives it the ability to make a good guess, like a human expert.
- Inference engine – a set of rules on which to base decisions and most of these rules have the 'if-then' structure. It is the part of the expert system that does the reasoning by manipulating and using the knowledge in the knowledge base.
- A user interface – the user interface presents questions and information to the operator and also receives answers from the operator.

How expert systems work

Expert systems use a problem-solving model that organises and controls the steps that need to be taken to solve the problem. One part of this model is the use of IF-THEN rules to form a line of reasoning. These problem-solving methods are provided as part of the inference engine.

The knowledge base is all the information an expert uses when arriving at a decision or diagnosis. The more knowledge and experience a human expert has in the field, then the more knowledge can be added to the knowledge base. Because knowledge is often incomplete or uncertain, a rule can sometimes have a confidence factor or weight.

A user of the expert system is asked a series of questions which may include the results of tests and on the basis of the answers, the expert system can arrive at an answer or diagnosis.

Expert systems continued

Expert system shells

There are two ways to create an expert system. You can:

- build the expert system from scratch using a software language suited to this task
- use a piece of development software called an expert system shell.

An expert system shell is a generic piece of software used for creating expert systems. The word generic means that the user can use the software in different ways for different applications. The system shell consists of an inference engine and the user interface but the knowledge base is not supplied. Instead the knowledge base is created by the person/expert who is building the expert system.

The reason for the word 'shell' is because the user has to build the knowledge base themselves, so the expert system is not considered complete until this is done. The shell enables people who know little about programming to create expert systems, although you still need to know quite a lot about expert systems to create them this way. This is why many expert systems are created by knowledge engineers (the people who actually build the expert systems) in consultation with the human experts.

Software languages

Programming languages have been developed that are specialist languages for the development of expert systems. These languages use English-like statements which are facts along with results and questions.

Two software/programming languages used for the development of expert systems are:

- PROLOG
- ASPRIN.

These languages can also be used to build systems that make use of artificial intelligence.

Medical uses of expert systems

Much of medicine is based around the making of decisions based around certain facts so expert systems find many uses in this field. Here are details of some of the expert systems used for patient healthcare.

MYCIN

MYCIN was the earliest expert system used in medicine and uses a patient's blood tests and results to enable doctors to pinpoint the correct organism, from many, that is responsible for a blood infection. Until the development of this expert system, it was necessary to grow a culture of the infecting organism, which took 48 hours, and if the doctors waited until the results came through, the patient could be dead. By identifying the correct organism using the system, specific drugs can be given to the patient that will treat that particular organism. Using the system means that junior doctors can make an accurate diagnosis with the accuracy of an expert doctor in the field and this means patients can be put on the correct medication immediately.

Features of the MYCIN system include:

- The expert system uses around 500 rules.
- The system will ask for further information such as 'has the patient recently suffered burns?'
- The system will ask for certain additional laboratory tests if needed.
- The system will suggest the best medication to treat the infection.
- The system will give a list of drugs with probabilities of the drug working.
- The system will make a final choice of the drug based on a series of questions the system asks about patient allergies.

The success of any expert system can be judged by comparing the system to human experts. With MYCIN they found that the system compared equally with a human specialist in blood infections and better than general practitioners.

NEOMYCIN

Neomycin is the name of another expert system used in medicine which was developed in order to train doctors. The system took the doctors through various example cases, checking the doctors' conclusions and then explaining, if they went wrong, where they went wrong.

Advantages and disadvantages of expert systems

The advantages and disadvantages of expert systems are:

Advantages

- Consistency – they provide consistent answers for repetitive decisions.
- Cheaper – they are cheaper than using a human expert such as a doctor or consultant.
- The expert system can consult a much larger pool of knowledge compared to a human expert.
- The expert system is available 24/7 and is never on holiday or off sick when needed.
- The computer uses all the information it has, unlike a human expert who may forget and make mistakes.

Disadvantages

- No common sense – so if the MYCIN system was used with a patient who had been shot and was bleeding to death, the system would look for a bacterial infection as the cause.
- Can make absurd errors – if data is incorrectly input, for example a person's age and their weight are swapped around – then absurd doses of drugs could be given.
- Not able to provide a creative response – human experts can produce creative responses in certain situations, which an expert system would be unable to do.
- Not being able to realise when no answer is available to a problem.
- Relies on the rules and knowledge base being correct. Any mistakes in these could cause incorrect diagnoses.

Case studies

 Case study | pp. 98–99

A computerised drugs trolley

Charing Cross Hospital is a large teaching hospital in London and is one of the hospitals using a new bar coding system which links patients to a computerised drugs trolley.

There is always a danger that a patient can be given the wrong drugs from the drugs trolley, and this new system reduces significantly the likelihood of this happening. Bar coded wrist bands containing patient details are worn by all patients. When nurses bring the drugs trolley around for the patient's medications, the bar code on the wristband is scanned, which then opens that patient's drawer on the drugs trolley containing their medications.

There are two other ICT systems in the hospital which are linked to the drugs trolley system. The first is a prescription writing system where doctors use PCs to type in the patient's prescriptions. This then is used to control a robotic picking arm in the hospital pharmacy which then puts each patient's drugs into the drugs trolley drawers ready for giving to the patient.

The system increases medication safety because it takes away the human element, and saves money because medication errors are prevented.

1 (a) Patients often wear bar coded wristbands in hospitals. Explain why. (2 marks)

(b) As well as containing machine readable bar codes, the wrist band also contains typed information.

(i) Suggest two items of information that would be included in the typed information. (2 marks)

(ii) Give one reason why typed information is included on the bar code. (1 mark)

2 The ICT system described in the case study prevents patients from being given the wrong medication. Explain briefly how the system works. (3 marks)

 Case study | pp. 100–101

Salford Royal Hospitals NHS Trust's electronic patient record (EPR) system

Salford Royal Hospitals NHS Trust uses an electronic patient record system across the Salford health community. There are over 3500 users of the system who under strict security measures can access patient records from over 2500 terminals.

Medical staff such as doctors and nurses can access patient information and update it at the patient's bedside using wireless devices. Medical staff can get test results, make referrals to specialities such as physiotherapy or the district nurse team, record patient care details and get all the information held about the patient.

Without ICT all these details would have been recorded on paper and retrieval of this information was difficult.

ICT and clinical staff were involved in the EPR project and this meant that clinical staff could say what would improve working practices and bring better care for the patient.

The security issues of patient data were controlled by a role-based security system, where users had to have a legitimate role with the patient in order to see the details. For example, ward clerks in the ward the patient was in could access some of the patient details such as name and address and relative details but they could not access clinical details.

When a patient's details are accessed there is also an audit facility which records who has opened the record and also the date, time and the workstation used. Queries over the privacy and security of a patient's record are therefore easily investigated. This also acts as a deterrent to staff who might abuse the system.

The use of electronic patient records has speeded up certain processes. For example, in the past when a patient had a blood test, the nurses had to wait for a paper record to arrive at the ward before the drugs to help the patient could be administered. This meant nurses had to chase the lab results up by ringing the lab. The new system means that the blood sample is processed and the results updated on the electronic patient record system in a few hours. As soon as the information is added, it can be accessed by the appropriate medical staff. To the patient this means they get the correct drug for their condition sooner which can be life-saving.

The trust also makes use of an intranet which includes the hospital telephone directory and list of e-mail contact details, the bleep details and the records of shift details so staff can find who is on call on a particular day and time.

1 An electronic patient record system offers many benefits to healthcare workers and the patients. Describe three ways in which the paperless system benefits healthcare in general. (3 marks)

2 Medical databases contain sensitive patient medical details. Explain two ways in which the EPR system prevents unauthorised access to these details. (2 marks)

3 Someone has illegally accessed the medical record of a celebrity patient and has passed the details to a tabloid newspaper. The hospital has conducted an investigation into this security breach. Explain how the audit facility of the EPR system will help them. (2 marks)

4 An EPR system relies on the security of data in databases as well as the secure transmission of data using networks. Explain three disadvantages in using an EPR system. (3 marks)

▶ Case study pp. 102–103

Monitoring patients

'Track and trigger systems' are used in hospitals to identify patients with heart problems who are too ill for surgery or are deteriorating following surgery. These systems rely on accurate measurements of the patient's condition being taken at regular intervals by nurses so that the doctors can identify these patients and can treat them appropriately. The data from the patient is normally added to a chart which is situated near the patient's bed. If the surgeon needs this information from another ward or even on another site at the hospital then this is not possible.

The new ICT system which runs on PDAs, tablet PCs and the hospital's intranet, allows nurses to enter the patient vital signs data directly into the system as the measurements are taken. The software will then analyse the data – pulse rate, blood pressure, respiratory rate, temperature, neurological status, urine output and oxygen saturation along with data such as biochemistry and haematology stored in other hospital databases. It can then identify those patients who are priority patients for care and an urgent alarm is sounded if the patient needs urgent medical attention. A doctor or surgeon can be bleeped automatically from any part of the hospital. Data validation methods are used to make sure only correct data is processed. The ICT system even tells the medical staff how often the vital signs readings need to be taken by nurses.

All the readings taken at the patient's bedside are sent automatically to the central hospital server using a wireless network. The data and other patient details can be viewed on the hospital intranet using tablet PCs or PDAs by any clinical staff anywhere in the hospital and even at home.

Backup and recovery procedures are in place to ensure the system is operational even if the network fails or if there is a power cut.

By allowing surgeons to monitor their patients almost in real time, the system allows them to be notified immediately if a patient's condition deteriorates, so that they can do something about it. The most important thing about this system is that it saves lives and makes sure the quality of care for the patient is improved.

1 In this system sensors are used to take measurements that indicate a patient's condition. Give three measurements that could be taken. (3 marks)

2 In the case study it mentions that 'Backup and recovery procedures are in place to ensure the system is operational even if the network fails or if there is there is a power cut'. Explain briefly how the problem with a power cut could be overcome. (2 marks)

3 This hospital system makes use of many wireless devices such as tablet PCs and PDAs. Give one reason why wireless devices are used in this system. (1 mark)

Questions

▶ Questions 1   pp. 98–99

1 Hospitals all use ICT extensively to help with administration and most use electronic patient record (EPR) systems to store details about patients.
   (a) Describe two advantages in storing patient data electronically rather than on paper. (2 marks)
   (b) Patient identification is extremely important in hospitals. Explain how patients can be identified in hospitals so that the correct treatment is given to the correct patient. (2 marks)

2 Hospitals have to track blood to ensure that the correct blood is given to the correct patient and hospitals use a computerised ICT system for this purpose.
   (a) Explain why hospitals have adopted a blood tracking system that makes use of bar coding. (2 marks)
   (b) Explain two ways in which hospital staff can use the Internet to help with patient care. (2 marks)

▶ Questions 2   pp. 102–105

1 ICT equipment is used to monitor a patient's medical condition automatically.
   For example, ICT is used to monitor a patient's condition in the intensive care unit (ICU) where sensors are used to monitor vital signs such as heart rate and temperature.
   Identify other patient vital signs that may also be recorded using sensors and describe the advantages in using sensors for this purpose. (5 marks)

2 Hospitals use computer-controlled diagnostic equipment to find out what is wrong with patients and to decide how best to treat them.
   (a) Give the names of the two main body scanning devices which are used to aid diagnosis, and discuss in detail, using appropriate examples, the main benefits of these devices. (4 marks)
   (b) Describe two future uses for ICT in the health service. (4 marks)

3 Sensors are used in patient care to monitor a patient's condition 24/7.
   (a) Give the names of three sensors used to monitor a patient's condition. (1 mark)
   (b) Using sensors allows a patient to be constantly monitored '24/7'.
   Give two other benefits of using sensors in patient care. (2 marks)
   (c) Explain two backup and recovery procedures that a hospital might employ in order to ensure the 24/7 availability of patient data. (4 marks)

▶ Questions 3   pp. 106–108

1 A medical expert system has been developed for diagnosing certain illnesses, which will enable inexperienced doctors to make accurate diagnoses. Briefly explain how it would be possible to test an expert system to check that it is coming to the correct conclusions. (2 marks)

2 An expert system shell consists of the following three components:
   Knowledge base
   Inference engine
   User interface
   Explain briefly the purpose of each of these three components. (3 marks)

Exam support

Worked example 1

1 Expert system shells are important in the development of medical expert systems.
   (a) Describe the three main parts of every expert system. **(3 marks)**
   (b) Describe, using examples, two advantages of using an expert system in medicine. **(2 marks)**

Student answer 1

1 (a) Database
      Inference engine
      GUI
   (b) It enables an inexperienced doctor to do the job of a
       consultant
       It saves time

Student answer 2

1 (a) Knowledge base
      Inference or reasoning engine
      User interface
   (b) They can base their diagnosis on a lot more facts than a
       human can
       They will go through steps that a human expert may forget
       to take to arrive at a more accurate diagnosis

Examiner's comment

1 (a) Database is not correct. The correct answer
      is 'knowledge base' which consists of factual
      knowledge and information about making good
      judgements.
      GUI (graphical user interface) is one type of
      interface that can be used as the interface
      between the user and the system. However, the
      correct answer is 'user interface' so this mark
      would not be given.
      One mark for the correct answer 'Inference engine'.
   (b) There is no way the inexperienced doctor becomes
      a consultant through using an expert system.
      Expert systems are only used in a small area of
      medicine usually to aid diagnosis. 'Saving time' on
      its own gains no marks. Here the student should
      have said in what way the system saves time.
      (1 mark out of 5)

Examiner's comment

1 (a) All correct answers here. Both the answers
      'Inference or reasoning engine' are correct.
   (b) Both of these answers are distinctly different
      and correct so full marks for this part.
      (5 marks out of 5)

Examiner's answers

1 (a) One mark each to a maximum of three for:
         Knowledge base
         Inference engine
         User interface
   (b) One mark each to a maximum of two marks for:
         Leaves doctors/specialists more time to concentrate on serious cases
         The knowledge base can be kept more up-to-date.
         Ordinary doctors can use the system to make an expert diagnosis without needing to contact a specialist.
         There is faster diagnosis for patients so patients get better quicker.
         It is cheaper to use the expert system than train doctors in the specialist area.
         A human may forget to consider a certain fact but the expert system will consider all the facts to arrive at a
         correct diagnosis.

Worked example 2

2 Hospitals make extensive use of ICT systems for keeping patient records. Apart from contact details such as name, address, postcode and telephone numbers, give four distinctly different fields that would be included and describe why they are needed. (10 marks)

Student answer 1

2 E-mail address so that the hospital can contact the patient quickly in case there has been a cancelled operation and they can be fitted in and they cannot be contacted by phone.

Doctor who is responsible for the patient. This is important as a patient who is seriously injured in a car accident will see many doctors but one doctor is given the main responsibility.

Next of kin so that they can give permission for operations or organ donations.

NHS number to act as the primary key to uniquely identify the patient in the database. This field will mean that patients who have the same name and live at the same address can be distinguished.

Examiner's comment

2 E-mail along with the description is not a valid answer here as the question asks for a field 'apart from contact details'.

The next three fields described are all fields which could be used in a patient record system. The descriptions given are relevant to the field and provide a clear explanation as to why the field is needed.

There are no spelling mistakes and the grammar and punctuation are accurate.

The student cannot get the mark range 7–10 marks because they have only given three correct fields and descriptions. **(6 marks out of 10)**

Examiner's answers

2 Candidates must supply a sensible field in the context of a patient record and a correct explanation. Any contact details for the patient gain no marks.

Next of kin – in case they need to be contacted re deteriorating condition, death, etc.

Allergies – so doctors can ensure certain drugs are not given that the patient is allergic to

Medication – doctors can see the drugs the patient is taking to make sure suitable drugs are prescribed

NHS number – used to identify a particular patient to the computer system

Operations – details of any operations the patient has had so the doctors are able to make a correct diagnosis

Student answer 2

2 Patient number is used to identify the patient to the electronic patient record system and is important because there can be many patients with the same name but the patient number is unique. Patient number acts as the primary key in this database.

The DOB (date of birth) is an important field because it can be used to calculate the patient's age and so the age is always up-to-date. This is important because you need to know the age of the patient to work out the dosage of certain drugs.

Medical details are important as the doctors need to know about existing illnesses.

Next of kin is needed so that they can be kept up-to-date with the patient's condition and there is someone to contact when the patient is discharged.

GP details are required so that treatment details can be passed to the family doctor, so they know what treatment is needed when they return home.

Examiner's comment

2 All the fields mentioned are correctly identified and described and they have used terminology correctly. The answer displays correct spelling, punctuation and grammar.

This is a very good answer and fits the mark range 7–10 marks. **(9 marks out of 10)**

Medical conditions – doctors treating one medical condition will need to know other conditions the patient suffers from

7–10 marks

Candidates give a clear, coherent answer fully and accurately describing and explaining at least four distinctly different fields and why they are needed. They use appropriate terminology and accurate spelling, punctuation and grammar.

4–6 marks

Candidates give some explanation of some fields and why they are needed, but the responses lack clarity or relevant examples. There are a few errors in spelling, punctuation and grammar.

0–3 marks

Candidates simply list the fields or give a brief explanation of one or two fields and why they are needed. The response lacks clarity and there are significant errors in spelling, punctuation and grammar.

Summary mind maps

Medical databases

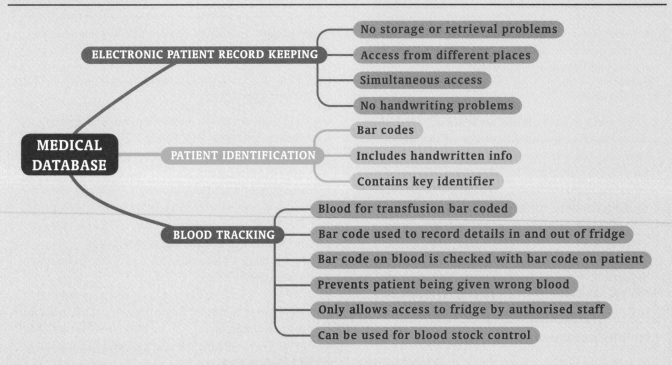

Use of the Internet, intranets and extranets

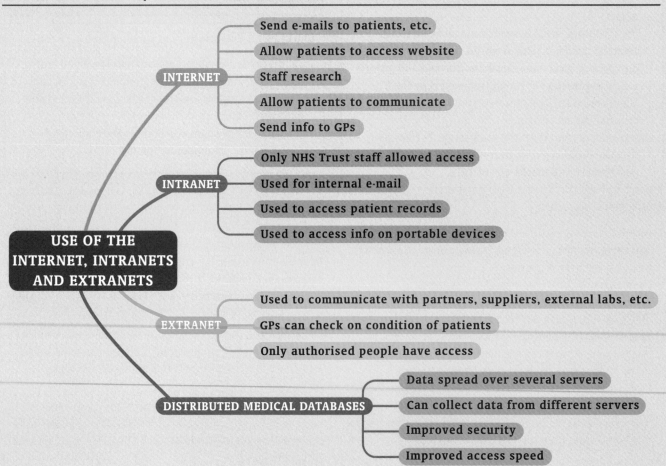

Scanning, life support and computer-controlled equipment

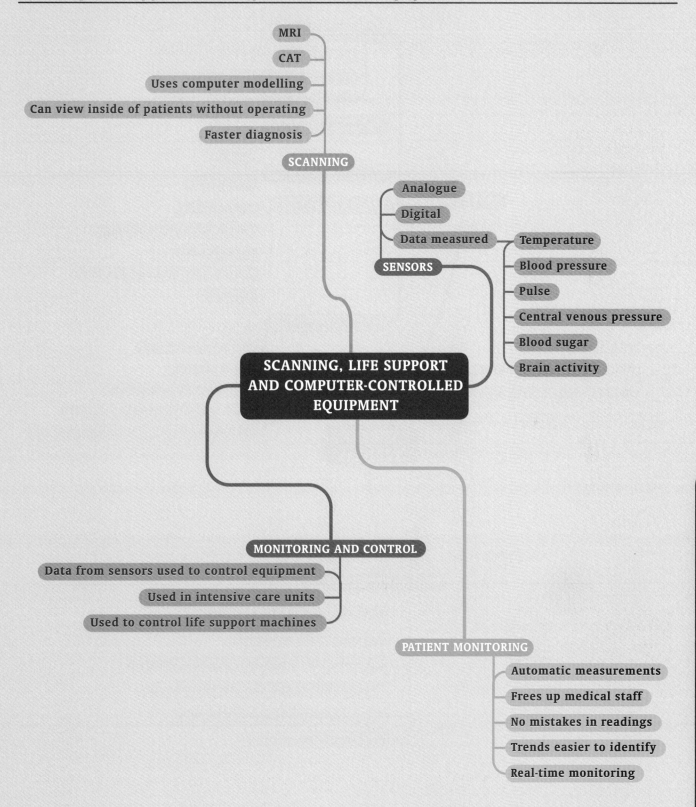

MRI

CAT

Uses computer modelling

Can view inside of patients without operating

Faster diagnosis

SCANNING

Analogue

Digital

Data measured

SENSORS

Temperature

Blood pressure

Pulse

Central venous pressure

Blood sugar

Brain activity

SCANNING, LIFE SUPPORT AND COMPUTER-CONTROLLED EQUIPMENT

MONITORING AND CONTROL

Data from sensors used to control equipment

Used in intensive care units

Used to control life support machines

PATIENT MONITORING

Automatic measurements

Frees up medical staff

No mistakes in readings

Trends easier to identify

Real-time monitoring

Expert systems

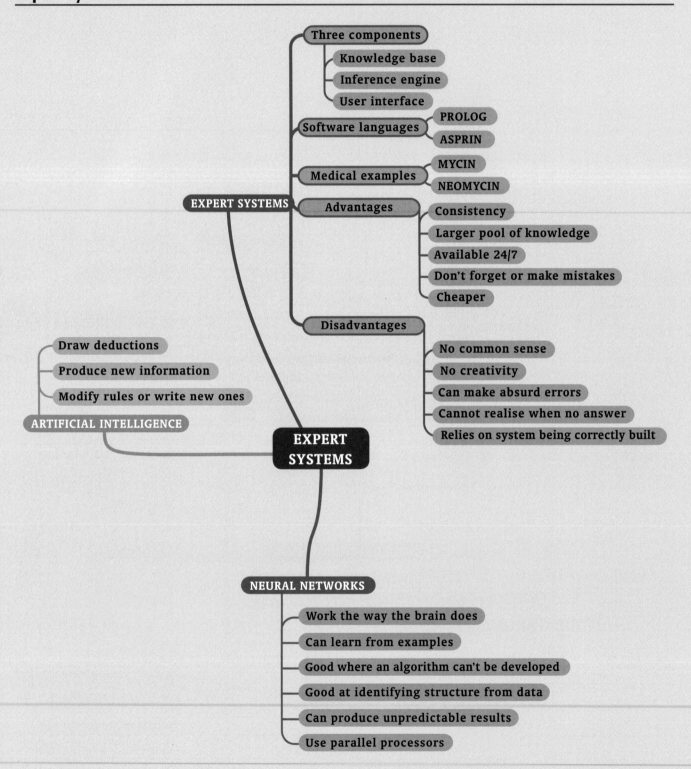

EXPERT SYSTEMS

- Three components
  - Knowledge base
  - Inference engine
  - User interface
- Software languages
  - PROLOG
  - ASPRIN
- Medical examples
  - MYCIN
  - NEOMYCIN
- Advantages
  - Consistency
  - Larger pool of knowledge
  - Available 24/7
  - Don't forget or make mistakes
  - Cheaper
- Disadvantages
  - No common sense
  - No creativity
  - Can make absurd errors
  - Cannot realise when no answer
  - Relies on system being correctly built

ARTIFICIAL INTELLIGENCE
- Draw deductions
- Produce new information
- Modify rules or write new ones

EXPERT SYSTEMS

NEURAL NETWORKS
- Work the way the brain does
- Can learn from examples
- Good where an algorithm can't be developed
- Good at identifying structure from data
- Can produce unpredictable results
- Use parallel processors

The way people entertain themselves has changed. Many people use computers for their entertainment and spend hours on the Internet or playing computer games. The use of ICT has enabled a huge increase in the number of television channels that can be viewed.

ICT has had a huge influence on how people spend their leisure time. Many people are now turning off their televisions and are instead using the Internet as their main source of entertainment. Computer games are popular with the young. Some people spend their time editing photographs obtained from their digital cameras, or desktop publishing. Older citizens use the Internet to keep in touch with family and friends and also to keep in touch with others who may have the same medical problems as themselves.

ICT has also changed the way that we obtain music. Downloads are becoming more popular as people want to store music on their portable MP3 players such as iPods and mobile phones. Many people now choose to bank from home. They can transfer money between accounts from the comfort of their own home.

In this topic you will learn about how ICT can be used in the home for entertainment and home banking.

▼ The key concepts covered in this topic are:

▶ The use of ICT systems in the home for entertainment

▶ The use of ICT systems in the home for on-line banking

CONTENTS

Unit IT1 Information Systems

Entertainment

Introduction

Many more people use their home computers for entertainment. Fast broadband access to the Internet has now made it possible to listen to the radio or music over the Internet as well as watch music video, films and programmes that you missed.

Many people spend time communicating with friends using chat rooms, instant messaging, social networking sites, text messaging, e-mail, etc.

Others use the ICT for the playing of games either individually or playing games as a team.

The use of ICT for playing games

Many computers are used by all ages to play games, which vary from traditional games such as chess, cards, backgammon to flight/racing car simulations to fast-moving arcade type games.

Games are important drivers in the computer industry and many home computers used to play games have more processing power than many computers used in a business setting.

For fast action computer games it is necessary to use:

- a fast processor
- a large screen
- a large amount of RAM
- a disk drive with plenty of storage capacity
- a high quality graphics card
- a high quality sound card
- large powerful speakers.

Advantages of computer games include:

- young children can learn from them
- can make learning fun
- some games are played on-line as a team, so it encourages team work
- can lead to well-paid employment as a games designer, programmer, etc.

Disadvantages of computer games include:

- can be addictive
- often a sedentary activity where little physical activity takes place and this can lead to obesity
- can be very violent and some people think that this can cause teenagers to act violently
- wastes time – school work can suffer through the time spent playing games
- health problems – repeated use of input devices such as a joystick or mouse can lead to repetitive strain injury (RSI), also incorrect posture when sitting can lead to back ache.

> **KEY WORDS**
>
> **Download** – to copy files from a distant computer to the one you are working on
>
> **MP3** – there are lots of ways to compress a music file but the most popular way is by using MP3

▼ You will find out

▶ About the use of ICT for playing games

▶ About the use of ICT for photography

▶ About the use of ICT for the downloading and playing of music

▶ About the use of specialist music systems such as MIDI, sequencers, notators and sound wave editors

▶ About the use of ICT for pay-to-view services

▶ About the use of ICT for home/interactive shopping

▶ About the use of ICT for cinema and theatre booking

▶ About the use of ICT for e-mail

▶ About the use of ICT for interactive services such as gambling, voting and dating

▶ About the use of Teletext services

▶ About the use of mobile phones

Here the photographer has failed to notice the bottle in the foreground. Editing software can help.

The use of ICT for photography

In a similar way that word-processing software allows people to produce professional-looking documents, digital cameras and computers with image editing software have allowed people to produce inexpensive high quality photographs.

Most people own a digital camera or a mobile phone with a camera and store their photographic images on their home computer. Many people like the flexibility offered by digital images. For example:

- they can be shared by attaching them to e-mails
- they can be sent via mobile phones
- they can be passed to social networking sites such as Facebook
- they can be edited.

Using image editing software and by cropping the image, the bottle can be removed, as shown above.

Using editing software and a digital image you can:

- copy part of an image
- add text
- re-size
- crop (i.e., only use part of the image)
- remove red eye
- alter the file format
- apply filters (i.e., alter the colours in an image).

Many people use digital video cameras for personal use and these can be edited and added to websites or sent to friends and relatives.

Music – downloads from the Internet

Most singles are purchased as downloads off the Internet but albums are usually bought as physical CDs.

Downloads have become very popular owing to:

- the ease with which they can be obtained
- the ability to just download tracks that you want – you do not need to buy the whole album

- you can still burn the tracks to a CD provided they are only for personal use
- the ease with which they can be loaded onto portable players such as i-Pods, MP3 players and mobile phones.

There are a number of problems with downloads including:

- many people use file sharing sites to avoid having to pay for downloaded music tracks
- people who download music or films illegally will be cut off from the Internet by their Internet service providers
- you do not have a physical CD which can be sold at a car boot sale or on e-Bay.

Copyright 2005 by Randy Glasbergen.
www.glasbergen.com

"I KNOW IT'S ILLEGAL TO DOWNLOAD MUSIC FROM THE INTERNET... BUT YOU SAID THE STUFF I LISTEN TO ISN'T MUSIC!"

Image editing software can be used to crop an image.

Entertainment continued

Making music – MIDI, sequencers, notators and sound wave editors

By using the latest technology it is possible for home users of ICT to compose and hear their own music using a variety of technologies such as the following.

MIDI (Musical Instrument Digital Interface)

Hardware and software designed to MIDI standards are able to send digital messages to MIDI devices such as keyboards, musical synthesisers and drum machines. These digital messages contain information about pitch, loudness, vibrato and the tempo.

It is important to realise that MIDI is a protocol or standard that is used by the music industry to allow musical data files to be shared between devices.

Sequencers

Sequencers are hardware or software used to create and manage electronic music. Examples of sequencers include:

- Drum machines – these are electronic musical instruments that simulate the sound of a drum and sometimes other percussion instruments. Drum machines are sequencers because they create and manage the drum beats.
- Music workstations – a piece of electronic equipment that allows a musician to create electronic music using a single piece of equipment.
- Music workstations consist of the usual computer but with a large screen so that all the controls such as knobs, sliders, buttons and sampling information appear on the screen. Some music workstations make use of touch screens.

Notators

A notator is a piece of software that allows you to compose your own music and you do this by entering notes into the computer via:

- the keyboard
- a MIDI system
- scanning a piece of music on paper using a scanner.

Once the notes are entered into the system, the musician can experiment by changing notes, loudness, tempo, etc. The main advantage is that the notator allows the musician to experiment. The notator can also be used to create the music for individual musical instruments, which can then be played together to produce the final piece of music.

Sound wave editors

Sound wave editors are software that allows the editing of sound waves. Using the software sound waves can:

- be edited
- be cut, copied and pasted.

Sound wave editors can also be used to alter a person's speech pattern, so it can be used to disguise a person's voice or even simulate another person's voice.

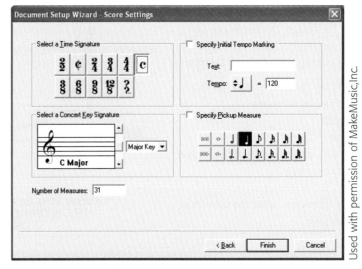

A notator being used to compose music.

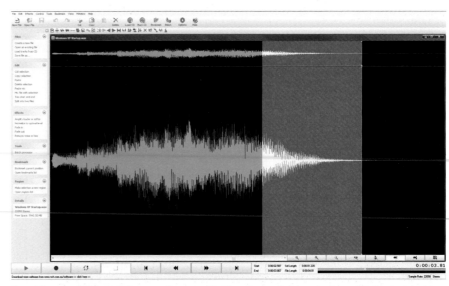

Sound wave editing software allows a digitised sound wave to be edited.

Interactive digital TV services

Digital TV may be free or it may be offered as a pay-to-view service. Either way digital TV offers many interactive features that were not possible before. These include:

- joining in with programmes by sending in comments
- seeing extra new stories and sports coverage
- booking cinema and holiday tickets
- playing games
- shopping
- placing bets
- using e-mail
- placing votes for programmes – there are plans to use this service for voting in parliamentary elections
- interactive advertisements.

Some problems caused by interactive services:

- may encourage young children to play games on their TV rather than play more energetic games
- could cause addiction to checking and sending e-mail, playing games, etc.
- gambling services could cause addiction to gambling.

Pay-to-view services such as Sky allow you to watch many live football matches for a monthly fee.

Pay-to-view services

Pay-to-view TV services are subscription based services where you pay a monthly fee for digital TV services which include:

- satellite channels and other services
- cable TV and other services
- digital terrestrial TV and other services (bit like ordinary TV but with an encrypted signal).

Additional services offered by the TV companies include:

Pay-per-view services

Even though you subscribe to the pay-to-view services there are other services where you pay a one off payment each time you wish to view. Pay-per-view services include:

- video on demand – where you can view a film from a selection
- some major sporting events – football, boxing, etc.

Home on-line/interactive shopping

Many people now use their home computer with an Internet connection to shop on-line from the comfort of their own homes. On-line shopping was looked at in detail in Topic 6(a).

On-line booking systems

There are many instances where you need to make bookings and here are some of them:

- booking a theatre or concert ticket
- booking a flight or holiday
- booking a train ticket
- booking car hire.

When people book the above there can be a large difference in prices and some of the best savings and special offers can be found on the Internet. Many of these services keep in touch with their customers by e-mail to let them know of the special offers available.

The Internet has changed the way people book flights and holidays. Using the Internet you can:

- check the availability and prices of some flights and holidays
- make savings when you book direct
- read reports of people who have been on the same holiday that you intend to book
- arrange your own travel and accommodation
- find out about the resort before you go.

Because the customer enters the details into the booking system themselves, they are less likely to make a mistake plus you do not have to pay them. In many of these systems, they do not have to print and send you tickets, as you just print out a voucher or the confirmation e-mail on your own printer. The savings for the companies are large, as there are no intermediary commissions to pay and no input staff to pay, so some of these savings are passed to the customer.

Travel agents may become a thing of the past as more people book their holidays direct. Some people even reckon that the package tour will eventually become a thing of the past as more people want to create their own holidays by booking travel and accommodation separately.

Entertainment continued

E-mail

Many people like to keep in touch with friends and family using e-mail. Once people have paid for their Internet use, e-mails are free, no matter how many are sent. This cheap form of communication is ideal for families who want to keep in touch, particularly if they are in different parts of the world. Being able to attach files to e-mails means that photographs or even short video clips can be exchanged.

Advantages and disadvantages of using e-mail

In America more e-mails are sent than traditional letters and we will soon see this happening in the UK. Here are the advantages and the disadvantages of using e-mail compared to using traditional letters.

Advantages

- It is very fast – e-mail is sent immediately and a reply can be sent as soon as the receiver checks their e-mail. Ordinary post takes several days.
- Quick to write. E-mails lack the formal structure of a letter so they are quicker to write.
- Saves time searching for the original e-mail – you can attach a copy of the sender's e-mail with your reply, so this saves them having to search for the original message.
- Cheaper than a letter – no stamp, envelope or paper is needed. There is also a time saving, so this makes e-mail cheaper. Even if the e-mail is sent across the world it will not cost any more than a local e-mail.
- No need to leave the house – no need to find a post box.
- No time wasted shopping – you do not have to waste time shopping for stamps, envelopes and paper.

- File attachments – if it can be stored as a file, then it can be attached to and sent with an e-mail.
- Document/diagram is in digital form – this means that it can be worked on and sent back immediately.

Disadvantages

- Not everyone has the equipment to send and receive e-mail. However, with Internet access from televisions, land line phones and mobile phones, it will soon take over from traditional post.
- Junk mail is a problem. You can waste time looking through e-mails that are just adverts.
- E-mails can be intercepted or hacked into, which can make them less secure than traditional letters.
- The system relies on people checking their e-mail regularly.
- Older people may feel left out because they feel that they are too old to learn.
- The equipment to send and receive e-mail is quite expensive compared to traditional methods.

Interactive services (e.g., betting, voting and dating)

There are a large number of interactive services available using the Internet and some of the cable/satellite systems. Here are a few of them.

On-line betting

If you go onto any sports website on the Internet you will notice the large number of on-line betting sites. Some of these sites concentrate on casino-style games such as poker and roulette and others offer betting on sporting events such as football, horse racing, boxing and almost any other event.

Advantages of on-line betting:

- you do not have to leave the house – handy for older or disabled people
- special Internet offers – there are special offers to tempt you to gamble more
- no need to pick up your winnings – they are simply added to your credit or debit card
- faster – you do not need to travel to a high street betting shop.

Disadvantages of on-line betting

- a credit or debit card is needed – you have to create an account using a card before you are allowed to bet
- it can become addictive – for most people gambling is just a bit of fun but others can lose their family and home through excessive gambling
- people may gamble more than they would when using cash – the use of credit cards may encourage people to bet larger amounts.

Dating

There are a huge number of dating sites on the Internet and many people choose to date this way because it offers them convenience in their busy lives. By looking at people's pictures and learning about their interests, you may feel that you know more about them than you would just chatting in a bar.

On-line voting

One problem that governments have is that many young people are turned off politics and therefore do not vote. Maybe it is just too hard for younger people to vote. If they could vote using the Internet then many more of them may have voted. Putting crosses on bits of paper in a church hall or a school may not appeal to them.

"I never realized how self-centered I am until ten online dating services matched me with myself!"

If the weather is bad then it is found that the turnout (i.e., the percentage of the people who actually vote out of those who are eligible to vote) is low. If people could vote using the Internet then they could vote without leaving the house.

One of the problems with cyber elections is that it is hard to make sure that they are fair. Each voter would be given a PIN (personal identification number) but these could be given or sold to others. The other problem is that not everyone is on the Internet, so you would still need some traditional polling stations.

Cyber elections have some big advantages that include:

- It eliminates the need to print paper ballot forms.
- Votes would be counted much faster and more accurately.
- Voters could vote from anywhere in the world.

Cyber elections have their disadvantages which include:

- Not everyone has access to the Internet, so polling booths will still be needed.
- The system is more open to abuse by hackers, fraudsters, etc.
- Older people may not understand the new system.

Teletext services

Teletext is a broadcast service which means it comes to our TVs as a television signal and because of this, and unlike the Internet, it does not slow down when more users access the service. Teletext is really a predecessor of the Internet but it is still a useful service for finding information such as weather, news, share prices, holiday offers, TV programme listings, etc.

"At election time, I'll base my vote on modern issues that really matter — which candidate has the coolest YouTube video and the most friends on their MySpace page!"

Unlike the Internet, Teletext only offers quite a limited number of pages but all TVs come with the ability to receive Teletext so it is effectively free. Also, Teletext is non-interactive, which means that you have to cycle through a series of pages to get to the information you want.

Mobile phones

Mobile phones are one of the most popular modern day inventions. Most people would be lost without them. When they were first developed they were simply the mobile equivalent of an ordinary telephone, so their main use was for having telephone conversations. The development of the Internet and other messaging systems means that mobile phones offer many new ways of communicating.

Mobile phones now offer a huge range of features and these are being added to all the time. Here are some of the many things you can do using mobile phones:

- send and receive text messages
- make phone calls
- take digital photographs
- take short video clips
- surf the Internet
- watch live TV
- send and receive e-mail
- download and listen to music
- download and play games
- send text messages
- send picture messages
- play videos.

Mobile phones offer many new ways of communicating.

Topic 6(d) Uses of ICT in the home

On-line banking

Introduction

Many people now use their home computer and Internet access for home banking. Short of getting money out of a cash dispenser, many of these people never go inside a bank branch.

In this section you will look at the ICT systems and the advantages and disadvantages of on-line home banking.

What a bank does

There are a number of things a bank does and here are the main ones:

- Keeps your money safe and allows you to withdraw it when needed.
- Issues you a cheque book so that you can pay bills using the post.
- Allows you to apply for loans and mortgages (mortgages are loans to buy a house).
- Issues you with credit cards/debit cards.
- Allows you to take out money using ATMs. These are the hole-in-the-wall cash dispensers.
- You can set up standing orders and direct debits so that payments for bills are made automatically without you having to remember.
- Provides insurance services.

Chip and PIN cards require a secret number to be entered to verify that the person with the card is the genuine cardholder.

You may have noticed that many bank branches have recently closed and are now restaurants or wine bars. Banks are not closing because they have too few customers or because banking is not as popular as it used to be. Instead, they are closing because their customers are banking in a different way. Rather than use branches, they can bank from home by making use of either the Internet or a telephone. They find it more convenient to do so. They do not have to find somewhere to park for a trip to the bank and they do not have to wait in a long queue. Another big advantage is that they can bank 24 hours per day, 365 days per year.

Banking from home is called home banking and it has changed the way people bank in many ways. In the past people opened a bank account when they first started work and stayed with their bank. Now the use of ICT has made it much easier to move your account, mortgage or loan. Many customers look for the best deal and change account if they need to. Banks now have fewer loyal customers. It is common for credit card companies to entice new customers with offers such as 0% interest for the first six months.

There are some problems with home banking. Generally the more well-off people are the ones who are able to take advantages of the higher saving rates and lower borrowing rates offered. The poorer people may see their local branch shut down. Because there is no costly branch network for the banks to pay for, they can offer customers more interest and cheaper mortgages and loans.

EFTPOS (electronic funds transfer at point of sale) and EFT (electronic funds transfer)

EFTPOS is the method used by stores to transfer money from customers' credit or debit cards directly to the store bank account. This means that the money is taken out of one account (the customer's) and deposited in another account (the store's) and all this occurs electronically. When a debit card is used, the customer is often asked at a store if they would like cash back, which takes money from their bank account and gives them cash.

EFTPOS is an extension of the service provided by the banking system called electronic funds transfer (EFT), which allows the movement of money from one bank account to another electronically. Many people now use EFT when they pay bills on-line using their bank's on-line banking facility.

Advantages of on-line banking

- banking services are available 24/7
- no need to keep paper statements as statements can be viewed on-line
- you can import the data in bank statements into spreadsheet software or budgeting software to help work out finances
- you do not need to spend time travelling to banks and waiting in queues to perform routine transactions
- you can move money between accounts quickly so you get the best rate of interest
- often the specialist on-line banks offer better rates of interest than the high street banks
- you can make payments to others by transferring money directly to their bank account without leaving home
- on-line banking produces no paperwork so there is less likelihood of identity theft.

Disadvantages of on-line banking

- on-line bank accounts could be hacked into and your money stolen
- you cannot get cash so you still need to visit a cash machine
- older people may prefer the personal service offered by a conventional bank.

Card services (credit and debit cards)

Credit and debit cards

The most popular electronic payment method for on-line payments is by credit or debit cards. Using this payment method you simply key in your card details and the payment is made. This works well with businesses you know and trust but you do have to be careful making payments to individuals or businesses you know little about, particularly if they are from abroad. Once someone has your personal details and your credit card details then they can be used fraudulently.

Most credit/debit cards are chip and PIN to help prevent fraud.

Most credit/debit cards are chip and PIN which means there is a small chip on the card containing encrypted data that only the reader in the store can read. This means that when you enter your PIN (personal identification number), the store can be sure that you are the correct owner of the card.

Credit/debit cards are used to make purchases either over the phone or using the Internet. In both these cases the customer is not present when they pay for their goods.

Instead they give certain details such as name, address and their card details.

Chip and PIN has reduced card fraud when a card is being used in ordinary stores but owing to the rise of transactions where the customer is not present (e.g., when buying goods or services over the Internet) there has been a total increase in credit/debit card fraud.

A chip and PIN reader: the customer inserts their card then enters their PIN.

PayPal

PayPal is simply an on-line banking system which was set up for users of the on-line auction site e-Bay to pay for goods they had bought. Anyone who has an e-mail address can send and receive payments using PayPal.

PayPal is very useful for consumers who wish to pay for goods quickly from e-Bay and do not wish to give credit card details to firms or individuals they know nothing about. Instead they can open an e-Bay account and pay money into it using a credit card or bank account and this money can be passed from PayPal to the person who is selling goods or services. If a business sells products or services, they can use PayPal to receive payment from their customers. This is particularly useful for small businesses, when they want the money from their customers quickly but have not set up a credit card payment system. The customers can pay the money into the business's PayPal account.

Nochex

Nochex is a company a bit like PayPal but unlike PayPal, it is UK based. Nochex provides a secure on-line payment service, so payments can be made to anyone with an e-mail address. Like PayPal, Nochex allows you to send payments to other people without giving them your card details. This is particularly important if you are paying for goods bought from on-line auction sites or new Internet companies you do not know much about. Basically the system works like this:

- You create an account with Nochex.
- You put money into your Nochex account using your credit or debit card.
- You buy goods on-line and then transfer the money from your Nochex account to the seller.

As you can see, only Nochex has your credit card details, not the seller of the goods or services.

It is also possible to use Nochex for one-off payments without creating an account. You simply go onto the Nochex account, put in your credit/debit card details and information about the amount and who you want to pay. The payment is then made. Nochex is free to the person making the payment but the person selling the goods or service is charged a fee.

Splash Plastic

The Splash Plastic prepaid Maestro® card from 360money can be used to make payments in the same way as any bank card, including shopping on-line. The card is aimed at anyone who does not have a bank account or bank cards. Splash Plastic is available to under 18s who are too young to have a credit card but want to shop on-line and use their card abroad. The card may be topped up by a credit or debit card (great for parents who want to help their teenagers' budget) or with cash from many stores displaying the Pay Point sign and any Post Office branch in the UK.

Credit or debit cards

SECURE ON-LINE PAYMENT SYSTEM SUCH AS **PayPal or Nochex**

How on-line payment services work.

The Splash Plastic card can be topped up using credit/debit cards, wage/bank transfers, or by using cash at any shop displaying the PayPoint logo. The cards can also be topped up at any Post Office branch in the UK.

Card crimes and methods of prevention

Card crime is one of the fastest growing areas of crime and it is performed on a large scale. Card crimes include:

- **Lost and stolen card fraud** – cards being physically stolen and then someone posing as you buying goods and services using them. Chip and PIN has reduced this type of crime because if the card is used in the UK they would need to know the PIN.
- **Counterfeit cards** – here a clone of your card is made. A piece of equipment is used to read the data on the magnetic strip and then transfer the information to a fake card which has been embossed with the same card number. This is called skimming. The fake card is then used fraudulently to pay for goods and services.

- **Card not present fraud** – this type of fraud occurs when criminals find card details in your rubbish, by adding a program to your computer, or by using fake e-mails from your bank asking you for the information. This is now the largest type of fraud because chip and PIN cards mean that the above two crimes are hard to commit. The problem in countering this fraud is the fact that neither the card nor the cardholder is present at the till point. This means that signature or PIN verification cannot be used to verify that the cardholder is genuine.

- **Phishing** – this is where fraudsters send random e-mails asking people who are using the on-line banking system to update their account details. When the user clicks on the link in the e-mail or copies the URL into their browser, they are taken to a fake website which looks similar to the proper bank site. The user is then asked to type in personal information such as name, address, credit or bank details and password. Once this has been done, the fraudster has access to the bank and credit card details.

Identity theft

Identity theft occurs when a criminal uses your fraudulently obtained personal information to open or access banking services or credit cards. In many cases the criminal will use your information along with stolen or false documents (utility bills, bank statements, etc.) to open accounts in your name.

By obtaining this information, the criminals are able to take over the running of your account. They can start by telling the bank that they (i.e., you) have changed address and they may even apply for credit cards or loans.

How can I prevent this from happening? Here are some tips:

- Be very suspicious of any e-mails sent to you. The Internet e-mail system is very insecure and you should never divulge personal information in an e-mail or follow a link to a site from an e-mail and divulge personal information.

- Always view official looking e-mails with scepticism despite them having the right logos and using official language. Do not be tricked into inputting the details even if they say things like 'your account will be suspended unless you enter these details'. If necessary send the bank a copy of the e-mail.

- Always shred any paperwork containing personal information.

- Do not leave personal information such as utility bills, bank or credit card statements lying around for others to see.

- Do not write down banking information such as passwords.

- Install a firewall in order to prevent hackers from gaining access to personal details held on your computer.

Banks impose home chip and PIN machines to fight fraud

Most fraud occurs when credit cards are used on-line, so most banks are starting to supply customers with their own home chip and PIN devices to help identify them when they are accessing on-line bank accounts or using cards for on-line purchases. Banks hope that the devices will beat fraudsters because they will be independent of a user's computer. This will prevent scams such as key logging where Trojan software records the keystrokes a user makes such as passwords and security information required for on-line payments.

Chip and PIN means that rather than a signature, a PIN is used to verify that the cardholder is genuine.

www.chipandpin.co.uk

Copyright 2003 by Randy Glasbergen.
www.glasbergen.com

"We're looking for someone who can help us crack down on identity theft. Fill out this application and don't forget to include your Social Security number, date of birth, phone number, home address and mother's maiden name."

Case studies and Activities

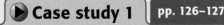

▶ **Case study 1**   pp. 126–127

Phishing – tricking people to part with account information

Phishing is where fraudsters set up a fake website, which looks the same as a bank website, and then send out lots of e-mails to attract people to the site. When these people go to the fake site, they are asked to supply personal/financial details, which can be used to steal their identity and money. The name phishing arises because they are 'fishing' for personal information. Shown below is an example of a 'phishing' e-mail.

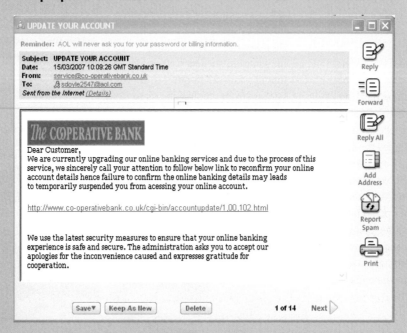

The phishing e-mail looks genuine, but read it and see if there is anything that would make you suspicious.

When you click on the link in the e-mail, you are directed to the following website:

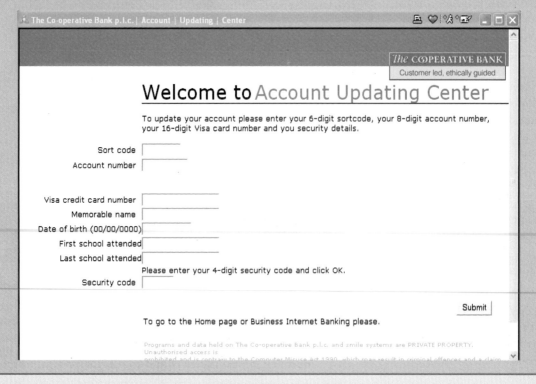

If you were to supply this personal information, the fraudster would have enough detail to be able to steal your identity and buy goods and services using your credit card. Notice that there is no indication that encryption is going to be used to scramble the information entered.

To combat phishing, banks now address you by name when sending you an e-mail and also write down the last few numbers of your account. Anyone sending you these fake e-mails would be unlikely to have these details normally, so you can be sure you are looking at an e-mail from your bank.

Banks would never send you e-mails to confirm or change your security details, account numbers, card numbers, PINs, or expiry dates.

1   As more people use the Internet for banking and buying goods and services on-line, there has been a huge increase in phishing. Describe the meaning of the term phishing and give an example of how it works. (2 marks)

2   When credit card or other personal/financial details are sent over the Internet, they are always encrypted before sending.

(a) Explain what is meant by the term encryption. (2 marks)

(b) Give **one** reason why encryption is necessary. (2 marks)

(c) Many banks ask a security question before a transaction can be completed. Give an example of a security question. (1 mark)

3   Banks and credit card companies are very worried about the increase in phishing. Give **two** pieces of advice you would give to people who buy goods/services or who bank on-line, to help prevent them falling for these fake e-mails and sites. (2 marks)

▶ Activity 1 The dangers of identity theft

There has been much in the news recently concerning identity theft and how it is likely to affect one in ten people. You have been asked to produce a self-running presentation on identity theft and the dangers it poses.
For the presentation you will need to use your own knowledge of the subject with material you can find from research using the Internet.
Identity theft is a major problem for society, so you should be able to find plenty of information about it.
To help you, you should consider using the following sources for your information:
*   On-line newspaper sites (Guardian, Daily Telegraph, Daily Mail, etc.)
*   The BBC news site at www.bbc.co.uk
*   The sites of the major banks (e.g., Lloyds, Barclays, etc.)

▶ Activity 2 Peer-to-peer file sharing

In this activity you are going to research peer-to-peer networks and peer-to-peer file sharing.
Use the Internet and access the following website: http://www.kazaa.com/us/help/glossary/p2p.htm
Look through the glossary until you have a good grasp as to what peer-to-peer is, how it works and why it is useful, and then answer the following questions:

1   Explain how a peer-to-peer network differs from a client-server network.
2   Peer-to-peer networking using the Internet is very popular. Give **two** things you can do using a peer-to-peer network.
3   People often have on their computers personal files that they would not want to share with others. How does the Kazaa P2P file sharing system deal with this?
4   File sharing systems are not popular with music publishers.
    (a) Give the name of the Act which protects musicians and music publishers from having their work copied.
    (b) Give **one** reason why musicians may not like systems such as Kazaa.
    (c) Some groups trying to get on the ladder might like systems such as Kazaa. Give **one** reason why.
5   Give **two** reasons why a user might be worried about the security implications of the Kazaa system.
6   Kazaa can be downloaded free from the website: http://www.kazaa.com/us/index.htm
    Explain how Kazaa can be provided free, yet Kazaa can still make money from the venture.

Questions

▶ Questions 1 pp. 118–123

1 (a) ICT has had a huge impact on the way children spend their leisure time. Describe three ways in which ICT has had an impact on the way a child spends their leisure time. **(4 marks)**

  (b) Discuss, by giving two examples, some of the problems that ICT has brought to the parents of young children due to their child's use of ICT. **(4 marks)**

2 It has been suggested by a computer expert that the home games market has driven recent advances in ICT.

  (a) Describe, by giving two relevant examples, how the human–computer interface can be improved by the use of specialist input devices for games. **(4 marks)**

  (b) Describe two health problems that the prolonged playing of computer games could cause. **(2 marks)**

3 Many people use their computers and digital cameras for digital photography.

  (a) Give three reasons why digital photography has become a popular use of computers for home users. **(3 marks)**

  (b) Many of these home users will use digital image editing software with their digital images. Give three features of image editing software and describe why each of them is useful to a home computer user. **(3 marks)**

  (c) Discuss the specialist input and output requirements for digital photography. **(4 marks)**

4 The use of the Internet has opened up a whole new source for music, music downloads.

  (a) Explain how the use of ICT has made it possible to load, store and transfer music files. **(4 marks)**

  (b) Storing music files in digital format has raised some issues. Explain one legal issue and one ethical issue presented by music downloads. **(2 marks)**

5 People use the Internet to access booking systems. By referring to a relevant example, explain how an Internet booking system works and the advantages in being able to book tickets/seats on-line. **(5 marks)**

6 Discuss the advantages and the disadvantages that the use of mobile phones has brought to society. **(6 marks)**

▶ Questions 2 pp. 118–127

1 The rise in the use of the Internet has led to a huge increase in the number of people who use ICT for their entertainment or home banking.

  (a) Discuss, by referring to four relevant examples, the rise in the use of the Internet for home entertainment. **(8 marks)**

  (b) Discuss the advantages and disadvantages of using home banking services. **(4 marks)**

2 On-line banking is very popular with home users of ICT.

  (a) Name and describe three services offered by on-line banking. **(3 marks)**

  (b) Some people are sceptical about on-line banking. Describe two worries that people might have with on-line banking. **(2 marks)**

  (c) Describe one way that the banks can address one of the worries you have described in part (b). **(1 mark)**

Exam support

Worked example 1

1 Many people now choose to bank on-line because of the time savings it offers. They do not have to travel to the bank and then probably queue up.

There are other advantages of on-line banking. Discuss the other advantages and possible disadvantages to the bank customer. (6 marks)

Student answer 1

Quicker – it is much quicker to use on-line banking

Easier – you can sit at home and do it

Safer – you can pay money without the need to draw cash out to pay bills

The worry of hackers accessing your bank account may make it not worth your while having an on-line account.

Examiner's comment

1 In the question the student was asked to 'discuss' the advantages and disadvantages. This means that they are expected to answer in sentences and not simply give a list of points.

In addition to this, the student has fallen into the trap of using the words 'Quicker' and 'Easier' without saying why. There are no marks for the first two points.

Safer is a valid answer because it is safer not to carry cash around so this part gains one mark.

The last point is made in a sentence and this is a valid disadvantage. **(2 marks out of 6)**

Examiner's answer

1 Candidates may discuss a range of the following:

Advantages

A customer can move money between current and savings accounts quickly in order to take the best advantage of better rates of interest

Customers can check all their statements on-line rather than have to store paper statements

On-line accounts frequently have better rates of interest

You can pay bills or put money directly into another account from your home

On-line accounts offer 24/7 access so you can bank outside normal banking hours

There is no paperwork with account numbers on to discard, so there is reduced risk of identity theft

You can apply for loans, overdrafts and credit cards without having to visit a bank

It allows you to pay for goods and services without using cash or cheques, which is easier

Student answer 2

1 On-line accounts often give the best rates of interests because the banks' operating costs are lower than high street banks.

Customers do not have to waste time travelling to banks and queuing up to do simple transactions that they could do from the comfort of home.

Customers no longer have to store their own paper bank statements as they can all be viewed on-line.

Goods are often bought by mail-order or over the Internet. It is possible to pay by transferring money to another person's account using on-line banking which saves having to write a cheque or reveal credit card details.

Some customers will be worried about unauthorised access to their on-line account by hackers who could commit fraud.

Examiner's comment

1 The student is awarded no marks for the second point as these are the points mentioned in the question. The rest of the answers are correct and have been given in proper sentences and they have discussed three advantages and disadvantages in detail. Their explanation of these was very clear. **(4 marks out of 6)**

Disadvantages

On-line bank accounts could be hacked into and your money stolen

You cannot get cash, so you still need to visit a cash machine

Older people may prefer the personal service offered by a conventional bank

4–6 marks

Candidates give a clear, coherent answer fully and accurately describing and explaining at least four advantages/disadvantages.

2–3 marks

Candidates give explanations of two or three advantages/disadvantages.

0–1 marks

Candidates simply give one advantage or disadvantage.

Exam support continued

Worked example 2

2 There has been a huge increase in peoples' use of ICT in the home, particularly in the area of entertainment. Many traditional activities such as sport and reading have been replaced by new forms of entertainment making use of ICT.
  (a) Discuss, by giving four distinctly different examples, the benefits that ICT developments have brought to home entertainment. (8 marks)
  (b) There are a number of disadvantages in using ICT for entertainment. Discuss by giving two distinctly different examples, two such disadvantages. (4 marks)

Student answer 1

2 (a) One benefit is downloads where you can select which tracks you want, instead of having to buy the whole CD. This saves you money and using play-lists you can choose to listen to all your favourite tracks together.
    Another benefit is Internet shopping where for a small fee you can select all the goods that you want from the comfort of your own home and get them delivered to your house at a certain time.
    Word-processing is useful at home because you can type in all your letters, school work, CVs, etc., and print them out on your home printer.
    Cable TV is ideal because you can watch films by paying a small fee which means you do not have to visit a video shop anymore as the film data is sent along a cable. You can also watch repeats of old series or even programmes that you wanted to watch the previous week.
  (b) You can become lazy just watching TV all day and you can end up not making friends or communicating with other people.
    There are dangers in meeting strangers from chat rooms, especially for young children who may meet without their parents' knowing. They could meet a paedophile who pretends to be a child when on-line.

Examiner's comment

2 (a) The first two benefits are well explained and the examples given are sensible and relate to the benefit.
       A third answer gives a benefit of word-processing, as a form of entertainment. This is stretching the word entertainment a bit too far, so credit is not given for this answer.
       The fourth answer is correct as it describes a pay-to-view service provided by a satellite or cable TV service.
   (b) Just because people watch TV does not make them lazy and this is far too general to be given any marks. The Examiner should not have to read anything into an answer in order to award it marks.
       The second part of the answer is good as it clearly identifies the disadvantage and the problems it creates.   **(8 marks out of 12)**

Student answer 2

2 (a) Many people use their home ICT equipment for digital photography. Digital photography, allows them to experiment by taking pictures, which they would not have been able to do with traditional film owing to the expense of getting them developed. They can edit these pictures, attach them to e-mails and send them to friends and family and print them in colour using ink-jet printers.

Some use the interactive facilities of their TV service or the Internet to gamble from their own home, using a credit card. It makes it more interesting when watching a football match to put some money on your favourite team. Using the Internet to do this is much easier than having to go to a high street betting shop.

You can use the Internet to play computer games. It is possible, for example, to play a game of chess over the Internet with your opponent in a different country. The good thing about this is that there is always someone to play with.

Mobile phones are great because you can do so much with them. For example, you can send and receive text messages, send and receive e-mail, surf the Internet, use your phone as an MP3 player, take digital photographs and even have a telephone conversation!

(b) You have to be careful when using the Internet, as there is a tendency to slouch in your chair. This is likely to cause you back ache in the future. Also, the repeated use of the mouse, joystick and keyboard could lead to repetitive strain injury (RSI).

Computer games can cause a problem because young children cannot seem to leave them alone so their school work suffers as a result.

Examiner's answer

2 (a) Any four from the following list. (One mark for the name of the item and the second mark for further amplification by describing the hardware or explaining what it has allowed the user to do.)

MP3 player – allowing people to listen to a choice of thousands of tracks on a small portable player.

Music downloads – allows users to pick only the tracks they want rather than have to buy the entire CD.

Digital photography – allows users to become much more proficient at taking photographs by allowing them to immediately see the results.

Interactive TV – allows people to shop, check e-mail, book holidays, bet, etc.

Chat rooms – allows people to make new friends with people all around the world

Mobile phones – can communicate with friends in a large number of ways such as text message, voice and e-mail.

Betting – can place bets without leaving your home and also you do not need to pick up your winnings as they are put back on your card.

Dating – meeting new dates is made easy by viewing the on-line pictures and profiles.

Games – can play computer games on long journeys to help relieve boredom.

Editing digital images – bad digital photographs can be improved by making use of image/photograph editing software.

On-line shopping – people are able to pick up bargains at many of the on-line stores which offer special discounts to on-line shoppers.

Examiner's comment

2 (a) This is a good set of answers which are all different and are clearly explained. Full marks were given for this part of the question.

(b) The first answer was more comprehensive than the second, and therefore deserves two marks. The second answer could have been explained in more detail, so only one mark is given for this part. **(11 marks out of 12)**

On-line booking – many people now choose to book flights, hotels and car hire separately as it is more flexible and often cheaper.

Voting – you can place votes for TV shows using the Internet and this will eventually mean that you will be able to vote in local and general elections in this way.

Improved hardware – home users are by far the biggest users of computers, so their demands are used to produce new improved hardware such as sound cards, video cards, etc.

Speakers – the demand for high quality sound from gamers and watchers of TV has led to the design of surround sound systems.

(b) Any two from the following list. (One mark for the name of the item and the second mark for further amplification by describing the resulting problems.)

Computer games – can be addictive and this can affect schoolwork.

Computer games – playing computer games is often a sedentary activity and so can lead to obesity.

Health problems – incorrect posture can lead to back ache; repeatedly using joysticks can lead to RSI.

Chat rooms – young children could be groomed in order to meet undesirable people.

Summary mind maps

Computer games

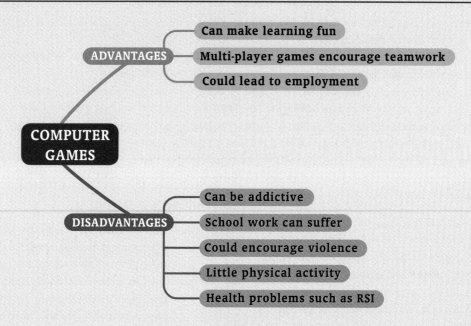

COMPUTER GAMES

ADVANTAGES
- Can make learning fun
- Multi-player games encourage teamwork
- Could lead to employment

DISADVANTAGES
- Can be addictive
- School work can suffer
- Could encourage violence
- Little physical activity
- Health problems such as RSI

Playing and creating music

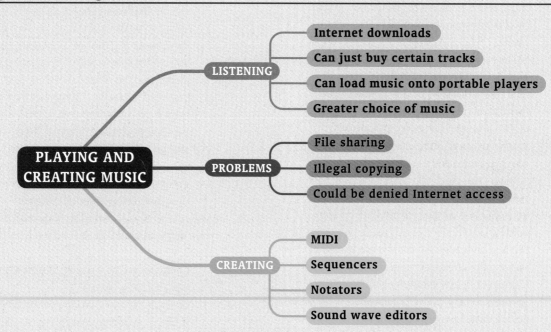

PLAYING AND CREATING MUSIC

LISTENING
- Internet downloads
- Can just buy certain tracks
- Can load music onto portable players
- Greater choice of music

PROBLEMS
- File sharing
- Illegal copying
- Could be denied Internet access

CREATING
- MIDI
- Sequencers
- Notators
- Sound wave editors

TOPIC 7: Presenting information

In this topic you will learn about the need to present information in a certain format, using a certain media or a combination of media for a particular audience. You will learn how to tailor information based on its subsequent usage and the needs of the recipient. You will also look at the use, key functions and advantages and disadvantages of a range of software such as word-processing/DTP, presentation, database and web authoring software.

▼ The key concepts covered in this topic are:

▷ Understand the need for the correct format, media and audience for information

▷ Understand the use, key functions, advantages and disadvantages of word-processing/DTP, presentation, database and web authoring software

CONTENTS

Formats, media and audience for information

▼ You will find out

▶ About the need to think about your audience

▶ About the different formats for information

▶ About the different media for information

Introduction

Data is processed by ICT systems to produce information, and before the information is given to someone, you need to decide on the format of the information, the media you intend to use for its presentation and the audience your information is aimed at.

In this section you will cover the formats, media and audience for information and find out why each of them is important.

Thinking about the audience

The audience are the people your information is aimed at. You need to make sure that the design of the document is appropriate for the people who will be reading it. For example, a poster advertising a school disco for 14–16 year olds would need a different design compared to a poster advertising a drink driving campaign. If you are talking about ICT to others who also know about ICT, then you can use technical terms without explaining them. Information in business needs to match the requirements of the person who has asked for it. For example, a director or owner of a company would need information which conveys an overall picture rather than fine detail.

In many cases, such as with websites, the information is aimed at a whole range of audiences. It is difficult to please and satisfy all audiences, so you need to produce a website that would be understandable and useable by the majority of users.

Formats for information

Information can be presented in many different formats which include:

- text
- tabular (i.e., presented in a table)
- graphics (graphs, charts, diagrams, photographs, etc.)
- audio
- animations
- video.

In books, reports and other printed media, only text and graphics are used, but information can now be conveyed using multimedia in presentations and websites so the full range of formats can be used.

Factors affecting the choice of format

There are a number of factors which cover the choice of format and these include:

- **The particular needs of the user** – a user may be partially sighted or blind so information as audio would need to be used rather than text.
- **The complexity of the information** – complex information can be explained better pictorially. Figures can be presented as graphs and charts so that comparisons can be made and trends spotted.
- **Whether the material is to be presented on-line** – animations and video can be added to multimedia presentations or websites.

There are many different formats in which information can be presented.

⬇ KEY WORDS

Format – the style in which the information is organised and presented

Media – the means by which information is communicated

Table – a more visual way of displaying data, especially numeric data

Multimedia – making use of many media such as text, image, sound, animation and video

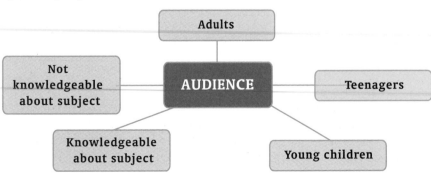

Media

We now live in a multimedia world, and information can be given in a wide range of media. Just think about all the different ways you can get football results. You can get them:

- on teletext
- as a video showing the highlights of the match
- as a text message to your mobile phone
- as audio on your radio
- on a website
- in printed form in a newspaper.

There is a range of media to choose from and in many cases to catch the majority of your audience for the information it is usually necessary to use a range of the media shown below.

Examples of media include:

- Paper-based media – sometimes called hard copy. This is a common and more traditional media where information is given as text and graphics on paper. Examples include newspapers, books, magazines, brochures, posters, catalogues, etc.
- Paper-based media are ideal for detailed information that needs to be taken away and studied and for information that does not change too often.
- Screen-based media – information which needs to be read only the once and does not need to be studied, can be viewed on screen. For example, if you wanted to check the train times, you could do this by viewing a website using a screen.
- Audio – information can be given using speech. For example, a message could be left using voice mail on a computer. You can download an audio file from the Internet to a portable media player such as mobile phone, iPod or MP3 player.
- Video – can be used to convey information. For example, a speech videoed during a meeting or conference can be sent digitally to people who could not attend.
- Multimedia – means many media. Usually multimedia means more than just text and graphics, so this means that a normal book or magazine would not be considered multimedia.

The types of media that can be used in multimedia are shown here:

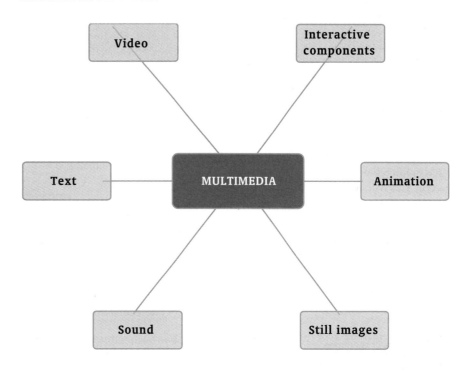

Factors affecting the choice of media

There are a number of factors which cover the choice of media and these include:

The nature and complexity of information

Some information is easy to understand and quick to read. Information of this sort can be presented on the screen. Lists of tabulated information, such as the sales figures for every month over the last five years, are complex and need quite a bit of analysis in order to understand them. This information would be best printed out and then studied to identify trends, etc. Complex information can be further processed to produce reports containing graphs, findings, etc.

Time to study

Material which needs to be studied at length needs to be hard copy (i.e., printed out).

The needs of the recipient

The person who has asked for information is not always the same person that actually does the searching for it. In many cases a manager will ask a member of their staff to find information and report back. It is therefore essential that the person who conducts the search for the information understands the purpose of the information and how it will be used. The supplier of the information must therefore bear in mind the needs of the recipient.

Lifespan of information

Some information changes by the minute or even the second, such as share prices, currency prices and commodities such as oil and gas. Even the prices in a supermarket can change, as price increases from suppliers are passed onto customers.

The lifespan of some information is short and it is important to use a medium for this information that can react almost instantaneously to the changing information. Websites and on-line systems are the best solution for information that is changing regularly.

Stock lists printed out on paper will only represent the stock at the time of the printout. It is always important that any reports and other printouts contain a date, otherwise you would not be able to trust the information they contain.

Word-processing/ DTP software

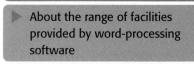
Introduction

You will already have a good knowledge of features of word-processing software but in this section you will come across some of the more advanced features as well as the familiar ones. When you have to produce a document there is a choice between word-processing and desktop publishing software. In many respects both pieces of software can be used for the same tasks if they are relatively simple in terms of design. It is important to be able to choose the most appropriate software for the task and to be able to do this you have to have a good understanding of the capabilities of desktop publishing software and word-processing software.

Word-processing

Word-processing packages are used to produce documents containing text such as letters, reports, etc., and for preparing text for other applications. For example, text could be typed in using word-processing software and then the file could be imported into desktop publishing software.

Before starting any document you need to consider the page layout/format which consists of the following:

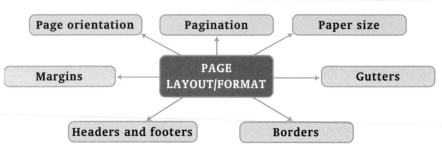

Once text has been entered it can be formatted to add structure and emphasis. Text can be formatted by altering the characteristics of the font. The formatting text features are shown here:

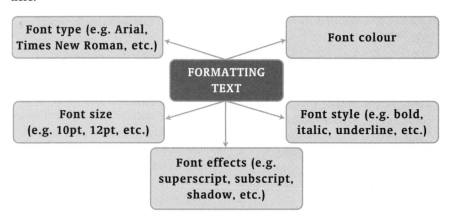

Formatting paragraphs/blocks of text

Blocks of text or paragraphs can be formatted in a number of ways which are shown below:

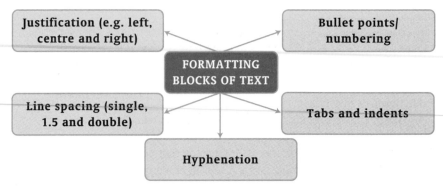

Additional features of word-processing software

There are a number of more advanced features of word-processing software that can be used:

- **Templates** – used to specify the structure of a document, such as fonts, page layout, formatting and styles.
- **Mail merge** – combining a list of names and addresses with a standard letter so that a series of letters is produced with each letter being addressed to a different person. The list of data used for the mail merge can be created using the word-processing software or it can be imported from a database or spreadsheet.

- **Indexing** – allows words to be highlighted so that they can be used to form an index. The word-processing software keeps a record of the words along with their page number and, when instructed to, it will create the index.
- **Macros** – these are used to record a series of keystrokes so that, for example, your name and address can be added to the top of the page simply by pressing a single key or clicking on the mouse.
- **Thesaurus** – allows a word to be chosen and the word-processor will list synonyms (i.e., words with similar meanings). This is useful in creative writing where you do not want to repeat a word.

- **Spellchecker** – word-processing software has a dictionary against which all words typed in are checked. There is usually the facility to add words, which is important if you use specialist terms.
- **Grammar checker** – used to check the grammar in a sentence and to highlight problems and suggest alternatives.

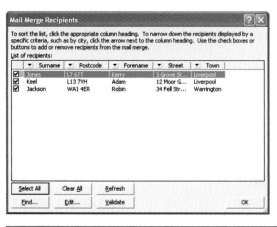

A list of mail merge recipients is produced or obtained. Notice the field names at the top of each column of data.

«Forename» «Surname»
«Street»
«Town»
«Postcode»

Dear «Forename»

As you know you will soon be taking your end of year examinations.

A letter is written containing the fields for the variable information. Part of the letter is shown here.

Kerry Jones
3 Grove St
Liverpool
L7 6TT

Dear Kerry

As you know you will soon be taking your end of year examinations. For those of you in year 11, these will be your GCSE exams. We will be holding a revision club on Mondays and Wednesdays from 4 p.m. to 6 p.m. A variety of staff will be on hand to help you with your revision questions. You should take advantage of this as it is completely free.

There will be a meeting on Wednesday 3rd May at 4 p.m. in the hall for any of you interested in taking up the offer.

Happy revision and good luck.

The variable information is now inserted to perform the mail merge.

Word-processing/DTP software continued

DTP (desktop publishing) software

Desktop publishing software is used to produce documents consisting of more than just text. For example, the documents can contain artwork, such as photographs, diagrams, clipart, cartoons, graphs as well as text.

Most of these items are prepared using different software and are then imported into the DTP software. DTP software therefore needs to be able to deal with lots of different types of file. For example, DTP software would need to be able to cope with the following:

- graphics (e.g., clipart, photographs, etc.) from a drawing or graphics package
- images from a scanner
- frames from a digital video camera
- still images from a digital camera
- text from a word-processor.

The differences between home DTP software and word-processing software

If the home user needs to produce a simple document, such as an advertisement or a simple newsletter, they will probably decide to use the software that they are most familiar with. This is likely to be word-processing software, because they already understand most of it. Word-processing software does have many features that you would also find in DTP software such as:

- newspaper/magazine type columns
- the ability to add vertical lines between newspaper type columns
- the ability to create an index
- the use of templates.

Features of professional DTP software

Professional DTP software is used by large publishing houses to produce complex designs for magazines, catalogues, newspapers, books, etc.

As professional DTP is used to design publications just like home DTP packages, the people using the professional package will use their own designs and will not want to make the compromises that need to be made in the home DTP software.

Here are some of the ways in which the large-scale DTP packages differ from a home DTP package:

- Professional level typesetting options – such as kerning, where you can finely adjust the spacing between characters.
- Plug-ins – extensions can be bought for the software which can be used for a particular industry. For example, you can buy a plug-in specifically for the production of newspapers.
- Ability to program the DTP software – in the same way that applications can be built by programming using a database as the core, some DTP packages can be programmed. For example, newspaper companies have a team of programmers who program more functions into the DTP software.
- Curving text along a line.
- A more standard file format – this makes it much easier to for printers to use the files directly without adjustment.

More advanced features of word-processing/DTP software

There are many more advanced features of word-processing/DTP software and here are just some of them.

Style sheets or cascading style sheets (CSS)

Style sheets separate the content (text, images, etc) from the way that the content is presented (font, font size, font colours, borders, position, etc.). This means that if a font for a heading needs to be changed throughout the document, then this can be done in the style sheet. As the formatting for all the other pages is taken from the style sheet, the changes are made automatically for all the pages, slides, screens, etc., for the entire document. This can save a huge amount of time as without style sheets it would be necessary to look at each page for headings and then change the font manually. In web authoring, style sheets are often called cascading style sheets (CSS).

Templates

Templates are pre-designed documents that we can use to create brochures, posters, exam papers, advertisements, school prospectuses, etc. They are partly completed documents which contain placeholder text and graphics just to mark the position on the page.

You can replace the placeholder text and graphics with your own and it makes it easy to use and will be ideal for staff who are beginners in using DTP who are not used to designing DTP documents. The main advantage in using templates is that you do not have to start from scratch and worry about the design of the page and the content. With a template you only need worry about the content.

Using templates you can design advertisements, brochures, catalogues, reports, etc.

There is a disadvantage in using templates in that your design can look like those of everyone else who has used the same template. You can, of course, create your own template but this takes time and you probably need some design skills.

Advantages of desktop publishing

Here are just a few of the advantages of DTP for preparing books, magazines, advertisements, posters and leaflets, compared with word-processing alone:

- More control over the way the page is laid out – DTP packages are more flexible in the way that text can be formatted and arranged on the page.
- Better at integrating files from other packages – DTP packages are not usually used for the creation of text or graphics. Instead they bring together the files of these items created in other packages and bring together the elements on the screen.
- Text and graphics can be put in boxes – this allows the boxes containing the text and graphics to be moved and positioned on the screen. Although word-processing software has text boxes, you cannot position them accurately or rotate them like you can with DTP packages.
- You can produce files that a professional printer can use directly – DTP can be used to produce the output in a certain way with a certain file format so that it can be sent to professional printers for printing.
- You can have text flow around irregular shapes.
- You can position each letter in text with much more precision.

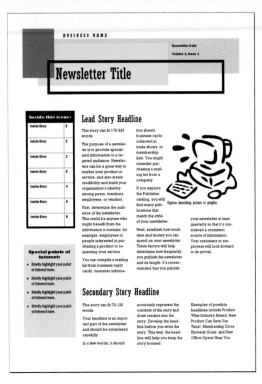

One of the many templates in the DTP software Microsoft Publisher. If the user is happy with the design, they simply change the content (headings, text, artwork, etc.) to their own.

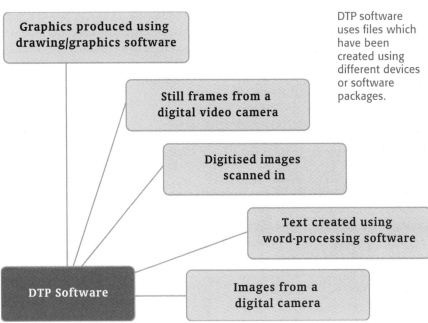

Graphics produced using drawing/graphics software

Still frames from a digital video camera

Digitised images scanned in

Text created using word-processing software

DTP Software

Images from a digital camera

DTP software uses files which have been created using different devices or software packages.

DTP is the only software to consider if you want to design and produce a multi-page document with lots of eye-catching design elements such as a brochure or magazine.

Presentation software

Introduction

Most of you will have used presentation software for your Key Stage 3 and 4 courses of study and you will have seen your teacher present material using presentation software. In this topic you will be learning about the key functions as well as the advantages and disadvantages of presentation software.

Presentation software

Presentation software is not just restricted to viewing a series of slides containing content. You can actually build a multimedia application such as a multiple choice or other type of computer-marked test using presentation software. In this type of problem you would use the feature of presentation software of being able to hyperlink one slide to another. This means that the slides do not have to be displayed in only one particular order. There are many other features of presentation software and these are shown in the diagram below.

Creating a show

A show is simply a series of slides, which are put together using presentation software. The designer of the presentation is able to choose the way slides can be timed to appear. For example, the slides can appear on a mouse click from the presenter or they can be timed so that one slide moves on to the next automatically. Some slideshows do not even have a presenter: you may have seen such slideshows being used in stores to present a particular product. Here the slide show is looped so that as soon as it ends it goes back to the beginning again and repeats. Usually there is some form of narration, which is saved as a sound file with the presentation.

You can also create interactivity in slide shows, so the user can determine the order in which elements of the show happen. It is possible to create quizzes using presentation software.

Animated transitions

The movement from one slide to another is called a slide transition. There are a number of different animated slide transitions. To make your slide transitions more interesting, you can:

- alter the way the slide appears on the screen
- alter the speed at which the slide appears
- get the computer to make a sound during the transition.

Warning – be careful with animations. If you overdo them, they can make your presentation look amateurish.

Exporting files

Exporting files means formatting the data in some way so that it can be used by another application. This means that the two different pieces of software are able to share the same data. An example would exporting an image file created using photo editing software so that it is in a format that can be used on a webpage.

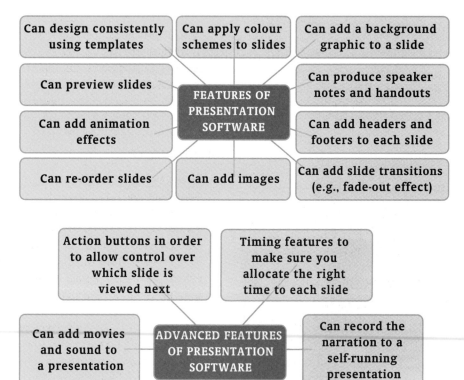

Can design consistently using templates — Can apply colour schemes to slides — Can add a background graphic to a slide — Can preview slides — **FEATURES OF PRESENTATION SOFTWARE** — Can produce speaker notes and handouts — Can add animation effects — Can add headers and footers to each slide — Can re-order slides — Can add images — Can add slide transitions (e.g., fade-out effect)

Action buttons in order to allow control over which slide is viewed next — Timing features to make sure you allocate the right time to each slide — Can add movies and sound to a presentation — **ADVANCED FEATURES OF PRESENTATION SOFTWARE** — Can record the narration to a self-running presentation — Animation effects – can add each object to a slide one-by-one — Ability to hyperlink (e.g., to another slide, webpage or file)

KEY WORDS

Compression – storing data in a format that requires less space. Bitmapped graphics such as photographs are usually compressed to a fraction of their normal file size

Importing files

Importing means the ability of one piece of software to read and use the data produced by a different piece of software. For example, when performing a mail merge using word-processing software, the data source that provides a list of variable information can be produced using spreadsheet software or database software. The files can be imported into the word-processing software. Another example would be a user importing their e-mail address book into the latest version of Microsoft Outlook.

When you create a presentation that includes images, sounds or movies, care needs to be taken when exporting the file. This is because if you just export the presentation file, the other files such as images, sounds or movies won't be accessible because the link to them is lost. It is therefore essential to export all the files used by the presentation as well as the actual presentation file itself.

Data compression techniques

If images are to be used on a website or a presentation, they can take time to load, so it is best to use compressed images. Compressing files makes the file size smaller which makes it quicker to load and also to copy onto other media. If the presentation is to be provided as a download on a website, it will be quicker to upload (i.e., save onto the server) and to download by users.

Audio files, such as files containing speech or music, are extremely large and these are normally saved in MP3 format, which compresses the file and makes the file more manageable.

Movie/video files are even bigger than audio files and so need to be compressed. When a file is compressed it:

- enables more files to be stored on the storage medium (e.g., DVD, memory card, hard disk, pen drive, etc.)
- makes it much faster to upload to put it on a webpage
- makes it much faster for others to download it from a webpage
- makes it faster to load when viewed with any software used to view or edit it
- makes it faster to transfer as an e-mail attachment.

File compression software such as WinZip is available which reduces the sizes of files. This process is called zipping. A zip file is an archive file and can contain one or more files. You will have come across zip files when downloading files from the Internet. Here they are zipped to reduce file size and download times. Before a zip file can be used it needs to be unzipped and this is done automatically when you click on the zip file.

The following diagrams show how compression reduces the file size.

Bitmap image
1280 × 960 pixels

File size:
3150 KB (3.5 MB)

Compression

JPEG image
1280 × 960 pixels

File size:
292 KB

Keep your slides simple like this one. People often include too much information.

The advantages and disadvantages of presentation software

There are a number of advantages and disadvantages in using presentation software and these are summarised below.

Advantages

- The use of presentation software makes the presenter look more professional.
- It encourages the presenter to summarise what they are saying in a number of bullet points.
- The presenter can print out the slides so the audience have some information to take away and digest.
- The presenter is able to make use of full multimedia capability in their presentation.
- Presentations can be stored and transferred to people who were unable to attend the presentation.
- Presentations can be shown using a projector, whiteboard, TV or on a desktop or laptop computer screen, so the presenter has flexibility in the way the presentation is delivered.
- The presenter's notes facility provides a set of notes that the audience cannot see, in case the presenter is not sure what to say next.

Disadvantages

- The files for presentations containing video are extremely large and need a lot of memory and storage for them to run successfully.
- The audience can get fed up seeing all the special effects that people tend to put in their presentations.
- Good presentations can take a long time to set up.
- Sometimes people concentrate more time on presenting the information than they do on gathering the information in the first place. This means that the information is sometimes incorrect.
- Sometimes the sound effects and animation used in presentations can annoy the audience.

Database software

▼ You will find out

▶ About what is meant by the term database

▶ About the advantages of databases over other storage systems

▶ About the disadvantages of databases over other storage systems

▶ About the import/export of data to and from databases

▶ About what a query is

▶ About what a report is

Introduction

Database software allows data to be entered and stored in a structured way, which aids its retrieval.

Database management systems keep the data separate from the programs themselves, so once the data has been created, it can be accessed using different software. This is important as when a business or organisation expands, it may decide to use different database management software and will not want to have to input all the data again.

Databases used by businesses and organisations are called relational databases with the data being held in lots of different tables with links called relationships between the tables.

What is a database?

A database is an organised collection of data or information. From this definition, you can see that the data does not necessarily have to be stored on a computer. Most large collections of data are now computerised and the main advantages of using a computerised database are that is gives more flexibility in organising, displaying and printing and it is much faster than any manual system.

Computerised databases may be divided into two types: the limited flat-file database suitable for only a few applications, and the much more comprehensive and flexible relational database.

▶ KEY WORDS

Relational database – database where the data is held in tables with relationships established between them. The software is used to set up and hold the data as well as to extract and manipulate the stored data

Relationship – the way tables are related to each other; they can be one-to-one, one-to-many or many-to-many

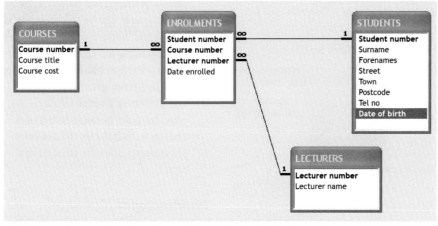

This shows the way the data is stored in a relational database. There are four tables in this database (represented by the boxes) and the links (correctly called relationships) are drawn as lines between the tables.

Computer-based databases are replacing paper-based storage systems.

The advantages of databases over other storage systems

The main advantages of a computerised database are:

- You only have to enter the data once. All the other applications can make use of this centralised pool of data.
- Files/tables are linked and this means that if the data is changed in one application, then the database will be automatically updated for other applications.
- If you find that due to changes in the organisation it is necessary to change the structure of the database, then this is easily done. With a manual system this would be very difficult to do, as it would involve a lot of work.

- Access to the information is very fast, which means you do not wait long to get the information you require.
- Complex search criteria can be constructed and these may be saved and used again or even modified.
- Everyone uses the same data, so that data consistency is ensured.
- Validation checks may be performed on the data as it is entered, thus protecting the integrity of the database.

There are a few disadvantages:

- If the file server containing the database breaks down, then none of the applications that use the data can be used.
- Security needs to be considered carefully as all the data is now held centrally.
- Users of the system will need careful training and this can be expensive.

Import/export

The data in a database may have taken years to collect and create and is a very valuable commodity to the organisation. Database software and other software used to manipulate the data may change over the years. It is therefore important that the data is easily imported and exported between different software. For example, names and addresses from a customer database can be imported into word-processing software in order to produce a mail merge. Sometimes, data is transferred between a supermarket and their suppliers, and in order to do this the software used by each must be capable of understanding the same set of data.

Query

The whole point in storing data in a database is the fact that it is easy to perform searches to extract data satisfying certain criteria, such as people over the age of 65, women in the production department who have not had health and safety training, etc.

One way of searching for the data in a database is to use commands written in a language called Structured Query Language (SQL). SQL consists of a small number of commands and, like programming language commands, they must be carefully constructed and this can be frustrating for inexperienced users.

If we had a database containing employee records, we might want to obtain a list from the database of employees in the production department earning £25000 or over per annum. We could do this using the following series of SQL commands.

```
SELECT EMPLOYEE_NAME
WHERE DEPARTMENT =
'PRODUCTION'
AND SALARY >= 25000
```

Query by example (QBE)

Query by example provides a simple way of running queries without having to worry about the way the statements are constructed, as you do when you are using SQL. Instead you use a simple way of selecting the columns you want to display and you can also specify simple search conditions and orders. Basically, it allows inexperienced or novice users to access the power of the relational database without having to bother about the syntax of SQL.

Report

A report is a printout of the results from a database. In most cases a report is produced on paper by printing the results but a report can also be produced on the screen. If there is a lot of detail in a report then it may be better to print it out so that it can be taken away and studied.

Reports give the user control over what and where the information they want is output; printed on paper or to the screen.

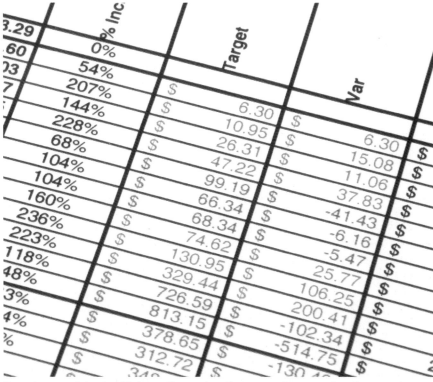

Reports are printouts of information and as these are often complex, they need to be taken away and studied. This report looks at the comparison between the values of actual sales against the values of targets set.

Web authoring software

Introduction

Web authoring software is the name of the software used to create websites.

In this section you will learn about the software that can be used to create websites and the components of websites that the software is used to create. You will learn about the range of software that can be used for web authoring including specialist web authoring software.

Web authoring software

In order to develop a website, web authoring software is needed. This need not be specialist software, as there are many common packages that could be used provided the site is not too complicated.

Generic software which could be used to develop websites includes:

- Word-processing software (e.g., Microsoft Word)
- Desktop publishing software (e.g., Microsoft Publisher).

Web authoring software has many more functions and is more difficult to use but the end result will be more professional. It includes packages such as:

- Microsoft FrontPage
- Adobe Dreamweaver.

In order to develop websites, many more pieces of software will be needed:

- Word-processing software – it is easier to word-process pieces of text using word-processing software.
- Scanning software – old photographs may need to be digitised so that they can be added to a webpage. Large amounts of text could be scanned in and then recognised using optical character recognition (OCR) software.
- Photo/image editing software – images sourced may not be the right shape or size for the space on the webpage so they will need to be edited. Contrast or brightness can also be altered.

- Browser software – needed to check how the webpage/website will look on the screen. Usually more than one browser is used to make sure the webpage looks as good in each browser.

Features of websites

Simple websites can be developed in packages such as Word or Publisher but for a better website it is advisable to use specialist web authoring software.

You will probably have created your own website using a suitable package at either Key Stage 3 or 4.

Simple design features of web authoring software

- Ability to add and format text.
- Just like in word-processing software, text can be added and formatted with different sized headings and sub-headings, etc.
- Adding tables to help layout text and images.
- Ability to import data from other packages.
- Ability to add hyperlinks to other webpages.
- Ability to use anchors to link to different sections in the same webpage.
- Ability to add a mailto link. This allows a viewer of a website to send an e-mail by opening the user's e-mail application.
- Ability to preview the website in different browsers for testing purposes.

Hyperlinks

Hyperlinks are used to jump from one place to another. Using hyperlinks you can:

- move from one place to another on the same webpage or slide
- move to another page on the same website or slide
- move to a completely different website or slide.

Hyperlinks can be textual or graphical:

Textual hyperlinks – are simply words on a website which are in blue and underlined. When you click on them you are moved to a different place.

Graphical hyperlinks – these are graphics (pictures, photographs, etc.) which you click on to move to a different place. They look just like ordinary graphics except when the cursor moves over them, it usually turns into a pointing hand.

Hyperlinks are also available in the presentation software PowerPoint. Action buttons are used to navigate between different slides and also between files stored on the hard drive or webpages on the Internet. Hyperlinks can be used to create interactive presentations where the user is able to decide which slide appears next rather than view them in a single sequence.

Formatting

Web authoring software can format text in a similar way to word-processing or DTP software. Using web authoring software you can:

- alter fonts (font and font size)
- produce bulleted lists
- create columns of text
- create tables
- add borders and shading.

Frames

Frames are used to split a window into sections. Using frames you can display two or more webpages at a time. You do not need to have whole webpages in a frame as you can just use part of each page in each frame.

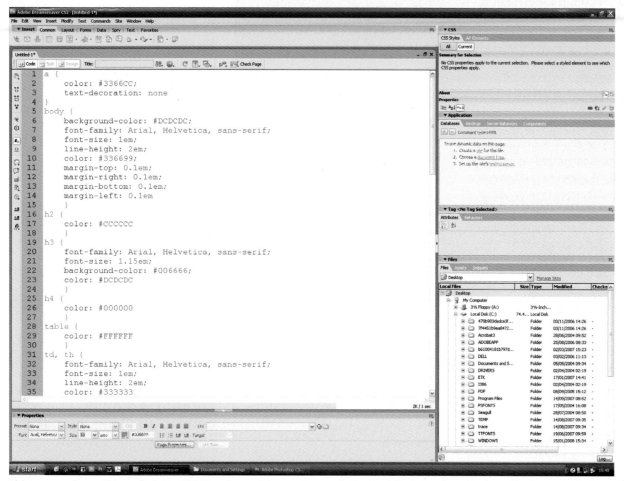

This screen shows the underlying HTML code used to create a website. Luckily the web authoring software protects you from the intricacies of this, so you do not need to know anything about HTML to create a website.

Frames are not used with all websites as they tend to be a bit confusing for the user, as when they are printed, only the active frame will print out.

HTML

HTML (HyperText Markup Language) is a series of instructions used to format and display text and images on the World Wide Web. You use it to specify the structure and layout of a webpage and website.

HTML is the instructions to the browser on how to present the content on the webpage to the user. HTML is complex and takes a lot of understanding and it is best left to the professional web designers who are using it all the time.

Most people who are not professional website designers prefer to use a web authoring package which is far more user friendly. Ultimately, any website you create using the package is turned into HTML code but the web authoring software does this automatically.

Advanced features of web authoring software

Cascading style sheets (CSS)

It is hard to keep consistency from one webpage to the next but the use of cascading style sheets helps with this. Instead of applying certain formatting to each block of text, you can apply an existing cascading style sheet to it. This means that this block of text will have the same font, font size and colour as defined in the CSS. The use of these sheets can save a huge amount of time when building websites.

The cascading style sheets are a way of separating the content from the presentation (e.g. font size, positioning, colours, etc.).

Ability to create a webpage using frames

Creating a webpage using frames means that you can have multiple webpages in a single browser window. By doing this the user can select a link in one frame that loads content into another existing frame, thus enabling the user to stay in the same browser window.

Ability to create a form and use it to collect data

Forms can be created which enable you to collect data from a user. For example, you could collect name and address details for a person asking for further information about a product. You could also ask the user to sign a guestbook and add their comments to a feedback page.

Ability to look at the HTML code

When a website is being developed using web authoring software, behind the scenes the program is generating a series of HTML codes that are the instructions that explain how you want the website set out.

Some website developers prefer to alter the HTML codes because it offers them more flexibility than using the website design package on its own.

Web authoring software continued

Use of animation

Many websites make use of animation but the animation is usually produced in a specialist graphics or animation package and then imported into the website. One such package you may have come across has the trade name Flash.

Flash enables you to:

- produce multimedia graphics on the web
- create interactive movies on the web.

You have probably heard of Flash. Lots of websites use it to produce impressive results. Flash has these advantages:

- Flash images are very fast to load
- you can create interactive animated images using Flash
- you do not need to know anything about programming to use it.

You need to make sure that any special animation effects you use can be viewed by almost everyone. To view Flash movies, Macromedia Shockwave Player is needed. Luckily it is included with most operating systems and browser software such as AOL, Internet Explorer, etc.

It is easy to produce animation using Flash. Before you start animation, you need to understand how animation is achieved. The simplest animation is where you draw a picture, erase it and then quickly draw the same picture in a slightly different position. The process is repeated until the picture has moved to its desired location.

If the change from one picture to another happens slowly, the human eye will see the separate pictures. If the picture is moved 24 times per second, then the human eye will be tricked into seeing that the picture is moving continuously.

Here are the steps you would need to take to move a red ball across the screen:

1. Draw the red ball
2. Erase it
3. Draw the red ball a little to the right
4. Erase it
5. Draw the red ball a little further to the right, etc.

The ball will appear to move (provided the process happens quickly).

When most people think of animations, they think of cartoons and particularly the Disney cartoons. These cartoons are frame by frame animations which means they are made up of thousands of separate frames with each frame slightly different from the last.

Creating a simple animation using animation software

To create an animation you need a start point and end point, which because of their importance, are called keyframes. Frames that hold new content are also called keyframes. In old Disney animations each frame would usually contain different content, so there were lots of keyframes.

You could create lots of different keyframes in animation software but it would take you ages. If you think you are going to be able to produce Disney-style animations then you will be disappointed.

Frame-by-frame animation has two major problems:

- it takes a lot of time and effort
- it produces very large files which can take a while to load on a website.

Tweening offers another way of producing simple animations. Basically the computer fills in the in-between frames once it knows the start and end frames. You can only do simple animations using tweening such as producing a smooth moving shape in different paths along the screen.

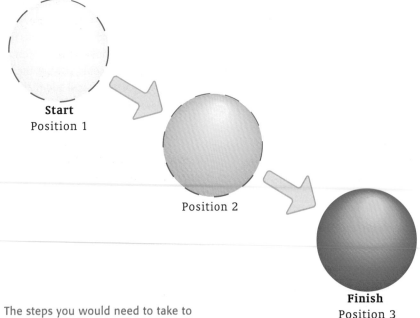

Start
Position 1

Position 2

Finish
Position 3

The steps you would need to take to move a red ball across the screen.

Questions and Activities

▶ Activity 1

Macros can be found as an advanced feature of most software. Using the software manuals or on-line help menus to help you, find out how to write a macro for a task that you find tedious when using your spreadsheet or word-processing software.

Produce an easy-to-understand set of instructions which you could give to a friend who needs to perform the same task.

▶ Activity 2

For this activity you are required to investigate the templates available in the word-processing and DTP packages that you are familiar with.

You are then required to produce a report outlining your findings.

▶ Activity 3

Using word-processing software, produce a template for a document for a holiday company. The holiday company would like to use this template to reply to people who have been dissatisfied with their holiday. The template will need to be tailored to their complaints so there needs to be quite a bit of space for the variable information to be inserted.

After completing the template you will need to prepare a short user guide to explain how the template should be used.

▶ Questions 1 pp. 138–141

1 What is a macro and why are they useful? (3 marks)
2 DTP software is used to produce a catalogue of products for an engineering company.
   (a) Discuss the factors which the company could use to determine whether home DTP software or professional DTP software should be used. (4 marks)
   (b) (i) Other than the computer itself, describe with reasons two other pieces of hardware that the company should buy. (2 marks)
       (ii) Give the names of two other pieces of software that the company would be likely to use in conjunction with the DTP software. Do not give brand names. (2 marks)
3 An author is writing a science book for GCSE. The book has a complex design, which makes use of a variety of fonts for headings, sub-headings, etc. There are also many different font sizes. The publisher of the book has suggested that the author use a style sheet.

   (a) Explain what is meant by a style sheet and explain, by giving an example, how the style sheet would be useful to the author. (3 marks)
   (b) The publisher has also suggested that macros can save the author time. Explain clearly what a macro is and give an example of how the author might use a macro to save time. (4 marks)
4 An administrator in a hospital uses word-processing software to send out letters to patients. Explain how mail merge could be used to save the administrator time. (5 marks)
5 Compare and contrast the features of desktop publishing and word-processing software, explaining how a user might choose between them. (6 marks)
6 Explain clearly the difference between a style sheet and template. (3 marks)
7 Give three reasons why desktop publishing software might be better than word-processing software for producing a brochure for a company. (3 marks)

▶ Questions 2 | pp. 136–137

1 (a) Information can be conveyed using a variety of media.
Give three types of media which could be used for promotion of a new pop group. (3 marks)

(b) Information can be displayed in a variety of different formats.
Describe two formats for information and for each give an example of a situation where each format would be appropriate. (2 marks)

(c) Explain, by giving a suitable example, why the audience must always be considered when giving them information. (1 mark)

2 A car company is promoting a new model of a car and needs to use ICT to help with this promotion. They intend to use a variety of different media. Give three types of media which could be used and explain why each medium would be appropriate. (3 marks)

▶ Questions 3 | pp. 142–143

1 A science teacher in a school uses presentation software in her lessons.

(a) Explain how the use of templates will help her produce a set of slides on a certain topic in less time. (3 marks)

(b) Describe two features of the presentation software that will add interest to her presentation. (2 marks)

(c) The teacher has been asked to produce an interactive presentation at a parents evening. Describe two features that this interactive presentation should have. (2 marks)

2 (a) Like most software, presentation software needs the facility of the user being able to import and export files.
By using suitable examples, define each of these terms, making sure that you clearly differentiate between them. (5 marks)

(b) Data compression techniques are often used with files associated with presentation software. Explain what data compression is and why it is used in this case. (3 marks)

▶ Questions 4 | pp. 144–145

1 A supermarket uses a database containing details of all the products and their prices.

(a) (i) Describe what is meant by the word query. (1 mark)

(ii) Describe one query that the store could perform on the data in the database. (2 marks)

(b) Data in a database often needs to be either imported or exported.

Explain clearly a situation in the supermarket where this would be likely to occur. (2 marks)

(c) (i) Explain what is meant by the term report. (1 mark)

(ii) Describe two situations in a supermarket where a report would be required and for each one explain what the report would include. (2 marks)

▶ Questions 5 | pp. 146–148

1 Websites are often interactive as they allow users to decide what they want to do next.
Presentations can also be made interactive by the use of hyperlinks.

(a) Explain what is meant by a hyperlink and give an example of how a hyperlink could be used in a presentation. (2 marks)

(b) Other than hyperlinks, describe two features of interactivity in websites. (4 marks)

2 Web authoring packages are used by web designers to design and build websites for their clients.
Other than the formatting of text and graphics, explain three features of a web authoring package. (3 marks)

Exam support

Worked example 1

1 A school office uses word-processing and DTP software for the production of documents such as letters, reports, posters, newsletters, etc. Define each of the following functions of the software and give an appropriate example of how each could be used by the school.
   (a) templates
   (b) style sheets
   (c) mail merge. (6 marks)

Student answer 1

1 (a) Templates are pre-designed documents that you can use to produce brochures, newsletters, pricelists and so on. You can replace the text that is already there with your own text. The graphics and all the design features are already present.
   (b) Everyone has their own style when writing a document. So style sheets allow you to write your document in your own style.
   (c) Mail merge involves combining a list of names and addresses with a standard letter so that a series of similar letters is produced, each addressed to a different person.

Examiner's comment

1 (a) This is a reasonable answer and the student has clearly identified that there is placeholder text. However, they have said that the graphics and the design features are present, which is true, but they have failed to say that these graphics and design features can be altered by the user. They student has also failed to mention an example of templates being used for a task in a school.

   (b) This answer is completely wrong, and it looks as though the student has guessed.

   (c) For this, the student has clearly given a direct and well thought out definition of the word mail merge. However, they have failed to give any further explanation or an example in the context of a school.

Students must make sure that they answer all parts of the question, as it is so easy to miss a part out. It is clear from the definition that they fully understand, mail merge and could easily have given an answer in the context of a school.

Because of the lack of examples and the fact that one of the answers is completely wrong, the mark range applicable to this answer is 0–2 marks (see Examiner's answer for details of this). Some of the answers are quite good and the whole answer deserves a mark at the higher end of the mark range. The clarity of expression and the good grammar, spelling and punctuation also justify a higher mark in the range. **(2 marks out of 6)**

Exam support continued

Student answer 2

1 (a) Rather than create a design from scratch, you can use a design that has already been created. These designs are called templates and they have placeholders (grid lines, boxes, dummy text) for key elements – text and graphics. The school staff can add their own text and graphics and choose the appropriate typefaces and not have to worry about the design.

(b) Style sheets allow the creator of a document to maintain consistency. They also allow a person to make quick changes to headings or sub-headings, fonts and font sizes, and formatting such as bold and italics, throughout the document. This means that if the school secretary wants to change all the headings to a different font then this can just be done in one go, by applying the change to the style sheet.

(c) If a school secretary needed to send the same letter out to all parents, she could create a standard letter. This letter could then have spaces which can use information from the school database about the parents' names and addresses, to send each person an individualised letter. This would save a lot of time and effort.

Examiner's comment

1 (a) The student's answer is almost perfect, the student has clearly defined what a template is and how it can be used by the school. The student has also mentioned an advantage to the staff in using templates.

(b) Here, the student has explained how the style sheet is used to maintain consistency across the pages in a document. They have, however, omitted to explain exactly what a style sheet is. Instead, they have explained how it can be used. Students need to look at the wording of the question very carefully. The example the student has given is very good.

(c) Again the student has given an example rather than explain exactly what the term means. Giving an example in this way is fine provided you have defined the term as well. The example given by the student is good. **(4 marks out of 6)**

Examiner's answer

1 (a) Candidates define the function and give one example that is relevant to a school.
Templates are pre-designed documents that we can use to create brochures, posters, exam papers, advertisement, school prospectuses, etc.
You can replace the placeholder text and graphics with your own and it makes it easy to use and will be ideal for school admin staff who are beginners in using DTP as it means they are able to produce professional documents.

(b) Style sheets allow you to specify the formatting of a document so that you can maintain consistency in a document. It also means that to change the formatting you only need to change the formatting in the style sheet, and not go through the whole document changing the format of individual items. This will give documents like the school prospectus a standard look from page to page and section to section. It will also save the school admin staff time because they will not need to worry about formatting once the style sheet has been created.

(c) Mail merge involves combining a list of data from, for example, a database containing names and addresses, with a standard letter so that a series of letters are produced, each addressed to a different person. This could be used in a school for sending letters to parents about parents' evenings, school trips, truancy, etc.

5–6 marks

Candidates give a clear, coherent answer fully and accurately defining the term, the function of the software and an example of how it may be used. They use appropriate terminology and accurate spelling, punctuation and grammar.

3–4 marks

Candidates give definitions of two of the terms and how they might be used, but the examples given lack clarity. There are a few errors in spelling, punctuation and grammar.

0–2 marks

Candidates only give brief definitions of one of the terms and fail to give sensible and relevant examples as applicable to a school. The response lacks clarity, and there are significant errors in spelling, punctuation and grammar.

Worked example 2

2 A tourist information office decides to produce a self-running presentation of all the local attractions.

   (a) Define each of the following functions of the presentation software, and explain, using an appropriate example, how each function could be used in this situation.
       (i) Templates
       (ii) Animated transitions. (4 marks)

   (b) The tourist information office decides to also put much of this information on a website so that it can be accessed over the Internet from any computer.
       To produce the website, web authoring software is used.
       Give three functions of web authoring software, and for each function explain how the function may be used in this situation. (6 marks)

Student answer 1

2 (a) (i)   Templates are designs that you can put your own work into. This means you don't have to start from scratch so it saves you time.

       (ii) Animated transitions are transitions that move a bit like a cartoon. They make it fun for your audience to watch and can liven up a presentation.

   (b) Hyperlinks – they allow you to jump from one part of a webpage to another part. It makes the website interactive.
       Graphics – you can put pictures, maps and photographs of the local area and its attractions on the website.
       Text – you can describe all about the attractions and which ones are worth going to see.

Examiner's comment

2 (a) (i)   The definition is not quite clear but the second sentence makes it worth one mark as no example is given.

       (ii) The student has latched onto the word animation but does not know how it applies to presentation software. No marks here.

   (b)   Hyperlinks do not just allow you to jump to different parts of the same webpage. You can jump to a webpage on a different site. No example given so just about worth one mark.
              Graphics are a feature of the content and are not a function of the web authoring software, so no marks for this part.
              Text is content and not a function of web authoring software so no marks here.
              (2 marks out of 10)

Student answer 2

2 (a) (i) Templates allow you to set out the formatting for a multi-page website. For example, you can specify the font and the size of the font for all the various headings and subheadings for the webpages. This means that if you decide to change them, you only have to change them in the template.

(ii) Animated transitions are the way in which one side is replaced by another in a slideshow. For example, the slide can appear from the left, right, top or bottom of the page. It is also possible to animate the bullet points as they appear on the slide. The animations add interest to the slide show and will catch tourists' eyes when they are in the office.

(b) Cascading style sheets. It is important to keep consistency from one webpage to the next. Instead of applying the formatting to each block of text, you can set out all the formatting on a style sheet. What style sheets do is they separate the content from the formatting. If you need to change something such as a font, it only needs to be changed in the style sheet.

Hyperlinks. Hyperlinks allow you to link to other webpages, which may be on the same website or a different website. When a user clicks on the hyperlink they are taken automatically to the new webpage. For example, the website could have a hyperlink to an art gallery so that users can check the opening times and where exactly it is.

Mailto link. A mailto link allows a user to e-mail the owner of the website. For example, if a link wasn't working properly, then the user could let the tourist information office know so that it can be fixed.

Examiner's comment

2 (a) (i) The student is getting mixed up between style sheets and templates and they have given a definition of a style sheet. Remember that style sheets determine the style (i.e. the formatting of the document) whereas a template is a whole document where you can change the text, graphics, etc.
No marks for this part.

(ii) This is a clear definition of the term animated transitions and they have given a good example of their use so two marks are given here.

(b) This is a clear description of the function of cascading style sheets with a good example.
The functions of hyperlink and mailto have been clearly explained and the student has explained clearly how the functions could be used in the web authoring software.
Full marks are given here. **(8 marks out of 10)**

Examiner's answer

2 (a) (i) One mark for the definition and one mark for the example.
Templates are partly prepared documents which contain placeholder text and graphics which you can replace with your own to save you from starting from scratch.
An example would be to have a slide, containing the logo for the tourist information office, a graphic, a certain background colour and some text, which can be replaced quickly when a new slide needs to be produced.

(ii) One mark for the definition and one mark for the example.
Animated transitions refer to the way slides can appear on the screen or it can refer to the way individual components such as text or graphics appear on the screen.

For example, the slides for different attractions could appear from different directions to add impact to the slide show.

(b) One mark for the function and one mark for explaining how it might be used on a tourist information office website × 3.
The ability to add hyperlinks to other webpages.
The ability to use anchors to link to different sections of the same webpage.
The ability to use mailto links so that e-mails can be sent to the tourist information office.
Hotspots. Graphics or parts of maps that you can click on which act as hyperlinks.
Keyword search. This allows the website to be searched for a certain word or phrase.
The use of pull-down menus to make selections.
The use of interactive buttons.

Summary mind maps

Things to consider when presenting information

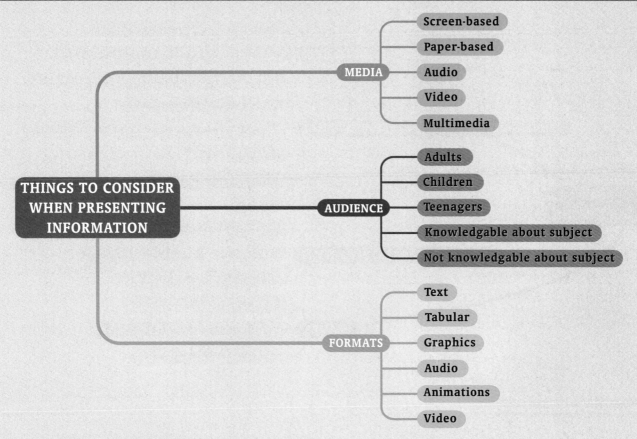

THINGS TO CONSIDER WHEN PRESENTING INFORMATION

- **MEDIA**
  - Screen-based
  - Paper-based
  - Audio
  - Video
  - Multimedia
- **AUDIENCE**
  - Adults
  - Children
  - Teenagers
  - Knowledgable about subject
  - Not knowledgable about subject
- **FORMATS**
  - Text
  - Tabular
  - Graphics
  - Audio
  - Animations
  - Video

Word-processing software

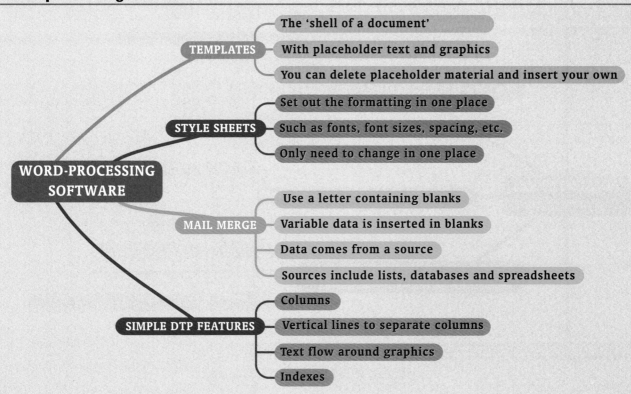

WORD-PROCESSING SOFTWARE

- **TEMPLATES**
  - The 'shell of a document'
  - With placeholder text and graphics
  - You can delete placeholder material and insert your own
- **STYLE SHEETS**
  - Set out the formatting in one place
  - Such as fonts, font sizes, spacing, etc.
  - Only need to change in one place
- **MAIL MERGE**
  - Use a letter containing blanks
  - Variable data is inserted in blanks
  - Data comes from a source
  - Sources include lists, databases and spreadsheets
- **SIMPLE DTP FEATURES**
  - Columns
  - Vertical lines to separate columns
  - Text flow around graphics
  - Indexes

Summary mind maps continued

DTP software

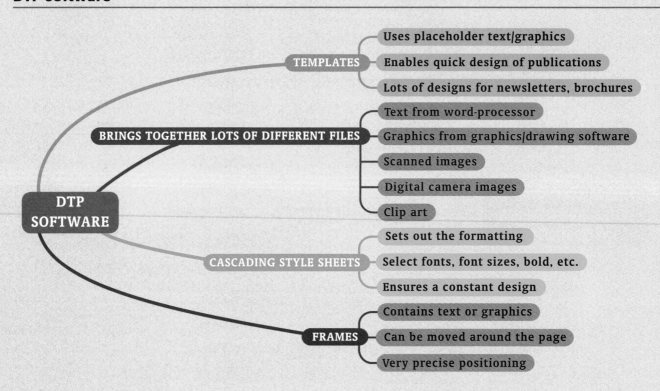

- **TEMPLATES**
  - Uses placeholder text/graphics
  - Enables quick design of publications
  - Lots of designs for newsletters, brochures
- **BRINGS TOGETHER LOTS OF DIFFERENT FILES**
  - Text from word-processor
  - Graphics from graphics/drawing software
  - Scanned images
  - Digital camera images
  - Clip art
- **DTP SOFTWARE**
- **CASCADING STYLE SHEETS**
  - Sets out the formatting
  - Select fonts, font sizes, bold, etc.
  - Ensures a constant design
- **FRAMES**
  - Contains text or graphics
  - Can be moved around the page
  - Very precise positioning

Presentation software

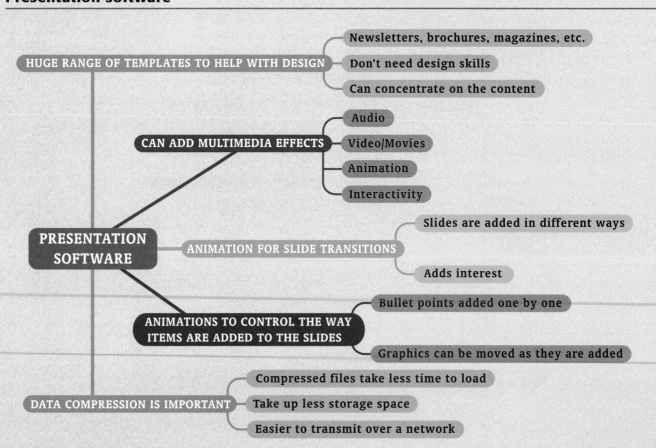

- **HUGE RANGE OF TEMPLATES TO HELP WITH DESIGN**
  - Newsletters, brochures, magazines, etc.
  - Don't need design skills
  - Can concentrate on the content
- **CAN ADD MULTIMEDIA EFFECTS**
  - Audio
  - Video/Movies
  - Animation
  - Interactivity
- **PRESENTATION SOFTWARE**
- **ANIMATION FOR SLIDE TRANSITIONS**
  - Slides are added in different ways
  - Adds interest
- **ANIMATIONS TO CONTROL THE WAY ITEMS ARE ADDED TO THE SLIDES**
  - Bullet points added one by one
  - Graphics can be moved as they are added
- **DATA COMPRESSION IS IMPORTANT**
  - Compressed files take less time to load
  - Take up less storage space
  - Easier to transmit over a network

Databases

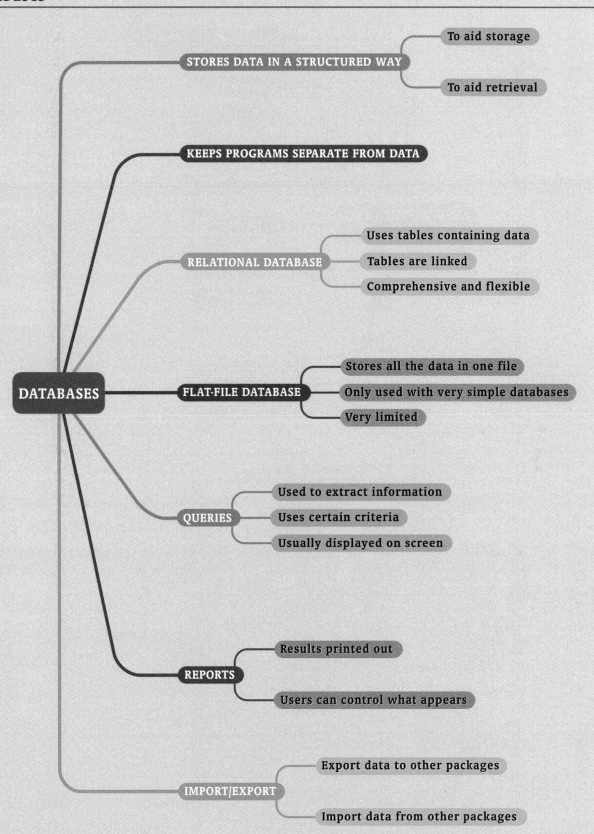

- **STORES DATA IN A STRUCTURED WAY**
  - To aid storage
  - To aid retrieval

- **KEEPS PROGRAMS SEPARATE FROM DATA**

- **RELATIONAL DATABASE**
  - Uses tables containing data
  - Tables are linked
  - Comprehensive and flexible

DATABASES

- **FLAT-FILE DATABASE**
  - Stores all the data in one file
  - Only used with very simple databases
  - Very limited

- **QUERIES**
  - Used to extract information
  - Uses certain criteria
  - Usually displayed on screen

- **REPORTS**
  - Results printed out
  - Users can control what appears

- **IMPORT/EXPORT**
  - Export data to other packages
  - Import data from other packages

Summary mind maps continued

Features of web authoring software

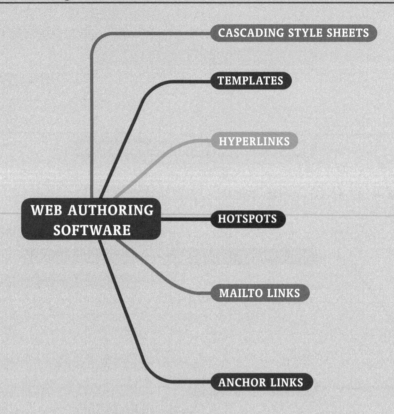

TOPIC 8: Networks

Nowadays most computers are connected to a network. If you connect your personal computer at home to the Internet then your computer becomes part of the network.

If a computer is used on its own without any connection (wireless or wire) to a network (including the Internet), then it is said to be a stand-alone computer.

The importance of being able to transfer data is the most important advantage in using a network and it is why networks are used in organisations of all sizes such as banks, schools, hospitals and shops as well as homes.

In this topic you will learn about the differences between networked and stand-alone computers and about LANs and WANs and the uses of the Internet, intranets and extranets.

▼ The key concepts covered in this topic are:

▶ Basic elements of an ICT network: network components

▶ Networks and stand-alone computers

▶ LANs and WANs

▶ The Internet, intranet and extranet

CONTENTS

Unit IT1 Information Systems

Basic elements of an ICT network: network components

▼ You will find out

▶ About communication devices

▶ About networking software

▶ About data transfer media

▶ About standards and procedures

Introduction

A basic network consists of a collection of computers and other hardware devices such as printers and scanners that are linked together so that they can communicate with each other.

Basic elements of an ICT network

There are four basic elements of an ICT network in addition to the computers themselves:

- communication devices
- networking software
- data transfer media
- standards and procedures.

Communication devices

Communication devices are those pieces of hardware that are needed to turn stand-alone computers into networked computers.

Network interface card (NIC)

Before a computer can be connected to a network it will need to have a network interface card. Most modern computers have these when you buy them. A network interface card is simply a card containing circuitry along with a socket. The socket allows the connection between the computer and the cabling. The card is simply slotted into the motherboard (the main circuit board) of the computer. The purpose of the network interface card is to convert the data from the form in which it is stored into a form that can be transmitted through the network media (e.g., metal cable, fibre optic cable or air).

Basically, a network interface card:

- prepares data for sending over the network
- sends the data
- controls the flow of data from the computer terminal to the transmission medium.

The socket on the NIC provides the connection to the transmission medium.

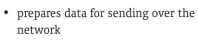

A network interface card (NIC).

Hub

A hub is a simple device which is used to join computers in a network so that they are able to share files and an Internet connection.

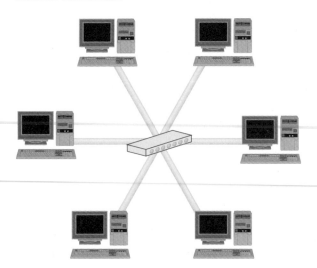

A simple network makes use of a hub.

Switches (network switches)

Switches are similar to hubs in that they are used to join multiple computers together in a network. Switches, however, contain more intelligence because they are able to inspect packets of data so that they are forwarded appropriately. Because a switch only sends a packet of data to the computer it is intended for, it reduces the amount of data on the network, hence speeding the network up.

Routers

Routers are hardware devices that join several wired or wireless networks together.

Routers are usually a combination of hardware and software which often act as gateways so that small home computer networks can be connected to the Internet using a single connection.

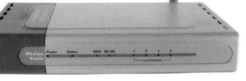

A wireless router.

Networking software

Networks need software to tell the connected devices how to communicate with each other.

Network operating systems software

Small networks can be run using existing Windows software, but for larger client-server networks, specialist network operating systems software is needed.

Network operating systems have more complexity because they need to coordinate the activities of all the computers and other devices connected to the network.

Examples of network operating system software include:

- UNIX
- Linux
- Novell Netware – this is a very popular client-server network operating system.

Network management software

If you were the network manager responsible for a network consisting of several hundred computers, you would need help in looking after them all to keep the network running.

Luckily there is software called network management software that will help you do this.

Some tasks the network management software would help with include:

- Making sure that all the computers have up-to-date software with the latest security patches, so that hackers cannot get into the network.
- Keeping track of the software being run on each computer and checking that there are licences for all the software being used.
- Keeping all application software up-to-date.
- Providing remote control facilities so that help-desk staff can sort a user's computer problem out by seeing exactly what is on the user's screen.
- Checking that bandwidth is being used correctly.
- Finding out if a user has installed non-licensed software without permission on a networked computer.
- Checking the speed of the processor and the memory used for a particular computer on the network. This can be useful to identify computers that need upgrades.

Data transfer media

Data transfer media is the material through which data travels from one computer to another in a network. For small, simple networks, this is usually wire, but many networks are now implemented wirelessly. Wires add considerably to the cost of a network, especially the cost of installing them.

The main forms of data transfer media are:

- metal wires
- fibre optic cable
- wireless.

Metal wires

Metal wires offer a high transmission speed but they do need to be installed

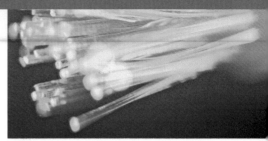

Fibre optic cable.

and this can be expensive. There are three different types of wire.

Unshielded twisted pair

The main features are:

- thin wires are twisted to help cancel out interference
- thin wires mean easier installation
- only suitable for small networks.

Shielded twisted pair

The main features are:

- wires are twisted
- wires have a copper braiding which protects the data signals from outside interference/corruption
- more expensive than unshielded twisted pair
- greater transmission speeds than unshielded twisted pair.

Non-metal cables

Light travels faster than electricity, so this is why in many networks pulses of light are used to carry data.

Fibre optic cable

In fibre optic cable, the data being passed is encoded as pulses of light through a very thin glass fibre. Bundles of fibres are used to carry the data to and from the network.

The main advantages of fibre optic cable are:

- speed – the data travels much faster
- small size – a huge amount of data can travel through a very small cable
- lack of electrical interference – they do not suffer from interference like metal wires.

The main disadvantage is:

- cost – the devices needed to connect up the cable and the cable itself are more expensive.

Basic elements of an ICT network: network components continued

No cables at all

Many computers are now able to connect to the Internet or communicate with other computers in a local area network wirelessly. With wireless communication, the data transfer medium is the air through which the radio waves travel.

Wireless

Wireless networks enable people to connect to the Internet or to a LAN wirelessly. This means they can work anywhere they can get a radio signal for their network.

Many people, especially people who travel a lot, need to access the Internet regularly. There are many public places where the Internet can be accessed wirelessly using a person's laptop computer or other portable devices such as mobile phone or PDA.

These places where you can access the Internet using Wi-Fi are called hot spots.

To set up a small Wi-Fi network you would need:

- a broadband connection to the Internet
- a router
- Wi-Fi enabled computers (most computers have a wireless adapter installed in them). You can buy wireless adapters for older computers.

Coffee bars

Airports

Train stations

HOT SPOTS

Hotels

Bars

Restaurants

Wireless Router   Power   Status   WAN   WLAN   1   2   3   4
Local Network

A wireless router used to set up a small wireless network in the home or office.

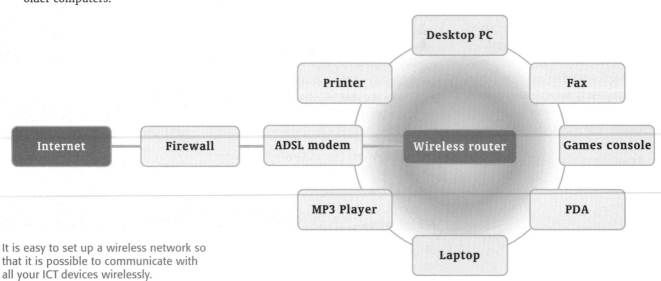

It is easy to set up a wireless network so that it is possible to communicate with all your ICT devices wirelessly.

Hot spot – a region where the Internet can be accessed wirelessly

Wi-Fi – a trademark for the certification of products that meet certain standards for transmitting data over wireless networks

How Wi-Fi works

1. The router is connected to the Internet by a high-speed broadband connection.
2. The router receives data from the Internet.
3. It transmits the data as a radio signal using an antenna.
4. The computer's wireless adapter picks up the signal and turns the radio signal into data that the computer can understand.

When sending data, the above processes work in reverse.

Advantages of Wi-Fi:

- allows inexpensive LANS to be set up without cables
- allows people the freedom of working anywhere a signal can be received
- ideal for networks in old listed buildings where cables would not be allowed to be installed
- global set of standards – you can use Wi-Fi all over the world.

Disadvantages of Wi-Fi:

- power consumption is high – which means laptops soon exhaust their rechargeable batteries
- there may be health problems in using Wi-Fi
- there may be security problems even when encryption is used
- home networks have a very limited range (e.g., 150 ft)
- can get interference if wireless network signals start to overlap.

Network standards and procedures

For devices to communicate with each other in a network certain standards need to be used. Standards are important because without them, one device could be sending data to another device in a form that the other device does not understand.

Manufacturers of devices that are connected to networks agree these standards so that the devices can work together. In order for a network to run properly it is necessary to adopt certain procedures and make sure that all users are aware of them. Without proper procedures:

- the security of the network may be compromised
- the network may run slowly
- users may fall foul of legislation (e.g., Data Protection Act, Computer Misuse Act, etc.)
- work may be lost
- actions may inconvenience or annoy other users
- actions may cost the organisation time in terms of employee time needed to sort out problems.

Wi-Fi zone sign.

Many users wish to free their computers of wires to connect them to the Internet. They want to be able to connect to the Internet from wherever they are.

Networks and stand-alone computers

▼ **You will find out**

▶ About the characteristics of networks and stand-alone computers

▶ About the relative advantages and disadvantages of networks

Introduction

In this section you will be looking at the characteristics of networks and stand-alone computers and the relative advantages and disadvantages of networks. You will see that the advantages far outweigh the disadvantages.

The characteristics of networks and stand-alone computers

When a computer is used on its own without any connection to other computers, it is said to be being used in a stand-alone environment. If data needs to be passed to another department, then it needs to be printed out on paper, or copied onto disk before being transferred by person to the other person for entry into their computer system. Information flow occurs all the time in organisations, so it makes sense to have a method that makes information exchange easier and faster,

such as by connecting the computers together by means of cables. A group of computers connected together in this way is called a computer network.

Advantages of a stand-alone environment

A stand-alone environment is where each computer is set up and used separately. Each computer will need its own copy of the operating system and the applications software being used. In addition they will use an individual set of data and if data needs to be passed from one computer to another then this will need to be performed manually.

There are some advantages in using stand-alone machines:

- Cheaper hardware and software – the wires, network cards and software needed to run a network are expensive, so stand-alone machines provide a cheaper option.

- Less IT knowledge needed – a greater degree of IT knowledge is needed to run a network successfully and this may mean a network manager/administrator should be employed.

- Fewer problems with viruses – virus infection will be less of a problem with stand-alone machines unless data and programs are transferred from one computer to another.

- Not as hardware dependent – less dependence on hardware. With some types of network, if the file server can't be used because of a technical problem, then this affects the whole network.

Disadvantages in using stand-alone computers

- Transfer of files between computers is sometimes necessary – users often work together on a project which means they need to transfer data from one computer to another using portable media such as CDs or flash drives. This is wasteful if CDs are used.

- Hard to keep data up-to-date – if two people are working with the same set of data, then care needs to be taken that two different versions are not produced, which can cause confusion. With a network only the one set of data is produced, so there is no such confusion.

- Harder to install software – with stand-alone computers, software has to be installed on each computer, whereas with a network you only install software on one computer, so time is saved during the installation.

Computers connected together so they are able to communicate with other computers are called networks.

- Harder to update software – you have to update the software on each computer with stand-alone computers.
- Backups need to be kept by each user – users of each computer have to be relied upon to take their own backups of their data.

Relative advantages and disadvantages of networks

There are many advantages of networking computers and they far outweigh the disadvantages. Advantages include:

Ability to share files – no need to make copies of files as all the files can be accessed by all the computers on the network if needed.

Ability to share hardware resources – no need to have a printer for each computer as any hardware device (e.g., printer, scanner, plotter, etc.) can be shared.

Ability to share software – software can be shared, meaning that everyone will be using the same version. Maintaining software by keeping it up-to-date is made much easier.

Lower software costs – it is cheaper to buy one network version with a licence for so many users compared to buying individual copies for each computer. It also saves time as only one copy needs to be installed on the server.

Improved security – it is easier for network managers to control access from computers to the Internet. It is much easier to make sure that any material from the Internet is checked with the latest virus checking software.

Easier to implement acceptable use policies – centralising applications software simplifies the process of implementing software policies in an organisation. Software policies refer to what software may be installed on computers and how it may be used.

Easier to back up files – backing up is performed by the network manager rather than the individual users. This means backing up is taken seriously and users are less likely to lose data.

Improved communication – networks have e-mail facilities which will improve communication between workers.

Central maintenance and support – new upgrades to software need only be added to the server. Network managers and support staff can see what the users are looking at on their screen, so they can be given help if they are having problems with a task.

Disadvantages include:

Technical knowledge needed – more IT knowledge is needed to run a network so specialist staff are usually needed.

Lack of access when file server fails – if a file server fails (i.e., goes down) the entire network may fail, which means that users might not be able to access files and data.

Cost – although a network will save money over time, there is the initial high cost of all the network equipment and training needed.

When you connect a stand-alone computer to the Internet using wires (or wirelessly), your computer will become part of a network. This laptop is connected using a cable but many laptops are connected wirelessly.

LANs and WANs

Introduction

Networks can be classified over the geographical area that they occupy and also whether or not they use third party telecommunications equipment or services.

In this section you will be looking at two different types of network called a LAN and a WAN.

ICT networks for different geographical scales and uses

ICT networks can be divided into two types:

- Local area networks (LANs)
- Wide area networks (WANs)

The geographical area covered by each of these networks is different with LANs being confined to a single building or site and WANs being distributed over multiple sites, even in other countries.

LANs

The main features of LANs are:

- Confined to single building or site – the hardware and communications equipment is contained in one building or site.
- Ownership of the communications equipment – the organisation actually own all the communications equipment (such as wiring, etc.) that links the terminals.

WANs

The main features of WANs are:

- Hardware is spread over a wide geographical area – devices (computers, point-of-sale terminals, storage, etc.) are spread over a wide geographical area. The devices are spread over multiple buildings and sites.
- Third party telecommunications equipment is used – hardware in a WAN is situated in many sites, which can be in different countries. Telephone, radio and satellite communications are needed, which are supplied by a third party (e.g., BT). The organisation with the WAN has to rent these services from a telecommunications supplier.

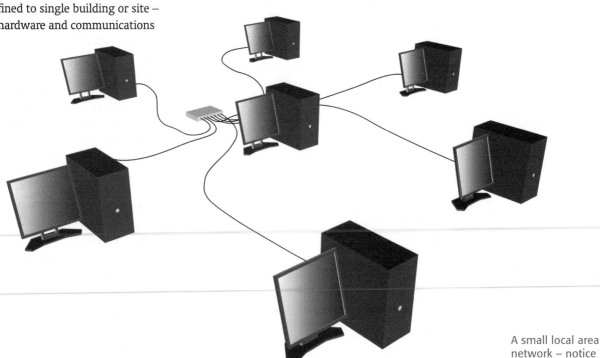

A small local area network – notice the central server

The Internet, intranet and extranet

▼ **You will find out**

▶ About the differences between the Internet and the World Wide Web

▶ About the characteristics of intranets and extranets

Introduction

In this section you will be looking at types of network that use Internet technology and the Internet itself. You will also be looking at the difference between the commonly used words the Internet and the World Wide Web.

The differences between the Internet and the World Wide Web

The Internet and the World Wide Web are not the same thing. Look carefully at the differences between the following definitions:

Internet – the Internet is a huge group of networks joined together. Each of these networks consists of lots of smaller networks. This means that the Internet consists of hardware.

World Wide Web (WWW) – the World Wide Web, simply called the Web, is a means of accessing information contained on the Internet. It is an information-sharing model that is built on top of the Internet. The World Wide Web uses HTTP, which is one of the languages used over the Internet, to transmit information. The World Wide Web makes use of browser software to access documents called webpages.

The Internet provides more services than accessing webpages.

Using the Internet you have:

- e-mail facilities
- instant messaging
- Usenet news groups
- FTP (file transfer protocol), which is a way of exchanging files between different computers connected to the Internet
- P2P (peer-to-peer) networking, which allows you to exchange files (usually MP3 files) with other users.

All of the above services require different protocols to that required by the World Wide Web.

The Internet is therefore the actual network whereas the World Wide Web is the accessing of webpages using the Internet. It is important to realise that the World Wide Web is only one of the facilities based on the Internet.

Intranets

An intranet is a private network that uses the same technology as that used by the Internet for the sending of messages around the network. The main use of an intranet is to share organisational information and share resources.

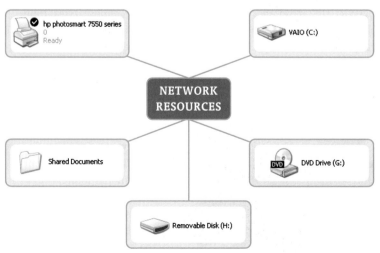

Some of the resources you can share on a network.

KEY WORDS

Extranet – extranets are intranets opened to select groups of users outside the company such as customers, suppliers, etc.

Intranet – private internal network which allows employees of an organisation to access information resources within the organisation

The concepts of client and server are used for the computers in an intranet along with the same protocols (HTTP, FTP and e-mail) as used by the Internet.

The main feature of an intranet is that only employees of the organisation are able to use it.

Please note that an intranet need not be confined to a single site and it is still possible for people on an intranet to access the Internet.

Extranets

The use of an intranet is restricted to employees of the organisation, whereas with an extranet, customers, suppliers and other partners, as well as the employees of the organisation, can access the information. Extranets are not accessible by the general public and this is ensured by the use of usernames and passwords. Because the people who need access to the information are not on the same site, data needs to be sent using third parties for the communication lines. Data can be sent via the Internet or it can be sent using the more expensive private communication lines which offer more security and performance.

If the Internet is used for the sending of the data in an extranet, the following security measures have to be put in place:

- gateways
- firewalls
- encryption
- user authentication.

The Internet, intranet and extranet continued

The Internet

Definition

The best way to describe the Internet is to call it a network of networks, enabling people to exchange and share data. There is no one person or government involved in the administration of the Internet and to many people this is one of its attractions. There are security problems with viruses, pornography, etc., but for most people the advantages of being able to reach other people all over the world and exchange ideas and information, far outweigh the disadvantages.

Benefits and developments

The Internet uses multimedia and interactivity extensively. Using multimedia means that you can access not only written words, but also pictures, music and sound effects. Interactivity means that the user can choose what they want to see just by the click of a mouse. The computer 'asks' users questions which they can then answer.

There are a huge number of benefits of the Internet and these include:

- more methods of cheap communication such as e-mail, text messaging, chat rooms, videoconferencing, webcam services, etc.
- video such as TV programmes, music video, instructional video, user-produced video (e.g., YouTube), video advertisements, etc.
- the ability to listen to almost any radio station around the world
- the ability to send and receive files
- the ability to run/download educational games and programs
- the ability to research information for school projects and business

- the opportunity to communicate with people from all around the world
- the opportunity to share resources and ideas with people that have the same interests
- the opportunity to shop on-line around the world without leaving your computer.

Disadvantages of the Internet

There are huge benefits obtained by Internet use but these come at a price because there are also some disadvantages with the Internet. Many of these disadvantages arise because there are no regulations or controls on the material that is placed on the Internet. Disadvantages of Internet use include:

- The ability to access inappropriate material – it is very easy for children to access inappropriate information and/or images by accident when performing searches. This material could include pornographic images or scenes of violence or cruelty.
- Children inadvertently forming 'friendships' with strangers – many paedophiles use chat rooms to form friendships with children.
- Cyberbullying – this is the use of the Internet or mobile phones to harass or intimidate another person.
- Advertising pressures – constant bombardment of advertising material by e-mail, etc., encourages people to take credit or buy goods they do not really want or need.

- Health problems – using the Internet extensively requires a lot of mouse movements and clicks, and this can lead to some health problems such as RSI (repetitive strain injury). Internet users often slouch in their chairs which can lead to back ache. Lack of exercise can lead to obesity.
- Privacy is eroded or lost – an Internet user has their privacy eroded because their surfing habits are watched and their e-mails are stored.
- Gambling addiction – there are a large number of sites devoted to on-line gambling, which is made much easier than traditional gambling, because you do not have to leave your house.
- Incorrect and inaccurate information – there are many sites on the Internet which deliberately set out to mislead you. Anyone can set up a site on the Internet and put their own information on the site which may be wrong. Only use trusted and reliable sites for information.

Communications

The Internet offers lots of different ways of communicating. For example:

- Instant messaging – where you can type in messages and receive replies almost in real time.
- Webcam services – where you can see and hear who you are chatting too.
- Cheap phone calls – you can make cheap Internet phone calls to anywhere in the world using a service called VOIP (voice over Internet protocol)
- Chat rooms – you can chat with your friends and family or people with similar interests to you.
- Text messaging – you can send and receive text messages to and from phones (mobile or landline) using the Internet.

The Internet is a global network.

E-mail services

An e-mail is an electronic message sent from one communication device (computer, telephone, mobile phone or PDA) to another. There is a huge range of e-mail services provided and these are covered in the next section.

Search

Search allows you to find an e-mail using keywords in the title or you can search for all the e-mails from or to a certain e-mail address.

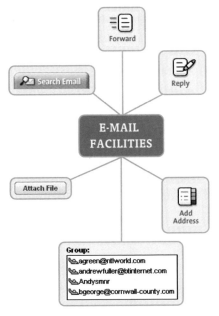

There are many e-mail facilities but the ones show here are the main time-saving ones.

Reply

This allows you to read an e-mail and then write the reply without having to enter the e-mail address. As the recipient can be sent both the original e-mail and your reply they can save time because they know what your e-mail is about.

Forward

If you are sent an e-mail that you think others should see, you can forward it to them. An e-mail, for example, sent to you by your boss, could be forwarded to everyone who works with you in a team.

Address book

In the address book are the names and e-mail addresses of all the people to whom you are likely to send e-mail. Instead of having to type in the address when writing an e-mail, you have just to click on the e-mail address or addresses in the address book.

You can get the e-mail software to automatically add people to your address book if they have sent you or you have sent them e-mail.

The screenshot on the next page shows an address book. Rather than type in the e-mail address of the recipients and maybe make mistakes, you can simply click on their address. Notice the facility to create groups.

Groups

Groups are lists of people and their e-mail addresses. They are used when a copy of e-mail needs to be distributed to people in a particular group. For example, if you were working as part of a team and needed to send each member the same e-mail, then you would set up a group. Every time you needed to send the members of the group e-mail, then you could just send the one e-mail to the group, thus saving time.

File attachments

You can attach files to e-mails. For example, you could attach a file containing a photograph of yourself obtained from a digital camera, a piece of clip art, a picture that you have scanned in, a long document, etc. Basically, if you can store it as a file, then you can attach it to e-mail.

You can attach more than one file to e-mail, so if you had six photographs to send, then you could attach and send them all at the same time.

Before you attach a file you must first prepare an e-mail message to send, explaining the purpose of your e-mail and also giving some information about the files that you are sending (what their purpose is, what file format they are in, etc.).

Once the e-mail message has been completed, you click on the file attachment button and select the file you want to send. A box will appear to allow you to select the drive, folder and eventually the file that you want to send.

If you want to send more than one file, repeat the file attachment process. Usually, if there is more than one file to send, then the files will be compressed to reduce the time taken to send them.

Voice mailboxes

Voice messages may be sent using a communications network where they are transformed into a digital form, which may be stored in the same way as for e-mail. When the user logs on to the system, they are informed that there is voice mail waiting for them and they may play this message back.

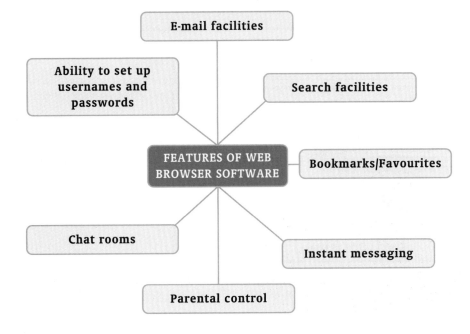

The Internet, intranet and extranet continued

Sharing data and ideas

The Internet allows people to work collaboratively (i.e. together) even if they are separated by a distance, as work is easily shared by file transfer or e-mail attachment. The Internet has made it possible for people around the world to share data and ideas. For example, doctors can hold videoconferences to learn about new surgical techniques.

Accessing information

Without leaving your home you can access the world's largest libraries for information. You can access dictionaries, encyclopaedias, atlases, thesauruses, research papers, timetables, etc. Generally speaking, if it is published, you will probably find it on the Internet.

Benefits of e-mail

- Virtually instantaneous – mail is sent immediately and a reply can be received as soon as the recipient checks their e-mail box.
- No need for the familiarity of a letter. E-mail is meant to be quick, direct and to the point. You do not need to worry about the odd typing or spelling mistake.
- You can easily attach a copy of the sender's message with your reply, which means that they do not have to search for the original message.
- If you discount the hardware and software which the user will probably already have, then an e-mail is virtually free to send.
- E-mails can be accessed using a large number of devices from mobile phones to television.
- More environmentally friendly, since less energy is used in delivering the mail from source to destination.

Disadvantages of e-mail

- Not everyone has e-mail, so ordinary post is still used.
- It may make users more casual about their approach to business and they may not realise that anything they say might be legally binding as if they had written it in a more formal document such as a letter or a contract.
- Junk mail is a problem, although there are software solutions that filter junk mail out from your important mail.
- There are worries about security aspects.

- The system relies on people checking their e-mail boxes regularly.
- E-mails, and particularly those containing file attachments, can contain viruses.
- E-mail is not secure and e-mails can be intercepted and read.

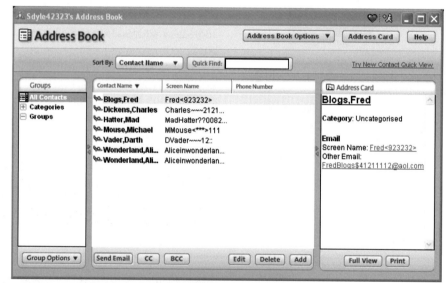

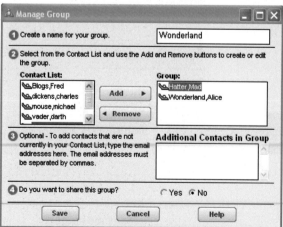

Using e-mail you can set up an address book and create groups of people who need to be sent the same e-mail.

FTP (file transfer protocol)

FTP, short for file transfer protocol, is a method (called a protocol) for exchanging files over the Internet. FTP transfers files in a similar way to the way webpages are transferred from the file server to the user's web browser when the user is viewing information using the Internet.

File transfer protocol transmits any type of file: computer programs, text files, graphics, etc., by a process which collects the data into packages. A package of data is sent and when received, the receiving system checks the package to make sure that no errors have been introduced during transmission. A message is than sent back to the sender system to let it know that the package is OK and that it is ready to receive the next package of data.

Newsgroups

A newsgroup is a place where data is stored in the form of messages from different users at different locations. Usually a newsgroup is a discussion group where people are able to post messages or replies to messages on a whole variety of topics. Basically, if you talk about it, then there will probably be a newsgroup about it.

Weblogs have replaced some of the uses of newsgroups.

Chat rooms

Chat rooms allow users to conduct real-time on-line conversations with others. They are usually provided as part of the many features offered by an Internet service provider and also by social networking sites such as MySpace.

Some chat rooms offer more than just text, as they can offer audio and video communication, for which a microphone, speakers and webcam are needed, which allows people to hear and see each other.

Webcams are often used in conjunction with chat rooms.

On-line shopping

Most people now do some on-line shopping, even if it is just for a few items such as books, CDs or music downloads. On-line shopping offers lots of advantages and there are a number of disadvantages. On-line shopping was looked at in detail on pages 65 and 121.

Accessing information using on-line databases

When you are searching for a holiday or flight, or even doing some on-line shopping, you are usually accessing an on-line database. On-line databases are used by companies to store the details of the services or stock. For example, when you book a flight you enter the dates, and the database is interrogated to extract the information.

Search engine selection

One way of finding information on the Internet is to use a search engine. A search engine is an Internet tool which will search for Internet sites containing the words that you designate as a search term. It provides results back to you in the form of links to those sites that have the term(s) you are looking for.

It is important to understand that search engines do not search the Internet itself. Instead they search databases of information about the Internet. Each search engine looks through a different database and that's why they each will reach different results from exactly the same terms. The detail recorded by search engines varies greatly. This is only one way in which search engines differ. Another difference is in the level of sophistication employed by the search engine when it looks through its database.

Using a search engine allows you to search for:

- webpages
- images
- other types of file.

There are a number of search engines in use and it is always worth looking at each to see the differences between them. Most people, however, usually use just the one and get used to using it.

When you enter your flight details into a website, you are actually setting out your search criteria for the on-line database of flights.

Questions

▶ Questions 1 | p. 166

1 At the central office of a landscape gardening company there are six employees. Each employee has a stand-alone computer system and printer. The company director commissioned a business survey which indicated that it would be more efficient if the six PCs were formed into a network.
State three benefits that the company would gain from networking their computer systems. **(3 marks)**

2 A local doctors surgery uses a number of stand-alone computer systems to manage patient records, appointments, staff pay and all financial accounts. The surgery manager is considering changing to a local area network.
Compare the relative advantages of using stand-alone computers and a local area network. **(6 marks)**

3 Give the names of three devices whose resources may be shared using a network. **(3 marks)**

4 An organisation has now decided that it needs a network.
By giving suitable examples, other than sharing hardware devices, and the sending and receiving of e-mail, describe three benefits that networking would give the organisation. **(3 marks)**

▶ Questions 2 | p. 166

1 Give two differences between a local area network (LAN) and a wide area network (WAN). **(2 marks)**

2 Most schools use networked computers to form a LAN rather than use stand-alone computers.
(a) Explain the difference between computers in a LAN and stand-alone computers. **(2 marks)**

(b) Describe two advantages to the students in using a LAN rather than using stand-alone computers. **(2 marks)**

(c) Describe two disadvantages to the students in using a LAN rather than using stand-alone computers. **(2 marks)**

▶ Questions 3 | pp. 167–171

1 Intranets and extranets are now very popular networks for large and small organisations.
(a) Give two features of an intranet. **(2 marks)**
(b) Give two features of an extranet. **(2 marks)**

2 (a) Intranets are very popular in organisations such as schools. By giving appropriate examples, describe how an intranet is useful to a school. **(4 marks)**
(b) Most schools allow the students restricted access to the Internet. Explain, by giving suitable examples, how the Internet is useful to students in schools and colleges. **(6 marks)**

3 Explain what a search engine is and how it is useful to someone using the Internet to find information such as train or flight times. **(3 marks)**

4 There is a lack of control over the Internet, and this causes a number of social problems, particularly for parents who have young and impressionable children. Discuss the problems caused by the Internet, and in your discussion you should cover chat rooms, e-mail and the appropriate use of search engines. **(6 marks)**

5 A teacher with a good knowledge of ICT in a primary school has decided to create an intranet for the school.

(a) Explain clearly, what is meant by an intranet. **(2 marks)**
(b) Give one advantage to the teaching staff in having an intranet. **(1 mark)**
(c) Give one advantage to the administration staff in having an intranet. **(1 mark)**
(d) Give one advantage to the students in having an intranet. **(1 mark)**

6 A software developer is working as part of a team of ten developers who are developing new software for an on-line loan company. The team members work in different parts of the country.
The developers need to keep in touch with each other and need to pass work (mainly programs, screen designs, etc.) to each other.
(a) Explain three advantages of the developers contacting each other by e-mail rather than by post. **(6 marks)**
(b) Describe two facilities provided by e-mail software that will make it a lot easier to work as a team. **(4 marks)**

Exam support

Worked example 1

1 (a) Explain what is meant by the term intranet. (2 marks)
   (b) Explain what is meant by the term extranet. (2 marks)

Student answer 1

1 (a) An intranet is an internal network and can be used for sending internal data. Internal data could include internal mail and information about the organisation.
   (b) An extranet is an external network and can be used for sending external data.

Examiner's comment

1 Part (a) is correct about the internal network but the second part needs to be more specific to gain the second mark. They needed to say, for example, that '... for sending internal data such as e-mails'.

In part (b) the main point that needs to be made is that data needs to be shared by people who are external to the organisation yet still need shared data. This is not specific enough to gain any marks.
(1 mark out of 4)

Examiner's answers

1 (a) One mark for what it is and one mark for how it can be used.
       An intranet is an internal network that can be used by all the employees of an organisation for the sending of internal e-mail, sharing diaries, sharing data, etc.
   (b) One mark for what it is and one mark for how it can be used.
       An extranet is an external private network which is made available to an organisation and their trading partners so they can share information about orders and payments.

Student answer 2

1 (a) An intranet uses the same technology as the Internet but is used internally within an organisation for the sharing of data such as internal e-mail, internal phone directories, health and safety policies and other information about the internal workings of the organisation.
   (b) An extranet again uses Internet technology and is used to allow trading partners such as customers and suppliers, who are outside the organisation, to access certain data. In order to access the extranet, someone outside the organisation will need the relevant permission and will need to have a user-ID and a password.

Examiner's comment

1 Part (a) is a good answer. They should have said it is a network – it is always best to assume that you are explaining it to someone with only a basic knowledge. This part is still worth the two marks.
Part (b) is a good answer but needed to mention that it is network and that it is a private network and only authorised persons are able to access it.
Still worth two marks though. **(4 marks out of 4)**

Worked example 2

2 A kitchen design company has 12 employees and each of them has their own stand-alone computer with ink-jet printer. CAD and other popular software is stored on all of the computers and users store their files on their own computers.
The owner of the company has suggested that it might be better to network these computers.
Discuss the likely benefits to the company from networking the computers. (6 marks)

Exam Support continued

Student answer 1

2 It is much easier for the staff to share files over a network as all the files can be accessed from any of the computers on the network. This means that several people can work on the same plan at the same time.

The staff can also send each other e-mails, and they will also have Internet access, which will allow them to do all sorts of things.

Security will be improved because there is no need to take backups as someone else will do it for you.

When the boss is not around, you will be able to use the Internet for downloading games or doing your shopping.

Examiner's comment

2 The first two sentences refer to the ability to share files and work collaboratively. The third sentence about e-mail is correct, but there is a vague statement about 'all sorts of things'. The student needs to be precise about what they mean here. The security aspect is poorly expressed and what they probably meant to say is that the network manager would take backup copies of the data that would be centrally held on the network. The last statement which refers to what they might do when the boss is not around is obviously not an advantage to the kitchen design company. The student needs to make sure that they are only giving advantages to the company.

There are probably only two distinct benefits explained here. However, only one of them provides a comprehensive description of the benefit.

From the mark banding information at the bottom of the Examiner's answer, you will see that this answer is worth three marks. **(3 marks out of 6)**

Examiner's answer

2 Students may include a range of the following:

It is much easier to work collaboratively

You do not need to spend time installing the same software on multiple machines

It is easier to update software centrally rather than have to add the updates to each machine

Staff would not need to use portable media to exchange files between machines which will save time

Network managers take backups centrally

It is easier for a technician to see if any upgrades are needed because they can see this from one central place

Can share hardware devices such as printers and plotters

Network versions of software are often cheaper than buying multiple stand-alone versions

Student answer 2

2 Hardware resources, such as laser printers, plotters, scanners, fax machines, etc., may be shared by all the users and this will mean that fewer but better quality pieces of hardware can be purchased. There will be central maintenance and support. For example, if new upgrades are needed then these need only be added to the file server, instead of updating all the stand-alone machines.

There will be improved communication between users. All networks can use electronic mail, which means it is quick and saves paper. Network versions of software are available, making it cheaper than buying individual copies for stand-alone machines. Data files can be shared amongst all the users without any need for duplication. This means they will not have to copy files onto removable media such as CD or flash drives to transfer the files between computers.

Internet access will also be provided, which means that e-mails, with file attachments such as plans, can be sent direct to clients for their comments.

Examiner's comment

2 This is a very good answer. Not only does it contain three clear and relevant advantages, it is also well written, with correct grammar and spelling.

Correct terminology has been used where relevant, and the whole discussion is well structured.

This is the type of answer produced by a very strong student who clearly understands the topic well.

Looking at the banding for the marks in the Examiner's answer, you will see that this answer is worth between five and six marks.

As the Examiner thinks this is a very good answer, full marks are given. **(6 marks out of 6)**

5–6 marks

Candidates give a clear, coherent answer fully and accurately describing and explaining at least three distinct benefits. They use appropriate terminology and accurate spelling, punctuation and grammar.

3–4 marks

Candidates give explanations of some benefits, but responses lack clarity. There are a few errors in spelling, punctuation and grammar

0–2 marks

Candidates simply list up to three benefits or give a brief explanation of one or two. The response lacks clarity and there are significant errors in spelling, punctuation and grammar.

Summary mind maps

Basic elements of an ICT network: network components

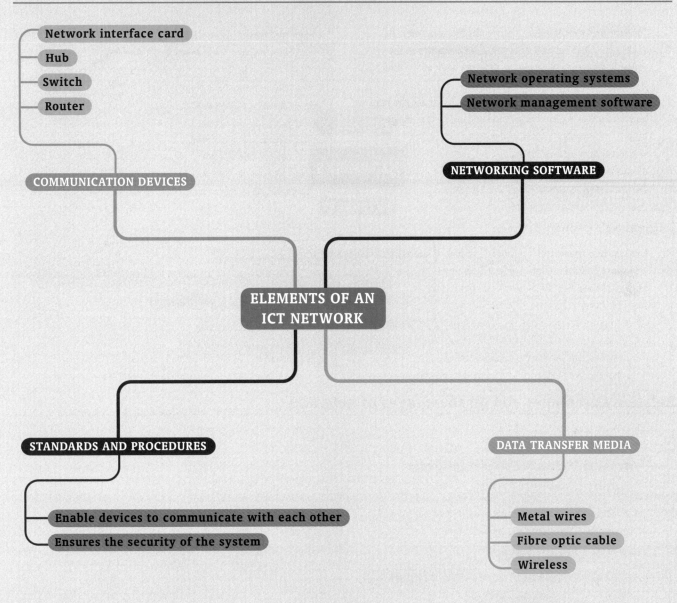

Intranets and extranets

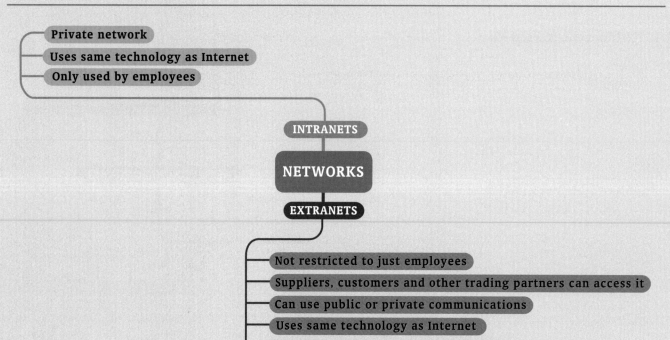

- Private network
- Uses same technology as Internet
- Only used by employees

INTRANETS

NETWORKS

EXTRANETS

- Not restricted to just employees
- Suppliers, customers and other trading partners can access it
- Can use public or private communications
- Uses same technology as Internet
- Need user-ID and password to access

Relative advantages and disadvantages of networks

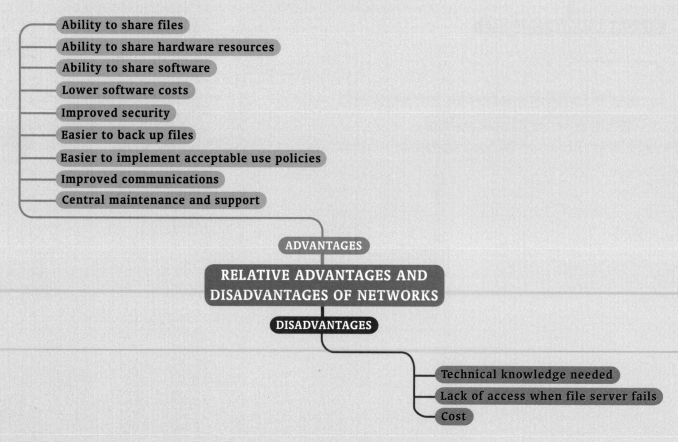

- Ability to share files
- Ability to share hardware resources
- Ability to share software
- Lower software costs
- Improved security
- Easier to back up files
- Easier to implement acceptable use policies
- Improved communications
- Central maintenance and support

ADVANTAGES

RELATIVE ADVANTAGES AND DISADVANTAGES OF NETWORKS

DISADVANTAGES

- Technical knowledge needed
- Lack of access when file server fails
- Cost

ICT systems are designed for people and are used by people for a particular purpose. In this topic you will be looking at the characteristics of users and how ICT systems need to take these characteristics into account. You will also be looking at how users interact with ICT systems and why this is important when providing systems that should communicate effectively with users. You will look at different types of user interface and their relative advantages and disadvantages.

▼ The key concepts covered in this topic are:

▶ The need for effective dialogue between humans and machines

▶ Appropriate interface design to provide effective communication for users

▶ The need to design human–computer interfaces that take into account the task, user experience, user preference and resources

CONTENTS

Unit IT1 Information Systems

Human–computer interface requirements

You will find out

▶ About the need for effective dialogue between humans and machines

▶ About the need for appropriate interface design to provide effective communication for users

▶ About the need to design human–computer interfaces that take into account the task, user experience, user preference and resources

▶ About general features of the human–computer interface

Introduction

Humans need to interact with ICT systems and this needs to be done in the most effective way, taking into account the characteristics of the users. There needs to be an effective dialogue between humans and machines. The commonest interface involves using a graphical user interface (GUI), with the user issuing instructions and making selections using the mouse. In this section you will be looking at the different types of user interface and how user interfaces can be designed to provide effective communication between the ICT systems and users.

The need for effective dialogue between humans and machines

When using any ICT device, there needs to be a dialogue between the machine and the human user. The user needs to be able to issue instructions to the device to tell it what to do and the device needs to tell the user what to do or, if there is a problem, what that problem is.

Human–computer interfaces provide the means by which the user can tell the computer what to do and at the same time the computer can interact with the human user by giving them a response. These interfaces are important because they determine how easy it is to use the ICT system to do a certain task.

The standard interface for the human inputting data into the computer is via the keyboard with the computer giving its response on the screen. This is not the only type of human–computer interface, although it is fair to say that it is the most common. There are many other systems that make use of ICT and need another type of interface. Process control screens, digital TVs, mobile phones,

computer games, cockpit controls on fly-by-wire aircraft, information systems that can be used by members of the public, all make use of innovative user interfaces.

Appropriate interface design to provide effective communication for users

If you are playing a game such as simulating driving a Formula One racing car around the track, then you would want the game to be as realistic as possible. You can easily show the view of the cockpit on a computer and it is easy to show the indicators and the instruments on the screen. All this adds to the realism. The part that would let the game down might be the human–computer interface. The worst interface would be using the cursor keys and other keys to steer the car, change gear, accelerate and so on. A better interface would be to use a joystick, although this will not be ideal as cars are normally fitted with steering wheels, gear sticks and foot pedals. You can actually buy these to make the interface as near to the real thing as possible.

The interface must be designed to enable the user to communicate effectively with the device and to also enable the device to communicate with the user.

The need to design human–computer interfaces that take into account the task, user experience, user preference and resources

When designing a human–computer interface the following need to be taken into account:

- task
- user experience
- user preference
- resources.

Specially designed input devices rather than the traditional keyboard and mouse are used with games.

Task

Different tasks require different human–computer interfaces. For example, a person using a CAD workstation will usually have attended training courses on how to use the software. They will be using the software on a daily basis, so their requirement will be to produce the diagrams and plans in the least amount of time. They will want to have as much on the screen as possible, so it does not matter if the screen is cluttered – they are used to it.

Software to teach a primary school pupil about words would have to have a very simple interface that is easy to understand and uncluttered. A games interface would have to be realistic, so in a racing car simulation, for example, you would expect to steer with a steering wheel rather than a joystick.

User experience

A user with lots of experience will want to complete the tasks in as little time as possible. They will want to accomplish the task in as few keystrokes as they can. Beginners will not be too bothered about how long the tasks takes, the main thing is to provide an easy to use interface that will enable them to complete the task.

User preference

Experienced users may prefer to issue commands at the keyboard if it is faster than pulling down menus or clicking on icons. Most software offers different ways of using it, so that the needs of novice and experienced users are both satisfied. For example, in Microsoft Office software, you can usually use icons, pull-down menus and issue commands using the keyboard to do the same thing. The user is then free to choose which they prefer.

Resources

Sophisticated human–computer interfaces require more processing power and memory, and this might be a problem when using older computers. Some specialist biometric input devices are very complex and are therefore expensive. Some software, such as speech recognition software, can be expensive.

General features of the human–computer interface

The human–computer interface is provided by a combination of hardware and software. If the software only uses keyboard input, then the design of the software alone will decide the ease of use of the interface.

The following is a list of things which should be considered when designing a human–computer interface:

Use of appropriate input methods

- reduce the use of the keyboard to avoid the onset of RSI
- use an ergonomic keyboard
- use an ergonomically designed mouse to avoid the likelihood of contracting RSI
- reduce to a minimum the number of mouse movements to carry out a task.

Use of colour

- pastel shades are easier on the eye, so avoid bright-coloured interfaces unless they have young children as their main users
- use appropriate text and background colour with plenty of contrast
- avoid using certain colours such as red and green for which some people are colour blind
- colours can make things easier to learn.

Icons (small pictures) are used with most graphical user interfaces.

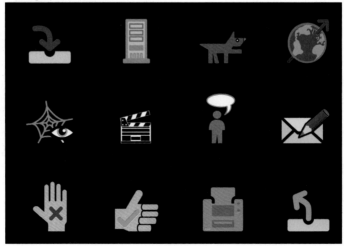

Consistency

- there should be consistency between similar pages, as this makes the system easier to learn
- similar pieces of software in the same range, should have similar human–computer interfaces as this makes it easier to learn
- objects (buttons, menus, icons, etc.) should be positioned in the same place, as users expect to see them in the same position, even though it is different software.

Use pictures/icons

- young children associate better with pictures, rather than words
- they help children choose the correct option
- they make the interface easier to learn.

Use of text

- use a font that is easy to read
- use an appropriate font size
- if the interface is aimed at children, do not use language that young children will not understand
- for interfaces designed for young children, keep sentences short
- do not give users too much to remember.

Sound

- add sound to make the interface more interesting
- allow sound to be turned off in case it distracts
- sound is essential for partially sighted users.

Types of human–computer interface

▼ You will find out

▶ About the need to provide the user with a method of communicating with the computer

▶ About the different types of interface

▶ About the relative advantages and disadvantages of each type of interface

▶ About the main features of a graphical user interface

Introduction

Software has to be able to communicate in some way with the user in order to be effective. It is important that the hardware and software allow this interaction in the easiest and most efficient way for the user.

There are three main types of interface:

- Command line/driven interface – here you have to type in a series of commands. This type of interface is very hard to use.
- Menu-driven interface – here you are presented with a list of things to do and you have to choose one of them by typing in either a number or a letter. These are easy to use but are limited in the sorts of things you can do with them.
- Graphical user interface (GUI) – these are very easy to use and have all the features such as windows, icons, menus, pointers, etc.

There are also other interfaces such as natural language interfaces and form-driven interfaces.

Command line/driven interfaces

Command line interfaces are interfaces where you have to type in commands in a certain language (a bit like a programming language) in order to get the computer to do something.

The commands had to be precise and correctly worded in order that the computer understood them. This was their problem. It made it difficult for an inexperienced user to use them.

> List Employee No, Surname
> For Job = "Production"

When commands are entered like this, a common interface is used.

Advantages of a command line interface:

- Quicker – in some instances you can do a task quicker by typing a command line rather than using the mouse and all the features of Windows.

Disadvantages of a command line interface:

- Very difficult for beginners to use – you have to learn the structure (called the syntax) of commands.
- Have to remember instructions – hard to remember the instructions/ commands you need to do a particular task.

Graphical user interfaces (GUIs)

Graphical user interfaces (GUIs) are very popular because they are easy to use. Instead of typing in commands, you enter them by pointing and clicking at objects on the screen. Microsoft Windows and Macintosh OS are examples of graphical user interfaces.

The main features of a GUI include:

- Windows – the screen is divided into areas called windows. Windows are useful if you need to work on several tasks.

- Icons – these are small pictures used to represent commands, files or windows. By moving the pointer and clicking, you can carry out a command or open a window. You can also position any icon anywhere on your desktop.
- Menus – menus allow a user to make selections from a list. Menus can be pop-up or pull-down and this means they do not clutter the desktop whilst they are not being used.
- Pointers – this is the little arrow that appears when using Windows. The pointer changes shape in different applications. It changes to an 'I' shape when using word-processing software. A mouse can be used to move the pointer around the screen. Other input devices can be used to move the pointer such as light pens, touch pads and joysticks.
- Desktop – this is the working area of the GUI and where all the icons are situated.

Windows is a graphical user interface.

- Drag and drop – this allows you to select objects (icons, folders, files, etc.) and drag them so that you can perform certain operations on them such as drag to the recycle bin to discard, add a file to a folder, copy files to a folder and so on.
- Taskbars – show the programs that are open. This facility is handy when working on several programs together.

Important note – although most systems software makes use of a GUI, this can be used with any software. For example, most applications software uses a GUI. Other examples of devices making use of a GUI include mobile phones, satellite navigation systems, etc.

Advantages of GUIs:

- No language needed – in the past you had to type in certain instructions to communicate with the computer.
- Use of icons – novice users can simply select programs or things they want to do by pointing and double clicking.
- Easier to use a mouse – most users would prefer to use a mouse to point and click rather than use the keyboard.

Disadvantages of GUIs:

- More memory is needed – sophisticated GUIs have large memory requirements so older computers may need upgrading or new computers bought.
- Increased processing requirements – faster and more powerful processors are needed to run the latest GUIs. This could involve upgrading the processor or buying new computers.

EXAM TIP

Make sure that you use the technical language in your answers. This is AS-level and you cannot get away with general answers – use the Key words correctly.

Menu-driven interfaces

Here a user is presented with a list of options and they type in the letter or number of their selection.

Advantages:

- A simple interface which is very easy to use.

Disadvantages:

- Only suitable where there are a few items to select from on the menu.

A menu-driven interface.

Form-driven interfaces

Form-driven interfaces are used to collect information from a user in a step-by-step manner. The user supplies this information by typing it into a form. Validation checks ensure that the customer only enters valid data into the form and that all the important fields are completed.

The form below is an on-line booking form for a holiday. Notice the red asterisks next to some of the fields. These fields contain presence checks, which means the user always has to enter data for these fields for the booking to be continued to the next stage.

Natural language interfaces

This is an interface that allows the user to interact using natural written or spoken language (e.g., English) as opposed to computer language and commands. It has the advantage that learning how to use it is easy because it uses words we are all familiar with and can remember.

The main problem with a natural language interface is that natural language is so ambiguous at times so it is necessary to restrict the language to certain words.

EXAM TIP

Natural language interfaces do not always use voice recognition – in many you have to type phrases the way you would do in ordinary language to extract information from an ICT system.

Passenger Details

Please enter passenger names to match those shown on your passports.　　　　　　　Pay ▶

	Title	First Name		Initial	Surname	
Adult 1	Mr ▾		*			*	Lead Passenger (Must be 18 years or over)
Adult 2	Mr ▾		*			*	

Please provide Lead Passenger Details

House Name		Daytime Phone No.		*
House No		Mobile Phone No.		
Address		*		
		Email Address		*
Town/City		*	Re-enter Email Address		*
County				
Post Code		*	All fields marked * must be completed	

Example of form-driven interface

Voice interfaces

Voice interfaces are becoming more popular as voice is the main way humans communicate with each other. Speech systems often involve two parts – the part where the system recognises what you are saying and the part that gives you instructions or information.

Voice/speech recognition systems

Voice/speech recognition systems allow you to enter data via a microphone directly into a computer. Basically you dictate the data into the computer. The only additional resources needed in addition to a computer are a microphone and the voice recognition software.

Voice recognition is ideal for entry of data into word-processing software or into a structure such as a database by people such as lawyers, doctors, etc., who only use ICT systems as part of their job. Voice recognition can also be used to dictate and send e-mails as well as enter commands into the operating system.

Voice recognition software turns voice into text.

Advantages of voice recognition include:

- Faster than typing – (up to 160 words per minute, which is three times the average typing speed).
- 99% accuracy – provided time has been spent teaching the computer about your voice.
- Cheap – many computers come with a microphone, so the only cost is the cost of the software.

A pen tablet.

Disadvantages of voice recognition include:

- Takes a while to get used to – can be frustrating for beginners to use.
- Not accurate at first – you may need to train the system about your voice. This is done by entering data and then correcting the mistakes the system has made.
- Errors due to background noise – few people have their own offices. Usually there is lots of background noise (people talking, telephones ringing, etc.). These can cause errors as the system tries to interpret these sounds.
- Does not work with all database software.

Speech synthesis

Speech synthesis enables a computer to read text that has been typed in or it can be used to give some sort of response such as the direction instructions in a satellite navigation system.

Graphical devices

Using a keyboard or a mouse can be difficult especially if you want to produce a doodle or a rough diagram, or maybe you want to mark comments on a design on the screen. The pen tablet shown here works the way a human would, using a pen and paper. Graphics pads are often used with CAD workstations or other design software to enter shapes, patterns, lines, etc., rather than use menus on the screen. The main advantage is that all of the screen can be used as the working area for the design and is not taken up by menus, toolbars, etc.

Game-playing devices

There are a number of input devices used with games that improve the human–computer interface by making it more realistic. Here are just some of them:

Joysticks allow control of games. This one is cordless and contains many different buttons which can be programmed by the games software.

A cordless games controller makes it easier to use the game rather than use a mouse and keyboard or even a joystick.

A steering wheel for a racing car simulation.

Proper clutch, brake and accelerator pedals improve the HCI.

A gear change will make the HCI even more realistic.

Output devices

There are also some output devices to make games more realistic:

Large plasma screens to make the game more realistic by it being life-size.

Surround sound speakers add realism to many games.

A gaming headset acts as an input device with the microphone used to issue commands and also the ear pieces to hear the realistic sound.

Touch-sensitive screens

Touch-sensitive screens allow a person to make selections by simply touching the screen. They are used as input devices for purchasing train tickets or used as information points in tourist information offices, art galleries and museums. They can also be used to provide information on services provided by banks and building societies. Mobile phones use them, as do satellite navigation systems.

The main advantage of the touch screen as an input device is that it is so simple and capable of being used by almost anyone. Touch-sensitive screens are often used as part of point-of-sale terminals in petrol stations and restaurants such as McDonalds because of their ease of use compared to keyboards.

Many mobile phones make use of a touch screen.

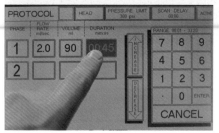

This process control system uses a touch screen for the human–computer interface.

Satellite navigation systems.

Biometric devices

There are many ICT systems that can recognise a particular person by certain biological properties of that person such as:

- the pattern of blood vessels on the retina at the back of the eye
- fingerprints
- hand prints
- voice
- face.

Any one of these can be used to identify a person to the computer system. This is an ideal human–computer interface, as it does not involve anyone having to understand how to type and there is nothing to remember such as a swipe card.

Biometric devices are used for:

- registration systems in schools and colleges
- recording employees as they arrive at and leave work
- limiting access to computers only to authorised staff.

Future uses include:

- passport control
- admission to clubs/bars.

Information kiosk.

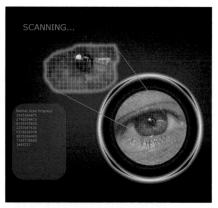

Iris recognition is used to identify a person using the pattern of blood vessels on the back of the eye, which is unique to each inividual.

Fingerprint recognition can be used to gain access to rooms or computers as well as for registration systems in schools or colleges.

Questions

● **Questions 1** pp. 178–181

1 UNIX is a make of operating system and it uses both a GUI and a command line interface.
   (a) Explain the meaning of the term operating system. (2 marks)
   (b) What does the abbreviation GUI stand for? (1 mark)
   (c) Briefly explain **one** difference between a GUI and a command line interface. (1 mark)
   (d) New users tend to prefer a GUI, whilst an experienced user may prefer to use a command line interface. Give **one** reason for this. (1 mark)

2 For users to interact with computers there needs to be an interface. An interface can be hard or easy to use and the most popular interface is the graphical user interface (GUI).
   State **three** factors of a GUI and for each one describe briefly how it aids the communication between the user and the computer. (6 marks)

3 A website designer is developing a website aimed at retired people.
   State, giving reasons, three things they would need to consider in their design of the human–computer interface for these users. (3 marks)

● **Questions 2** pp. 182–183

1 Speech recognition systems are more accurate and easier to use than in the past.
   (a) Give two advantages to a user in using a speech recognition system. (2 marks)
   (b) Describe two different ways in which a speech recognition system could be used. (2 marks)
   (c) Speech recognition systems are sometimes not 100% accurate. Give two possible reasons for this. (2 marks)

2 Touch screens can often be seen at tourist information offices. Give one advantage of using a touch screen as an input device for use by the general public. (1 mark)

3 A different human–computer interface would be needed for each of the following users:
   (i) a young child in a primary school
   (ii) a partially sighted adult
   (iii) a person who works on complex plans and drawings produced using CAD.
   For each of these uses, describe and justify features of the human–computer interface that are needed. (6 marks)

Exam support

Worked example 1

1 There are an increasing number of computers in the home being used by young children to help them learn.

  (a) Discuss the importance in having a human–computer interface that is appropriate for the use of young children. In your discussion you need to refer to appropriate examples and discuss the aspects of both hardware and software that will improve the interface for these users. **(6 marks)**

  (b) There is a worry that repeated use of ICT by young children could lead to a number of health problems. Name one such health problems and suggest how the use of an appropriate human–computer interface could help prevent it. **(2 marks)**

Student answer 1

1 (a) Use a large mouse as an input device so that young children can use it.

Picture hot spots and icons need to be large, as young children cannot move the mouse on the correct part as easily as adults.

Use plenty of colour, as young children like lots of colour.

Make sure that the icons, pictures and text are uncluttered on the screen.

(b) Repetitive strain injury (RSI) caused by repeated clicks and movements of the mouse. To solve this problem they should be given an ergonomic mouse, which has been specially designed to prevent RSI from occurring.

Examiner's comment

1 (a) The first answer gains no marks because they have only named the device and have not given any detail for the exact reason why young children find it easier to use a larger mouse. The second answer is better, because it identifies the fact that children are not as dextrous as adults. The third answer gains no marks, because they have not properly explained the advantages in using colour with young children. The fourth answer is worth a single mark. The student has not answered this with a discuss-style answer. They should not have answered it in the way they have with a series of points.

(b) This is a good answer and is worth two marks. **(5 marks out of 8)**

Student answer 2

1 (a) Young children do not like too much reading, so it is better to use as little text as possible, and you can do this by using pictures, sound, animations and so on. A font should be carefully chosen so that it is easy to read, and the size of a font needs to be large. Any coloured text should be combined with an appropriate background colour to add contrast, but certain colour combinations should be avoided.

Young children can usually use a mouse more easily than the keyboard. Keyboard entry should be avoided because of the future RSI implications. Any screen design should be uncluttered and there should be consistency between the screens so that the software is easier to learn and use. Wherever possible, a graphical user interface should be used, which makes use of pictures and icons rather than menu selections and commands.

(b) An ergonomic mouse should be used by young children in conjunction with a mouse mat containing a wrist rest. This will hopefully solve the problem of repetitive strain injury in future life. RSI is a painful condition which is caused by repeated movements of a mouse or by using a keyboard for long periods.

Examiner's comment

1 (a) This is a very good answer, which has been answered in the correct discussion style. There is a logical structure to the answer and the factors involved have been identified with a clear indication of how the interface can help. This answer is hard to fault and has therefore been given full marks.

(b) In this answer the student has clearly identified the health problem and how it is caused and a possible solution to the problem. Again, this part of the question deserves full marks. **(8 marks out of 8)**

Examiner's answer

1   (a)   There is no mark given for naming the factor or the feature of the human–computer interface.
Two marks are given for two related features/factors.
Use of appropriate input methods
  • reduce the use of the keyboard to avoid the onset of RSI
  • use an ergonomically designed mouse to avoid the likelihood of contracting RSI
Use of colour
  • use appropriate text and background colour with plenty of contrast
  • avoid using certain colours such as red and green for which some people are colour blind
  • colours can make things easier to learn
Consistency
  • there should be consistency between similar pages, as this makes the system easier to learn
  • similar pieces of software in the same range, should have similar human–computer interface as this makes it easier to learn
Use pictures/icons
  • young children associate better with pictures, rather than words.
  • they help children choose the correct option

  • they make the interface easier to learn
Use of text
  • use a font that is easy to read
  • use an appropriate font size
  • do not use language that young children will not understand
  • keep sentences short
  • do not give them too much to remember
Sound
  • add sound to make the interface more interesting
  • allow sound to be turned off in case it distracts
  • sound is essential for partially sighted users

   (b)   No marks for simply stating the issue (e.g. RSI)
One mark for a full description of the health problem and how it is caused and one mark for explaining a method of prevention.
RSI/back ache – caused by sitting for long periods at a poorly designed workstation
Solved by using the correct posture, an adjustable chair, an ergonomic mouse/keyboard, a wrist rest, etc.
Eye strain caused by spending too much time working on the computer or by poor lighting. Ensure there is no glare on the screen. Ensure there is suitable lighting.
Other health problems such as obesity and epileptic fits are acceptable.

Worked example 2

2 When software is developed, great care is taken in deciding which human–computer interface to use.
The main types of human–computer interface are:
Graphical user interface (GUI)
Menu-driven interface
Command line/driven interface
(a) Describe two features for each of these types of interface. (6 marks)
(b) Explain how the software developer could decide on a suitable HCI. (4 marks)

Student answer 1

2   (a)   A graphical user interface makes use of a graphical interface and this makes it much easier to use. A GUI makes use of WIMP. A menu driven interface is an interface that uses menus. The user can make selections using the menu.
Command-driven interfaces work by the user issuing commands and the software doing what it is told.

   (b)   He could find out the age of the users to make sure that the HCI is appropriate.
He could see if the HCI is suitable by getting them to use it.

Examiner's comment

2   (a)   For the answer for the GUI, the student has given an answer that almost anyone could have guessed at. The mention of WIMP does not gain any marks as there is no explanation as to what it means. The other answers to this part of the question are equally as bad with guesses made and no proper understanding.
No marks at all for this part of the answer.

   (b)   Only one mark is awarded here for the first answer. **(1 mark out of 10)**

Student answer 2

2 (a) GUI
Makes use of the mouse as the main input device.
Uses buttons, icons, pull-down menus, windows and toolbars
which makes it easier for novice users to use.
Menu-driven interface
Presents selections as a list from which you select by clicking
on the menu item.
If a touch screen is used, menu selections are shown on
the screen and the user simply selects one by pressing the
screen.
Command-driven interface
Commands are typed in at the keyboard to make selections.
The user has to remember commands.

(b) The age of a typical user should be considered. Using a
keyboard would be inappropriate for very young children.
The task should be considered. Designing a game would
require a realistic interface.
The experience of the user. An experienced user will want
to do things more quickly and will not be bothered about
having to remember commands.

Examiner's comment

2 (a) Two features of each interface are given for both
the GUI and the menu-driven interface, so this
section gains four marks. Only the first part of
the answer for the command driven interface
gains a mark. The second part about the user
having to remember commands is not a feature
of the interface but more a disadvantage, so
only one mark is given for this part.

(b) The first three answers are good. The 'how' and
reason are clear.
There are only three explanations given so only
three marks are given. **(8 marks out of 10)**

Examiner's answer

2 (a) The answers must be features of the interface and not simply an
advantage or disadvantage of the interfaces.
One mark for an explanation of the feature up to a maximum of 6 marks.

GUI
Uses windows, icons, menus, pointers, etc.
Uses a mouse rather than a keyboard
You point and click at objects on the screen, such as icons,
pictures, text, etc.
Menu-driven interface
Provides a list of items to select
Selections are made by keying in a letter or number
Can also make selection by clicking on the item in the list
Can make use of a touch-sensitive screen
Command line/driven interface
Commands are typed in
Makes use of a keyboard as the input device
Commands have to entered precisely

(b) One mark each, for four distinctly different points such as:
Task – CAL software for teaching primary school children would use
a GUI with a mouse rather than a keyboard.
User experience – experienced users just want the job completed in
the least time, whereas beginners want to be guided more.
User preference – users should preferably be given a choice. For
example, the same piece of software could allow different ways of
accomplishing the task.
Resources – interface needs to be within the budget of the user.

Summary mind maps

Types of human–computer interface

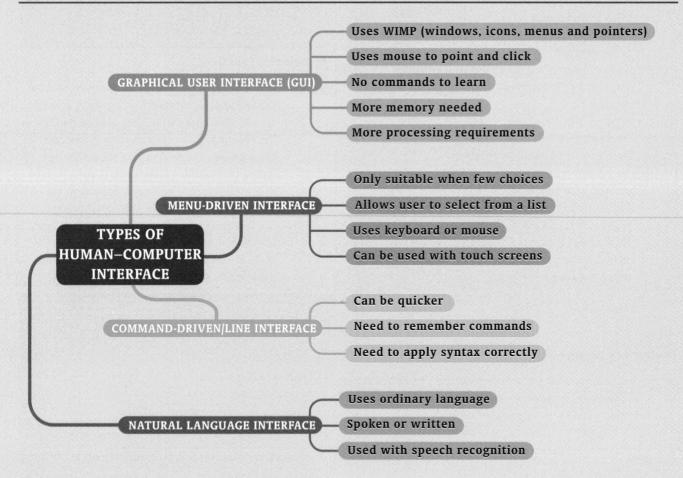

GRAPHICAL USER INTERFACE (GUI)
- Uses WIMP (windows, icons, menus and pointers)
- Uses mouse to point and click
- No commands to learn
- More memory needed
- More processing requirements

MENU-DRIVEN INTERFACE
- Only suitable when few choices
- Allows user to select from a list
- Uses keyboard or mouse
- Can be used with touch screens

TYPES OF HUMAN–COMPUTER INTERFACE

COMMAND-DRIVEN/LINE INTERFACE
- Can be quicker
- Need to remember commands
- Need to apply syntax correctly

NATURAL LANGUAGE INTERFACE
- Uses ordinary language
- Spoken or written
- Used with speech recognition

TOPIC 10: Social issues

You will need to understand the current health and safety problems associated with working using ICT systems and how health problems are caused and how the risks from them can be reduced with correct working practices or properly designed equipment.

There are a number of ways in which ICT equipment and services can be abused and you will learn about these. You will learn about the acceptable use of ICT equipment and services and the difference between malpractice and crime.

You will learn about the responsibilities employers have when introducing new hardware and software in the workplace.

▼ The key concepts covered in this topic are:

▶ Understand the health and safety issues associated with ICT

▶ Understand the health problems and what can be done to alleviate them

▶ Understand the need for health and safety legislation

▶ Understand the nature of abuses of ICT equipment and services

▶ Understand the legislation covering the use of computers

CONTENTS

Unit IT1 Information Systems

Health and safety issues associated with ICT

▼ **You will find out**

▶ About the need for health and safety legislation

▶ About how to apply the health and safety legislation

▶ About the things you can do to prevent health problems when using ICT

Introduction

Using computer equipment is a safe occupation but there are a number of health problems which can pose a hazard to users. In this section you will be looking at what these health problems are and how it is possible to prevent them.

The health problems

The main health problems that may occur when working with ICT systems are:

- Back ache
- Repetitive strain injury (RSI)
- Eye strain
- Stress
- ELF (extra low frequency) radiation.

Back ache

Back ache is mainly caused by sitting with incorrect posture. Slouching in a chair whilst using the computer can lead to back problems. Sitting awkwardly at a desk is another cause.

To help prevent back problems:

- Use an adjustable chair (NB in workplaces this is a legal requirement but you need to ensure that the chair you use at home is adjustable).
- Always check the adjustment of the chair to make sure it is suitable for your height. Use a foot support called a footrest if necessary.
- Sit up straight on the chair with your feet flat on the floor.
- Make sure the screen is lined up and tilted at an appropriate angle.

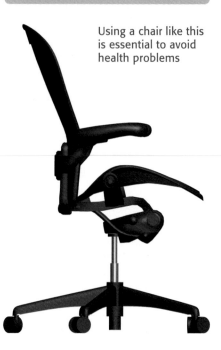

Using a chair like this is essential to avoid health problems

Repetitive strain injury (RSI)

Repetitive strain injury (RSI), sometimes called ULD (upper limb disorder), causes aches and pain in hands, wrists, arms and neck. Usually the symptoms do not last but they can be persistent and eventually disabling.

RSI can be prevented by good workstation design and good working practices.

To help prevent RSI:

- adjust your chair to the correct seating position for you
- make sure there is enough space to work comfortably
- use a document holder
- use an ergonomic keyboard/mouse
- use a wrist rest
- keep your wrists straight when keying in
- position the mouse so that it can be used keeping the wrist straight
- learn how to type properly – two-finger typing has been found to be much worse for RSI.

If you slouch in your chair, you may end up with back ache.

GLASBERGEN

**'It's an ergonomic ankle support
designed to help you be more productive.'**

Stress is often caused by too much work to do in too little time.

Eye strain

Eye strain causes blurred vision and headaches. It is caused by using the screen for long periods, glare on the screen, dirt on the screen and working without the best lighting conditions.

To avoid eye strain:

- keep the screen clean so it is easy to make out the characters on the screen
- use appropriate lighting (fluorescent tubes with diffusers) and blinds to avoid glare which can cause headaches
- take regular breaks to avoid stress and give your eyes a rest
- have regular eye-tests (NB if you use a screen in your work, then your employer is required by law to pay for regular eye-tests and glasses if they are needed)
- ensure you are not sitting too near the screen, to avoid the possible risks of radiation.

Stress

Using ICT systems can be stressful, especially when things go wrong.

The people who produce ICT systems for others to use (e.g., websites, databases, on-line ordering systems, etc.) have a responsibility to us all to make them simple to use.

Stress can come from:

- the pace of work (e.g., too much to do in too little time)
- worry about using the new technology – older people feel they cannot cope
- software that is frustrating to use because it has not been designed properly
- losing work, problems with viruses and technical problems.

Stress can be reduced by the following:

- good management of workload
- training for users in new systems and software
- provision of help-desks to help prevent users wondering how to do things
- correctly designed software that is not frustrating to use
- use of anti-virus software, firewalls, etc., that help prevent loss or corruption of data.

ELF radiation

Extra low frequency (ELF) radiation is given out by all electrical devices including computers and computer equipment. Some researchers believe that such fields could contribute to such conditions as leukaemia, tiredness or general fatigue. Others are not sure whether they are dangerous or not. ELF radiation can be reduced by careful screening in the design of the computer, laptop, mobile phone or other electrical device and by keeping the strength of any signals low.

Stress caused by unreasonable workloads is a problem for many employees.

The application of current health and safety regulations

▼ You will find out

▶ About how the Health and Safety at Work Act 1974 ensures safe working conditions and methods

▶ About how the Health and Safety (Display Screen Equipment) Regulations 1992 governs the design of ICT equipment that can be used in the workplace

Introduction

Because of the problems identified in the previous section, the health and safety regulations were applied to the use of ICT equipment in the workplace. The Act in force which applies to the use of ICT equipment is called the Health and Safety at Work Act 1974.

Health and safety legislation

Under the Health and Safety at Work Act 1974, employers have a duty to minimise risks to employees in the workplace. Employees need to have a safe place to work and have a safe system of work.

The Health and Safety at Work Act 1974 is fairly general and more specific regulations covering the use of computer equipment are contained in the Health and Safety (Display Screen Equipment) Regulations 1992.

The regulations made it law for employers to take certain measures to protect the health and safety of their employees who use ICT equipment.

The Health and Safety Executive (HSE) are the government department responsible for health and safety in the workplace. Part of their job is to promote good health and safety practice in the workplace and they produce many leaflets (both on-line and paper) to this effect.

Health and safety regulations apply to computer screens.

Computer screens

Computer screens should:

- tilt and swivel
- be at an appropriate height for the user
- display a stable image with no flickering
- have brightness and contrast control
- be free from reflections
- be of an appropriate size for the software application being run (e.g., CAD (computer-aided design) needs a large screen because there is so much displayed on the screen at one time).

Appropriate training

There should be training of employees so that they:

- know how to make adjustments to the screen (i.e., alter the brightness and contrast)
- understand the need for taking regular breaks
- adjust the size of text and other screen elements so that they can be read easily
- understand the importance of keeping the screen clean.

Chairs

There is a tendency to slouch in chairs when using computers and especially when surfing the Internet. This should be avoided because prolonged slouching will almost certainly lead to back problems in the future. Chairs should be:

- adjustable in height so that the feet can be placed flat on the floor. If this is not possible because a person is short, then a footrest should be provided
- have seat backs which provide proper back support (i.e., they should have adjustable height and tilt)
- have five feet with castors for stability and to ensure that it is easy for the chair to be moved closer to and further away from the desk.

Desks or workstations

Desks or workstations should:

- be big enough for computer equipment and paperwork
- have a matt surface to reduce glare.

Keyboards

The keyboard design we are used to has evolved from the development of the typewriter. If a keyboard were to be designed today, from an ergonomic point of view, the keys would not be arranged in this way.

There have been many attempts at putting the keys in different orders but getting users to use them has been difficult.

This keyboard isn't broken. It is one of many ergonomic keyboard designs.

▶ Activity: Workstation health and safety

The diagram below shows a user sitting at a workstation. This user is adopting good practice.

Label this diagram with as many examples of good practice as you can spot. You should be looking for a minimum of 7.

© 1998 Randy Glasbergen.

If the QWERTY keyboard were arranged ergonomically, it would have this arrangement of keys. This arrangement reduces the finger travel distance for keystrokes which helps reduce RSI.

Research sites

The Health and Safety Executive is the government department responsible for publicising and enforcing health and safely legislation. Their site can be found at: *http://hse.gov.uk*

The TUC's site offers useful advice on RSI: *http://www.tuc.org.uk/h_and_s/ tuc-7697-f0.cfm%20*

'Suspending your keyboard from the ceiling forces you to sit up straight, thus reducing fatigue.'

Health and safety guidelines covering new software

▼ **You will find out**

▶ About the problems with software that can cause stress in users

▶ About how software can be designed so that it does not cause stress in users

Introduction

The health and safety guidelines cover the design and introduction of new software as this is frequently a source of stress amongst employees. Employees are often given little input into the design of software, even though they may be using it for long periods each day. Software that is poorly designed or frustrating to use causes employee stress. In this section you will be looking at what can be done to minimise the problems.

Making software less stressful to use

Software can be designed ergonomically so that it is easier and less stressful to use.

Software designers can make software less stressful to use by ensuring:

- that software is bug free and does not cause the computer to freeze or crash, sometimes resulting in the user losing work
- that fonts and font sizes are chosen carefully to make text easier to read
- that information is displayed in a logical order on the screen – important items are displayed at the top left of the screen
- that the software is intuitive so that it behaves in a way users would expect it to behave
- help screens tell the user what to do in a way they understand and do not leave the user more frustrated
- methods which minimise the amount a user has to key in should be used in order to reduce the likelihood of RSI
- any music or any animations can be switched off or skipped past by the user
- shortcuts should be used wherever possible to minimise mouse clicks.

How do you know you are stressed?

Pressure can be good for you in small amounts, but if the pressure gets too much, you may experience stress. You know you are stressed if you:

- are smoking or drinking excessively
- are rushing and hurrying from place to place
- are doing several jobs at once
- are missing breaks and taking work home with you
- have little time for exercise and relaxation
- are not sleeping properly.

Prolonged stress can lead to physical and/or mental ill health and everything should be done by employers to try to reduce the stresses on employees.

The top five ICT-related stress triggers

Using computers can be very frustrating at times. In a survey, the following were identified at the top five stress triggers:

1 Slow performance and system crashes
2 Spam, scams and too much e-mail
3 Pop-up ads
4 Viruses
5 Lost or deleted files

Shortcuts enable programs to be launched in the least possible time.

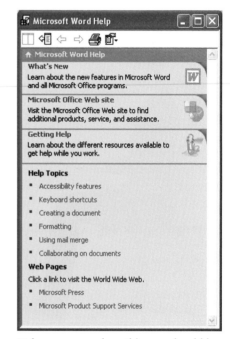

Help screens such as this one should be easy to use and get users back on task as soon as possible.

Software should be thoroughly tested so that it is bug free.

Other things can be done to make the use of software less stressful

There are other things apart from the correct design of software that will help make the use of ICT systems less stressful. These include:

- having a help-desk to help with user problems
- training users fully in all the ICT systems they use
- a procedure of logging problems as they arise so that they can be corrected.

How software can be designed so that it does not cause stress in users

Software design is not simply about getting the software to complete a task. When designing the software it is very important to remember that people will be using it on a day-to-day basis. Here are some of the things that should be considered:

- Ensure that the order of material on each screen is logical and that the important items always come first.
- Ensure that all software is thoroughly tested so that it does not crash.
- Software should be tested by users so that any frustrating user-identified problems can be eliminated.
- Try to minimise the mouse movements needed to make selections to save a user time and to reduce RSI. Use drop-down menus where possible.
- Keep consistency from one screen to the next, which will make the software easier to learn.
- Put items such as buttons, menus, etc., on the screen where users would expect them.
- Help screens should be written simply. This should be tested by novice users.

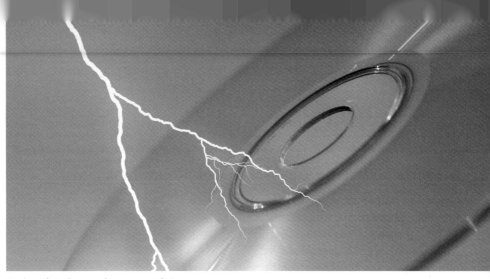

Losing data is a major cause of stress.

Chatting to a usability engineer

Amy Hawkes is a usability engineer whose job is simply to eliminate problems in software that makes users grit their teeth. She improves all those confusing messages, eliminates links that don't work, and makes menus less confusing.

Amy explains: 'It is my job to make users' jobs easier and less stressful. For example, it should not take six steps to do something that could take three.'

She goes on to say: 'As part of the training for my job I have to understand how people learn and remember. I also trained to understand layouts of the screens and the psychology of colours.'

In order to increase the efficiency of users, Amy looks at users to see what they are likely to want to do next after completing a task. The idea is to increase the efficiency of the user.

Amy uses real users to see if she was right. Amy says: 'I do this by making paper prototypes of the design. I then use graphics software to create a model of what the screens, icons and menus will look like.'

Amy explains: 'I then ask the user to point to the icons they need to do the work on the paper. Depending on which icon they use, I can then quickly give them another piece of paper. I can get a feel for the design of the solution by doing this.'

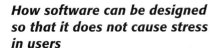
Not knowing what is happening is a cause of stress.

Acceptable use of ICT equipment and services

You will find out

► About users' responsibilities relating to the appropriate use of ICT equipment

► About users' responsibilities relating to the appropriate use of networks

► About users' responsibilities relating to the appropriate use of the Internet

Introduction

Users of ICT equipment and services have a responsibility to others. This means that they should not do anything to harm or distress or inconvenience anyone else. In the workplace most organisations will set out clearly what may and may not be done on the organisation's computers. For example, organisations will not allow users to load their own software on the computer because this can frequently be a source of viruses, and the organisation would be responsible for any copyright violations.

In this section you will be looking at what the responsibilities are.

User responsibilities

Users of ICT facilities have a variety of moral, ethical and legal responsibilities. Since, when at work, an organisation is responsible for the acts of its employees, it is important that all staff members are aware of what these responsibilities are. Even though the organisation did not know about the acts of some of their employees in breaking the law, it could still be held liable. If it was proved that it had taken sufficient steps, then it may not be prosecuted.

Appropriate use of ICT equipment

Here are some rules which might apply for the use of ICT equipment. Users should:

- report broken equipment and not leave it to others to do it
- not store games or other unauthorised software on computers
- keep regular backups of their work on stand-alone computers
- not alter the hardware and software settings.

Appropriate use of networks

Here are some rules which might apply for the use of networks. Users should:

- not use the organisation's networks to send inappropriate e-mails and file attachments to others
- log off the system if they leave the workstation
- not reveal customer or confidential details to others
- not load their own programs on the network
- change passwords on a regular basis
- not reveal their passwords to others
- not write their passwords down where others are likely to find them.

Appropriate use of the Internet

Here are some rules which might apply for the use of the Internet. Users should:

- not download games, music or video and store it on the organisation's computers
- not open file attachments if their source is unknown
- not use the Internet to download programs without permission
- not use the Internet to access inappropriate material
- not use the Internet for misuses such as hacking, spreading of viruses, etc.
- not use the Internet for violation of copyright (e.g., sharing music using file sharing sites).

Inappropriate use of ICT

ICT is used by many people and not all of them are using it for good. Here are some of the things that might be considered inappropriate whilst at work or in school or college:

- deliberately damaging hardware or software

- using ICT to commit fraud
- blackmail
- downloading offensive/ pornographic images
- sending offensive e-mails to others
- engaging in chat in chat rooms whilst at work
- stealing company data
- deliberately altering company data
- not logging off a network when going for a break
- using the network to find information for a friend (e.g., finding where an ex-partner is living, how much money someone has in their account, etc.)
- divulging passwords to others
- performing personal tasks using the Internet, such as your weekly shopping
- hacking into another person's computer
- spilling a drink over the keyboard
- leaving an untidy workstation for someone else to use.

The difference between malpractice and crime

There are lots of different types of activities which human users might or might not do which cause a threat to ICT systems. Malpractice means improper or careless use or misconduct. Crime obviously means all those acts which are against the law. There is a bit of blurring with the word malpractice, as this can also involve illegal acts according to the strict dictionary definition; however, for the exam you need to make the distinction that malpractice is not against the law, whereas crime is.

Examples of malpractice

Examples of malpractice include:

- accidentally deleting data
- not taking backup copies
- not scanning for viruses regularly
- copying an old version of data over the latest version
- allowing your password to be used by others
- not logging off the network after use.

Examples of crime

Examples of crime include:

- hacking
- deliberately distributing viruses
- illegally copying data or software
- stealing hardware.

Acceptable use policy

Misusing the ICT facilities in an organisation by their own staff can lead to a number of threats. For example, downloading music onto the firm's computers can introduce viruses.

In order to prevent their own staff from misusing the ICT systems in an organisation, many organisations have an acceptable use policy. This policy makes it clear to all employees or users what is acceptable use and what isn't. The policy will usually make it clear about what disciplinary action will be taken if the ICT systems are abused.

An acceptable use policy protects both the organisation and individuals by providing clear guidelines as to what constitutes use and abuse. There can then be no ambiguity as to how the ICT systems can be used. There are six main areas on a typical IT acceptable use policy:

1 Introduction – this gives general information about the organisation and also outlines the main reasons for having the IT acceptable use policy.
2 General computer use – information here about general use such as

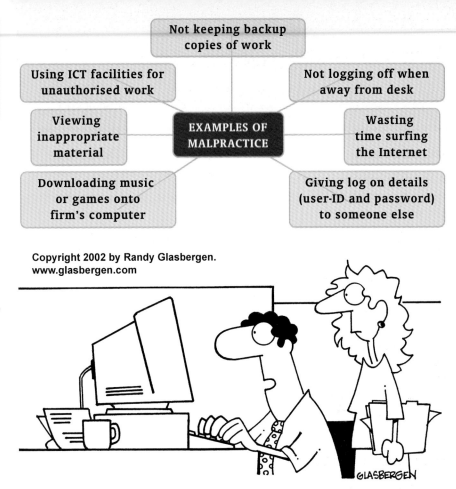

Not keeping backup copies of work

Using ICT facilities for unauthorised work

Viewing inappropriate material

Downloading music or games onto firm's computer

EXAMPLES OF MALPRACTICE

Not logging off when away from desk

Wasting time surfing the Internet

Giving log on details (user-ID and password) to someone else

Copyright 2002 by Randy Glasbergen.
www.glasbergen.com

'We don't pay much attention to information security.
We're hoping our competitors will steal our ideas
and become as unsuccessful as we are.'

health and safety information, advice about keeping workstations clean, eating and drinking near computer equipment, etc.
3 Network and Internet usage – information about network security – passwords and usernames, logging on and off, warnings about visiting undesirable and non-work-related sites. Warnings about downloading files from sites and doing non-work-related tasks.
4 E-mail – ensuring that e-mails sent internally and externally

are appropriate. Warnings about opening e-mails from unknown sources which could contain viruses.
5 Security – outline of the Data Protection Act if personal data is being processed. Details about access and unauthorised access. Security measures that must be followed.
6 Training – training must be offered so that all staff understand all aspects of the IT acceptable use policy. They will also need training in all the legislation that applies to ICT use.

Software piracy

Deliberate destruction of data

Deliberately writing and spreading computer viruses

Hacking

EXAMPLES OF CRIME

Running unlicensed software

Identity theft

Fraud

Theft of hardware, software or data

Topic 10 Social issues

Legislation: personal data and the Data Protection Act 1998

▼ You will find out

▶ About the need for the Data Protection Act 1998

▶ About what is meant by personal data

▶ About the eight Data Protection Principles covered in the Data Protection Act

▶ About the meaning of certain terms used in the Data Protection Act

▶ About what constitutes processing under the Data Protection Act

Introduction

With the development of ICT systems, new laws had to be passed by parliament in order to protect the individual against misuses of personal data held about them. New laws also needed to be passed to cover other misuses such as writing and spreading viruses, illegally accessing computer resources (i.e., hacking), etc.

The Data Protection Act 1998

The widespread use of ICT has made the processing and transfer of data much easier and to protect the individual against the misuse of data, a law was passed called The Data Protection Act 1998.

Another reason for the Act was the fact that all Member States in the European Economic Area (EEA) had data protection laws, so the UK had to have them as well. This would allow the free passage of personal data from one Member State to another, which is essential when conducting business.

The Data Protection Act 1998 covers the misuse of personal data, whether by the use of ICT systems or not. The Act gives rights to the individual to find the information stored about them and to check whether it is correct. If the information is wrong, they can have it altered and may be able to claim damages if they have suffered loss resulting from this wrong information.

What data is classed as personal data?

The Data Protection Act 1998 refers to personal data. Personal data is:

• data about an identifiable person
• who is alive
• and is specific to that person.

The data subject must be capable of being identified from the information. Usually this would mean that the name and address would be part of the data but it could be that the person could be identified simply by other data given. Data specific to a particular person would include:

• medical history
• credit history
• qualifications
• religious beliefs
• criminal records.

The padlock/signpost symbol is used to alert individuals to the fact that their personal information is being collected. The symbol directs them to sources that will explain how their information is to be used.

Personal data held about you

Personal data is particularly important to people who are trying to sell you something. Generally this marketing data can be put into the following data types: demographic data (where you live) and lifestyle data (what your interests are, what you spend your money on, etc.).

Marketing people need to know more about our personal lives in order to target us for advertising and promotional material.

➤ KEY WORDS

Data controller – the person whose responsibility it is in an organisation to control the way that personal data is processed

Data subject – the living individual whom the personal information is about

Information Commissioner – the person responsible for enforcing the Act. They also promote good practice and make everyone aware of the implications of the Act

Personal data – data about a living identifiable person, which is specific to that person

Credit card details are personal details and must be protected.

If you see a lock (🔒) on the web browser address bar then you should also see that the website starts with HTTPS as opposed to HTTP, in which case the page is using secure socket layer and is secure from a third party being able to see your information as it is being transmitted.

The Data Protection Act balances the rights of individuals with the needs of organisations.

The eight Data Protection Principles

The Data Protection Act 1998 contains the following eight principles:

1 Personal data shall be processed fairly and lawfully.
2 Personal data shall be obtained only for one or more specified and lawful purposes, and shall not be further processed in any manner incompatible with that purpose or those purposes.
3 Personal data shall be adequate, relevant and not excessive in relation to the purpose or purposes for which they are processed.
4 Personal data shall be accurate and, where necessary, kept up to date.
5 Personal data processed for any purpose or purposes shall not be kept for longer than is necessary for that purpose or those purposes.
6 Personal data shall be processed in accordance with the rights of data subjects under this Act.
7 Appropriate technical and organisational measures shall be taken against unauthorised or unlawful processing of personal data and against accidental loss or destruction of, or damage to, personal data.

8 Personal data shall not be transferred to a country or territory outside the European Economic Area (EEA) unless that country or territory ensures an adequate level of protection for the rights and freedoms of data subjects in relation to the processing of personal data.

Processing personal data

The Data Protection Act refers to the processing of personal data. Processing can mean:

• obtaining data (i.e., collecting data)
• recording data
• carrying out any operation or set of operations on data.

Summary of the eight Data Protection Principles

The eight Data Protection Principles require that data shall be:

1 fairly and lawfully processed
2 processed for limited purposes
3 adequate, relevant and not excessive
4 accurate
5 not kept longer than necessary
6 processed in accordance with the data subjects' rights
7 secure
8 not transferred to countries outside the EU without adequate protection.

Mobile phone companies keep records of all calls.

Information Commissioner's Office

The Information Commissioner's Office is the UK's independent authority set up to promote access to official information and to protect personal information.

Personal data should not be transfered to a country outside the EEA without data protection.

Legislation: the working of the Data Protection Act 1998

You will find out

▶ How notification that an organisation is processing personal data takes place

▶ About the exemptions from notification

▶ About how data subjects can apply for access to personal data held about them

▶ About how mistakes in personal data can be rectified

▶ About the exemptions from subject access

Introduction

The Data Protection Act 1998 is used to protect personal data from misuse. In order to do this it requires certain procedures to take place.

Notification

Notification is the process of letting the Information Commissioner's Office know that an organisation is storing and processing personal data. The person in the organisation who is responsible for the processing of the data (i.e., the data controller) will inform the Information Commissioner of certain details such as:

- Company registration number (a unique number given to each company/organisation).
- The name and address of the data controller.
- The classes of the data that is held (e.g., medical details, financial details, employment details, etc.).
- A general description of the reasons for storing the personal data (debt collection, research, criminal investigation, etc.).
- A description of the data subjects who the data are about (e.g., pupils, patients, customers, etc.).
- Lists of other organisations to which the data is passed (e.g., police, HM Revenue and Customs, universities). These are called recipients.

- Information about whether the information is passed to other countries outside the EEA (European Economic Area).

Notification can be done:

- by post using a special form
- over the Internet
- by phone to the Information Commissioner's Office.

Once these details have been supplied, they will be added to a register that will be made available to the public. This will allow the public to find out about organisations processing their personal data.

It is an offence for an organisation to process personal data without notification.

Exemptions from notification

There are some exemptions from notification under the Data Protection Act. The implication of this is that the data subjects no longer have the right to see the data, have it changed or claim compensation. Data is exempt:

1 Where data is being held in connection with personal, family or household affairs or for recreational use.
2 Where data is used for preparing the text of documents. This is often referred to as the 'word-processing exemption'. This would cover references for jobs, universities, etc., stored on a computer.
3 Where the data is used for the calculation of wages and pensions, or the keeping of accounts or keeping records of purchases and sales for accounting purposes only.
4 Where the data is being held in the interests of national security.
5 Where data is being used for mailing lists, provided that only names and addresses are stored

and the individuals must be asked if they object to personal data being held by the user.

Subject access

Under the Data Protection Act, data subjects (i.e., the people whom the personal information is about) can ask to see the information held about themselves. To do this, they have to write to the organisation they believe is processing the data. There is a fee payable to the organisation of up to £10 but if it is a credit reference agency, then the fee is £2. A reply from the organisation must be within 40 days and if the reply comes from a credit reference agency, then it must come within 7 days.

The purpose of subject access is so that the data subject can see the personal information to check that it

KEY WORDS

Data subject – the person whom the personal information is about

Information Commissioner – the person responsible for the Information Commissioner's Office and the administration of the Data Protection Act 1998

Notification – the process of letting the Information Commissioner's Office know that personal data is being processed

When you see the following padlock next to a form you are filling in, either on the computer or otherwise, you know that personal data is being collected.

is accurate. Many decisions, such as being able to borrow money, whether you are suitable for a job, what medical treatment you are given, etc., are based on this information, so it is very important that the information does not contain errors.

What happens if the personal data is wrong?

The whole point of the Data Protection Act is to allow subject access to allow a person to check the data held about them. If the data subject finds wrong information about them they:

- have the right to compensation for financial loss or injury caused by the incorrect data
- have the right to the data being corrected or even deleted.

Exemptions from subject access

Unless the data falls into one of the categories for exemption from notification, all other personal data must be notified. Notification will allow data subjects to access the personal information about them, but there are exemptions.

These exemptions mean that if the personal data being stored and processed falls into one (or more) of the following categories, then the data subject may be refused access to the personal data. Data where subject access could be refused includes:

- data used for the prevention or detection of crime
- data used for the apprehension or prosecution of offenders
- data used for the assessment or collection of tax or duty.

Consent to process and pass personal information to others

You can consent to allowing your personal details to be processed and passed to other organisations.

When returning from a holiday you may have been asked to fill in a questionnaire to give the holiday company feedback on the sort of holiday you had. You may at first glance think that this form is entirely about collecting information on your opinions of the holiday but there are some questions about things that are unconnected to the holiday such as the date your house or car insurance is up for renewal. Personal information is valuable, especially if the person has consented to it being passed to others.

The Information Commissioner

The Information Commissioner is the person responsible for the Information Commissioner's Office. The Information Commissioner's Office is the UK's independent authority set up to promote access to official information and to protect personal information. Duties of the Information Commissioner include:

- responsibility for administering two Acts: The Data Protection Act 1998 and the Freedom of Information Act 2000
- to promote good information handling
- to investigate complaints
- to provide guidelines
- to bring legal proceedings, if necessary.

The Freedom of Information Act 2000

The Information Commissioner is responsible for another Act called the Freedom of Information Act 2000. This Act gives the right of access to information held by public authorities. Using this Act, an individual can access information such as e-mails, meeting minutes, research reports, etc., held by local authorities. Typically this information would be about:

- how public authorities carry out their duties
- how they make their decisions
- how they spend public money.

Public authorities include:

- central government and government departments
- local authorities
- hospitals, doctors' surgeries, dentists' surgeries, etc.
- schools, colleges and universities
- police and prison service.

Unlike the Data Protection Act, the Freedom of Information Act is not restricted to personal information. It covers all types of information provided that the information is not covered by the following exemptions:

- where the information could jeopardise the prevention or detection of a crime
- where the release of the information would harm the public more than not releasing the information.

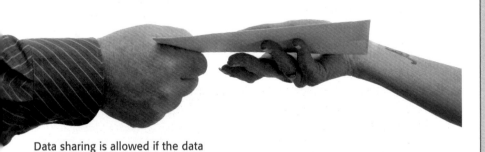
Data sharing is allowed if the data subject has agreed to the sharing.

EXAM TIP

Although the Information Commissioner is responsible for both the Freedom of Information Act and the Data Protection Act, do not get confused between the Acts when answering questions. Basically, the Freedom of Information Act does not concern itself with personal information but instead it concentrates on information about public authorities.

Legislation: The Computer Misuse Act 1990

Introduction

Other Acts had to be produced to deal with some of the misuses that started to cause problems after ICT systems became more widespread.

The Computer Misuse Act 1990

The Computer Misuse Act 1990 was passed to deal with a number of misuses as the use of computers became widespread. The Act makes it an offence to:

- deliberately plant or transfer viruses to a computer system to cause damage to programs and data
- use an organisation's computer to carry out unauthorised work
- hack into someone else's computer system with a view to seeing the information or altering it
- use computers to commit various frauds.

Problems with gaining prosecutions under the Computer Misuse Act 1990

In order to prosecute someone under the Computer Misuse Act 1990 the police would need to prove that they did the misuse deliberately. In other words, the person committing the crime knew what they were doing and knew it was wrong to do it.

Proving this intent is very difficult. For example, if you had a virus on your flash drive from home and took it to work and put it into a computer and it transferred a virus, this is an easy thing to do unknowingly. It would be difficult and almost impossible to prove whether or not this had been done deliberately.

Some organisations would not want others (especially the media) to know that their security has been compromised, so many cases go unreported and unpunished.

Spreading computer viruses is illegal.

It is necessary to protect against hackers by using firewalls.

Offences under the Computer Misuse Act 1990

There are three sections that define the three offences under the Act.

It is useful to summarise the three sections:

Section 1

A person is guilty of an offence if:

(a) he/she causes a computer to perform any function with intent to secure access to any program or data held in any computer;

(b) the access he/she intends to secure is unauthorised; and

(c) he/she knows at the time that it is unauthorised.

The maximum sentence for an offence under this section of the Act is six months' imprisonment.

Section 2

A person will be guilty of an offence under Section 2 of the Act if he/she commits an offence under Section 1 of the Act with the intent of committing a further offence such as blackmail, theft or any other offence which has a penalty of at least five years' imprisonment. They will also be guilty if they get someone else to do this further offence.

The maximum sentence for an offence under this section of the Act is five years' imprisonment.

Section 3

A person is guilty of an offence under this section of the Act if he/she does any act which causes an unauthorised modification of the contents of any computer, and at the time that he/she knows that the modification is unauthorised and he/she has the requisite intent. The requisite intent is intent to cause a modification and by so doing:

(a) to impair the operation of any computer;

(b) to prevent or hinder access to any program or data; or

(c) to impair the operation of any program or reliability of any data.

The maximum sentence for an offence under this section of the Act is five years' imprisonment.

Users can spend lots of time trying to sort out misuses such as hacking and virus attacks. This can be extremely stressful.

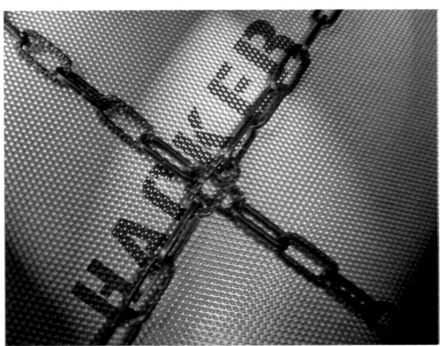

Hacking is an offence under the Computer Misuse Act 1990.

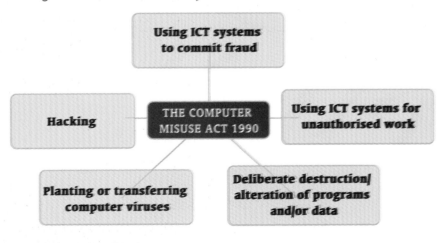

A summary of the offences under The Computer Misuse Act 1990.

Legislation: The Copyright, Designs and Patents Act 1988

▼ **You will find out**

▶ About The Copyright, Designs and Patents Act 1988

The copyright symbol shows that the software is copyright protected.

Introduction

Many people make a living out of writing software and manuals for others to use. These people are protected from having their work copied, in the same way as the writer of a best-selling novel is protected.

Copyright and licensing

There are the following problems with computer software:

- it is very easy to copy
- it is very easy to transfer files over the Internet
- people don't view copying software as like stealing goods from a supermarket.

There are the following problems with copied software:

- not entitled to technical support
- do not qualify for upgrades

- software may be incomplete
- it may contain viruses.

The process of illegally copying software is called software piracy.

The Copyright, Designs and Patents Act 1988

This Act makes it a criminal offence to copy or steal software. In addition if you copy software illegally then you are depriving the owner of the software of some of their income/profits and they will be able to sue you.

The Copyright, Designs and Patents Act 1988 allows the software owner to copy the software and also allows someone else to copy the software provided they have the owner's permission. It is not just programs that are protected by this Act; databases of data, computer files and manuals would also be covered.

Remember that you can legally copy software if you have the permission of the owner. This is necessary in order to take backup copies of software for security purposes.

Under the Act it is a criminal offence to:

- copy or distribute software or manuals without the permission or licence from the copyright owner
- run purchased software covered by copyright on two or more machines at the same time unless there is a software licence which allows it
- compel (i.e., force) employees to make or distribute illegal software for use by the company.

Consequences of breaking this law

Offences under this Act are considered serious and the consequences could include:

- unlimited fines and up to 10 years' imprisonment
- you could lose your reputation, promotion prospects and even your job
- you could be sued for damages by the software owner.

Software piracy

Software piracy is the illegal copying of software and data. Just like software, data has a value and many companies would love to get their hands on their competitors' data. It has been

Piracy is the illegal copying of software.

Piracy – the process of illegally copying software

Software licence – document (digital or paper) which sets out the terms by which the software can be used – it will refer to the number of computers on which it can be run simultaneously

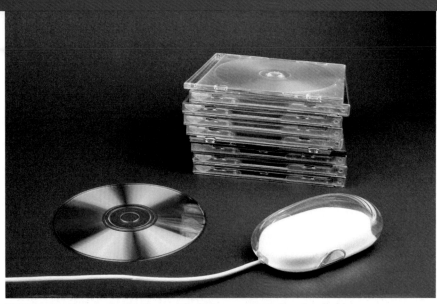

FAST (Federation Against Software Theft) is an organisation funded by software manufacturers to help combat illegal copying of software.

estimated by FAST (Federation Againt Software Theft) that around 27% of the software used in Britain is illegal.

Software piracy means unauthorised copying of software. In many cases this copying will be for personal use but in some cases the people making the copies will sell them at car boot sales, computer fairs, etc. Such copying is illegal since it deprives the software manufacturer of the revenue they would have received had they sold the software.

There are other infringements of the law that are less blatant. For example, a company may have a site licence for 20 computers to use the software when the actual numbers are more than this. Nevertheless, this is still illegal and if caught doing this, the company can face being sued by the manufacturers for loss of sales revenue and fines or even imprisonment for the employees.

The consequences of malpractice and crime on information systems

Malpractice and crime can cause all sorts of problems to organisations, and financial loss is just one of them. Here are some of the consequences:

- complete loss of data
- prosecutions under the Data Protection Act 1998 for failing to keep personal data safe
- loss of money due to fraud
- sensitive company data falling into the hands of competitors
- loss of ICT facilities while problem is sorted out
- loss of customer confidence
- bad publicity in press
- possibly lives put in danger.

Selling pirated copies of software at car boot sales or on eBay

Sharing digital music illegally using peer-to-peer file sharing software

Copying images or text without permission

ILLEGAL ACTIVITIES UNDER THE COPYRIGHT, DESIGNS AND PATENTS ACT

Running multiple copies of software not allowed by the licence

Forcing others to illegally copy files

EXAM TIP

When software is bought, you do not own it, you only have a licence to use it. Make sure that in exam questions you specify what site licences usually allow you to do.

Never say in an answer that you are not allowed to copy software – this is not true.

Case studies

▶ Case study 1 | pp. 190–193

Computers 'could disable children'

Children use computers early on and this could put them at risk of permanent injury.

The problems include neck and back ache as well as numbness and tingling in the fingers caused by RSI.

A doctor worried about the problem said: 'this is the first generation of children who have used computers since early childhood while their muscles and bones are developing'.

One child complained of severe pain in their neck and back which gets worse after prolonged sessions on the computer. They complained that: 'no matter which way you sit or lie, you just cannot get comfortable'.

Some lawyers have suggested that schools need to train children to use computers in a safe way in order to avoid legal action from pupils and their parents. They also need to check workstations for problems.

1　You have been asked by the headteacher of a primary school to look at the workstations and ICT equipment in order to identify any issues that could give rise to health problems.
Describe **four** things you would look for and for each one give a reason why it is important. (4 marks)

2　(a)　Give the meaning of the abbreviation RSI. (1 mark)
　(b)　RSI can be caused by computers. Describe **two** things that a user might do which would make them more susceptible to RSI. (4 marks)

3　The Health and Safety (Display Screen Equipment) Regulations 1992 only apply to the workplace and do not apply to students/pupils in schools and colleges but they do apply to staff.
Give **one** reason why the regulations do not apply to pupils/students attending schools and colleges. (1 mark)

▶ Case study 2 | pp. 190–195

Is working in an office making you ill?

Working in an office could be making you ill. The way you work in an office affects your general well-being.

Back pain is a big problem with office workers with many people unable to work with it and others having to take long periods off sick with it. Health and safety advisors say that they are amazed at the chairs people who work with computers have to sit on. They say that a good chair should fit you individually and should be adjustable, have five feet and should be able to move freely.

'Repetitive strain injury (RSI) is a real problem' says the safety advisor and to prevent the problem 'you need to support your wrists with wrist rests which the employer should provide'.

Eye strain is caused by long periods staring at a computer screen. Reflection from windows and lights can cause headaches as it makes text more difficult to read.

Rising stress levels are also worrying and so much so that it has become the largest health and safety problem.

1　(a)　Give the meaning of the initials RSI. (1 mark)
　(b)　Give **two** precautions a user can take in order to reduce the likelihood of them contracting RSI through the use of ICT equipment. (2 marks)

2　Eye strain can cause headaches. Eye strain can be caused by glare on screens. Describe **two** things that can be done to eliminate the glare on computer screens. (4 marks)

3　Stress has been identified in the article as a major health problem. Give **one** thing that an employer can do in order to reduce employee stress when working with ICT systems. (2 marks)

Pupil hackers

Schools are having problems with school hackers breaching schools' firewalls to access forbidden material. They are using software and special techniques to crack passwords and special websites which can be used to bypass the firewall to access data held on the network.

In one school, a pupil had managed to hack into a teacher's e-mail account and then sent a message to her boyfriend dumping him.

There are a huge number of sites that hackers use to give them information about hacking or can give them access in some other way. Teachers try to block the pupils' access to such sites but it is difficult because there are so many of them and more are being created all the time.

Another way pupils are hacking into ICT systems is by standing behind a teacher and looking at what they are typing in for their username and password. Because of the slowness by which some teachers enter these details, they are able to follow the keystrokes.

Many pupils see Internet misuse as a challenge and almost a game but it does cause all sorts of problems and wastes a lot of time and money.

Security experts have said that there is a real need to educate pupils about their rights and responsibilities when using the Internet and the sanctions for misuse must be spelt out.

1 Briefly explain the purpose of a firewall. (2 marks)
2 Unauthorised access to computer resources is called hacking. There are many different ways a hacker can get access to a network. Briefly describe **two** such ways. (2 marks)
3 A school is likely to hold personal information about its pupils on the network.

Give **five** items of personal information that would be stored about a pupil. (5 marks)
4 Once a pupil has gained access to the school's network, outline **two** things they could do with the information. (2 marks)
5 A school should have an acceptable use policy governing the way the school's computer facilities should be used.

Outline **two** things that should be in the acceptable use policy that would help protect against the abuses outlined in the case study. (2 marks)
6 Hacking is illegal. Give the name of the law which covers hacking. (1 mark)

Cases brought under the Computer Misuse Act 1990

Some successful prosecutions have been brought under the Computer Misuse Act 1990. Here are some of the more interesting ones. Read them carefully and then answer the questions that follow.

1 A teenager bombarded his ex-employer's mail server with 5 million e-mails causing the e-mail server to crash. This caused a denial of service. He pleaded guilty and was sentenced to a two-month curfew.
2 A computer engineer deleted a company's files after a dispute over money he was owed. He was convicted and given an 18-month prison sentence.
3 A man who infected thousands of computers across the world with a fast spreading virus has been jailed for two years. The virus was sent as an e-mail which, when opened, put a virus on the computer hard drive. The e-mail was automatically sent to everyone in the e-mail address book, so the virus soon spread. The virus corrupted data on the computer's hard drive and 'seized-up' 27,000 computers worldwide.

To make a user open the e-mail it had the interesting title 'You have a secret admirer'!
4 A computer student was sentenced to three years psychiatric treatment after he hacked into websites and gained the details of 23,000 Internet shoppers around the world.

The judge said that he had a sense of humour after he sent a consignment of Viagra to Microsoft's founder Bill Gates after hacking his credit card details.

His activities brought FBI agents and Canadian Mounties to the small Welsh village where he lived where he was arrested and had his computer confiscated.

The cost of stopping all the credit card details and reissuing the new credit cards was in the region of £1.5million.
5 A female police officer used the Police National Computer to access the electoral rolls and car registration records to find the address of a woman who was having an affair with her boyfriend. She was sentence to three months' imprisonment.

Case studies continued

1 Case 1 was an example of a denial of service attack. Explain briefly what this means. (2 marks)

2 (a) Explain what is meant by a computer virus. (2 marks)

   (b) Computer viruses can cause annoyance to computer users in a number of ways. Describe **two** ways in which viruses cause annoyance. (2 marks)

3 Give **one** reason why users of ICT systems should never open e-mails from people or organisations they do not know. (1 mark)

4 The Computer Misuse Act 1990 has been around for many years, yet there have been relatively few convictions. Give **one** reason why this is. (1 mark)

5 State **three** actions by a computer user which are illegal under the terms of the Computer Misuse Act 1990. (3 marks)

 Case study 5 pp. 204–205

The Federation Against Software Theft (FAST)

FAST is the abbreviation for the Federation Against Software Theft.

The Federation Against Software Theft is an anti-piracy organisation who work to protect the work of software publishers. In 2006 FAST announced research findings that 79% of respondents would report someone they saw shoplifting but only 19% would report a colleague for sharing illegal software.

The person in charge of FAST said: 'In my opinion, digital software theft is exactly the same as walking out of PC World with a CD stuffed up your jumper – stealing is stealing, and I'm shocked at the blasé attitude of so many of our survey respondents. There seems to be a huge morality gap.'

Maybe people think they cannot be caught stealing software as there are no CCTV cameras or store detectives. However, FAST has developed ways of finding where illegally downloaded versions of software come from.

It has been estimated by FAST that a reduction in software piracy of 10% could create 40,000 additional jobs and contribute £6bn to the UK economy.

1 Give the meaning of the abbreviation FAST. (1 mark)

2 Explain what is meant by software piracy. (1 mark)

3 Give **one** way in which software piracy is morally wrong. (1 mark)

4 Give the full name of the organisation that helps protect software producers' rights. (1 mark)

5 Explain what is meant by a software licence. (2 marks)

6 Explain **two** things an organisation can do to help prevent staff putting illegal copies of software onto the organisation's computers. (2 marks)

7 The copying of software illegally without permission is covered by a law.
   Give the full name of this law. (1 mark)

Questions

▶ **Questions 1** pp. 190–191

1 The use of ICT systems has been associated with a number of health problems.
   (a) State **three** health problems that have been associated with the prolonged use of ICT systems. (3 marks)
   (b) In order to avoid computer-related health problems certain preventative actions can be taken. Describe **six** such preventative actions that can be taken to alleviate the health problems you have identified in part (a). (6 marks)

2 An employee who spends much of their time at a keyboard typing in orders at high speed is worried about RSI.
   (a) What do the initials RSI stand for? (1 mark)
   (b) Give **one** of the symptoms of RSI. (1 mark)
   (c) Write down **two** precautions that the employee can take to minimise the chance of contracting RSI. (2 marks)

▶ **Questions 2** pp. 192–193

1 A person employed in a telephone ordering department works for long periods typing order details into a computer using a keyboard. To ensure the health and safety of the employee, state, with reasons:
   (a) **Two** design features that the chair the employee sits on should have to minimise health problems. (2 marks)
   (b) **Two** design features that the screen the employee uses should have to minimise health problems. (2 marks)

2 (a) Give the name of the health and safety regulations which cover working with display screens. (1 mark)
   (b) The regulations lay down certain steps which employers must follow to protect their workers when they are working with computer equipment.
      (i) Give **two** features that a display screen must have when being used in the workplace. (2 marks)
      (ii) Give **two** features a workstation must have when being used in the workplace. (2 marks)

▶ **Questions 3** pp. 194–195

1 Poorly designed software can cause stress amongst employees. For example, the text on the screen may be too small for the user to read properly.
   Describe **three** other features in the design of a software package that could cause stress in a user. (6 marks)

2 You are designing an ICT system for use by others. Describe **two** things that can be done to check that the user interface is not frustrating to use. (2 marks)

3 Using ICT systems can result in user stress. Employers could be sued if they cause bad health owing to poor working practices.
   Describe **one** working practice that could result in a stress problem when working with ICT systems. (2 marks)

▶ Questions 4 | pp. 198–201

1 The Information Commissioner is the person responsible for the Data Protection Act 1998. Give **one** reason why you think the Information Commissioner is independent. (1 mark)

2 Under the terms of the Data Protection Act 1998, an organisation must notify their use of personal data.
  (a) Give **one** reason why this notification is necessary. (1 mark)
  (b) Give **three** pieces of information the data controller would need to give as part of the notification process. (3 marks)

3 A person applies for subject access under the Data Protection Act 1998.
  (a) Explain what subject access means. (1 mark)
  (b) Subject access is not always granted. Describe, by giving an example, a situation where subject access could be refused. (2 marks)

4 In the context of the Data Protection Act 1998, describe the meaning of the following terms:
  (a) The Information Commissioner (1 mark)
  (b) A data subject (1 mark)
  (c) A data controller (1 mark)
  (d) Notification (1 mark)

▶ Questions 5 | pp. 202–203

1 Give the name of the Act which is designed to allow organisations to prosecute anyone accessing their ICT systems illegally. (1 mark)

2 Explain, by giving an example, what is covered by the Computer Misuse Act 1990. (2 marks)

3 Passwords are one method used to protect against unauthorised access to ICT systems. Give **one** other way in which unauthorised access can be prevented. (2 marks)

▶ Questions 6 | pp. 198–201

1 Write down **three** different ways by which personal data could be obtained. (3 marks)

2 Explain simply what recording data would typically mean. (2 marks)

3 Describe **three** different operations that can be carried out on personal data. (3 marks)

4 (a) Give the name of the legislation that protects the privacy of individuals whose personal data is stored and processed by others. (1 mark)
  (b) Give two reasons why this piece of legislation was passed by parliament. (2 marks)

Exam support

Worked example 1

1 Health problems can be caused by poorly designed workstations.
   State **three** features of a well designed workstation and for each feature state the health problem that could be reduced. **(6 marks)**

Student answer 1

1 Make sure that the seat is comfortable so user is relaxed.
   Use blinds on the windows to reduce glare which can cause eye strain.
   Do not leave trailing wires which people could trip on and injure themselves.
   Have a dull desk surface to reduce glare.

Examiner's comment

1 The question refers specifically to the workstation and not the entire room.

   The chair answer is relevant but not appropriate. A settee is comfortable and gives a relaxed sitting position yet would be inappropriate for use with a workstation.

   The blinds and trailing wires answers refer to the room rather than the workstation so there are no marks for the first three answers.

   The last answer is ok for the feature but glare gives rise to a health problem and there is no mention of what this is (i.e. eye strain). A feature and the health risk the feature reduces is needed for two marks.
   (1 mark out of 6)

Student answer 2

1 There needs to be sufficient desk space to rest hands which will reduce the likelihood of the user contracting repetitive strain injury (RSI).
   The user could use an ergonomic mouse or keyboard which will reduce the likelihood of contracting RSI.
   The screen should be adjustable so that neck strain is reduced.
   An adjustable chair with five points should be used so that the user adopts the correct posture which will reduce future back ache.

Examiner's comment

1 This student has clearly identified a feature of a workstation and also clearly stated the health problem that the feature is likely to reduce. This is a perfect answer and gains full marks. **(6 marks out of 6)**

Examiner's answers

1 One mark for the feature and one mark for how the feature reduces the health risk. Note that the answer must be relevant to a workstation.
   • Sufficient desk space (1) to rest hands will reduce the likelihood of RSI (1).
   • Using footrests (1) if the person is short will reduce back ache (1).
   • Use a tiltable/adjustable screen (1) to reduce neck strain (1).
   • Use a screen with a matt surface (1) to reduce eye strain due to glare (1).
   • Use an ergonomic keyboard (1) to help reduce the likelihood of RSI (1).
   • Matt surface on the desk (1) reduces glare and hence eye strain (1).
   • Use an adjustable chair (1) which will reduce back ache (1).

Worked example 2

2 Software needs to be designed to be 'user friendly' in order to prevent health problems to users. For example, a software developer can design software having the function of clear error messages that will allow users to identify what is wrong and how to correct it thus reducing user frustration and stress.

Give **four** other functions that a software developer can provide in the software that will help prevent the health problem of user stress when using an ICT system. (8 marks)

Student answer 1

2 Choose a large font so that the text can be easily read.
Choose a font colour and a background colour that make the text easy to see.
Help is provided in easy to understand terms so that a user does not get stuck using the software which will increase their stress.
Use autosaving facilities so that if the computer is turned off by mistake or the power is switched off, the user has most of their work saved thus reducing the stress of losing a lot of work.

Student answer 2

2 Reducing the amount users have to type in by using drop-down lists, which will reduce the amount of typing users have to do, which will reduce the likelihood of contracting RSI.
Ensuring that the forms used on the screen match up with the paper forms being used to hold the data for input, which will reduce user frustration and reduce stress.
Messages on the screen after a set time to tell the user to take a break, which will reduce eye strain and fatigue.
Use short cut keys so that experienced users can use keys rather than menus, which will reduce the stress in using the software.

Examiner's comment

2 Here the question asked for a function of the software rather than simple features. A function of the software is the way that it performs. The first two answers about fonts and colours are really simple features rather than functions. Also there is no mention of the health problem and how the function helps prevent the health problem. There are no marks for the first two answers.

The next two answers are much better. Both answers give a function of the software and they also identify the health problem and how the function prevents it. So, full marks for each of these answers. **(4 marks out of 8)**

Examiner's comment

2 All the answers refer to the functions of the software. The functions described all do something. Also how the function helps reduce the health risk is clearly stated. This is a very good answer. **(8 marks out of 8)**

Examiner's answers

2 One mark for the function of the software (note must be a function and not a simple feature) and one mark for how the function prevents the health problem.
- Messages on the screen after a set time to tell the user to take a break (1) which will reduce eye strain and fatigue (1).
- Use short cut keys (1) so that experienced users can use keys rather than menus, which will reduce the stress in using the software (1).
- Suitable validation checks (1) during entry ensure that problems caused by processing incorrect data do not cause stress (1).
- Use drop-down lists (1) rather than type in data, which will reduce the likelihood of RSI (1).
- Use help screens (1), which will reduce stress when users get stuck (1).

Worked example 3

3 A health and fitness club would like to offer past members who have let their membership lapse special deals to rejoin the club. They use data they collected five years ago to decide what special deals and promotions should be offered.
   (a) Explain why the data from five years ago might not be suitable to decide on the offers made to past members today. (2 marks)
   (b) Explain the effect on the health club if they used this data from five years ago. (2 marks)

Student answer 1

3 (a) Data from five years ago would be out of date. For example, they could have changed address so they would not hear about the offers.
   (b) The health club would lose money and they could be prosecuted.

Student answer 2

3 (a) The data would no longer be accurate. Their circumstances could have changed and they may have a family and not have time to attend a health club.
   (b) The response rate for the offer would be low and not justify the time, effort and cost of letters sent out.

Examiner's comment

3 (a) A fairly simple question if it had been read carefully. This student has answered a completely different question such as 'what are the consequences of using out-of-date data?'. This answer does not answer the question – it needs to refer to the data being used to make a decision. **(0 marks out of 2)**
   (b) There are two marks here so at least two points are needed.
      General statements, such as 'lose money' without saying why, gain no marks.
      Again 'could be prosecuted' is too general to be given credit, without giving the reason why.
      (0 marks out of 2)

Examiner's comment

3 (a) There are two marks here. You are safer explaining two separate points rather than give a fuller description of a single point.
      This student should have given two points or made it clearer that the two points made are distinctly different. **(1 mark out of 2)**
   (b) Again there are two marks and one point is given.
      Answer is correct but two separate answers should have been given. **(1 mark out of 2)**

Examiner's answers

3 (a) One mark each for two of the following:
      Market conditions may have changed from five years ago, e.g. there may be more competition.
      People's tastes change so what attracted them five years ago might not attract them today.
      People will be five years older so could have more demands on their time, e.g. families.
   (b) One mark each for two of the following:
      They may waste time and money offering deals no-one wants.
      The price offered may be wrong owing to the competition being cheaper thus losing money.
      They would be in violation of the Data Protection Act 1998 for keeping data for longer than necessary and for processing out-of-date data.

Worked example 4

4 Under the terms of the Data Protection Act 1998 a data subject may ask to see the personal data held about them.
   (a) Give one reason why the Data Protection Act allows subject access. (2 marks)
   (b) It turns out that some of the data subject's personal information is wrong. Explain two things that the data subject could now do. (2 marks)

Student answer 1

4 (a) To let the Information Commissioner know that personal data is being processed.
   (b) Sue the firm
        Ask them to correct the data.

Examiner's comment

4 (a) The student is getting confused here and has supplied a definition of the notification process. Students often confuse terms in exam questions. **(0 marks out of 2)**

   (b) The firm can only be sued if it can be proved that the data subject has suffered loss in some way from the incorrect information.
        This answer is not in enough detail for a mark. The second point gains a mark.
        (1 mark out of 2)

Student answer 2

(a) Only the data subject would know whether the data is correct or not. For example, if the information said that they owed lots of money when they didn't, they could have it corrected. If they did not do this, it could affect them getting loans, credit cards, etc.
(b) Apply to have the incorrect data corrected.
     Sue the organisation for damages, if they have suffered as a result of the wrong information. They may not have been able to buy a house if the incorrect information had them as a bad credit risk.

Examiner's comment

4 (a) The two points made in the first two sentences are enough for two marks.
        The example is given to help explain, although it starts to answer the next part of the question (i.e., part (b)). It is good exam technique to always read the entire question before answering it. It stops you wasting time answering the next part of the question. **(2 marks out of 2)**

   (b) This is a good answer and is worth full marks.
        (2 marks out of 2)

Examiner's answers

4 (a) Need to mention that the person to whom the data refers is to look at the data and that the personal data is to be checked for accuracy.
        Two points (one mark each):
        To allow a data subject (1) to check the personal data held about them (1).
        So that the person who the data is about can check (1) the accuracy of the personal data held (1)

   (b) One mark each for two answers similar to:
        They can have the data changed if it is incorrect.
        They can have the data deleted if it is incorrect.
        They can sue the organisation if they have suffered loss as a result of decisions being made on the basis of the incorrect information.
        Have the right of compensation caused by incorrect data.

Summary mind maps

The need for current health and safety legislation

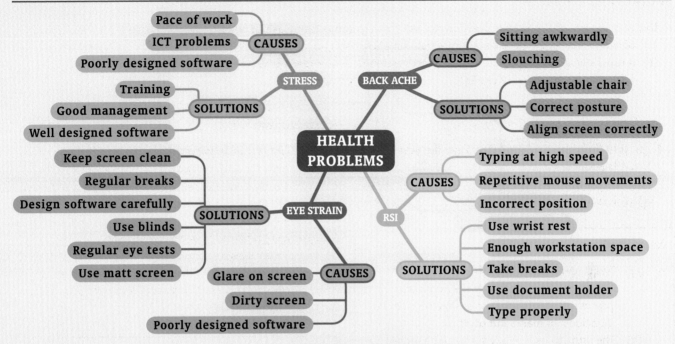

The application of current health and safety regulations

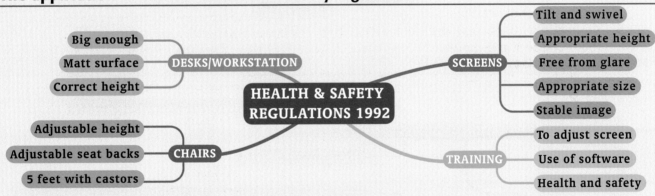

Health and safety guidelines covering the design and introduction of new software

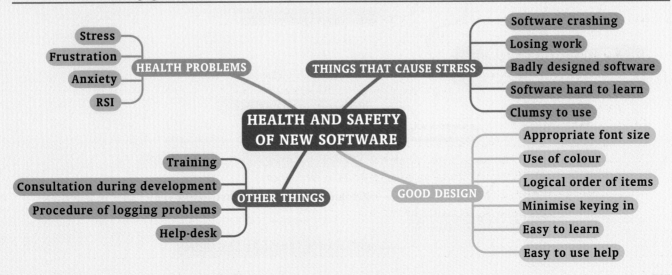

Threats to ICT systems: what they are

- **THREATS**
  - **INTERNAL**
    - Threats from within organisation
    - User mistakes
    - Theft
    - Hacking by employee
    - Negligence
  - **EXTERNAL**
    - Threats from outside organisation
    - Hacking
    - Arson
  - **MALPRACTICE**
    - Improper, careless use or misconduct
    - Wasting time surfing Internet
    - Not logging off
    - Divulging passwords
  - **CRIME**
    - Illegal
    - Punishable

Protecting ICT systems: methods

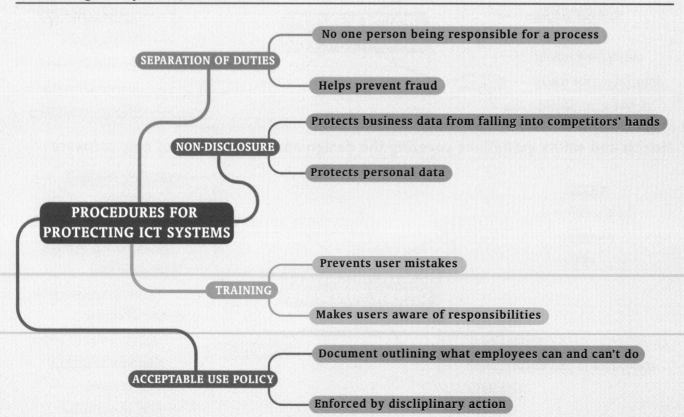

- **PROCEDURES FOR PROTECTING ICT SYSTEMS**
  - **SEPARATION OF DUTIES**
    - No one person being responsible for a process
    - Helps prevent fraud
  - **NON-DISCLOSURE**
    - Protects business data from falling into competitors' hands
    - Protects personal data
  - **TRAINING**
    - Prevents user mistakes
    - Makes users aware of responsibilities
  - **ACCEPTABLE USE POLICY**
    - Document outlining what employees can and can't do
    - Enforced by disciplinary action

TOPIC 11: Database systems

You will already have come across a brief introduction to databases in Topic 7: Presenting information, as well as coming across them in your Key Stage 3 and 4 work. This topic seeks to expand your knowledge about databases to cover the two different types of storage: the flat-file and the relational database. You will learn about the relative advantages and disadvantages of each and also learn about the security of database systems.

▼ The key concepts covered in this topic are:

▶ The definition of a database

▶ Database software

▶ Flat-file systems

▶ The problems of flat-file systems

▶ The difference between a flat-file and a relational database

▶ Advantages and disadvantages of a relational database over flat-files

CONTENTS

Unit IT1 Information Systems

page**217**

Databases

Introduction

All organisations need to hold a store of data and this data needs to be organised and stored in order to aid retrieval. This topic explains what a database is and the two ways in which data can be stored; by using a flat-file or relational database.

Definition of a database

A database is a large collection of data items and links between them, structured in such a way that allows it to be accessed by a number of different applications programs. Strictly speaking, the database itself is the collection of related records, whilst the software used to manipulate the data is called the database management system.

Database software

Database software allows data to be entered and stored in a structured way which aids its retrieval.

Database management systems keep the data separate from the programs themselves, so once the data has been created it can be accessed using different software. This is important as when a business or organisation expands, it may decide to use different database management software and will not want to have to input all the data again.

Databases used by businesses and organisations are called relational databases, with the data being held in lots of different tables with links called relationships between the tables.

Flat-file systems

Flat-file systems for storing data are little more than a computerised card box file, where a single card is used to store one record. A record is simply the complete information about a product, employee, student, order, etc. An item of information such as surname, date of birth, product number, product name, on a record is called a field.

Flat-files only contain one table of data, which limits their use to simple data storage and retrieval systems such as storing a list of names, addresses, phone numbers, etc. Flat-files are unsuited to business applications where much more flexibility is needed.

This flat-file has been set up using spreadsheet software to analyse the answers to questionnaires about recycling. Each row represents a record (i.e., the recycling details for one household) and the columns headings (in bold) represent the field names, with the data in columns below.

Simple flat-files, which are the same as databases with only one table, can be set up in either specialist database or spreadsheet software. If the data needs a lot of further analysis, it is easier to set it up using spreadsheet software.

The problems with flat-file systems

Flat-files store all the data in a single table. The disadvantages of using a flat-file are:

- You will find that there is a lot of duplicate data needed in the table. Time is wasted re-typing the same data.
- When a record is deleted, a lot of data, which is still useful, may be deleted.

The difference between a flat-file and a relational database

In a relational database, we do not store all the data in a single file or table. Instead the data is stored in several tables with links between the tables to enable the data in the separate tables to be combined together if needed. To understand this look at the following example.

A tool hire business hires tools such as ladders, cement mixers, scaffolding, chain saws, etc., to tradesmen. The following would need to be stored:

- data about the tools
- data about the customers
- data about the rentals.

Initial	Surname	Street	Postcode	No_in_house	Type	Garden	Paper	Bottles	Cans	Shoes	Carriers	Compost	Junk_mail
A	Ahmed	18 Rycroft Road	L12 5DR	1	S	S	Y	Y	Y	Y	Y	Y	10
R	Lee	1 Woodend Drive	L35 8RW	4	D	M	Y	Y	Y	N	N	Y	4
W	Johnson	42 Lawson Drive	L12 3SA	2	S	S	Y	Y	Y	N	N	Y	0
D	Gower	12 Coronation Street	L13 8JH	3	T	Y	Y	N	N	N	N	N	9
E	Fodder	124 Inkerman Street	L13 5RT	5	T	Y	N	N	N	N	N	N	12
R	Fowler	109 Pagemoss Lane	L13 4ED	3	S	S	N	N	N	N	N	N	5
V	Green	34 Austin close	L24 8UH	2	D	S	N	N	N	N	N	N	7
K	Power	66 Clough Road	L35 6GH	1	T	Y	Y	Y	Y	N	N	N	7
M	Roth	43 Fort Avenue	L12 7YH	3	S	M	N	N	Y	N	N	N	7
O	Crowther	111 Elmshouse Road	L24 7FT	3	S	M	Y	Y	Y	N	N	N	8
O	Low	93 Aspes Road	L12 6FG	1	T	Y	Y	Y	Y	Y	N	N	11
P	Crowley	98 Forgate Street	L12 6TY	5	T	Y	Y	Y	Y	N	N	N	15
J	Preston	123 Edgehill Road	L12 6TH	6	T	Y	Y	Y	N	N	N	N	2
J	Quirk	12 Leopold Drive	L24 6ER	4	S	M	Y	Y	N	N	N	Y	2
H	Etheridge	13 Cambridge Avenue	L12 5RE	2	S	L	N	Y	N	N	N	Y	5
E	James	35 Speke Hall Road	L24 5VF	2	S	L	Y	Y	N	N	N	Y	5
W	Jones	49 Abbeyfield Drive	L13 7FR	1	D	M	N	N	N	N	N	Y	5

Flat-file database.

Three tables are needed to store this data and these can be called:

Tools
Customers
Rentals

If the above were stored in a single table, in other words using a flat-file, there would be a problem. As all the details of tools, customers and rentals are stored together; there would be no record of a tool unless it had been hired by a customer. There would be no record of a customer unless they had hired a tool at the time.

Hence there are serious limitations in using flat-files, and this is why data is stored in a relational database, where the data is held in several tables with links between the tables.

Tables consist of columns and rows organised in the following way:

- the rows apart from the first row represent the records in the database
- the columns contain the database fields
- the first row contains the field names.

Each column represents a field of the database

Sex	Year	Form teacher
F	7	Miss Hughes
M	7	Mr Thomas ←
F	8	Dr Hick
F	7	Mrs Standford
F	7	Miss Taylor
M	8	Mr Smith

This row contains the set of fields. Each row is a record.

Important note
Records are always rows
Fields are always columns

Advantages of a relational database over flat-files

- Data may be combined more flexibly – if the data is stored in the tables or can be calculated from the data stored, any combination of information can be produced.

- No data duplication – data is only entered once and stored no matter how many applications use it.
- Data integrity is maintained – an update of the data in one place ensures that the data is up-to-date in all the applications that use the database.
- Much easier to search for specific information – relational databases have powerful search facilities, whereas flat-files have limited search facilities.
- Can build an application around the database – relational database software incorporates a special programming language so that a whole application can be built around the database.

Disadvantages of a relational database over flat-files

- Hard to set up – relational databases need to be carefully planned, and more specialist knowledge is needed to use the software.
- More expensive – simple flat-file databases can be created using spreadsheet software, which means another software package may not need to be bought.
- Inappropriate for simple lists – simple list-type stores of data do not require a relational database.

Database security

Data in databases needs to be secured against unauthorised access using a password system. People in an organisation are given a series of access rights which allow them to do their own job but not view or alter data that is not applicable to them. Access rights are determined by a hierarchy of passwords.

Hierarchy of passwords

Users can be allocated certain access rights to the data held on the database. What this means is that someone in the sales department could not access personnel details stored on the same database. Some users will be given access rights so that they are only able to see the data and not alter it. The database administrator will also be responsible for the allocation of access rights to each user.

A hierarchy system allows different people or different groups of people more control over what they can and cannot do with the data in the databases. The higher up the organisational ladder a person is, then the greater the information they need, so they have more access rights. When a user types in their username or user-ID, followed by their password, they have certain rights to access files in the database. Here is a summary of what these rights could be:

Access to certain files or groups of files:

- Access to certain groups of files – these rights allow users access to those files that are necessary for their job.
- Full access – some staff, such as senior managers, may need full access rights to all the files in the database.

Ability to perform certain operations:

- Read only – the user can only read the data and cannot alter it.
- Read and write – the user can not only read the data, they can alter it as well.
- Execute – allows a user to run a particular program. This could prevent users from copying files using the facilities offered by the system software.

Storage of data separate to programs

Most organisations now keep the data separate to the applications used to process the data, so this means that if the applications software is changed, then the data can be kept on its own so that it can be used with another application.

Questions

▶ Questions 1 | pp. 218–219

1 An organisation makes use of a computerised flat-file information storage and retrieval system. The organisation is experiencing problems due to the use of this flat-file system.
   Describe three benefits that the company would gain by using a relational database as opposed to a flat-file system. **(3 marks)**

2 The table below refers to a flat-file containing customer, tool and hire details for a tool hire company.

Customer number	Customer name	Equipment number	Equipment description	Hire date
1212	Hughes	1099	Angle grinder	09/08/09
1311	Ahmed	1200	Chainsaw	09/08/09
1212	Hughes	1987	Orbit sander	09/08/09
1976	Smith	1211	Mini mixer	10/08/09
1976	Smith	1655	Steam cleaner	10/08/09
1200	Green	1077	Steam wallpaper stripper	10/08/09
1212	Hughes	1499	Router	10/08/09

   (a) By referring to the data in this file, define each of the following terms:
       (i) A field.
       (ii) A record. **(2 marks)**
   (b) Each row in the table/file represents one piece of equipment being hired.
       By referring to the above table, give two reasons why storing data using a flat-file in this way is inefficient. **(4 marks)**

3 The following flat-file has been created using spreadsheet software:

Title	Forename	Surname	Street	Area	Postcode	Telephone No
Ms	Amy	Cheung	18 Rycroft Road	West Derby	L12 5DR	(0151)427-2384
Mr	Charles	Clare	1 Woodend Drive	Woolton	L35 8RW	(0151)456-9849
Mrs	Maureen	Criddle	42 Lawson Drive	West Derby	L12 3SA	(0151)755-6899
Mr	Raymond	Cropper	12 Coronation Street	Old Swan	L13 8JH	(0151)478-0371
Mr	Hugh	Davies	124 Inkerman Street	Old Swan	L13 5RT	(0151)478-0098
Miss	Paula	Edwards	109 Pagemoss Lane	Old Swan	L13 4ED	(0151)228-3142
Miss	Irenee	Gant	34 Austin close	Garston	L24 8UH	(0151)475-3351
Mrs	Angela	Gerrard	66 Clough Road	Woolton	L35 6GH	(0151)708-3445
Ms	Fiona	Harper	43 Fort Avenue	West Derby	L12 7YH	(0151)427-8777

   (a) By referring to the table below, explain what is meant by:
       (i) A field.
       (ii) A record. **(2 marks)**
   (b) Give one advantage in storing data such as this in a flat-file. **(1 mark)**
   (c) This database has been created using spreadsheet software. Give one reason why spreadsheet software may be more appropriate for creating simple flat-file databases rather than specialist database software. **(2 marks)**

4 Most modern organisations use a relational database to hold all the organisation's data. Explain two features of a relational database that make it suitable for use by large organisations. **(4 marks)**

5 Discuss how the use of hierarchical passwords allows access control to an organisation's data in a relational database. **(5 marks)**

6 (a) Explain two advantages and two disadvantages in using a relational database to store pupils' data in a school. **(4 marks)**
   (b) Explain how passwords can be used to limit access to pupil data in this database. **(4 marks)**

Exam support

Worked example 1

1 The manager of a tool hire company wishes to use a relational database management system (RDBMS) to help keep track of the business. The database stores the data in three tables, namely: Tools, Customers and Rentals.
   (a) Explain what a relational database is and what its main features are. (5 marks)
   (b) What are the main advantages to this manager in storing the data in a relational database rather than a flat-file database? (3 marks)

Student answer 1

1 (a) A relational database is a database that has relationships between it. The relationships mean that you can get all the data out of the database in whatever order you want. Relational databases are proper databases and are good for businesses that use them a lot.

  (b) The manager will be able to access the data from lots of different places.
      To put the data into the relational database requires less typing, as you only need to put the data in one file.
      The manager will be able to find out information such as which customer has which tool.

Examiner's comment

1 (a) The first sentence could be thought up by anyone using the term 'relational database', so it gets no marks. To obtain the marks, they would need to mention that the relationships are links formed between tables.
      The other sentences are vague statements and this student obviously knows little about these databases. No marks are awarded for this part of the answer.

  (b) In the first sentence the student looks as though they are getting mixed up with distributed databases.
      The second sentence is a main advantage in using relational databases and therefore gets one mark. The third sentence is not specific and is awarded no marks. **(1 mark out of 8)**

Examiner's answer

1 (a) One mark each for five features of a relational database such as:
      Databases that do not store all the data in a single table.
      They use several tables.
      Tables are linked together (or mention of relationships).
      Data in one table can be combined with data in any of

Student answer 2

1 (a) A relational database consists of a collection of data organised into different tables with each table containing a set of data that is relevant to the organisation. Three tables would be used here; a customers table, a tools table and a rentals table. The data is put into the separate tables but the tables are linked together, so it is possible to combine the information from data in all the tables.

  (b) He won't have to type as much in as there is not as much duplication of data as there would be with a flat file.
      If a customer changed their address, then with a flat file the manager would have to change the address in each current record where a piece of equipment has been hired. This means that if a customer has hired five different pieces of equipment, the address would need changing five times.

Examiner's comment

1 (a) There are three separate points made here so three marks.

  (b) This student has mentioned duplication of data and easier updating process and has explained each of these well. Two marks are given here. **(5 marks out of 8)**

the other tables.
Note they must be features and not advantages.

  (b) One mark each for three distinctly different advantages that must be relevant to this application.
      Full customer details do not need to be entered when a customer who has rented before rents again.
      If a mail shot needs to go out to customers, the manager will not need to go through all the orders extracting names and addresses as he can use the Customers table.
      An update is easier to make as the manager will only need to alter the data once in one of the tables.
      The data is stored more efficiently, so it will be faster to do searches and sorts.
      There will be fewer data errors since the data is only entered once, which means the manager can rely on the information produced.

Exam support continued

Worked example 2

2 A school uses a relational database for the day-to-day running of the school.

(a) Other than the pupils table, give the names of two other tables that this relational database system is likely to hold. **(2 marks)**

(b) Describe two features of a relational database that you would not find with a flat-file system. **(2 marks)**

(c) Databases store the data separate from the database program.
Give one reason for this. **(1 mark)**

(d) Pupil data is often sensitive personal data.
(i) Give an example of sensitive personal data that could be stored in the pupil table.
(ii) Explain one way in which the privacy of the data in this table can be assured. **(2 marks)**

(e) The school management system, which is based around a relational database, is protected by a hierarchy of passwords. Explain, with reference to this system, what is meant by a hierarchy of passwords. **(2 marks)**

Student answer 1

2 (a) Teachers table
Form table

(b) More than one table being used
Links between tables

(c) So that the data is easier to store

(d) (i) Health data such as illnesses and medications the pupil is taking
(ii) Passwords can be used to ensure there is no unauthorised access to the pupil data as this is a requirement under the terms of the Data Protection Act 1998

(e) Passwords can be used to decide who gains what access to the system and what they can do with the data in the system. For example, some users such as managers in the school can access and alter all the data in all the tables of the database. Teachers can only see the part of the data necessary for the performance of their jobs and they may only alter certain information.

Examiner's comment

2 (a) Both tables are applicable so two marks here.
(b) There is just about enough detail here so full marks.
(c) This is not a reason. Vague answers like this show no understanding and gain no marks.
(d) (i) and (ii) Two good points so two marks.
(e) This is well answered and worth two marks. **(8 marks out of 9)**

Student answer 2

2 (a) Teacher table
Student table

(b) Relationships
Tables

(c) So that the database program can be changed, and it can still use the existing data

(d) (i) Details of bad behaviour and detentions
(ii) Only allow certain people who need this information to access it
Use passwords, to prevent unauthorised access

(e) Some passwords are more important than others. For example, the head teacher's password would allow them to see all of the data, but a form teacher may only see the data about pupils in their own form. The passwords can also determine what you can do with the data in the database such as copy, alter, delete, and so on.

Examiner's comment

2 (a) Only teacher table is allowable for a mark here as student table is the same as pupil table.
(b) One word answers are not acceptable for a question, which asks the student to 'describe' so no marks are given here.
(c) The correct answer is given.
(d) (i) This is an acceptable answer.
(ii) Both of these answers are correct.
(e) This clearly explains that passwords can be used to limit access and control what a user can do with data. Two marks for this answer. **(6 marks out of 9)**

Examiner's answer

2 (a) One mark each for a table that is applicable to a school system.
Subject table
Teacher table
Form table
Room table
Class table

(b) One mark each for two features which must include a description and not simply a name.
More than one table
Links and relationships between tables
The ability to program the database

(c) One mark for a reason such as:
To enable the data to be imported or exported more easily
So that the data can be backed up separately
To make it easy to upgrade the software without altering the data

(d) (i) One mark for information such as:
Ethnic origin
Religion
Medical details

(ii) One mark for one of the following:
Appropriate training so staff understand responsibilities
Use of passwords
Access rights
Acceptable use policy

(e) Any two relevant aspects for two marks such as:
Passwords allocated to people according to their post
Passwords determine what files can be accessed
Passwords determine what can be done with the data once accessed
(e.g., read only, read/write, etc.)
Passwords used to limit access to programs that can be run

Summary mind maps

Databases

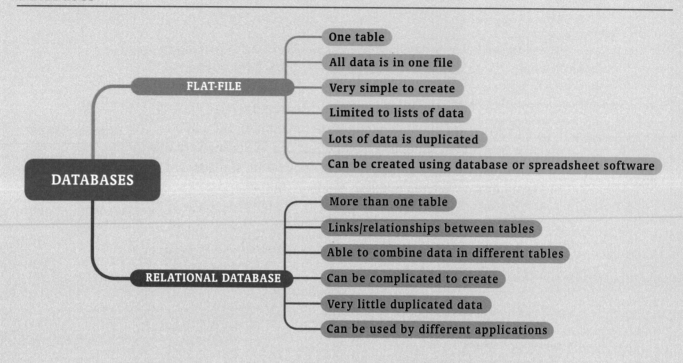

FLAT-FILE
- One table
- All data is in one file
- Very simple to create
- Limited to lists of data
- Lots of data is duplicated
- Can be created using database or spreadsheet software

DATABASES

RELATIONAL DATABASE
- More than one table
- Links/relationships between tables
- Able to combine data in different tables
- Can be complicated to create
- Very little duplicated data
- Can be used by different applications

Advantages and disadvantages of a relational database

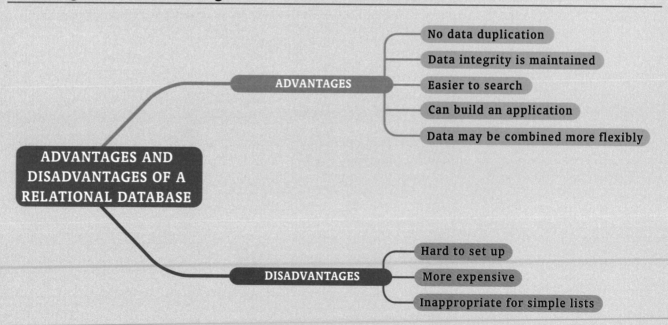

ADVANTAGES
- No data duplication
- Data integrity is maintained
- Easier to search
- Can build an application
- Data may be combined more flexibly

ADVANTAGES AND DISADVANTAGES OF A RELATIONAL DATABASE

DISADVANTAGES
- Hard to set up
- More expensive
- Inappropriate for simple lists

Introduction

In Section B of IT1, which accounts for 25% of the total marks for IT1, you will be required to prepare a spreadsheet on a specific topic. The topic will be given to you by WJEC well in advance of the examination. You will then prepare a spreadsheet which you will print out and take with you into the examination for IT1 and you will use your spreadsheet to answer questions in Section B of the examination. You will hand in the hard copy of the spreadsheet at the same time as your completed examination paper.

In this topic you will learn about spreadsheet features and functions, some of which you will need to use in the model you create. You will also learn about simulation modelling in general and how it is useful.

▼ The key concepts covered in this topic are:

▶ Understanding spreadsheet features and functions

▶ Understanding simulation modelling

CONTENTS

Spreadsheet features and functions

▼ You will find out

▶ About spreadsheet basics

▶ About formatting data

Introduction

You will already be familiar with many features and functions of spreadsheet software. This section seeks to revise some of the basics of spreadsheets but also seeks to let you know what other features are available in spreadsheet software and how they are used. This section does not seek to specifically teach you the actual commands and how they work. It does let you know the basic workings of them so that you can go away and use more specialist books or use the help information provided as part of the software. As you will be required to produce a solution to a problem using spreadsheet software, and this problem has to be quite complex, you will need to use a number of powerful functions and features that you may not have used before.

Spreadsheet basics

Just as a reminder here are the basics of spreadsheets.

The concepts of rows, columns, cells and cell references

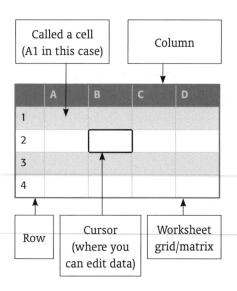

Called a cell (A1 in this case)

Column

Row

Cursor (where you can edit data)

Worksheet grid/matrix

Labels

Labels are the text next to cells that explains what it is that the cell contains.

You should never have a value on a spreadsheet on its own as the user will be left wondering what it represents.

Data formats

Data formats allow you to present the information in your spreadsheets more effectively.

Formatting text

Text can be made to stand out by formatting it in a number of ways:

- Font – changes the shapes of letters and numbers.
- Font size – used to make headings, sub-headings, etc., stand out.
- Bold, Italics, Underline – used to draw attention to text.

Borders and rotating text

Using borders you can:

- put a border around cells or groups of cells
- shade in certain cells or groups of cells.

Rotating text is useful when you want a narrow column but the column heading is wide.

Adding colour

Colour may be added to:

- text
- borders
- background colours for cells.

You should experiment with this menu to see what exactly the spreadsheet software is capable of.

Formatting numbers

There are lots of ways you will want to format numbers and here are some of them:

- Currency – numbers in normal money format with a pound sign added.
- Number – you can alter the number of decimal places to display.
- Date – there are lots of different formats for dates to choose from.

Common formulas/standard functions

A function is a specialised calculation that the spreadsheet software has memorised. There are many of these functions, some of which are very specialist.

A function must start with an equals sign (=) and it must have a range of cells to which it applies in brackets after it.

Average

For example, to find the average of the numbers in a range of cells from A3 to A10 you would use:
=AVERAGE(A3:A10)

Maximum

=MAX(D3:J3) displays the largest number in all the cells from D3 to J3 inclusive.

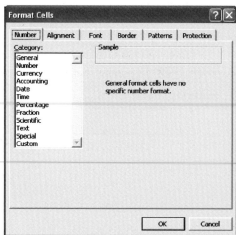

Minimum

=MIN(D3:J3) displays the smallest number in all the cells from D3 to J3 inclusive.

Mode

=MODE(A3:A15) displays the mode (i.e. the most frequent number) of the cells from A3 to A15 inclusive.

Median

=MEDIAN(B2:W2) displays the median of the cells from cells B2 to W2 inclusive.

Sum

=SUM(E3:P3) displays the total of all the cells from cells E3 to P3 inclusive.

COUNT

Suppose we want to count the number of numeric entries in the range C3 to C30.

We can use =COUNT(C3:C30).

Any blank lines or text entries in the range will not be counted.

COUNTA

To count a number of items or names of people we need to be able to count text entries.

To do this we can use =COUNTA(C3: C30).

You need to make sure that headings are not included in the range so that they are not counted as well. Again blank lines are not counted.

RAND

Sometimes it is necessary to include a random element into a model as completely unexpected events do happen. RAND generates a random number which is greater than or equal to 0 but less than 1.

It is more useful in models to generate a random number between any two values, in which case the following formula can be used:

=RAND()*(b-a)+a where a is the smaller and b is the larger of the numbers.

So, for a random number between 1 and 10 including only integers (i.e. whole number values) you would use:

=INT(RAND()*(10-1)+1)

Relative and absolute cell references

There are two ways in which you can make a reference to another cell and it is important to know the difference if you want to copy or move cells. An absolute reference always refers to the same cell.

The other type of reference, called a relative reference, refers to a cell that is a certain number of rows and columns away. When the current cell is copied or moved to a new position, the cell to which the reference is made will also change position.

To understand the difference we will look at two examples.

The first example shows relative referencing with cell B4 containing a relative reference to cell A1. This reference tells the spreadsheet that the cell to which it refers is 3 cells up and one cell to the left of cell B4. If cell B4 is copied to another position, say E5, then the reference will still be to the same number of cells up and to the left so the reference will now be to cell D2.

With absolute cell referencing, if cell B4 contains a reference to cell A1, then if the contents of B4 are copied to a new position, then the reference will not be adjusted and it will still refer to cell A1.

In most cases we will want to use relative cell references and the spreadsheet will assume that ordinary cell references are relative cell references. Sometimes we want to refer to the same cell, even when the formula referring to the cell is copied to a new position. We therefore need to make sure that the formula contains an absolute cell reference. To do this, a dollar sign is placed in front of the column and row number.

Cell B6 is a relative cell reference. To change it to an absolute cell reference we would add the dollar signs like this: B6.

More advanced spreadsheet modelling concepts

Introduction

This section covers some of the more advanced spreadsheet modelling concepts, some of which you will need to use when creating your own model for assessment.

The concept of a workbook

If you load spreadsheet software you will notice that there is a small tab like this at the bottom of the worksheet:

`\ Sheet1 / Sheet2 / Sheet3 /`

You can see here that there are three worksheets which can be chosen. A collection of worksheets is called a workbook and it is sometimes useful to group worksheets together. For example, you could use one worksheet for input, one for the processing and another to present the output.

`\ Input / Processing / Output /`

You can have more than three worksheets if you want. For example, you could set up a worksheet to show the sales for four quarters of a year.

`\ 1st Quarter / 2nd Quarter / 3rd Quarter / 4th Quarter /`

Lookup, VLOOKUP or HLOOKUP tables

Lookup function

Lookup functions are very useful. When you type in a number, such as pupil number, NHS number or product number, the spreadsheet looks through a table until it finds this number along with other important data. For example, if each different product in a shop is given a unique number, then we can store this number along with a description of the product, price, etc., in a table in another part of the spreadsheet. If we type in a product number in another part of the spreadsheet, the spreadsheet will search through the table until it locates the product number and related details.

The two types of lookup function

There are two types of lookup function: VLOOKUP and HLOOKUP. The one to use depends on whether the data in the table is arranged vertically or horizontally. In the worksheet shown below the data to look up is contained

▼ You will find out

▶ About the concept of a workbook

▶ About lookup (VLOOKUP or HLOOKUP) tables

▶ About facilities for data entry – spinners, list boxes and combo boxes

▶ About 3D referencing

▶ About macros to initiate automated routines

▶ About validation techniques and error messages

▶ About single IF functions

▶ About multiple IF functions

▶ About the DATE function

▶ About the ROUND function

➡ KEY WORDS

Workbook – a file that contains one or more worksheets

Worksheet – a single page showing the worksheet grid into which you can put data, formulas, etc.

in a vertical table with the headings at the top of the columns so the VLOOKUP function is used.

The HLOOKUP function is used when the data in the table to look up looks like this:

Level	KS3	GCSE	AS-Level	A-Level	Degree
Rate per hour	£25.60	£27.50	£29.00	£30.00	£41.00

The Lookup function being used to return product information when a product code is entered					
Product Number	1023				
Product Description	HB pencils				
Product Price	0.04				
Product Number	**Product Description**	**Product Price**			
1021	A4 paper	£5.45			
1022	Paper clips	£0.23			
1023	HB pencils	£0.04			
1024	Red pens	£0.28			
1025	Black pens	£0.28			

Facilities for data entry – spinners, list boxes and combo boxes

The main requirements for data entry into a spreadsheet model are that:

- it should be made as easy as possible for the user
- it will reduce the likelihood of incorrect data being entered.

Other than just typing, you can use the following facilities to enter data:

Spinners – these let you alter the value in a cell by clicking on an up or down arrow.

Here is a spinner used in a worksheet to alter the number of years:

List boxes – list boxes present a choice of data to be entered into a spreadsheet cell. All the items in the list are shown in the box unless the list is too long in which case the scroll bar is used to make them visible.

Combo boxes – these allow you choose an entry from a list which only appears when you click on the arrow to drop it down. They are useful because they can be used to enter more than one piece of data from a table of data.

Combo boxes are used when you have a fixed number of choices (e.g., days of the week, months of the year, certain sizes (S, M, L, XL), certain colours, etc.).

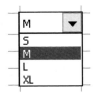

Logical (True or False) boxes – these are sometimes called check boxes and they return a true or false depending on whether they are selected or cleared. They are useful when there are only two possible settings such as on/off or true/false. Here is one where express delivery can be chosen by putting a tick in the check box.

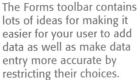

Option buttons – are used when the user has to select between alternatives. To the right is one where the user has to choose their age range:

3D referencing

3D referencing is used when you want to refer to the same cell or a group of cells which are contained on multiple worksheets within a workbook. For example, using the spreadsheet software Excel you could have a formula with a 3D reference like this:

$$=SUM(Sheet1:Sheet4!A6)$$

The above formula would add together all the contents of cell A6 in all the worksheets from worksheet 1 to worksheet 4. This would be useful if you had sets of sales figures for four years each on different worksheets and you wanted to produce a summary worksheet which compares the figures.

AutoFill lists

Suppose you want to type the days of the week or months of the year down a column or across a row. Excel is able to anticipate what you probably want to do by the first word alone. So, if you type Monday, then the chances are that you want Tuesday in the next column or row and so on. The main advantage in using AutoFill is that the data being entered is less likely to contain errors than if you type in the data yourself.

There are many other ways you can use spreadsheet software to fill in data for you, so use the help facility to find out more about AutoFill.

Macros to initiate automated routines

Macros are very useful features of software packages because they can save the user a lot of time. Using a macro you can instruct the computer to perform a large number of tasks at the press of a button.

The Forms toolbar contains lots of ideas for making it easier for your user to add data as well as make data entry more accurate by restricting their choices.

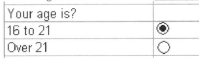

Basically, a macro is a set of commands that may be played back whenever you want to perform a simple task. For example, you could create a macro which will create a pie chart from a table of sales data. Instead of having to go though all the steps using the Wizard to create the chart from scratch, you can just run the macro.

When you are looking for things to automate using macros, you should think of all those tasks that take time and are repetitive in nature.

There are two ways you can produce a macro:

- using the macro recorder
- using the Visual Basic Editor.

Only the first method will be looked at here.

Using the macro recorder is the easiest method of recording macros, but the sorts of things you can do is limited. With the macro recorder, you use the recorder to record commands and options made using mouse clicks. You can then play back the commands or options in the order they were made, simply by accessing the macro from a menu. Alternatively, you can assign the macro to a toolbar.

Using the Visual Basic Editor is a more advanced way to create powerful macros that could not be created using the macro recorder.

When a macro is recorded, all the steps will be recorded, even the wrong ones if you make any mistakes. Before starting the macro, you need to be fairly clear about what you are trying to do and it is often worth going through the steps as a dummy run before you actually record the macro. It is also useful to write the steps down.

Always save your work before starting a macro, since you can go back to the saved version if something unexpected happens. You cannot use the Undo command with a macro, so stopping the macro and going back to a previously saved version of the worksheet is your only option.

Rather than go though the usual procedures for running a macro, it is easier to use a special button which you can set up for the purpose. To learn about how to do this you can look at the help provided with the software.

More advanced spreadsheet modelling concepts continued

IF function – the IF function tests a condition to see if it is true or not. This test could see if a cell is above a certain number (i.e. >), below a certain number (i.e. <), equal to a certain number (i.e. =) and so on. When the condition is tested, it can be true or false. If the condition is true, then one value will be returned, which will be the first one in the list. If the condition is false, then a different value will be returned, which will be the second value in the list.

Validation techniques and error messages

You learnt about producing validation checks and error messages in Topic 4 Validation and verification/4 on pages 36–39. You should look back at these pages to refresh your memory.

Sorting techniques

Using spreadsheet software, you can produce a flat-file containing data. The data in this file can be sorted according to any of the fields.

Filtering is also useful where only specific information is obtained. Here is a filter applied to a names and addresses database to extract all the names and addresses in the L12 postcode area.

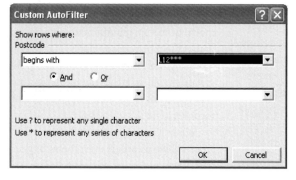

Search for specific criteria

You can search for a record using a single field or a number of fields in a flat-file. For example, the record for the person with the surname 'Harman' is being searched for here.

You can also add operators to your search criteria chosen from the following table.

Operator	Meaning
=	equal to
>	greater than
<	less than
<=	less than or equal to
>=	greater than or equal to
<>	is not equal to

Single IF functions

The IF function is called a logical function because it makes the decision to do one of two things based on the value it is testing. The IF function is very useful because you can use it to test a condition and then choose between two actions based on whether the condition is true or false.

The IF function makes use of something called relational operators. You may have come across these in your mathematics lessons but it is worth going through what they mean.

Relational operators (=, <, >, <>, <=, >=)

Symbol	Meaning	Examples
=	equals	5 + 5 = 10
>	greater than	5*3 > 2*3
<	less than	-6 < -1 or 100 < 200
<>	not equal to	"Red" <> "White" or 20/4 <> 6*4
<=	less than or equal to	"Adam" <= "Eve"
>=	greater than or equal to	400 >= 200

Enter one or more search criteria in these boxes.

Click on Find Next to display the whole record

Sheet1

		Criteria
Surname:	Harman	New
Forename :		Clear
Gender:		Restore
Date of Birth:		
Year Group:		Find Prev
Registration Group:		Find Next ◄
Admission Number:		Form
		Close

The most common operator by far is the equals sign but sometimes a comparison needs to be made between two items of data. For example, we may need to find a list of employees whose salaries are greater than a certain amount such as £20,000.

Operators can also be used with characters or character strings, so one character can be compared with another and since each character has a binary code (ASCII) associated with it, the computer can work out that A comes before B and so on. You can also test to see if the contents of a certain cell have a certain word in them. For example, you could test to see IF B6="Yes".

The IF function is structured like this:

=IF(Condition,value if true,value if false)

The value can either be a number or a message. If the values are messages, then they need to be enclosed inside quote marks (e.g. "High").

Here are some examples of the use of a single IF function:

=IF(B3>=50,"Pass","Fail")

This function tests to see if the number in cell B3 is greater than or equal to 50. If the answer is true, Pass is displayed and if the answer is false, Fail is displayed.

=IF(A2>=500,A2*0.5,A2)

This tests to see if the number in cell A2 is greater than or equal to 500. If true the number in cell A2 will be multiplied by 0.5 and the answer displayed (i.e. 250 will be displayed). If false, the number in cell A2 will be displayed.

Multiple IF functions

Multiple IF functions test for more than one condition to be met.

Combining conditions with AND

If you want to perform a calculation or produce a message only when two conditions are true, then you can use the AND() function.

Look at this function containing AND:

=IF(AND(B3="Yes",C3="Yes"), "Pass","Fail")

Notice how this formula works. The innermost brackets contain the two conditions to be tested. In this case we are checking to see if both cells have Yes in them. After these brackets, the message to be printed if the conditions in the brackets are true, is placed in inverted commas (i.e. "Pass"). After this comes the message for the false condition (i.e. "Fail").

Combining conditions with OR

If you want to perform a calculation or produce a message only when one or two of two conditions are true, then you can use the OR() function.

Look at this function containing OR:

=IF(OR(B3="Yes",C3="Yes"),"Pass", "Fail")

In this example either B3 or C3 or both need to contain the text "Yes" for the condition to be true and the message "Pass" to appear.

DATE function

There are many ways of writing a date, but when entering a date into a spreadsheet you are best using the format:

14/03/2009 (DD/MM/YYYY)

Dates in Excel are stored as numbers and the date 01/01/1900 (i.e. 01 Jan 1900) is represented by the number 1. This means that the date 02/01/1900 is represented by the number 2 and so on.

Representing dates in this way means that you can subtract two dates to find the number of days that have elapsed between them:

In the worksheet the formula in cell B4 is =TODAY() and a normal date is entered into B5. Cell B7 contains the formula =B4-B5 but this cell needs to be formatted to a number when the correct number of days is shown.

In order to see a date as a number, the cell must be formatted to number.

Here are two useful date functions:

=TODAY() is a useful function that returns the current date
=NOW() is a useful function that returns the current date and time.

ROUND

The ROUND function rounds a number correct to a number of digits that you specify. ROUND is used in the following way:

=ROUND(number,number of digits), where number is the number you want rounded off and number of digits is the number of decimal places.

Here are some examples:

=ROUND(3.56678,2) will return the number 3.57
=ROUND(5.43,1) will return the number 5.4

	A	B	C	D	E
1	Spreadsheet to work out the number of days between two dates				
2					
3					
4	Today's date	17/03/2008			
5	Your date of birth	04/07/1993			
6					
7	You have lived	5370	Days		
8					

Simulation modelling

Introduction

Modelling means producing a series of mathematical equations, which may be used to mimic a real situation. When values are put into the model or we exercise the model in some way we are said to be performing a simulation. There are many types of specialist modelling software, from games to flight simulators. Models can be created to describe the flow of traffic at junctions and the output from the model can then used to issue controls to the traffic signals to ensure that the traffic flows as smoothly as possible. Spreadsheet software can be used to construct models.

The components of a simple model

Models consist of the following components.

Input values

These are the values that are not preset within the model. Input values are usually entered by the user using keyboard entry. It is important that these input values are validated so that only valid data is processed.

Variables

Variables are those items of data that we are likely to change in the model. For example, in a model to show the effect of inflation on someone's savings, the amount they have saved, the interest rate they are getting and the rate of inflation are all variables. Variables should never be put directly into a formula, since for a user to change their value they would have to understand the formula.

Constants

These are those numbers which do not change or you want to keep the same. Be careful with constants because many quantities stay constant over a short period but not a longer period.

Constraints

A constraint is something that is imposed on a model. For example, you could have a credit limit imposed on you by the bank and your spending cannot go over it.

Rules (i.e., calculations and other operators)

Once data has been entered, it can be subject to a range of operators:

- Arithmetic ($+$, $-$, $\div$, $\times$, etc.)
- Relational ($=$, $<$, $>$, IF)
- Logical (AND, OR, NOT).

These calculations and logical operators are referred to as rules.

Startup user interface

A model is an application that is designed for others to use, which means it should have an easy to use human–computer interface. The user should not be wondering what they must do.

You need to ensure that all the worksheets that you use in the model can be accessed from a startup user interface which will be the first thing that users see when they open the spreadsheet file. Thought needs to be given to the best way of making sure that the user knows exactly what to do.

Many models can be created using spreadsheet software.

Applications of modelling

There are many examples of modelling other than the ones we have already looked at. Here are some of the popular types of model.

Economic and financial models

The state of the economy is important to all of us. It determines how prosperous the country is. The government use an economic model to predict what might happen if they raised taxes, reduced interest rates, increased the amount spent on public services, such as hospitals, schools, etc.

Like all models, the economic model consists of rules and variable data. In the economic model the rules consist of equations like this:

unemployment = people able to work – people actually working

The variable data might be the inflation rate, interest rates, the price of oil, and so on. By altering the values of the variables, economists can see what the likely consequences are.

Businesses often need to make predictions to help them plan, and they create models which mimic certain financial aspects of the business.

Here are some examples of financial models:

- sales analysis
- break-even analysis
- modelling the effects of inflation
- working out depreciation
- working out the value of a portfolio of investments
- profit and loss account
- cashflow forecast
- sales staff commissions
- breakdown of profit from each customer
- costings
- stock analysis.

To understand the above, you need to understand the underlying business concepts involved. When you produce a business model, you need to perform some research and this can be done by looking at business studies textbooks to give you some ideas.

This financial model has been created using spreadsheet software to work out the number of cups of coffee a large coffee bar must sell in a month in order to break even.

Games

Many games are models. For example, the board game Monopoly is a model of running a property business. Many computer games use models. For example, one game simulates running a theme park. Using this simulation you can add new rides, position ice cream kiosks and do all the things involved in running a theme park. The aim of the game is to make your park as profitable as you can.

Even action games use models to simulate driving a Formula 1 car, flying a fighter jet, playing football and so on.

Weather forecasting

Weather data such as wind speed, air temperature, ground temperature and humidity are logged continuously from remote weather stations throughout the world. The data collected from these stations are relayed back to the meteorological office. The data is then processed along with the data from satellite pictures to produce a weather forecast. The program that does this is a model. It uses the variables and lots of rules to try to predict what the weather is likely to be in the future.

Weather forecasts use models to help make predictions.

	A	B	C	D	E	F
1	**AromaBar model to find the break-even point**					
2	All the following figures are monthly figures					
3						
4	Selling price of a cup of coffee	£1.50				
5						
6	**Fixed costs**					
7	Rent of premises	£750				
8	Staff wages	£4,200				
9	Rates	£557				
10	Interest on loan	£345				
11	Total fixed costs	£5,852				
12						
13						
14	**Variable costs (per cup)**					
15	Coffee	£0.13				
16	Filter papers	£0.02				
17	Milk/Cream	£0.05				
18	Total variable costs (per cup)	£0.20				
19						
20						
21						
22	**Number of cups of coffee sold**	**Variable costs (£)**	**Fixed costs (£)**	**Total costs (£)**	**Sales revenue (£)**	**Profit/Loss (£)**
23	4491	£898.20	£5,852	£6,750.20	£6,736.50	£13.70
24	4492	£898.40	£5,852	£6,750.40	£6,738.00	£12.40
25	4493	£898.60	£5,852	£6,750.60	£6,739.50	£11.10
26	4494	£898.80	£5,852	£6,750.80	£6,741.00	£9.80
27	4495	£899.00	£5,852	£6,751.00	£6,742.50	£8.50
28	4496	£899.20	£5,852	£6,751.20	£6,744.00	£7.20
29	4497	£899.40	£5,852	£6,751.40	£6,745.50	£5.90
30	4498	£899.60	£5,852	£6,751.60	£6,747.00	£4.60
31	4499	£899.80	£5,852	£6,751.80	£6,748.50	£3.30
32	4500	£900.00	£5,852	£6,752.00	£6,750.00	£2.00
33	4501	£900.20	£5,852	£6,752.20	£6,751.50	£0.70
34	4502	£900.40	£5,852	£6,752.40	£6,753.00	£0.60
35	4503	£900.60	£5,852	£6,752.60	£6,754.50	£1.90
36	4504	£900.80	£5,852	£6,752.80	£6,756.00	£3.20
37	4505	£901.00	£5,852	£6,753.00	£6,757.50	£4.50

The advantages and disadvantages of using simulation models

There are many reasons why models and simulations are used and here are some of them.

The advantages

Cheaper

It can be cheaper to use a model/ simulation. For example, car engineers can use a computer to model the effect on the occupants during a crash and this is cheaper than using real cars with crash test dummies.

Crash test computer models replace the crash test dummies.

Safer

Flight simulators can model the effect of flying a plane in extreme situations. Extreme situations might include landing without the undercarriage coming down, or landing with only one engine working and so on. It would be far too dangerous to expect a pilot to try these in real life.

It can save time

Global warming models can be set up to predict what the likely effects of global warming will be in the future.

It is possible to experience lots more situations

Pilots using simulations can experience all sorts of extreme weather conditions such as sand storms, hurricanes, smoke from volcanic action, and so on. These would be almost impossible to experience any other way.

The disadvantages

The differences between simulation and reality

There will always be some differences between a model/simulation and reality. No model or simulation can ever be perfect because real life can be so complicated.

The accuracy of the rules and variables

The person designing the model may have made mistakes with the rules or the variable data.

Some situations are hard to model

Some situations are difficult to model because some aspects of the model are often open to interpretation. For example, experts on the subject may disagree about the rules that apply.

Simulations

Doing something with a model that has been created is called a simulation. Models consist of set of equations that are used to describe how the real thing behaves. When we perform a simulation we put values into these equations to see what happens. Sometimes we continually interact with the model such as in a flight simulator.

Flight simulators

You can buy flight simulator software for your computer. Obviously you will not get the feel of a real plane but it will give you some idea what the controls are. Real flight simulators move in the same way as the plane, so you can get the feel of the plane accelerating along the runway, climbing and descending, etc.

As well as the rules which make up the models being used, there are also some inputs needed into the system.

A motion simulator used at NASA flight research centres.

Inputs to a flight simulator

- type of weather (fine, snow, fog, thunderstorms, rain, etc.)
- the type of aircraft
- the total weight of the aircraft as this will affect the plane's performance
- any problems with the aircraft (e.g., loss of power from an engine, undercarriage not coming down, etc.)
- the terrain (i.e., what the ground looks like from the plane)
- whether it is day or night
- the approach scenery to the airport.

Examples of simulations

- games
- flight simulators for the training of pilots
- animated weather maps showing the path of a storm
- car crash simulations.

Car crash simulations

Simulations are used instead of actual crashes to find out design changes based on crash simulations when a new car is being designed. For more on this please see the Case study.

For a simulation for crash testing a car, the inputs might be:

- speed
- road conditions (rain, ice, snow, etc.)
- condition of brakes and tyres
- the make of cars (some cars are stronger in crashes than others)
- the direction of collision
- the number of occupants in the car.

Inside a flight simulator.

Issues relating to hardware used for simulation modelling

There are many complex simulation models that cannot be solved using ordinary computer systems. In this section you will look at how these problems are solved.

Parallel processors

Most computers have a single processor, which means they are only able to do one thing at a time. The high speed of computer processors means we are tricked into thinking they are working on more tasks, because they are able to move quickly between tasks.

The most powerful computers used for large-scale complex simulations have parallel processors, which means they are able to divide up a large complex task and carry out each task simultaneously.

Distributed processing

Distributed processing is the processing performed by any ICT system that uses more than one processor to run an application. This means that computers which use parallel processors are using distributed processing. Another way this can be achieved is when the processors of several computers connected in a network, such as a local area network (LAN), are combined so that the task can be worked on by the processor of each computer simultaneously.

A Cray supercomputer, one of the most powerful computers in the world makes use of parallel processors.

Questions and Case study

▶ **Questions 1** pp. 226–235

1 Many simulation models are used by accountants in businesses to model certain financial aspects of the business.
  (a) Describe what is meant by the term simulation model. (3 marks)
  (b) Discuss the reasons why spreadsheet software is often used by accountants for creating simulations models. (4 marks)
2 Simulation models are used in many applications.
  (a) Describe three main components of a simulation model. (3 marks)
  (b) Describe two distinctly different applications for simulation models other than for financial modelling. (4 marks)
  (c) Give one advantage and one disadvantage of using simulation models. (2 marks)

3 Large simulation models are used for weather forecasting, simulating climate change and car crash analysis.
  Describe the issues relating to the hardware used for these large-scale and complex simulation models. (4 marks)
4 Simulation models are often created using spreadsheet software.
  (a) Explain two features of spreadsheet software that makes it especially suitable for the production of these models. (2 marks)
  (b) It is essential that as far as possible only correct data should be processed by the simulation model. Describe two methods of validation you have used in a computer model to trap certain types of error. (2 marks)

▶ **Case study** pp. 232–235

Crash testing BMW 5-Series cars using virtual reality

A 5-Series BMW is driven into a concrete wall and the driver moves forward against the seatbelts and into the airbag. The car was travelling fast and the bonnet is crushed completely. This crash is not happening in real life, it is happening on a computer screen. The engineer uses the computer to model the crash.

The damage inside the car can now be seen by a click of the mouse. The inside of the car is now revealed, to see how the various parts have been affected by the crash. Most importantly the engineers can see the effect on the driver of the car. Because the car has been so well designed, the part where the driver sits has not collapsed, so the driver would not be injured.

Before a new car is built, it will have been crashed over a hundred times in different directions. A powerful computer takes days to work out the damage of just one crash because of the millions of calculations it needs to make. The effect of the crash can be seen in slow motion and the designers can make alterations to the design of the car if needed. In the past they would have had to make prototypes (almost complete cars) costing as much as £500,000 each and then crash them. A very expensive process bearing in mind that several cars would be needed! A crash using the computer costs very little.

1 The crash testing system used by BMW is an example of virtual reality. Explain what is meant by simulation. (2 marks)
2 Certain details about the car will need to be input into the computer before the crash takes place. Give three inputs that might be needed. (3 marks)
3 Give two advantages in using the simulation model rather than a real car to find out what happens during a crash. (4 marks)

Exam support

Worked example 1

1 A kitchen design company would like to use computer software to give customers quotations and to work out sales staff commissions.

Describe the benefits in using spreadsheet software to solve these problems. (4 marks)

Student answer 1

1 It saves time if you use a spreadsheet and it is also more efficient to enter details into the spreadsheet and let it do the work. You could get the spreadsheet to work out who gets what commission and then put it into a graph such as a bar chart showing a comparison of different salesmen's commissions so that each salesperson can assess their performance against others.

Examiner's comment

1 The first sentence gains no marks as it does not specify what it is that is more efficient or that saves time. The second sentence outlines the benefit and this is expanded to explain the way in which the spreadsheet is used. **(2 marks out of 4)**

Examiner's answer

1 Two marks for benefits and two marks for further explanation.

Maximum mark of three if only one benefit is given.

Ability to recalculate (1). If a customer adds items or takes items away from the design, the spreadsheet automatically recalculates the costs (1).

Student answer 2

1 Customers have a budget when buying a kitchen so they will often have to make changes to a kitchen design to fit their budget. For example, they may choose fewer units, cheaper fridges, freezers, etc. Using a spreadsheet allows them to make changes and use the spreadsheet software to recalculate the costs. They can then save the different versions using different file names in case they want to go back to them.

Examiner's comment

1 Here the student has only given one benefit. It is always best to use the mark scheme to gauge the number of marks for each part. The word 'benefits' was mentioned in the question so more that one benefit should have been given.

This is a good answer for a single benefit but can only gain a maximum of three marks according to the mark scheme. **(3 marks out of 4)**

Can perform 'what ifs' (1) to model the costs of different appliances, different tiles, etc. (1).
Can show graphically by producing graphs and charts (1) the comparisons between the different commissions of the sales staff in order to foster competition (1).
Accurate calculations of commissions (1) will increase efficiency and save time by preventing sales staff having to query errors (1).

Exam support continued

Worked example 2

For this question, the student must refer to their own spreadsheet

2 (a) Describe the purpose or function of two different formulas you have used in your spreadsheet. **(4 marks)**

   (b) Describe two methods you used in your spreadsheet to ensure as far as is possible that incorrect data is not processed by your spreadsheet. **(4 marks)**

   (c) Other than the calculations you have described in part (a) or (b) describe two completely different processes used in your spreadsheet. **(4 marks)**

Student answer 1

2 (a) I used the formula to add up the total costs in column A. The formula =SUM(B2:B15) was put in cell B16.
   Here is another formula I used:
   =IF(A2<0,"Account overdrawn","Account in credit") tests cell A2 to see if it is less than 0. If true the message "Account overdrawn" appears and if false the message "Account in credit" appears.

   (b) I verified the data by reading the sheet I used with all the numbers on that I needed to enter and checking that I did not introduce any errors during the typing in.
   I formatted the cells which meant I could specify the type of data that could be entered. For example cell C2 was formatted to currency and this means that only numbers can be entered and the Pound sign will be added automatically.

   (c) I used goal seek where I wanted to set the profit/loss in cell G5 to zero by altering cell B9 which contains the number of games sold.
   I worked out all the percentages in column D by using a formula.

Examiner's comment

2 (a) Students need to have experienced 'high level' spreadsheet work and in questions such as this they are best advised to explain the higher level work they have done.
   As SUM is a basic function, no marks are given here.
   The IF….THEN…ELSE formula is more complex and has been well explained and gains two marks.

   (b) The question states that the method is used in the spreadsheet which means that it is looking at validation rather than verification. No marks for this part.
   Formatting cells for a particular type of data is not the same as a data type check. For example, formatting a cell to currency will not prevent a word being entered. There is no mark for this part of the question.

   (c) Goal seeking is a process but there is only one mark allocated for the description.
   Percentages are calculations and the question is clear about not wanting any more calculations as advantages of processes, so no marks for this part. **(3 marks out of 12)**

Examiner's comment

2 (a) Although using the DATE function is fine, the student has made no reference to where this formula was used. It is best to include the cell references to which the formula applies and it is a good idea to also write down the formula. One mark is given for this description.
The second part of this answer is much better with the formula included and the purpose of the formula made clear. Two marks for this.

(b) Both these methods of validation are range checks. Students have to make sure that they give completely different checks.
Two marks are given here for the description of the range check.

(c) Both these process descriptions contain two points which can gain marks. Four marks are given here. **(9 marks out of 12)**

Examiner's answers

2 (a) If there is no spreadsheet evidence submitted, then no marks can be awarded.
Simply naming the type of formula or function will gain no marks but a full description of what it does or how it works will gain a max of two marks.
Examples include:

=IF(A1>=500,25,15) this formula means that if the charge is £500 or over then £25 will be placed in column B for the postage and if not then £15 is put in.

=IF(A3>5,A6+B2,A6-C2)

This means that IF the number in cell A3 is greater than 5 THEN the contents of cell A6 will be added to those of cell B2, otherwise (ELSE) the contents of cell C2 are subtracted from those in cell A6.
The formula in cell B5 is, =VLOOKUP(B4,A11:C14,2,FALSE).
B4 is where the data is entered to match a value held in the table of data. A11:C14 is the range of cells where the table of data is located. The number '2' then tells the computer it has to look at the second column in this table to find the data it needs to put into the cell where the formula is.

(b) One mark for the correct name of a validation check and up to three marks for describing the check.
I used a list box (1) which meant users were restricted in their choice of data (1) to the items in the list which they just clicked on to save time (1).
I applied a range check to cell C4 (1) by only allowing whole numbers between 11 and 19 to be entered (1). I created an input message so that users knew what data should be entered and I created an error message which popped up when data breached the rule (1).

(c) No mark for simply naming a different process but up to two marks for a detailed description.
I used 3D referencing with five worksheets in a workbook so that I could add up similar sales data for each quarter (1) contained in different worksheets (1) and compare and summarise the differences in a summary worksheet (1).
I used a macro to take the share data in the worksheet and produce line graphs using the chart wizard (1). I created a button so all the user needed to do, is to click on the button and the macro will be started (1).

Topic 12 Modelling

Summary mind maps

The benefits of using spreadsheet software for simulation models

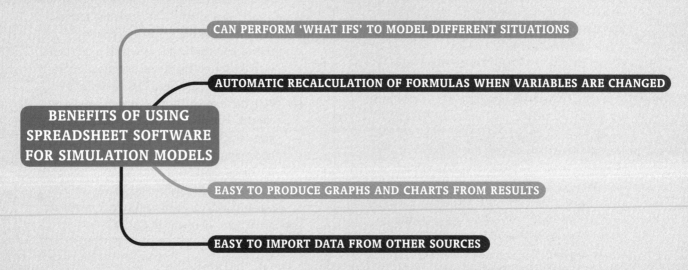

A summary of simulation models

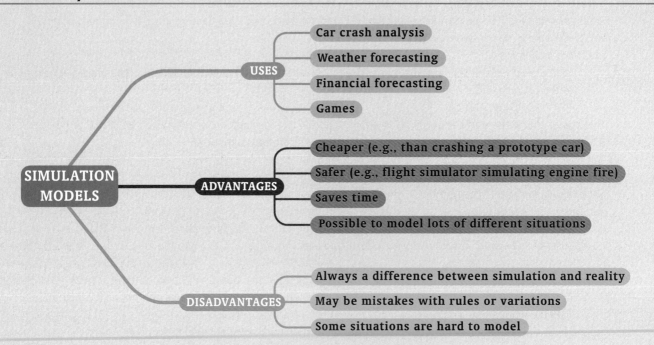

In this unit, you will be required to use ICT hardware and software applications to solve a problem involving three separate tasks:

1. a document such as a leaflet or magazine
2. a document containing automated routines such as a mail merged letter
3. a presentation to an audience such as a webpage or a slide-based show.

You will need to read each of the sections very carefully several times in order to understand exactly what you have to do.

▼ The key components of the assessment for IT2 are:

▶ Background – explains the background information to the organisation

▶ Analysis of data processing activities – where documents used by the organisation are investigated for house style, ethos and image

▶ Task 1 – Desktop publishing

▶ Task 2 – Automated documents

▶ Task 3 – Presentation

▶ Evaluation

▶ Compression and storage techniques

CONTENTS

Overview of the tasks

Introduction

Before looking at what you have to do for the three separate tasks, it is useful to have an overview of all the tasks and look at those things that apply to the whole project.

Choosing the context for the project

You have to choose your own context for the project as WJEC will not set a context and neither will your teacher/lecturer. You are not allowed to complete the project as a part of a group, so the work must be all your own.

Here is a summary of what you have to do, which is taken from the WJEC specification. Notice that the table shows the features (basic and advanced) that should be included in each task submission.

IT2 Presenting Information (Internally Assessed Task)			
Background			
Analysis of existing data processing activities			
Tasks	**Examples**	**Basic features**	**Advanced features**
	Candidates must attempt all tasks	Candidates should use *all* of these features	**At least five** of the following are required to access the higher mark ranges
Task 1 DTP Design and produce a document of at least two A4 sides and containing at least 150 words	• Leaflet or magazine	• Use of different styles • Use of different font sizes • Use of bold, centre and underline • Right or fully justify • Autoshapes • Bullet points • WordArt • Shading effects • Headers and footers • Use of at least two forms of electronic combination of graphical images, e.g. scanned images, graphics from the Internet, clipart from disc, digital camera images, graphs from a spreadsheet, graphics from a paint or CAD package • Tables	• Customised tables • Different paragraph formats • Different line spacing • Superscript and subscript • Page or frame borders • Set and use own tabs • Set and use own indents • Watermarks • Pagination • Use of layering (forward and behind) • Create own style sheets
Task 2 Automated documents Design and produce documents containing automated routines	• Mail merge letters including macros	• Import data from an external source • Design and use of professional format and layout for data • Ensure automated routines work	• Individual macros or modules created using internal programming capabilities of the software package • Individually designed templates (other than the normal template or standard templates provided by wizards in the software package)
Task 3 Presentation Design and produce a presentation of at least six slides/ pages for an audience	Either a • Slide-based presentation Or • Webpages	• Background styles • Animation effects • Transition effects • Hypertext • Hotspots • Bookmarks	• Use of sound • Use of original video • Use of original animation/Flash graphics

What you have to produce for background and analysis

The design stage

A builder would not start building a house without any designs or plans, so you should not start producing any work without carefully considering the design aspects.

Since you will be producing three separate documents, the design of each should be documented separately.

You need to consider each of the following:

Ethos, image and house style

Ethos

Ethos is the fundamental character or spirit of an organisation; the underlying sentiment that informs the beliefs, customs or practices of the organisation.

Image

Image is the general or public perception of a company, organisation, etc., especially as achieved by careful calculation aimed at creating widespread goodwill.

House style

Many different people in an organisation produce documents and these documents need to look similar – almost as if the same person had produced them all. House style concerns the following:

- Use of a logo – logos are used consistently (i.e., size, colour and position).
- Use of words – there are different ways to spell the same words, so there needs to be consistency.
- Use of colours – colour schemes can be identified and used consistently.
- Writing style – the way people express themselves needs to be consistent.
- Tone – certain documents need to adopt a specific tone.

Important note

Ethos or house style is not the same as age group or target audience.

Rules which you must obey

Here are some rules set by the examination board WJEC:

- You must choose your own topic.
- Your work must be distinctive (i.e., not like anyone else's).
- Do not put your work in ring binders – as it takes up too much space.
- Ensure that the pages can be detached if needed.

Advice that applies to all three tasks

The following advice applies to all three tasks:

- Do not waste time providing evidence that is not needed.
- Avoid cropping your work too much, as this sometimes destroys the evidence.
- Do not provide screenshots that are too small – the markers will need to be able to read them.
- You must produce proper design work – annotating (i.e., adding remarks) to implemented solutions is not proper design. Design must not be an afterthought.
- You should clearly explain or justify your ethos or house style. The ethos must be explained for all three tasks. The house style applies to all the documents and can be explained just once.

▶ **Activity: Looking at the house style for an organisation**

Imperial College London is a university and like all organisations they produce a huge range of documents authored by many different people. The university want to convey a professional image, so they need to make sure that all documents have a similar professional look to them. This is why they use a house style. To ensure all staff who produce documents know what the house style is, they have included it on a webpage. Look at this using this web address:

http://www3.imperial.ac.uk/graphicidentity/housestyle

You will find it useful to understand the typical components of a house style so that you can apply a house style to the documents you produce for your project.

Completing the tasks: Task 1

Introduction

The material that follows will help you identity what you need to do for your project. At the start of each section you will notice a table containing the component (i.e., the part of the overall project that is being completed), the criteria (i.e., what you have to produce to gain marks) and the mark allocated for each criterion along with a mark for the whole section.

Background

The background to the tasks is an important part of the overall project as it seeks to put the whole project into context. For this part you are required to describe the organisation and its values and how these can be conveyed in any documents it produces.

Components	Criteria	Mark
Background	Description of the organisation	2
	Ethos and house style	2

Description of the organisation

Here you need to describe:

- what the organisation is (including its name)
- where it is
- what it does
- its size.

Ethos and house style

Here you need to:

- Identify three types of document (NB each should have a different function) used by the organisation (e.g., letters, fliers, brochures, leaflets, catalogues, webpages, advertisements, slideshows, etc.).
- Include the three documents in your report (you can include originals, print them, scan them in, photograph them, etc.).
- Analyse all three documents collectively to determine the house style, ethos/image. Make sure that you understand the exact meaning of each term before you do this. You need to identify the philosophy, vision or persona being reflected by the document or justify why you used a particular icon or colour scheme.

Data processing activities within the organisation

For this part you are required to identify data processing activities used by the organisation as evidenced by certain documents of which you must obtain evidence.

Components	Criteria	Mark
Data processing activities within the organisation	Desktop publishing	2
	Automated documents	2
	Presentation or webpage	2

Desktop publishing

Here you need to:

- For two documents (they should be distinctly different and can be actual or automated) describe the main purpose of the document and its data and identify the purpose of the document (e.g., to advise, to sell, to remind, etc.).
- Identify and describe four techniques used in the documents, such as tables, bullets, watermarks, etc.

Important note

If you choose a website as a document then be wary about choosing different pages from the same website, as each document needs to have a different purpose.

Similarly, be careful about choosing different pages from a long document as two different documents – they must have a distinctly different purpose.

Automated documents

Automated documents can be documents that exist or that can be used as part of an ICT system. For example, membership card, questionnaire, application form, invoice, etc.

Here you need to:

- For each document state the purpose of the document.
- Explain for each document how the document can be used in an automated way (e.g., what fields could be merged, tick boxes, option boxes, option buttons, etc.).

Presentation or webpage

The presentation or webpage can be existing or potential. Here you need to:

- For either a presentation or webpage, describe the purpose or anticipated purpose.
- Describe the data needed or the special features which are or could be included, such as video, sound, animations, etc.

Task 1 Desktop Publishing

For this task you must design and produce a document of at least two A4 sides and containing at least 150 words. You must provide evidence, by using a word count, and ensure that this minimum word number is exceeded.

Design of document

For this part you need to plan the design of your document which you will implement (i.e. create) later.

Components	Criteria	Mark
Design of document	Purpose of document/intended user	1
	Image/ethos being conveyed	1
	Detailed design of document	4

Purpose of document/intended user

Here you should:

- Describe the purpose of the DTP document you intend to produce and identify who the audience for it is.

Image/ethos being conveyed

Here you should:

- Describe the image/ethos you are going to project with your document.

Detailed design of document

This is design so it is not where you actually produce your document (called implementation). Here you should:

- Include a sketch of the layout of the document (i.e., showing the position of text, graphics, tables, logo, watermark, etc. These can be shown as rectangles on the document).
- Include details of which text and pictures go where (e.g., picture of a person using a computer goes here).
- Include details of fonts and font sizes.
- Include details of eight features such as margins, tab settings, line spacing, paragraph styles, etc.

Important note

Do not include screenshots showing the implementation in this section. Only designs should be included.

Use of basic features

In this section you take your design and start to implement it.

Components	Criteria	Mark
Use of basic features	Use of different font styles and sizes	1
	Use of bold, centre and underline	1
	Autoshapes	1
	Right or full justification	1
	Bullet points	1
	WordArt	1
	Shading effects (e.g., shading tables, text boxes, text, shading in WordArt)	1
	Headers and footers (NB both these must be present on every page in the same position. Include the page number)	1
	Use of at least two forms of electronic combination of graphical images, *e.g. scanned images, graphics from the Internet, clipart from disc, digital camera images, graphs from a spreadsheet, graphics from a paint or CAD package* (NB make sure you include evidence for this)	2
	Tables	1

Here you should:

- Include the basic features shown in the table in the implementation of your DTP document as per your design.

Use of advanced features

In this section you take your design and start to implement it and add some of the more advanced features as shown in the following table:

Components	Criteria		Mark
Use of advanced features	Each of the following may be awarded 1 mark – up to a maximum of 5 marks for this section.		5
	Different paragraph formats	1	
	Different line spacing	1	
	Superscript and subscript	1	
	Customised tables	1	
	Page or frame borders	1	
	Set and use own tabs	1	
	Set and use own indents	1	
	Watermarks	1	
	Pagination	1	
	Use of layering (forward and behind)	1	
	Own style sheets	1	

Here you should:

- Add at least five advanced features to your document.

Important notes

- You must supply evidence of the above features in your report. The document will not always supply this on its own.
- You need to supply before and after evidence.
- Some features, such as watermarks and style sheets, will require construction evidence to show how you have actually used the software.
- Some features (e.g., customised tables, page or frame borders and pagination) can be clearly seen on the final printed document, so there is no need for extra evidence.
- Any feature you describe must appear in the final document and not just in the report.

Remember

Once you have produced your final document, do not forget to print it out.

Task 2 Automated documents

For the automated document task, you must produce a mail merge document.

Design of documents

Here you must plan the design of the documents you are producing checking that the correct image/ethos for the organisation is being conveyed.

Components	Criteria	Mark
Design of documents	Purpose of document	1
	Image/ethos being conveyed	1
	Detailed design of document	4

Purpose of document

Here you should:

- Describe the purpose of the mail merge document you intend to produce.

Image/ethos being conveyed

Here you should:

- Describe the image/ethos you are going to project with your document.

Detailed design of document

This must show evidence of design and must not be implementation with annotations. Here you should:

- Produce a design or designs showing the basic layout and page orientation.
- Produce a design which shows clearly the names of any mail merged fields.
- Produce a design which shows the macros.
- Include details of fonts and font sizes.
- Include details for contact data, logo/graphics and a description of data in the letter.

Use of basic features

For this part of the automated task you will be importing data from an external source in order to merge it with your document. You will also check that the mail merge works properly.

Components	Criteria	Mark
Use of basic features	Import data from an external source	2
	Use of suitable format and layout for data	2
	Ensure automated routines work	2

Import data from an external source

Here you should:

- Show the word-processed template document showing the fields incorporated into the document. The letter should not be cropped and should clearly identify both the merged fields and their position on the document; the contact details and the data in the letter/document.
- Provide evidence of the database used which could be in the form of a screenshot or printout.

Use of suitable format and layout for data

Here you should:

- Produce a letter which addresses all of the following:
  - Does it address the stated purpose?
  - Does it have contact details on?
  - If it is a letter, does it have a date?
  - Does the body of data contain all the required data (e.g. place and time) if applicable?
- Produce a letter in a suitable format and layout: There must be no mistakes in the letter. No capital letter or spelling mistakes in the letter or in the data imported from the database. Names and addresses in the database have to be realistic and not nonsense. Basic grammar must be correct, such as full stops at the end of sentences. Not a mixture, e.g. street, Street.
  - Not Dear Mr Davies and Dear Mr Davies,.
  - Not mr.
  - Not 123 6Ty – a mixture of upper and lower case in the postcode.
  - Layout should not be cramped.
  - Graphics such as watermarks should not obscure text.
  - No inconsistencies such as Beach Club/Beach club or headteacher/head-teacher.

Ensure automated routines work

Here you should:

- Produce printouts which should show at least three merged records.
- Ensure that there are no spacing errors in the merged data and if there are, you should go back and correct them.

Completing the tasks: Task 2 continued

Use of advanced features

Here you will create automated macros or modules as well as produce individually designed templates.

Components	Criteria	Mark
Use of advanced features	Individual macros or modules created using internal programming capabilities of the software package	3
	Individually designed templates (other than the normal template)	3

Individual macros or modules created using internal programming capabilities of the software package

There are two possible options for this:

Option 1: Provide three simple play and record macros

For this option you need supply both of the following pieces of evidence:

- Evidence of the three macros with the actual template letter in the background.
- Evidence of the code for the macros.

Option 2: Write your own individual code in Visual Basic

For this option you would need to:

- Write the macro using VB code.
- Provide written evidence of testing as evidenced by screenshots and printing the code out.
- Provide annotated code to show your understanding of the macro.

Individually designed templates (other than the normal template)

For this part you need to provide evidence for three of the following:

- Save the mail merge document as a template capable of being reused.
- Design your own button icon for one of the macros you have used and add it to the toolbar.
- Show a second use of the template document.
- Create your own style sheet.
- Create standard documents such as invoices, application or survey forms and questionnaires that contain automated features such as tick boxes, list boxes or automatically calculated fields.

Completing the tasks: Task 3

Task 3 Presentation

For task 3 you must produce a presentation containing at least six slides.

Design of document

In this design stage you will plan and design the structure of the presentation of the material.

Components	Criteria	Mark
Design of document	Purpose of document/intended user	1
	Detailed design of document	4
	Structure diagram showing pathways	1

Purpose of document/intended user

Here you should:

- Explain the purpose of the presentation.
- Describe the intended user/audience.

Detailed design of document

Here you should:

- Produce a design showing the basic background style and outline layout.
- Include details on the design showing details of both text and graphics including original and non-original graphics.
- Include details on the design of fonts and font sizes.
- Include details on the design of animation, transition, hotspots, hypertext, bookmarks, sound and video, animations, etc.

Important note

Make sure that this is design and not implementation. Annotating your printouts to explain the design is not acceptable – so no printouts or screenshots.

Structure diagram showing pathways

Here you should:

- Include a structure diagram showing pathways.

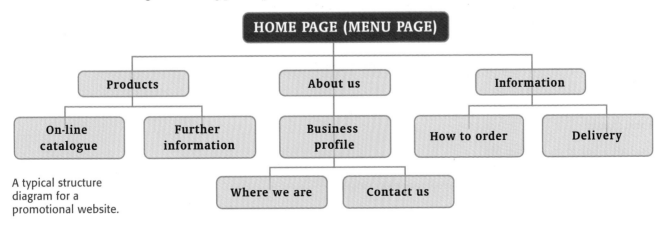

A typical structure diagram for a promotional website.

Structure diagrams show the structures of the webpages or presentations as a series of levels (a hierarchy). A home page of a website will be the first page that any customers or potential customers encounter, so it is on the first level.

Notice that the home page is the one visited first and the user then can decide which of the three paths to take to view Products, About us or Information. A user can select which path they want to take using a menu.

There are usually three ways a user will get around (i.e., navigate) a site with this structure. These are:

- moving backwards and forwards
- using a menu
- using Previous or Next buttons.

Use of basic features

In this section, you will use the basic features of the software to create slides or webpages.

Components	Criteria	Mark
Use of basic features	Background styles	1
	Animation effects	1
	Transition effects	1
	Hypertext	1
	Hotspots	1
	Bookmarks	1

Background styles

Here you should:

- Design your own style and not use a pre-defined template.
- Employ a consistent theme or house style (e.g., consistent colour scheme, presentation style, logo in same position on each slide, etc.).

Animation effects

Here you should:

- Add effects on slides or webpage and show appropriate evidence.

Transition effects

Here you should:

- Add effects on slides or webpage and show appropriate evidence.

Hypertext

Here you should:

- Include a link to an external file.
- Show the object and the URL address or directory.
- Ensure that this appears on the final presentation or webpage.

Hotspots (picture/graphic which links to internal or external object or file)

Here you should:

- Show the object and URL address or directory or slide.
- Ensure that this appears on the final presentation or webpage.

Bookmarks/anchor (link to internal slide/object or file)

Here you should:

- Show the object and URL address or directory or slide.
- Ensure that this appears on the final presentation or webpage.

Use of advanced features

In this section, you will use the advanced features of the software to create slides or webpages that include sound, video and original animation or Flash graphics.

Components	Criteria	Mark
Use of advanced features	Use of sound	2
	Use of original video	4
	Use of original animation/Flash graphics	2

Use of sound

Here you should:

- Provide evidence that you have used sound in the presentation or webpage (e.g., sound from a video, internal sound features of PowerPoint or importing sound files from disk).
- Show how the sound was captured (NB this should not be simply loading it from backing store). Examples would include: downloading from Internet, using the sound recorder in Windows, dictating sound commentary using PowerPoint, editing and creating own sound files, etc.).

Use of original video

Here you should:

- Produce your own video and incorporate it into your own presentation or webpage.
- Provide evidence in the form of a screenshot of the film in editing software.
- Provide evidence that you have planned your work (e.g., by using a storyboard, overview/outline of what happens in each frame, transcript of what was said, timings between frames, planned transition or special effects or titles and credits).
- Provide evidence of video editing effects put on frames (e.g., credits, or frame effects such as blurring, old fashioned effects, etc.). All effects should be annotated.
- Provide evidence of video effects put on transition between frames. All effects should be annotated.

Use of original animation/Flash graphics

Here you should:

- Include a simple animation such as a 'Flash' type animation using two commands or frames (e.g., create a ball and then make it bounce).
- For an extra mark, produce a more complex animation with at least three frames or commands.

Evaluation of the tasks

Evaluation

Here you will produce an evaluation of all the three tasks you completed.

Criteria	Mark
This section assesses your quality of written communication. The marks are only given for the following criteria if your response demonstrates: • legibility of text; accuracy of spelling, punctuation and grammar; clarity of meaning; • selection of a form and style of writing appropriate to purpose and to complexity of subject matter; • organisation of information clearly and coherently; use of specialist vocabulary where appropriate.	6
A detailed and critical evaluation of all three tasks which examines the data, system and suggests future modifications 5-6 marks	
A detailed evaluation of all tasks, which addresses the system and future modification 3–4 marks	
Not all tasks have been evaluated or only a brief evaluation of all three tasks and limited suggestions for future modifications 1–2 marks	

Important note

You should not produce a running commentary of what you did for the evaluation.

Compression and storage techniques

You will have used many different files and files types when producing the work for your three tasks. This section asks about the file types you used and the reasons for using them and also about the compression.

Criteria	Mark
Identification of methods used	2
Justification of chosen method	2

Identification of methods used

Here you should:

- Describe at least three compression and storage methods you used in your tasks.
- Ensure that the techniques you mention are relevant to the documents you have produced.

Justification of chosen method

Here you should:

- Justify your choice of why you used compression in at least three areas.
- Justify why storage techniques were used in at least two areas.
- Mention specific objects or files which appear in your documents.

Important note

Do not simply give a general description as to why compression is used.

Printouts of the three tasks

You need to remember to print out:

- your leaflet
- your letters
- your webpages or presentation.

Glossary

Acceptable use policy Document making it clear to all employees or users what is acceptable use of ICT systems and what isn't.

Access rights Restrictions to a user's access to only those files they need in order to perform their job.

Address book In the address book are the names and e-mail addresses of all the people to whom you are likely to send e-mail.

Append Users can add new records but they will be unable to alter or delete existing records.

Artificial intelligence (AI) Creating computer programs or computers that behave in a similar way to the human brain by learning from experience.

ASCII Code for representing characters in binary.

Backup Keeping copies of software and data so that the data can be recovered should there be a total loss of the ICT system.

Backup file A copy of a file which is used in the event of the original file being corrupted (damaged).

Bandwidth A measure of the amount of data that can be transferred using a data transfer medium.

Bar code reader Input device used to scan a series of lines (called a bar code).

Binary code Code made up from a series of binary digits – 0 or 1.

Bit Binary digit 0 or 1.

Blog A website providing commentary, personal thoughts or news on a particular subject. It is written in chronological order and can include text, images and links to other blogs and websites.

Blogger A person who posts their comments to a blog.

Bookmark Storage area where the URL (i.e. the web address) of a website can be stored so that it can be accessed later using a link.

Bug A mistake or error in a program.

Bullet point A block or paragraph of text that has a symbol placed in front to make the section of text stand out.

CAD (computer-aided design) A method of using the computer to produce technical drawings.

CAL (computer-assisted learning) Using ICT systems to help with learning.

CAM (computer-aided manufacturing) The use of computers to control the manufacturing process in some way by controlling manufacturing equipment such as lathes, drills, millers and robots.

Character Any symbol (letter, number, punctuation mark, etc.) that you can type from the keyboard.

Check digit Number placed at the end of the block of numbers used to check that the numbers have been entered correctly into the computer.

Chip and PIN reader Input device which has now replaced magnetic strip readers for the reading of credit or debit card details. Rather than signing to verify you are the correct owner of the card, you have to enter a four-digit personal identification number (PIN) to verify that you are the true owner of the card.

Compression Storing data in a format that requires less space. Bitmapped graphics such as photographs are usually compressed to a fraction of their normal file size.

Computer-based training (CBT) Use of ICT systems for training in the workplace usually by making use of PCs or portable devices.

Computer Misuse Act 1990 An Act which makes illegal a number of activities such as deliberately planting viruses, hacking, using ICT equipment for fraud, etc.

Cookie A small text file downloaded to your computer, used by websites to collect information about how you use the website.

Copyright, Designs and Patents Act 1988 An Act, which, amongst other things, makes it an offence to copy or steal software.

CPU (Central Processing Unit) The computer's brain. It stores and processes data. It has three parts: the artithmetic logic unit (ALU), the control unit and the memory.

Crime An illegal act.

Cross field checks Checking the data in more than one field with other fields to make sure they make sense.

Cybercrime Crime committed involving ICT systems as a major part.

Data Raw facts and figures or a set of values, measurements or records of transactions.

Data capture Term for the various methods by which data can be entered into the computer so that it can be processed.

Data controller The person whose responsibility it is in an organisation to control the way that personal data is processed.

Data Protection Act 1998 Law to protect the individual against the misuse of data.

Data subject The living individual whom the personal information is about.

Data type check Check to ensure the data being entered is the same type as the data type specified for the field.

Desktop The working area of the GUI and where all the icons are situated.

Distributed database A collection of information spread over two or more servers in a network. These servers are often in different locations. The user will not know that data is being obtained from different servers.

Double entry of data Two people use the same data source to enter the details into the ICT system and only if the two sets of data are identical, will they be accepted for processing.

Download To copy files from a distant computer to the one you are working on.

Drag and drop Allows you to select objects (icons, folders, files, etc.) and drag them so that you can perform certain operations on them such as drag to the recycle bin to discard, add a file to a folder, copy files to a folder and so on.

Driver A short specially written program that understands the operation of the device it controls/operates. It is needed to allow the systems or applications software to use the connected device properly.

Drum plotters Used when drawings, plans and maps need to be printed on large sheets of paper.

Electronic funds transfer (EFT) Refers to the payment for goods where the payment is made electronically from one account to another.

Encoding Producing a shorter version of the data to aid typing in and to aid validation of the data.

Encryption Coding data whilst it is being sent over a network so that only the true recipient is able to decode it. Should the data be intercepted by a hacker, then the data will be in code and totally meaningless.

Ergonomics An applied science concerned with designing and arranging things people use so that the people and things interact most efficiently and safely.

Erroneous data Data that is ridiculous or totally unsuitable.

Expert system An ICT system that emulates the decision making ability of a human expert.

Expert system shell Allows people to create their own expert systems without the need for programming skills or the need to start from scratch.

Extranet An external network that can be used by the customers, suppliers and partners of an organisation as well as the organisation itself.

Favourites Storage area where the URL (i.e. the web address) of a website can be stored so that it can be accessed later using a link.

Federation Against Software Theft An anti-piracy organisation who work to protect the work of software publishers.

Field An item of information such as surname, date of birth, product number, product name on a record.

File attachments Files that are transferred along with an e-mail.

File compression Used to compress files before storing or before being sent over a network.

File management software Part of systems software used to create folders, copy folders/files, rename folders/files, delete folders/files, move files/folders, etc.

File/Table lookups Used to make sure that codes being used are the same as those used in a table or file of codes.

Firewall Hardware and/or software that work in a network to prevent communication that is not allowed from one network to another.

Flash/Pen drives Popular storage media which offer cheap and large storage capacities and are ideal media for photographs, music and other data files. They consist of printed circuit boards enclosed in a plastic case.

Flat-file A way of storing data in a list or a single table.

Footer Text placed at the bottom of a document.

Format The style in which the information is organised and presented.

Format checks Checks performed on codes to make sure that they conform to the correct combinations of characters.

Forward If you are sent an e-mail that you think others should see, you can forward it to them.

Freedom of Information Act 2000 Act giving the right of access to information held by public authorities.

FTP (file transfer protocol) A method (called a protocol) for exchanging files over the Internet.

GIGO Abbreviation for garbage in garbage out. It means that if you put rubbish into the computer then you get rubbish out.

Grammar checker Used to check the grammar in a sentence and to highlight problems and suggest alternatives.

Graph plotter A device which draws by moving a pen. Useful for scale drawings and is used mainly with CAD packages.

Graphics tablet An input device which makes use of a large tablet containing many shapes and commands which may be selected by the user by moving a cursor and clicking. Basically it moves the toolbars onto the tablet rather than clutter up the screen when doing large technical drawings using CAD software.

Groups Lists of people and their e-mail addresses.

GUI (Graphical User Interface) An interface that allows users to communicate with ICT equipment by making use of icons and pull-down menus.

Hacker A person who tries to or succeeds in breaking into a secure ICT system.

Hacking The process of trying to break into a secure computer system.

Hard copy Printed output on a computer which may be taken away and studied.

Hardware The physical components of a computer system.

Header Text placed at the top of a document.

Health & Safety (Display Screen Equipment) Regulations 1992 Regulations making it law for employers to take certain measures to protect the health and safety of their employees who use ICT equipment.

Health and Safety at Work Act 1974 Law making sure that employees have safe working conditions and methods.

Hot spot A region where the Internet can be accessed wirelessly.

Icons Small pictures used to represent commands, files or windows.

ICT systems Hardware and software working together with people and procedures to do a job.

Identity theft/fraud Using your banking/credit card/personal details in order to commit fraud.

Implementation The process of producing the working version of the solution to the problem as identified by the client.

Importing The ability of one piece of software to read and use the data produced by a different piece of software.

Indexing Allows words to be highlighted so that they can be used to form an index.

Information Output from an ICT system or data that has been processed and gives us knowledge.

Information Commissioner The person responsible for enforcing the Data Protection Act. They also promote good practice and make everyone aware of the implications of the Act.

Ink-jet printer A printer that works by spraying ink through nozzles onto the paper.

Input Act of entering data into an ICT system.

Input device The hardware device used to feed the input data into an ICT system such as a keyboard or a scanner.

Input media The material on which the data is encoded so that it can be read by an input device and digitised so that it can be input, processed and turned into information by the ICT system.

Input message A message which when the field or cell is selected, gives the user some advice on the kind of data that should be entered.

Interactive Where there is a constant dialogue between the user and the computer.

Interface The point where two objects meet. In ICT this is usually between a device such as a computer, printer, scanner, etc., and a human.

Internal threat A threat to an ICT system that comes from inside an organisation.

Internet A huge group of networks joined together.

Internet service provider (ISP) The organisation that provides your Internet connection.

Intranet A private network used within an organisation that makes uses of Internet technology.

Just in time stock control Where goods are delivered to the stores as fast as they are being sold.

Knowledge Knowledge is derived from information by applying rules to it.

LAN (local area network) A network where the linked hardware is confined to a single office or site and where all the wires and other devices needed for the LAN are owned by the organisation.

Laser printer A printer which uses a laser beam to form characters on the paper.

Length check Checks to make sure that the data being entered has the correct number of characters in it.

Lookup table When you enter data, the spreadsheet looks through a table to find a match and other relevant data.

Macro Used to record a series of keystrokes so that, for example, your name and address can be added to the top of the page simply by pressing a single key or clicking on the mouse.

Magnetic Ink Character Recognition Input method making use of numbers printed onto a document such as a cheque in a special magnetic ink which can be read by the magnetic ink character reader at very high speed.

Magnetic media Media such as tape and disk where the data is stored as a magnetic pattern.

Magnetic strip Data is encoded in the magnetic strip and when the card is swiped the data from the card is used to record the transaction.

Magnetic strip reader Hardware device that reads the data contained in magnetic strips such as those on the back of credit cards.

Mail merge Combining a list of names and addresses with a standard letter so that a series of letters is produced with each letter being addressed to a different person.

Malpractice Improper or careless use or misconduct.

Media The means by which information is communicated.

Memory cards Thin cards you see in digital cameras used to store photographs and can be used for other data.

Menus Allow a user to make selections from a list.

MIDI (Musical Instrument Digital Interface) Used mainly to communicate between electronic keyboards, synthesisers and computers. MIDI files are compressed and the files are quite small.

Mind map A hierarchical diagram with a central idea, or image, at the centre of the map surrounded by branches that extend from the central idea.

Model A computer program/system that mimics a real situation.

MP3 Music file format that uses compression to reduce the file size considerably and this is why the MP3 file format is so popular with portable music playing devices such as iPods.

Multimedia A means of communication that combines more than one medium for presentation purposes, such as sound, graphics and video.

Natural language interface An interface that allows the user to interact using natural written or spoken language (e.g., English) as opposed to computer language and commands.

Network A group of ICT devices (computers, printers, scanners, etc.) which are able to communicate with each other.

Networking software Systems software which allows computers connected together to function as a network.

Neural network An ICT system that processes information in the same way that the human brain does. It uses a series of processing elements which work in parallel to solve a specific problem. They cannot be programmed but instead learn by example.

Newsgroup A discussion group where people are able to post messages or replies to messages on a whole variety of topics.

Non-volatile memory Memory stored on a chip which does not lose data when the power is turned off.

Normal data Entering data that should be acceptable to the solution.

Notification The process of letting the Information Commissioner's Office know that an organisation is storing and processing personal data.

On-line/e-learning Using ICT to help in the learning process.

Operating system Software that controls the hardware of a computer and is used to run the applications software. Operating systems control the handling of input, output, interrupts, etc.

Optical Character Recognition (OCR) Input method using a scanner as the input device along with special software which looks at the shape of each character so that it can be recognised separately.

Optical Mark Recognition (OMR) Input method using paper-based forms or cards with marks on them that are read automatically by a device called an optical mark reader.

Output The results from processing data.

Package software A bundle of files necessary for a particular program to run along with some form of documentation to help a user get the program started.

Password A series of characters which need to be typed in before access to the ICT system is allowed.

Peripheral A device connected to and under the control of the central processing unit (CPU).

Personal data Data about a living identifiable person, which is specific to that person.

Phishing Tricking people into revealing their banking or credit card details.

PIN (personal identification number) A secret number that needs to be keyed in when using a debit/credit card.

Piracy The process of illegally copying software.

Placeholder text Text included to show the position of text in a template and that you can delete and replace with your own text.

Podcasting Creating and publishing a digital radio broadcast using a microphone, computer and audio editing software. The resulting file is saved in MP3 format and then uploaded onto an Internet server. It can then be downloaded using a facility called RSS onto an MP3 player such as an iPod.

Pointer This is the little arrow that appears when using Windows.

Presence checks Check to make sure that data had been entered into a field.

Primary storage Storage in chips inside the computer.

Print preview Feature that comes with most software used to produce documents. It allows users to view the page or pages of a document to see exactly how they will be printed. If necessary, the documents can be corrected.

Printer driver Software that converts commands from the systems or applications software into a form that a particular printer can understand.

Privacy Being able to choose to keep certain aspects of your life private.

Process Any operation that transfers data into information.

Processing Performing calculations or arranging the data into a meaningful order.

Programmer A person who writes computer programs.

Proof reading Carefully reading what has been typed in and comparing it with what is on the data source (order forms, application forms, invoices, etc.) for any errors, which can then be corrected.

Protocol A set of standards that allows the transfer of data between computers on a network.

Query A request for specific information from a database.

RAID (Redundant array of inexpensive disks) A system used by networks to keep backups.

RAM (Random access memory) Used to hold the data temporarily whilst the computer is working on it. Contents are lost when the computer is switched off.

Range check Data validation technique which checks that the data input into the computer is within a certain range.

Read only A user can only read the contents of the file. They cannot alter or delete the data.

Read/Write A user can read the data held in the file and can alter the data.

Real-time processing The input data is processed immediately as it arrives. The results have a direct effect on the next set of available data.

Record The complete information about a product, employee, student, order, etc.

Relational database Database where the data is held in tables with relationships established between them. The software is used to set up and hold the data as well as to extract and manipulate the stored data.

Relationship The way tables are related to each other. Relationships can be one-to-one, one-to-many or many-to-many.

Reply Allows you to read an e-mail and then write the reply without having to enter the recipient's e-mail address.

Report The output from a database in which the results are presented in a way that is controlled by the user.

Resolution The sharpness or clarity of an image.

ROM (Read only memory) Memory stored on a chip which does not lose data when the power is turned off.

RSI Repetitive strain injury. A painful muscular condition caused by repeatedly using certain muscles in the same way.

Scams Setting up bogus companies with bogus websites and then making off with the money from customers' orders.

Scanner Input device that can be used to capture an image and is useful for digitising old non-digital photographs, paper documents or pictures in books.

Search engine Program which searches for required information on the Internet.

Secondary (or backup storage) Storage outside the computer.

Security Making sure that the hardware, software and data of an ICT system does not come to any harm.

Shockwave Audio format used for very high quality sound with very small file size.

Simulation An imitation of a system or phenomenon using computer software.

Software Programs which supply the instructions to the hardware.

Software licence Document (digital or paper) which sets out the terms by which the software can be used. It will refer to the number of computers on which it can be run simultaneously.

Sorting Putting data into ascending or descending order.

Spam Unsolicited bulk e-mail (i.e., e-mail from people you do not know, sent to everyone in the hope that a small percentage may purchase the goods or services on offer).

Spellchecker Facility offered by software where there is a dictionary against which all words typed in are checked.

Spyware Software which collects information about the user of a computer connected to the Internet without their consent.

Storage capacity How much data can the storage device/media hold? Usually measured in MB or GB.

Systems software Any computer software that manages and controls the hardware thus allowing the applications software to do a useful job. Systems software consists of a group of programs.

Table A more visual way of displaying data, especially numeric data, or a structure used to hold data in a relational database.

Taskbar Shows the programs that are open. This facility is handy when working on several programs together.

Teletext A broadcast service which means it comes to our TVs as a television signal. The service provides a limited number of pages such as news, weather, sport results on your TV screen.

Templates Document that has already been designed and you simply remove the placeholder text and images and replace with your own.

Test plan The approach that will be used to test the whole solution and consists of a suite of tests.

Thesaurus Allows a word to be chosen and the word processor will list synonyms (i.e., words with similar meanings).

Toner Black plastic particles used by laser printers as the 'ink'.

Topology The way a particular network is arranged. Examples include ring, star, mesh and bus.

Touch screen Screen that allows a person to make selections by simply touching the screen.

Transaction A piece of business, e.g. an order, purchase, return, delivery, transfer of money, etc.

Transaction processing Processing of each transaction as it arises.

Transcription error Error made when typing data in using a document as the source of the data.

Transmission medium The material which forms the connection between the computers in a network (e.g., air in the case of wireless, metal wire, optical fibre).

Transmission rate The speed of data flow in bits per second (bps) through transmission media.

Transposition error Error made when characters are swapped around so they are in the wrong order.

Trojans Lines of computer code stored in your PC without you knowing.

URL (Uniform Resource Locator) The web address used to locate a webpage.

User A person who makes active use of an ICT solution to solve an ICT problem.

Username A way of identifying who is using the ICT system in order to allocate network resources.

Utility Part of the systems software that performs a specific task.

Utility programs Software which helps the user perform tasks such as virus checking, file compression, etc.

Validation checks Checks a developer of a solution creates, using the software, in order to restrict the data that a user can enter so as to reduce errors.

Validation expression/rule Command that a developer must type in order to set up the validation for a particular field/cell.

Validation message A message which appears if the validation rule is breached.

Verification Checking that the data being entered into the ICT system perfectly matches the source of the data.

Videoconferencing ICT system that allows face-to-face meetings to be conducted without the participants being in the same room or even the same geographical area.

Virus A program that replicates (i.e. copies) itself automatically and usually carries with it some payload which causes damage.

VOIP (voice over Internet protocol) Service that allows you to make cheap Internet phone calls to anywhere in the world.

Voice recognition Voice recognition systems allow you to enter data via a microphone directly into a computer.

Volatile memory Memory which loses data when the power is turned off.

WAN (wide area network) A network where the hardware is spread over a wide geographical area and where the organisation does not own some or all of the telecommunications equipment used.

WAV Used with Windows for storing sounds. Files in this format are not highly compressed.

Web authoring software Software used to create websites.

Web browser The software program you use to access the Internet. Microsoft Internet Explorer is an example of a web browser.

Webcam A small video camera used as an input device to send a moving image over an intranet or the Internet.

Webpage Single document on the World Wide Web.

Wi-Fi A trademark for the certification of products that meet certain standards for transmitting data over wireless networks.

WIMP (Windows Icons Menus Pointing devices) The graphical user interface (GUI) way of using a computer rather than typing in commands at the command line.

World Wide Web A means of accessing information contained on the Internet. It is an information sharing model that is built on top of the Internet.

Worm A program that keeps replicating itself automatically, and as it does so it takes more and more disk space and also uses a greater proportion of the system's resources for each copy.

Index

Acknowledgements

Folens Limited would like to thank the following for giving permission to use copyright material.

P.3, argus/Shutterstock; p.3, Macs Peter/Shutterstock; p.4, Marco Rametta/Shutterstock; p.5, Chepe Nicoli/Shutterstock; p.5, Andresr/Shutterstock; p.12, amfoto/Shutterstock; p.13, RTimages/Shutterstock; p.13, Shutterstock; p.20, Phil Date/Shutterstock; P.21, Paul Herbert/Fotolia; p.22, www.statistics.gov.uk/ psi licence; p.23, Image Dictionary; p.23, Royal Mail; p.23, © Marc Dietrich/Fotolia; p.31,TheSupe87/Shutterstock; p.33, GreenGate Publishing; p.34, Kimberly Hall/Shutterstock; p.35, © thecarlinco/Fotolia; p.35, © Andres Rodriguez/Fotolia; p.36, © Tadija Savic/Fotolia; p.42, GreenGate Publishing; p.48, © Aloysius Patrimonio/Fotolia; p.48, © Valery Potapova/Fotolia; p.48, © 3dweave.com/Fotolia; p.48, © Stolbtsov Alexandre/Fotolia; p.48, © ivan kmit/Fotolia; p.48, © Edward White /Fotolia; p.49, © PressBoy/Fotolia; p.49, © David Hughes/Fotolia; p.49, © Real Deal Photo/Fotolia; p.52, ©ericsphotolab/Fotolia; P.60, Harris Walton Lifting Gear Ltd; p.61, Farnborough Kitchens; p.61, Kharpham.co.uk; p.61, Idea spectrum; p.61, Image courtesy of iCreate Ltd (www.icreate3d.com); p.61, © Baloncici/Fotolia; p.61, Assist; p.62, © Sascha Burkard/ Fotolia; p.62, 3dconnexion; p.62, hp; p.62, MultiCam Inc., photo by Mark Allen; p.63, Delcam; p.63, Lancashire Grid for Learning; p.64, © Edyta Pawlowska/Fotolia; p.65, Tesco; p.65, © Amy Walters/Fotolia; p.66, © Rob Pitman/Fotolia; p.67, www.cd-wow.com; P.68, GreenGate Publishing; p.68, Epson (UK) Ltd; p.69, © Flashgaz/Fotolia; p.70, Sebastian Kaulitzki/Shutterstock; p.70, Nrtpos; p.70, Tesco; p.71, Geminicad; p.71, Ideaspectrum; p.72, Ideaspectrum; p.74, LMG; p.78, © SamSpiro/Fotolia; p.83, Open University; p.83, © Training and Development Agency for Schools. p.84, BBC (bbc.co.uk/gcsebitesize); p.85, Glasbergen; p.85, promwebcast; p.86, drs; p.87, Drs; p.87, Petr Rehor/Shutterstock; p.87, Picture in public domain; p.88, © Ozgur Artug/Fotolia; p.88, Kirill R/Shutterstock; p.89, © Argus/Fotolia; p.89, Lorraine Kourafas/Shutterstock; p.90, Capita; p.98, Glasbergen; p.99, Zebra Technologies; p.99, © dazzi-b/Fotolia; p.99, thelearningclinic.co.uk; p.100, John Keith/Shutterstock; p.101, © vasco/Fotolia; p.101, Nikolay Iliev/Shutterstock; p.102, Ariadna de Raadt/Shutterstock; p.103, © Norman Chan/Fotolia; p.103, Draeger; p.103, Glasbergen; p.104, © weim/Fotolia; p.110, thelearningclinic.co.uk; p.118, Steve Doyle; p.119, Glasbergen; p.119, Steve Doyle; p.120, MakeMusic Inc.; p.120, nch software; p.121, Diego Cervo/Shutterstock; P.123, Glasbergen; p.123, © Akhilesh Sharma/Fotolia; P.124, © Rico Leffanta/Fotolia; P.125, © imagesab/Fotolia; p.125, www.chipandpin.co.uk; P.126, © Aloysius Patrimonio/Fotolia; p.126, LoopAll/Shutterstock; p.126, www.splashplastic.com; p.126, www.paypoint.co.uk/; p.127, www.chipandpin.co.uk; p.127, Glasbergen; p.128, Reproduced with kind permission from The Co-operative Financial Services; P.136, © pressmaster/Fotolia; P.136, © Daraban Oana Gabriela/Fotolia; P.136, © Lorelyn Medina/Fotolia; P.136, © Aloysius Patrimonio/Fotolia; P.136, © Ralf Kraft/Fotolia; P.136, © Aloysius Patrimonio/Fotolia; p.141, © hazel proudlove/Fotolia; p.143, Steve Doyle; p.143, © amaxim/Fotolia; p.144, frolovav/Shutterstock; p.145, Christopher Hall/Shutterstock; P.160, SnappyStock, Inc./Fotolia; p.160, © Marc Dietrich/Fotolia; p.161, © Sean MacLeay/Fotolia; p.161, PhotoDisk (Volume 85); p.162, © Nathalie Dulex/Fotolia; p.162, © dechefbloke/Fotolia; p.162, © Dominique LUZY/Fotolia; p.162, © Com Evolution/Fotolia; p.162, © jeff gynane/Fotolia; p.162, © Galyna Andrushko/Fotolia; p.162, © Sean MacLeay/Fotolia; p.163, © Stephen Finn/Fotolia; p.163, © Foto Factory/Fotolia; p.164, Dmitriy Shironosov/Shutterstock; p.165, Maxim Tupikov/Shutterstock; P.166, © digerati/Fotolia; p.168, © Sergey Ilin/Fotolia; p. 171, © Feng Yu/ Fotolia; p.178, © Nenad Djedovic/Fotolia; P.179, Christos Georghiou/Shutterstock; P.181, Thomson; p.182, www.wacom.com; p.182, www.logitech.com; p.183, www.logitech.com; p.183, © Andres Rodrigo Gonzalez Buzzio/Fotolia; p.183, © John Neff/Fotolia; p.183, © Gilles Parnalland/Fotolia; p.183, Protouch; p.183, © Michelle D. Parker/Fotolia; p.183, © Kirill Roslyakov/Fotolia; p.190, © Adam Borkowski/Fotolia; p.190, © Panagiotis Parthenios/Fotolia; p.191, Glasbergen; p.191, © Radu Razvan/Fotolia; p.191, © Mark Aplet/Fotolia; p.192, GreenGate Publishing; P.193, Ergoption; P.193, KB Covers; P.193, Glasbergen; p.194, Alexander Kuznetsov/Fotolia; p.195, © Stasys Eidiejus/Fotolia; p.195, © Anyka/Fotolia; p.197, Glasbergen; P.198, © Aloysius Patrimonio/Fotolia; p.199, © Stephen Coburn/Fotolia, p.199, © Sean Gladwell/Fotolia; p.199, © matttilda/Fotolia; p. 200, GreenGate Publishing; p.201, © Peter Baxter/Fotolia; p.202, © Vasiliy Yakobchuk/Fotolia; p.202, © kmit/Fotolia; p.203, Fotolia; p.203, © Moïse Parienti/Fotolia; p.204, © Feng Yu/Fotolia; p.204, © Tomislav/Fotolia; p.205, © Dana Heinemann/Fotolia; p.232, © Forgiss/Fotolia; p.233, © Gale Distler/Fotolia; p.234, © Alexander Sayganov/Fotolia; p.234, NASA; p.235, NASA; p.235, Image courtesy of Cray Inc.

Adobe product screen shot(s) reprinted with permission from Adobe Systems Incorporated.

Microsoft product screenshots reprinted with permission from Microsoft Corporation.

Every effort has been made to contact copyright holders of material used in this publication. If any copyright holder has been overlooked, we should be pleased to make any necessary arrangements.